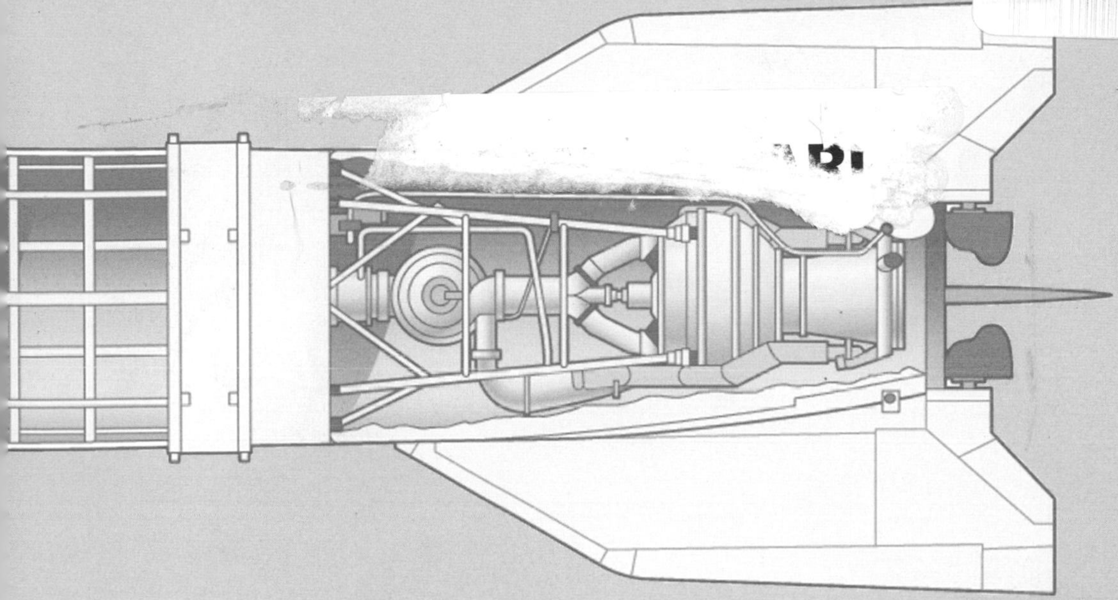

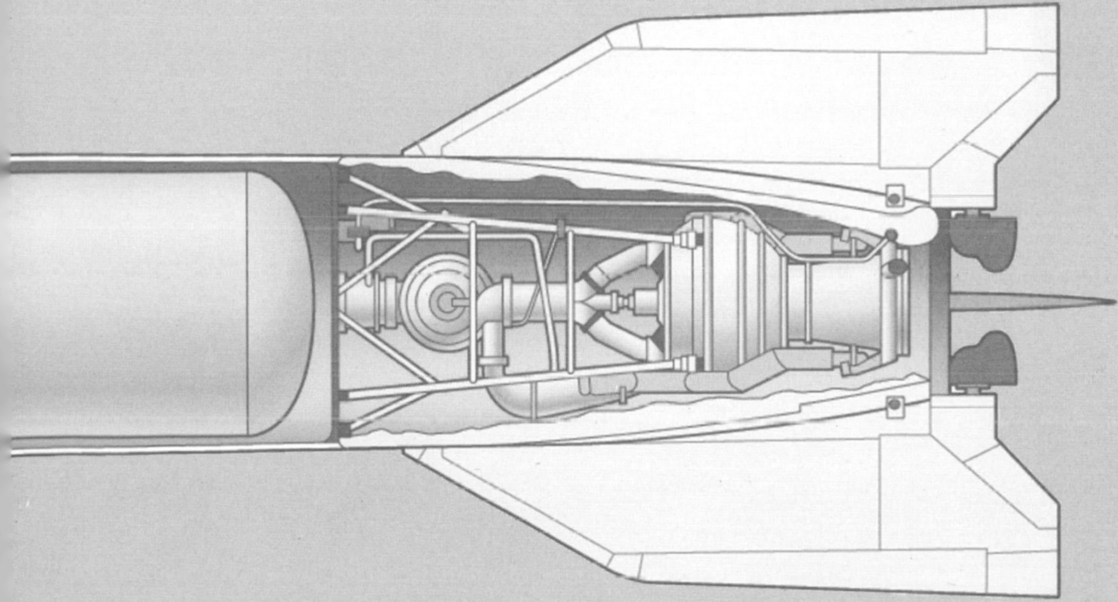

WORLD WAR II DATA BOOK

HITLER'S SECRET WEAPONS

1933–1945

THE ESSENTIAL FACTS AND FIGURES FOR GERMANY'S SECRET WEAPONS PROGRAMME

WORLD WAR II DATA BOOK

HITLER'S SECRET WEAPONS 1933–1945

THE ESSENTIAL FACTS AND FIGURES FOR GERMANY'S SECRET WEAPONS PROGRAMME

DAVID PORTER

amber BOOKS

First published in 2010 by
Amber Books Ltd
Bradley's Close
74–77 White Lion Street
London N1 9PF
www.amberbooks.co.uk

ISBN: 978-1-906626-74-7

Project Editor: Michael Spilling
Design: Hawes Design
Picture Research: Terry Forshaw

Printed in Thailand

PICTURE CREDITS

Art-Tech/Aerospace: 6/7, 17, 20/21, 39, 55, 74/75, 84/85, 96/97, 116/117, 119, 136/137, 163, 166/167
Art-Tech/MARS: 30/31, 32/33
Cody Images: 42/43, 81,152, 154
Corbis/Bettmann: 45
Library of Congress: 14
Photoshot: 87, 99, 111
Plbcr/Wikipedia Creative Commons: 95
U.S. Department of Defense: 144

Illustrations

Alcaniz Fresno's S.A.: 54 (both centre), 61 (bottom)
Amber Books: 129
Art-Tech/Aerospace: 11 (both), 18 (all), 28 (all), 47 (top, 2 centre), 49 (all), 50 (all), 54 (top, bottom), 61 (top, centre) 66 (top), 67, 77, 78, 83, 88, 102 (centre bottom), 105 (centre), 106 (both), 107 (top), 112 (centre, bottom), 114 (both), 116/117, 125 (top), 128, 133, 139 (top, centre), 142 (left), 153, 155, 157 (centre, bottom), 158, 159, 175, 181 (top, bottom), 182 (top, bottom), 184 (bottom)
Vincent Bourguignon: 9 (all), 47 (bottom), 63 (both), 65 (all), 66 (centre, bottom), 69 (all), 70/71 (both), 72/73, 89, 90, 102 (top, bottom), 105 (centre top, bottom), 107 (bottom), 112 (top), 123, 125 (centre, bottom), 135, 139 (bottom), 142 (right), 145, 157 (top), 181 (centre), 182 (centre), 184 (top)

All other illustrations and maps by Patrick Mulrey (© Amber Books)

CONTENTS

CHAPTER 1

Secret Weapons before 1939

The years between the proclamation of the German Empire in 1871 and the outbreak of World War I saw a massive increase in German industrial capacity, which especially increased its military output. These industries were largely powered by the Ruhr's coal production, which rose from 100 million tonnes (98 million tons) in 1894 to 191 million tonnes (188 million tons) in 1913. By the 1890s, Germany had the most advanced chemical industry in the world, which could readily switch from the production of civilian dyes and fertilizers to military explosives and poison gas.

Ironically, much of this technology was viewed with suspicion by most of the aristocratic and conservative officers who dominated the German military command structure in 1914. Such attitudes would change, but the delay in producing weapons that exploited emerging technologies contributed to Germany's defeat in 1918.

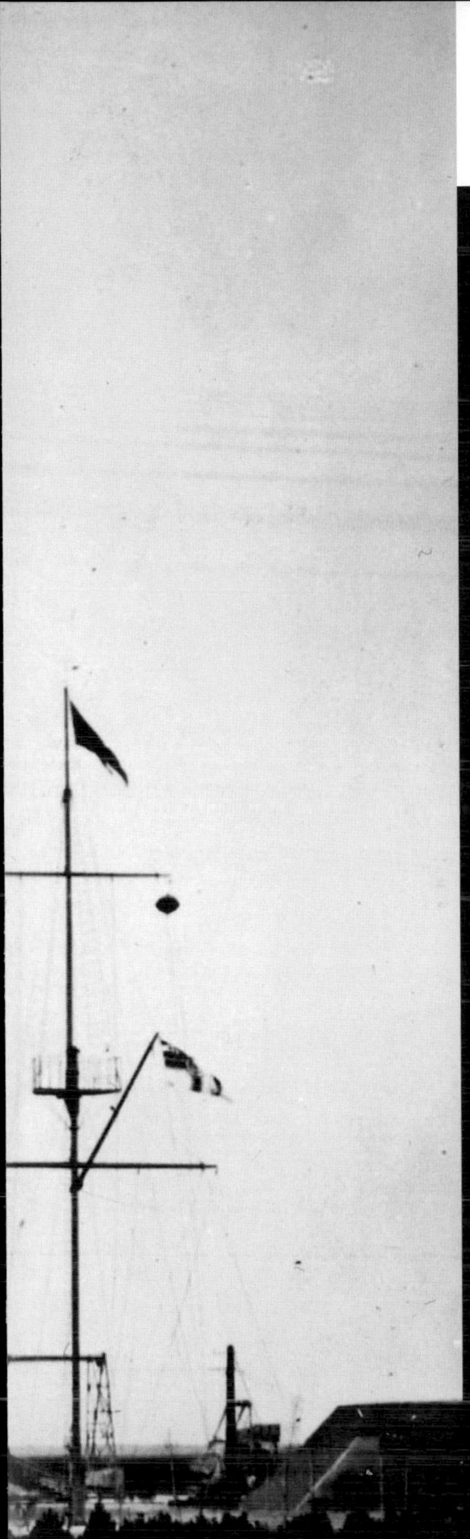

On the ranges – test-firing the Paris Gun, 1918.

The Early Years: 1917–18

German military innovators were given free rein to develop new weapons from the middle of World War I as it became clear that the Allied lead in military technology was costing Germany the war. In fact, many of the devices pioneered in 1917–18 reappeared in a far more sophisticated form in the arsenals of Hitler's Third Reich.

Germany's pre-war dominance in civilian chemical technology gave it a head start in gas warfare. The chemical companies BASF and Hoechst and Bayer (which formed the IG Farben conglomerate in 1925) had been producing chlorine as a by-product of their dye manufacturing. In co-operation with Fritz Haber of the Kaiser Wilhelm Institute for Chemistry in Berlin, these companies began developing methods of discharging chlorine gas against enemy trenches.

First attacks

The first large-scale German gas attacks of 1915 proved to be highly effective, but the Allies quickly produced gas masks to counter the threat and then retaliated with their own chemical weapons. For the remainder of the war, there was a race to produce new and more effective poison gases as well as provide troops with effective counter-measures. Indeed, on 15 October 1918 *Gefreiter* Adolf Hitler was admitted to a field hospital, temporarily blinded by a mustard gas attack. He never forgot the experience and refused to authorize the first use of battlefield chemical weapons during World War II.

The Kaiser's Panzers

Three years before the outbreak of World War I, an Austro-Hungarian army officer called Günther Burstyn drew up plans for a small armoured tracked vehicle armed with a turreted gun. He called this the Motorgeschütz *(Motor-gun).*

In October 1911, Burstyn sent the design and a scale model to Vienna, Austria, for consideration by the War Office there. The official response was encouraging and asked for a prototype to be submitted for military trials. However, Burstyn lacked the industrial contacts and funding to produce a pilot model so, instead, offered his design to the German War Department in Berlin, which had also expressed an interest in his proposals. Despite enthusiastic support from a leading German military magazine, Burstyn fared no better with the German authorities and dropped the idea after an abortive attempt to patent his design in 1912.

Although the *Motorgeschütz* failed to progress beyond the design stage, it is one of history's fascinating 'what ifs'. If his design had received more enthusiastic official backing, the Austro-Hungarian and German armies might have been able to develop and deploy operational tanks well before the Allies.

K-Wagen

The combat debut of Allied tanks in 1916 convinced German military thinkers that only bigger German tanks could reply to these weapons. In June 1917, they persuaded the German War Ministry to order the *K-Wagen*, a new 'super-heavy' tank for the breakthrough role. Design work was carried out by Joseph Vollmer, an engineer working for the army's *Verkehrstechnische Prüfungs Kommission* (Technical Trials Committee), and *Hauptmann* Weger.

As originally designed, the vehicle would have weighed 168 tonnes (165 tons), but this was reduced to a more practicable 122 tonnes (120 tons), including an impressive armament of four 77mm (3.08in) guns and six machine guns. Even so, the huge size and weight of the *K-Wagen* made it impossible to transport as a single unit, so it was split into six sections for transport by rail to an assembly point just behind the front line.

Although a total of 10 vehicles were ordered, only two neared completion at the Riebe-Kugellager factory in Berlin by the end of the war. Under the Treaty of Versailles, both were destroyed by the Allied Control Commission.

Sturmpanzerwagen Oberschlesien

In contrast to the archaic *K-Wagen*, the *Oberschlesien,* designed by

EARLY HEAVY TANKS COMPARED

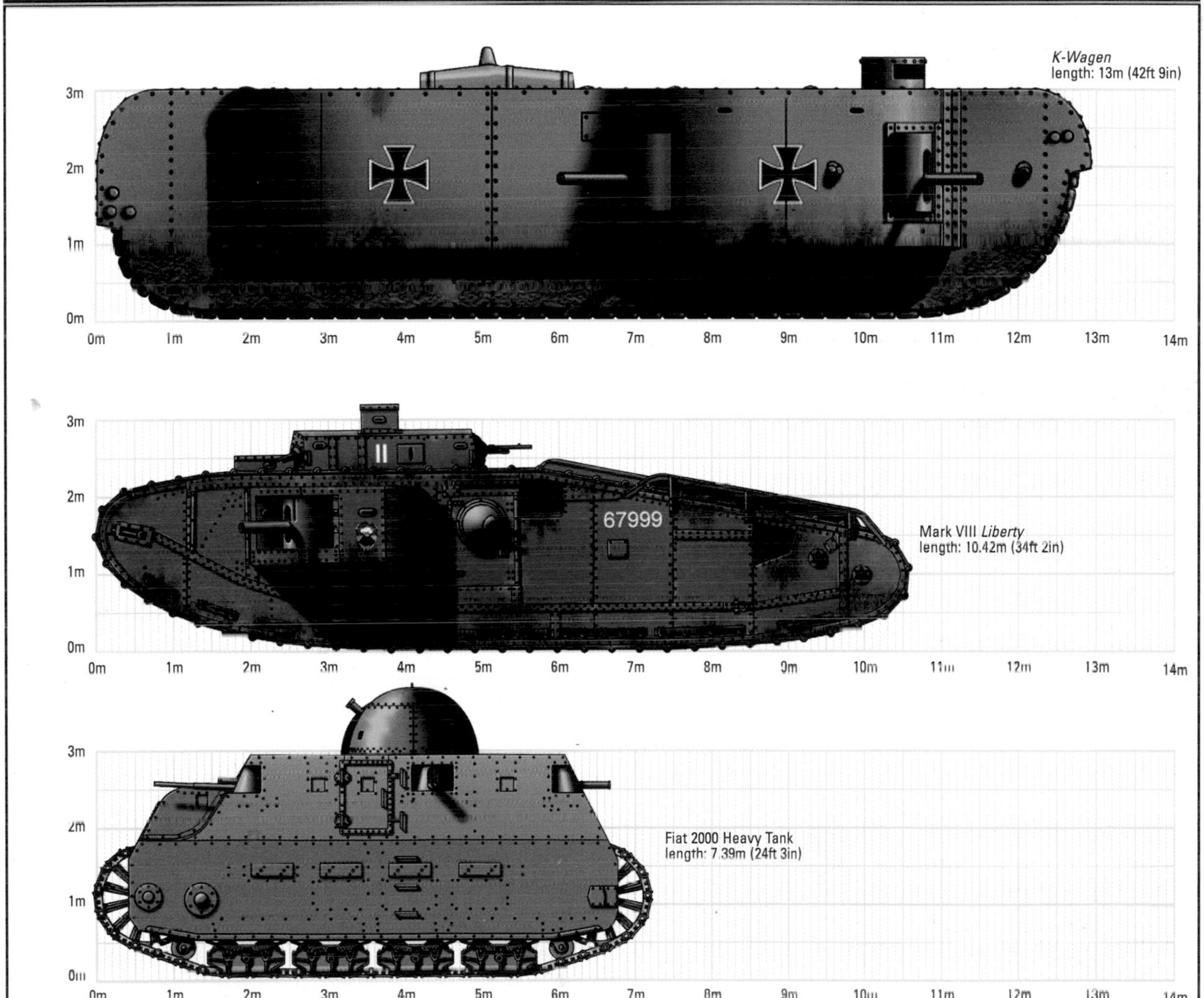
K-Wagen
length: 13m (42ft 9in)
Mark VIII *Liberty*
length: 10.42m (34ft 2in)
Fiat 2000 Heavy Tank
length: 7.39m (24ft 3in)
67999
0m 1m 2m 3m
0m 1m 2m 3m 4m 5m 6m 7m 8m 9m 10m 11m 12m 13m 14m

Hauptmann Muller, was a remarkably futuristic fast, lightly armoured assault tank. It was ordered from Oberschlesien Eisenwerk of Gleiwitzin. An order for two prototypes was placed in mid-1918, but both were only partially completed by the time of the Armistice in November.

Early Super-Artillery

The Boer War (1899–1902) and the Russo-Japanese War (1904–05) convinced German military planners that heavy artillery would be a decisive factor in future conflicts. To start, the army was equipped with 150mm (5.9in) howitzers, which gave it a distinct advantage over equivalent Allied formations at the beginning of World War I.

Good as the 150mm (5.9in) howitzers were, they could not penetrate the elaborate Allied trenches and strong-points that evolved as the front solidified in 1914–15. This problem had been anticipated and a 21cm (8.25in) howitzer had entered service in 1910 and a total of 216 had been completed by 1914. However, even these howitzers were dwarfed by the artillery's 'secret weapons'.

42cm (16.5in) *M-Gerat 14* Howitzer (Big Bertha)

This siege howitzer has a strong claim to be the first German secret weapon. It was produced in response to the lessons of the Russo-Japanese War in which the Japanese only succeeded in breaking through the Russian defences of Port Arthur after deploying 28cm (11in) coast defence howitzers. The Germans appreciated the need for even larger mobile siege artillery to deal with the formidable French and Belgian fortifications and developed a series of prototype weapons. By early 1914, two examples of the definitive 42cm (16.5in) *M-Gerat 14* howitzer were completed by Krupp's chief designer, Professor Fritz Rausenberger and were dubbed *Dicke Bertha* (Big Bertha) after Bertha Krupp, the wife of the owner of the Krupp armaments consortium.

The type proved its worth in the opening campaigns of 1914, rapidly demolishing the Belgian forts protecting Liège, Namur and Antwerp which had proved invulnerable to lighter artillery.

It seems likely that a total of 12 Berthas were built by 1918, some of which were fitted with L/30 30.5cm (12in) barrels to improve their range, albeit at the expense of shell weight. These weapons were known as the *Schwere Kartaune* or *Beta-M-Gerät*.

The Paris Gun

The increasing diversion of German naval resources to the U-boat programme led to suspension of work on the last two *Bayern* class battleships *Sachsen* and *Wurttemberg*. However, their 38cm (15in) guns had been completed and were converted to railway artillery pieces which were dubbed *Lange Max* (Long Max). At least five guns were used in the coastal batteries of Deutschland and Pommern on the Belgian coast. The Pommern battery near Dunkerque fired about 500 rounds between June 1917 and October 1918 at ranges of up to about 44,000m (48,000yd). Although their 750kg (1650lb) shells were a highly effective addition to the German heavy artillery, these guns lacked the range to shell Paris, the most prestigious target of all.

Krupp's design teams then pushed the technology of the era to its limits and managed to produce a weapon capable of reaching the range of 120km (75 miles) needed to shell Paris. The resulting 'Paris Gun' was an amazing technical achievement, although its inaccuracy made it a propaganda weapon rather than a practical artillery system.

It was a very large armament. The gun itself weighed 260 tonnes (256 tons) and was fitted to a special rail-transportable carriage mounted on a prepared concrete emplacement with a turntable. and had a 28m (95ft) long, 21cm (8.3in) rifled barrel, with a

BIG GUNS OF WORLD WAR I

42cm (16.5in) *M-Gerat* 14 howitzer (Big Bertha)

Weight: 43.55 tonnes (42.85 tons)
Shell Weight: 820kg (1807lb)
Length: 6.72m (22ft)
Barrel Length: 5.04m (16ft 6in)
Range: 12.5km (7.7 miles)
Calibre: 42cm (16.5in)
Elevation: 75°
Traverse: 4°

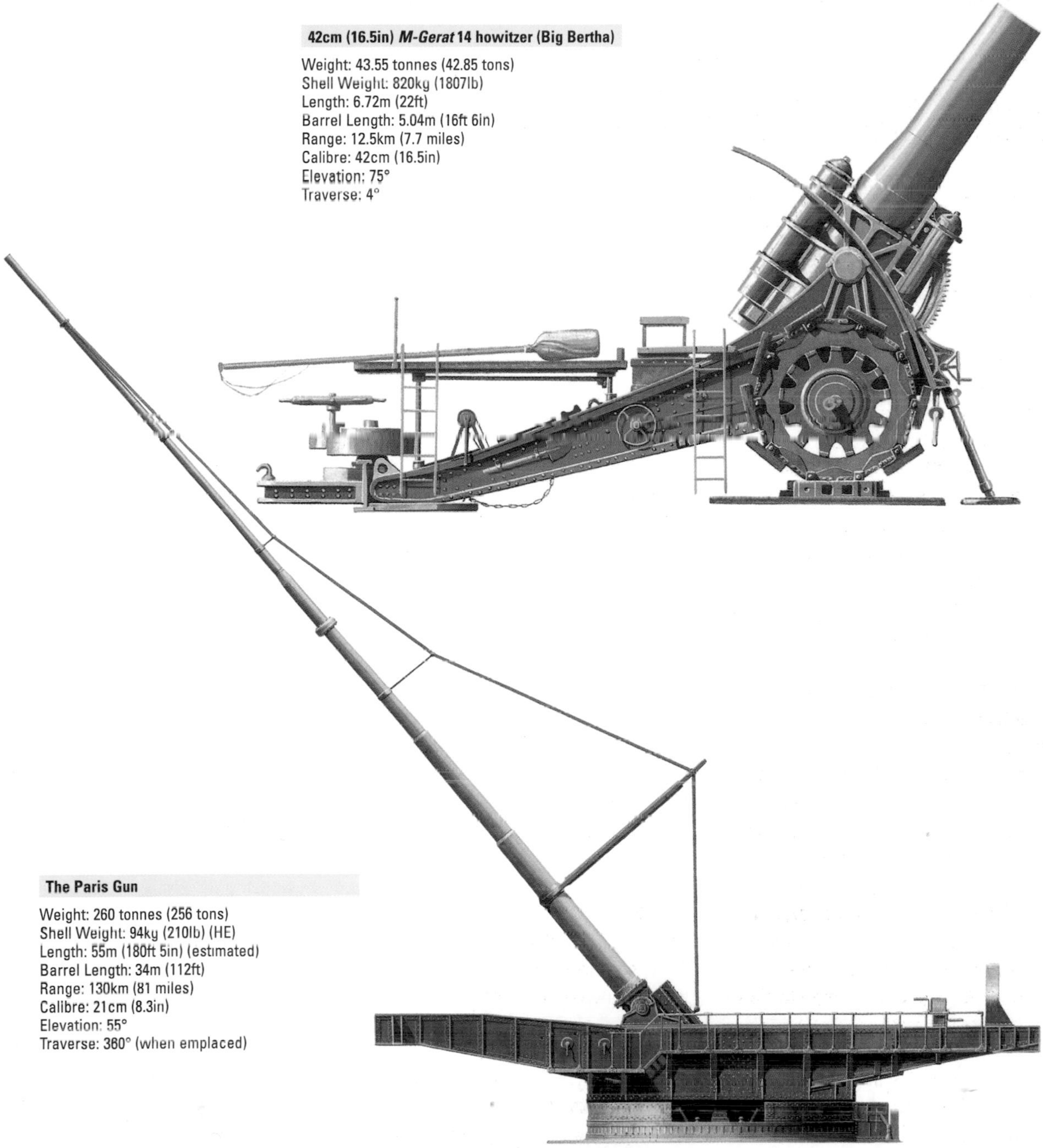

The Paris Gun

Weight: 260 tonnes (256 tons)
Shell Weight: 94kg (210lb) (HE)
Length: 55m (180ft 5in) (estimated)
Barrel Length: 34m (112ft)
Range: 130km (81 miles)
Calibre: 21cm (8.3in)
Elevation: 55°
Traverse: 360° (when emplaced)

6m (20ft) long smoothbore extension. This assembly was braced to counteract barrel droop and was fitted inside a 38cm (15in) *Lange Max* barrel.

The Paris Gun's shells were fired at such a high velocity that each successive round wore away a considerable amount of steel from the rifled bore. Each set of shells were sequentially numbered according to their increasing diameter, and had to be fired in strict sequence to avoid the risk of a burst barrel due to a round jamming in the

BIG GUNS COMPARED

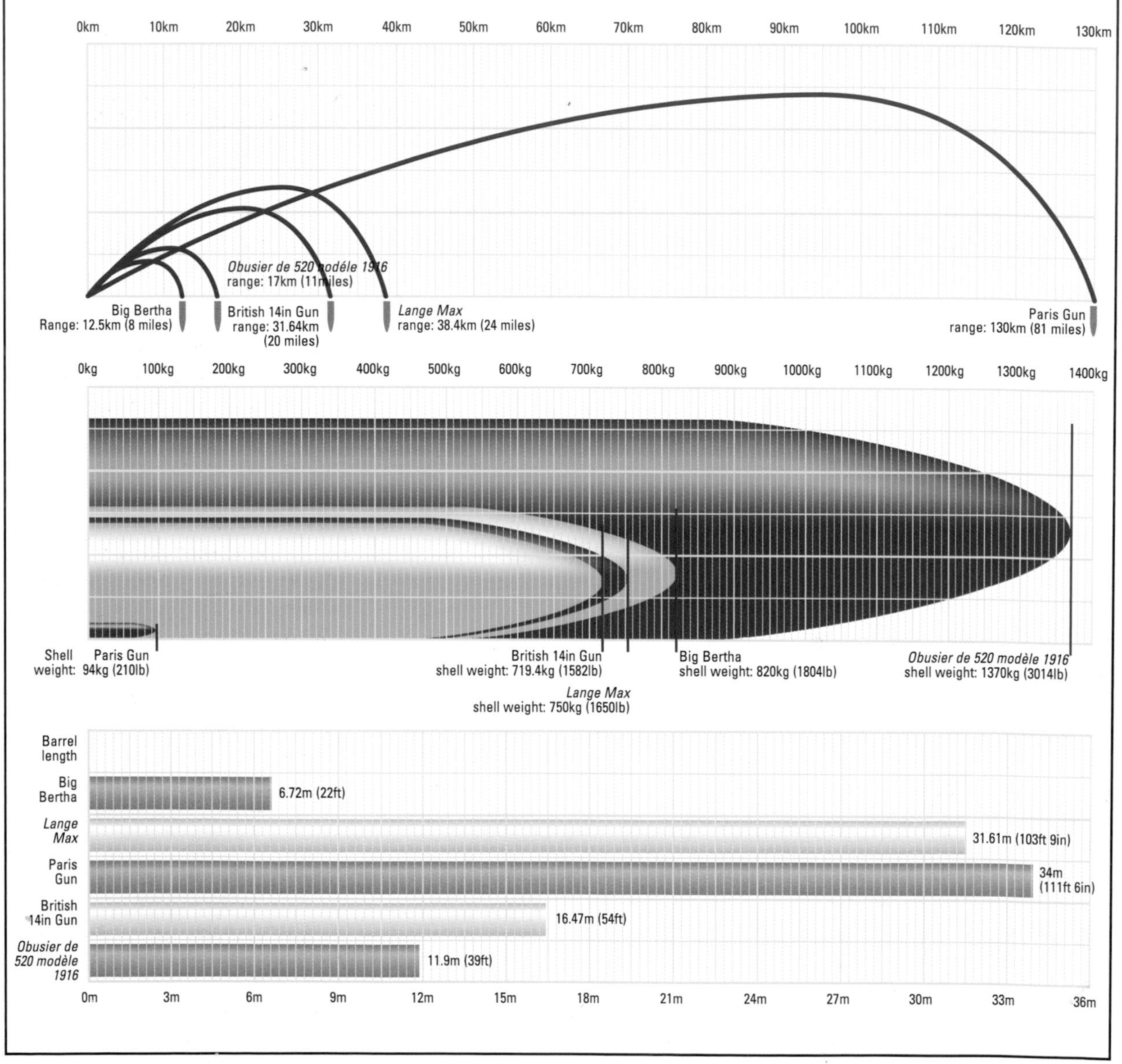
0km
10km
20km
30km
40km
50km
60km
70km
80km
90km
100km
110km
120km
130km
Obusier de 520 modèle 1916
range: 17km (11 miles)
Big Bertha
Range: 12.5km (8 miles)
British 14in Gun
range: 31.64km
(20 miles)
Lange Max
range: 38.4km (24 miles)
Paris Gun
range: 130km (81 miles)
0kg
100kg
200kg
300kg
400kg
500kg
600kg
700kg
800kg
900kg
1000kg
1100kg
1200kg
1300kg
1400kg
Shell weight:
Paris Gun
94kg (210lb)
British 14in Gun
shell weight: 719.4kg (1582lb)
Big Bertha
shell weight: 820kg (1804lb)
Obusier de 520 modèle 1916
shell weight: 1370kg (3014lb)
Lange Max
shell weight: 750kg (1650lb)
Barrel length
Big Bertha
6.72m (22ft)
Lange Max
31.61m (103ft 9in)
Paris Gun
34m
(111ft 6in)
British 14in Gun
16.47m (54ft)
Obusier de 520 modèle 1916
11.9m (39ft)
0m
3m
6m
9m
12m
15m
18m
21m
24m
27m
30m
33m
36m

bore. The huge propelling charges also rapidly wore away the gun's chamber, so that after each shot it had to be carefully measured to determine the difference in its length: even small changes would cause a great variance in the velocity, and with it, the range. Then, with the variation assessed, an additional quantity of propellant was added to the standard charge. After 65 rounds had been fired, each of progressively larger calibre to allow for wear, the barrel was returned to Krupp's and re-bored to 24cm (9.4in) and re-issued with a new set of shells.

Between March and August 1918, when they were withdrawn as the Allies advanced and the war neared its conclusion, the three operational guns fired a total of 367 shells, of which 183 hit various points across Paris, killing 256 civilians and wounding a further 620.

'Tin Donkeys', Giants and Glider Torpedoes

Innovation flourished in the Imperial German Air Service, which encouraged the production of some remarkable aircraft and weapons. The Navy's 'special forces' also pioneered concepts such as the Fernlenkboote *(Explosive Motor Boat), which reappeared in World War II.*

Fortunately for the Allies, by the time that many of these advanced weapons were ready for deployment in 1918, Germany lacked the resources to produce them in quantity. However, in many respects, they represented the shape of things to come in World War II.

The Junkers J.I

The general impression of World War I aircraft is of light, fragile biplanes and triplanes, but the Junkers J.I, which first flew in 1917, was the first all-metal military aircraft to enter series production. Even more remarkably, the entire forward fuselage, from nose to just aft of the rear gunner's position, was a single unit formed of 5mm (0.2in) thick armour. Although slow and unwieldy (dubbed 'Furniture Vans' or 'Tin Donkeys' by their crews), they were popular for their ability to withstand sustained attacks. A total of 227 machines were completed and saw action throughout 1918.

R-Planes

In 1914, the airship pioneer Graf von Zeppelin began development of a *Riesenflugzeug* (Giant Aircraft), or R-Plane. Designs were steadily developed into the *Zeppelin-Staaken R.VI*, 18 of which were completed by the end of the war. They carried out night raids over Britain and France in 1917–18, each carrying an average bomb load totalling 1000kg (2200lb). Four were shot down and six were lost in accidents (mainly crashes on landing).

Siemens Glider Torpedo

In October 1914, Dr Wilhelm von Siemens began work on an air-launched 'stand-off' torpedo to be carried by Zeppelins. Guidance signals were transmitted through a thin copper wire unrolled from a 4km (2.5 mile) reel above the fuselage and the airframe was fitted with flares to help the controller steer it within range of the target vessel before transmitting a signal to release the torpedo.

Extensive flight trials were carried out from Zeppelins between January 1915 and August 1918 using a variety of biplane and monoplane airframes. Eventually, a biplane design was adopted due to its greater carrying ability. This was intended for operational use by the new R.VIII bomber, but none of these aircraft or their glider torpedoes were delivered by the time of the Armistice.

FL-Boats

One of the least-known but most imaginative weapons of the Imperial German Navy was the *Fernlenkboote* (literally 'remote-controlled boat'), or FL-boat. It was a wire-guided 56km/h (30 knot) motorboat, 17m (56.1ft) long,

FERDINAND ADOLF HEINRICH AUGUST GRAF VON ZEPPELIN

■ **Zeppelin was attached to the Union Army as an official observer during the American Civil War when he was impressed by the use of observation balloons.**

Zeppelin appreciated the potential of air power and became the driving force in Germany's development of airships and multi-engine aircraft.

BIRTH:	8 July 1838
DEATH:	8 March 1917
PLACE OF BIRTH:	Konstantz, Grand Duchy of Baden
FATHER:	Friedrich Jerôme Wilhelm Karl Graf von Zeppelin
MOTHER:	Amélie Françoise Pauline (née Macaire d'Hogguer)
SIBLINGS:	Eugenia von Zeppelin; Eberhard von Zeppelin
PERSONAL RELATIONSHIPS:	Isabella Freiin von Wolff, married 7 August 1869. One daughter, Helena (Hella)
MILITARY SERVICE:	Wurttemberg Army, 1858–90
EDUCATION:	Stuttgart Polytechnic
KEY POSITIONS:	Owner of Luftschiffbau Zeppelin GmbH, the company that designed and built civilian and military Zeppelin airships (1908–17). Owner of Versuchsbau Gotha-Ost (VGO), also known as Zeppelin-Staaken, a consortium that designed and built multi-engine bombers (1914–17)

which carried a 700kg (1540lb) impact-fused explosive charge. The type was primarily developed for use against Royal Naval vessels shelling German positions along the Belgian coast. On 28 October 1917, the monitor HMS *Erebus* was struck amidships by an FL-Boat whilst bombarding Zeebrugge. The monitor's anti-torpedo bulge prevented critical damage, but *Erebus* was put out of action for two weeks.

A contemporary account of the FL-Boats and their attack on *Erebus* (here mistakenly referred to as her sister-ship, HMS *Terror*) was given by an RNR officer, Charles Lightoller, in his book *Titanic and Other Ships*:

They evolved what we called an Electric Motor Boat, commonly known as an EMB. These were driven by internal combustion, and directed electrically from the shore by a wire attached to the boat. In the stern was a reel of wire miles long which supplied direction. An aeroplane formed the guiding star and gave directions by wireless back to the station ashore. In the bows, the EMB. carried a high explosive charge and travelled at some 30 knots (56km/h). In consequence, it was almost impossible to hit her. With us Destroyers we could always get out of the way, by either heaving up, if there was time, or slipping our cables if there wasn't. With the unwieldy Monitors it was another matter, for they could neither slip, nor move quickly enough to dodge. The result was, they would see the feather of foam (which was all that could be seen of the EMB), and then they promptly loosed off with every gun they possessed, with every hope, but little prospect, of registering a hit. Of course, the Monitor had its blister, or bulge, round the water line, so there was really no fear of her being actually sunk. But, as in one case, the EMB came charging along everybody blazing away with really more danger to themselves than the precious boat – and hit the Terror*'s blister a glancing blow, leapt clean up and out of the water, exploding on her upper works. No small amount of damage ensued... Those boats... travelled at an angle of almost 30-degree tail down and nose up. That was how this one came to jump the* Terror*'s blister, and blow in her upper works.*

Rebuilding an Arsenal, 1919–39

Following Germany's defeat in 1918, the Treaty of Versailles imposed severe restrictions on the size and equipment of her armed forces. Almost immediately, German generals and admirals began to examine ways to circumvent the hated diktat *of Versailles.*

The ban imposed on key weapons such as tanks, aircraft and U-boats was partially evaded by setting up dummy companies based in Sweden and the Netherlands to continue development work on such weapons for foreign customers. In addition, Germany sought help from Russia, the other pariah state of Europe. In a secret annex to the Treaty of Rapallo, signed in 1922, the Soviet government authorized the establishment of German military and aviation bases within Russia.

These bases were primarily used for research and development and tactical training with weapons banned under the terms of the Treaty of Versailles. In return, Germany would allow the Red Army to conduct military exercises alongside the *Reichswehr* and would also share industrial and military technology.

A new generation

In 1925–26, the companies Rheinmetall-Borsig, MAN, Krupp and Daimler-Benz received orders from the *Reichswehr* for prototypes of light tanks of 10.2–12.2 tonnes (10–12 tons), and medium tanks of up to 23.4 tonnes (23 tons), under the cover name of 'tractors'. These were secretly tested in Russia at the *Panzertruppenschule Kama*, near Kazan, between 1930 and 1933. The light tanks were designated *Leichte Traktor* (VK 31) and were armed with a turret-mounted 37mm (1.45in) KwK L/45 gun and a co-axial machine gun. The medium tanks, initially known as *Armeewagen 20* (later renamed *Grosstraktor*) were fitted with a turret-mounted 75mm (2.95in) gun and three or four machine guns in two sub-turrets. While none of these vehicles were entirely satisfactory, they provided the German AFV design teams with invaluable data.

Development of the *Neubaufahrzeug* (New Construction Vehicle) began in 1933 when the *Reichswehr* issued a contract for the development of the *Grosstraktor* to both Rheinmetall and Krupp. The two designs closely resembled each other, the main difference being the weapons layout. Each had a main turret armed with a 75mm (2.95in) KwK L/24 main gun and co-axial 37mm (1.45in) KwK L/45. Rheinmetall's design mounted the secondary armament above the 75mm (2.95in) KwK L/24, while the Krupp design had it mounted next to the 75mm (2.95in) KwK L/24. Both designs had small machine-gun turrets derived from the Panzer I, mounted to the front and the rear of the main turret.

Rheinmetall's design was designated the PzKpfw NbFz V (*PanzerKampfwagen NeubauFahrzeug V*), and the Krupp design the PzKpfw NbFz VI. It was intended that these types would become the heavy 'breakthrough' tanks of the *Panzerwaffe*, but the design was too complex and unreliable. Development nevertheless continued in order to gain experience with multi-turreted tanks.

In 1934, Rheinmetall built two prototypes with their own turret design, and three more fully armoured prototypes were built with the Krupp turret in 1935–36. Three vehicles took part in the invasion of Norway in 1940, primarily to deceive Allied intelligence.

Henschel began development of more powerful modern heavy tank designs in January 1937 in response to a requirement for a *Durchbruchwagen* (Breakthrough Vehicle). These led to Henschel's final pre-war designs – the VK3001(H) medium tank and the VK3601(H) heavy tank. Both were potentially good combat vehicles which were able to mount high velocity 75mm (2.95in) guns or close support howitzers of up to 105mm (4.1in) (VK3001(H)) or 128mm (5in) (VK3601(H)).

However, the German victories of 1939–40 led to over-confidence and neither of the new designs entered service. Only the encounters with the T-34 and KV-1 in Operation Barbarossa shattered the illusion of Panzer invincibility and ended the inertia.

A New Navy: Pocket Battleships and Plan Z

In 1929, the revolutionary battleship, Panzerschiff Deutschland, *was laid down at Kiel. Although ostensibly within the 10,160 tonne (10,000 ton) limit for capital ships set by the Treaty of Versailles, it was 610 tonnes (600 tons) overweight on completion and the weight rose steadily as new equipment was fitted.*

Even so, it was a remarkable technological achievement, pioneering the large-scale use of hull welding instead of the then-standard rivets and diesel engines. The 28cm (11in) main armament was concentrated in two triple turrets, a development of a weight-saving idea first used in the Austro-Hungarian *Tegetthof* battleships just before World War I. The *Deutschland,* and the following vessels in the class, caused a sensation in the world's navies; theoretically they were capable of sinking any cruiser and could outrun any battleship. Only a handful of British battlecruisers, HMS *Hood, Renown* and *Repulse* could

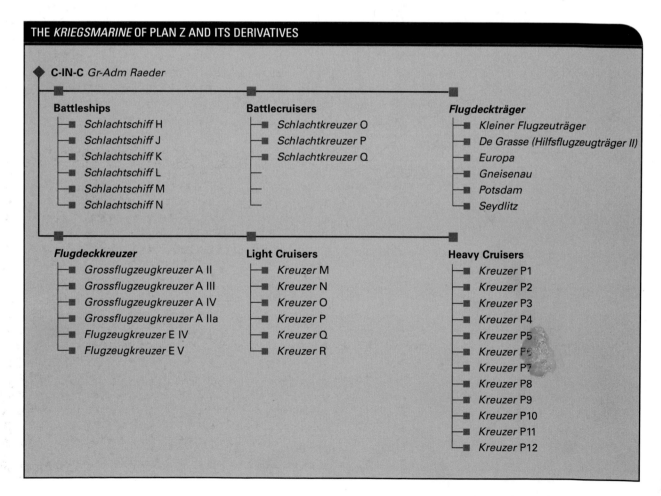

THE *KRIEGSMARINE* OF PLAN Z AND ITS DERIVATIVES

C-IN-C *Gr-Adm Raeder*

Battleships
- *Schlachtschiff* H
- *Schlachtschiff* J
- *Schlachtschiff* K
- *Schlachtschiff* L
- *Schlachtschiff* M
- *Schlachtschiff* N

Battlecruisers
- *Schlachtkreuzer* O
- *Schlachtkreuzer* P
- *Schlachtkreuzer* Q

Flugdeckträger
- *Kleiner Flugzeuträger*
- *De Grasse (Hilfsflugzeugträger II)*
- *Europa*
- *Gneisenau*
- *Potsdam*
- *Seydlitz*

Flugdeckkreuzer
- *Grossflugzeugkreuzer* A II
- *Grossflugzeugkreuzer* A III
- *Grossflugzeugkreuzer* A IV
- *Grossflugzeugkreuzer* A IIa
- *Flugzeugkreuzer* E IV
- *Flugzeugkreuzer* E V

Light Cruisers
- *Kreuzer* M
- *Kreuzer* N
- *Kreuzer* O
- *Kreuzer* P
- *Kreuzer* Q
- *Kreuzer* R

Heavy Cruisers
- *Kreuzer* P1
- *Kreuzer* P2
- *Kreuzer* P3
- *Kreuzer* P4
- *Kreuzer* P5
- *Kreuzer* P6
- *Kreuzer* P7
- *Kreuzer* P8
- *Kreuzer* P9
- *Kreuzer* P10
- *Kreuzer* P11
- *Kreuzer* P12

catch them and the threat posed by these new ships prompted the French navy to hastily authorize two new fast *Dunkerque* class battleships.

The prestige brought by the *panzerschiffe* led to the navy ordering two improved vessels, *Panzerschiffe D and E*. These became the *Scharnhorst* and *Gneisenau*, carrying nine, instead of six, 28cm (11in) guns. The Anglo-German Naval Agreement of 18 June 1935, which allowed Germany to build a navy equivalent to 35 per cent of British surface ship tonnage and 45 per cent of British submarine tonnage, boosted German confidence, marked by Hitler changing the name of the *Reichsmarine* to *Kriegsmarine*.

By 1938, Plan Z had evolved after much debate within the *Kriegsmarine* between the traditionalists, who favoured a battle fleet capable of taking on the most powerful foreign navies, and those who favoured using a large U-boat force to destroy enemy commercial shipping.

Ultimately, the traditionalists' views prevailed and the plan would have seen the completion of two battleships (*Bismarck* and *Tirpitz*) and three heavy cruisers (*Admiral Hipper, Blücher* and *Prinz Eugen*), then under construction. The following major units would then be built, with the majority being completed by 1945:

- Four aircraft carriers
- Six H-class battleships
- Three O-class battlecruisers
- Twelve *Kreuzer* P-class *Panzerschiffe*
- Two heavy cruisers (*Seydlitz* and *Lützow*)
- Four M-class light cruisers
- Two improved M-class light cruisers
- Six *Spähkreuzer* class large destroyers
- 249 U-boats

Construction began on the aircraft carrier *Graf Zeppelin* in 1936, with a second carrier laid down in 1938. In mid-1939, following the launching of *Bismarck* and *Tirpitz*, the keels of the first three improved battleships were laid, while orders were placed for navalized Messerschmitt Bf 109 fighters and Junkers Ju 87 dive-bombers for the carriers. However, with the outbreak of World War II, it was decided that these large projects required too many of the resources vital for the army and *Luftwaffe*. As a result, work on the ships was halted (despite the fact that *Graf Zeppelin* was almost complete) and the materials were diverted to the U-boat construction programme.

ERICH JOHANN ALBERT RAEDER

■ **Raeder was promoted to Germany's highest naval rank of Grand Admiral in 1939, the first person to hold the rank since Henning von Holtzendorff in 1918.**

Raeder was steeped in the traditions of the Imperial German Navy in which he served with distinction. After the German defeat in 1918, his exceptional administrative skills ensured his rapid promotion in the tiny post-war *Reichsmarine*. He strongly supported plans for rebuilding a powerful fleet, culminating in the ambitious 'Plan Z' of 1939.

BIRTH:	24 April 1876
DEATH:	6 November 1960
PLACE OF BIRTH:	Wandsbek, Schleswig-Holstein
FATHER:	Hans Raeder (school teacher)
MOTHER:	Gertraudt (née Hartmann)
PERSONAL RELATIONSHIPS:	One son, Hans
NAVAL SERVICE:	Officer Cadet (1894); Chief of Staff to Admiral Franz von Hipper (1912–17); Rear Admiral (1922); Vice Admiral (1925); Admiral (1928); *Reichsmarine* Chief of Staff (1928); Grand Admiral (1939); Admiral Inspector (Jan 1943); Retired (May 1943)

BATTLESHIPS COMPARED

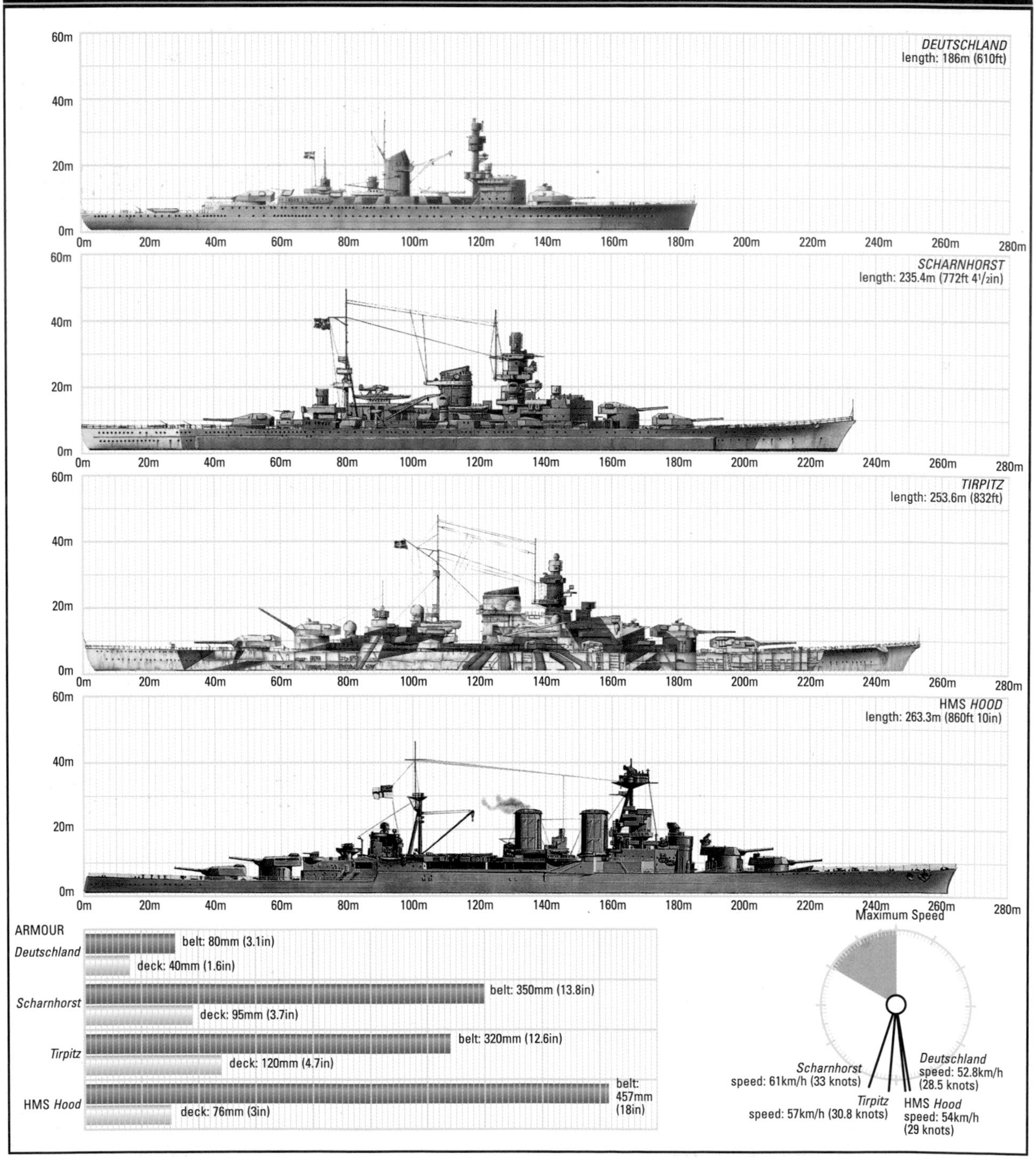
DEUTSCHLAND
length: 186m (610ft)
SCHARNHORST
length: 235.4m (772ft 4½in)
TIRPITZ
length: 253.6m (832ft)
HMS HOOD
length: 263.3m (860ft 10in)
0m 20m 40m 60m 80m 100m 120m 140m 160m 180m 200m 220m 240m 260m 280m
0m 20m 40m 60m
ARMOUR
Deutschland
belt: 80mm (3.1in)
deck: 40mm (1.6in)
Scharnhorst
belt: 350mm (13.8in)
deck: 95mm (3.7in)
Tirpitz
belt: 320mm (12.6in)
deck: 120mm (4.7in)
HMS Hood
belt: 457mm (18in)
deck: 76mm (3in)
Maximum Speed
Scharnhorst speed: 61km/h (33 knots)
Tirpitz speed: 57km/h (30.8 knots)
Deutschland speed: 52.8km/h (28.5 knots)
HMS Hood speed: 54km/h (29 knots)

A NEW ERA: OUTGUNNING THE OLD

In the table below, the broadside weights and ranges are given for main and secondary armaments – these represent the maximum weight of fire which could be brought to bear on a single surface target. In most cases, only half the secondary guns could fire on such a target. The maximum ranges of main armaments are largely theoretical, as even with radar fire control, the chances of hitting a target at maximum range were almost non-existent. In July 1940, HMS *Warspite* hit the Italian battleship *Guilio Cesare* at approximately 23,775m (26,000yd) and this is generally accepted as the longest range at which a hit was ever scored on a moving target in a naval action.

NEW BATTLESHIPS: WEIGHTS AND RANGES COMPARED

Battleship	*Armament*	*Type*	*Weight*	*Range*	*Rate of fire*
Deutschland	Broadside	6 x 28cm (11in)	1800kg (3968lb)	36,475m (39,890yd)	
	Secondary	4 x 15cm (5.9in)	181.2kg (399.5lb)	22,000m (24,060yd)	
	AA	6 x 105mm (4.1in)	15.1kg (33.3lb)	12,500m (41,010ft)	15–18rpm
		8 x 37mm (1.45in)	0.74kg (1.64lb)	4800m (15,750ft)	30rpm
		10 x 20mm (0.79in)	0.13kg (0.3lb)	3700m (12,140ft)	120rpm
Scharnhorst	Broadside	9 x 28cm (11in)	2835kg (6250lb)	40,930m (44,760yd)	
	Secondary	6 x 15cm (5.9in)	271.8kg (599.2lb)	22,000m (24,060yd)	
	AA	14 x 105mm (4.1in)	15.1kg (33.3lb)	12,500m (41,010ft)	15–18rpm
		16 x 37mm (1.45in)	0.74kg (1.64lb)	4800m (15,750ft)	30rpm
		10 x 20mm (0.79in)	0.13kg (0.3lb)	3700m (12,140ft)	120rpm
Tirpitz	Broadside	8 x 38cm (15in)	6400kg (14,109lb)	36,520m (39,589yd)	
	Secondary	6 x 15cm (5.9in)	271.8kg (599.2lb)	22,000m (24,060yd)	
	AA	16 x 105mm (4.1in)	15.1kg (33.3lb)	12,500m (41,010ft)	15–18rpm
		16 x 37mm (1.45in)	0.74kg (1.64lb)	4800m (15,750ft)	30rpm
		12 x 20mm (0.79in)	0.13kg (0.3lb)	3700m (12,140ft)	220rpm
		72 x 20mm (0.79in)	0.13kg (0.3lb)	3700m (12,140ft)	220rpm
HMS *Hood*	Broadside	8 x 38cm (15in)	7032kg (15,504lb)	29,720m (32,500yd)	
	Secondary	8 x 101.6mm (4in)	130.4kg (287.5lb)	19,476m (21,300yd)	
	AA	14 x 101.6mm (4in)	16.3kg (35.9lb)	12,192m (40,000ft)	16–18rpm
		24 x 40mm (1.6in)	0.9kg (2lb)	3960m (13,300ft)	100rpm

NEW BATTLESHIPS: MAIN BROADSIDE ARMAMENT RANGE

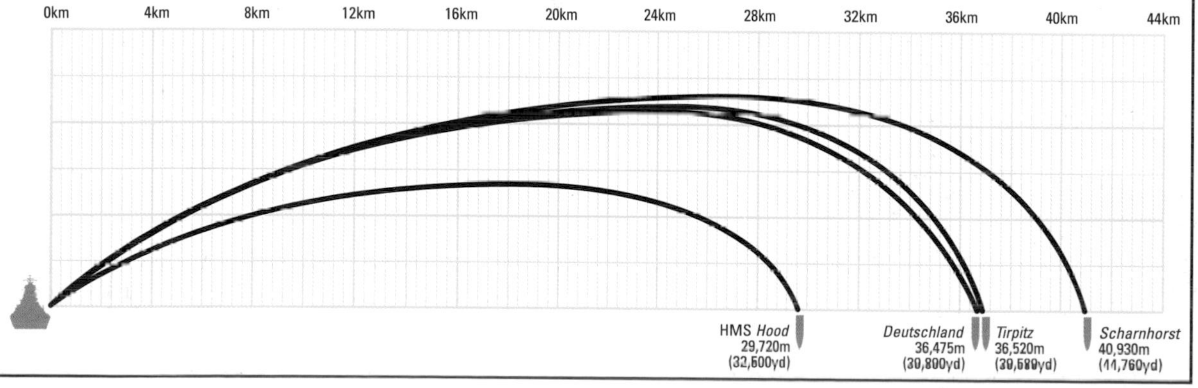
0km
4km
8km
12km
16km
20km
24km
28km
32km
36km
40km
44km
HMS Hood
29,720m
(32,500yd)
Deutschland
36,475m
(39,800yd)
Tirpitz
36,520m
(39,589yd)
Scharnhorst
40,930m
(44,760yd)

CHAPTER 2

Maritime Weapons Programme

The Kriegsmarine *was largely unprepared for the outbreak of war in 1939 which wrecked 'Plan Z', the programme for fleet expansion that was scheduled for completion in 1945–46. Despite the suspension of construction work on the major surface vessels to free resources for U-boat production, design studies for ever-larger capital ships continued throughout the war.*

In contrast to these grandiose projects, the growing need for weapons capable of combating Allied amphibious operations led to the rapid development of the 'semi-suicidal' Linse explosive motor-boats and a host of equally hazardous manned torpedoes and miniature submarines.

It is highly unlikely that any of these could have decisively altered the outcome of the war, but there was one class of vessel which had the potential to do just that – the revolutionary Type XXI U-boat.

Although less hazardous than the tiny *Biber* midget submarine, the *Molch* (Salamander) proved ineffective in combat.

New Battleships

In 1937, the Oberkommando der Kriegsmarine *(OKM) ordered a design study of new battleships to succeed the* Bismarck *class. Initial proposals were for enlarged and more powerfully armed developments of the basic* Bismarck *design that could be completed in time to meet the schedule imposed by Plan Z.*

The schedule began to slip, however. Hitler's love of big projects began to cause problems early in the design process as he was adamant that the ships should have a 50.8cm (20in) main armament, rather than the 40.6cm (16in) guns proposed by the naval design teams. He reluctantly authorized the smaller weapons after it was explained that any battleship with 50.8cm (20in) guns would be between 81,280 and 121,920 tonnes (80,000 and 120,000 tons) with an overall length of roughly 300m (1000ft). Vessels of this size would need new, greatly enlarged harbour facilities and would take far longer to design and build than more conventional capital ships.

As finally approved, the H-39 design was basically an enlarged version of the *Bismarck* class. The most recognizable feature of the new design was its twin funnel layout, in contrast to the single funnels of all the *Kriegsmarine*'s earlier capital ships. Internally, the H-39 was very different to *Bismarck* and *Tirpitz* as it was powered by 12 MAN diesel engines instead of the earlier vessels' steam turbines. It was calculated that the diesel engines would increase the H-39s' range by 60 per cent and give a top speed of 56km/h (30 knots), comparable to that of the battleships entering service in foreign navies.

The increased proportion of space occupied by the engines and funnels forced a redesign of the *Bismarck*'s aircraft-handling arrangements, which concentrated the hangars and catapult amidships. The chosen solution was to site hangars for four Arado Ar 196 seaplanes in the aft superstructure with rails running either side of the after turrets to allow the aircraft to be moved easily to a centreline catapult on the quarterdeck.

A total of six H-39 class battleships were ordered under Plan Z and construction contracts were placed with companies across Germany:

- *Schlachtschiff* 'H' to Blohm und Voss, Hamburg
- *Schlachtschiff* 'J' to Deutsche Schiff-und Maschinenbau AG, Bremen
- *Schlachtschiff* 'K' to Deutsche Werke, Kiel
- *Schlachtschiff* 'L' to the Kriegsmarinewerft, Wilhelmshaven
- *Schlachtschiff* 'M' to Blohm und Voss, Hamburg
- *Schlachtschiff* 'N' to Deutsche Schiff-und Maschinenbau AG, Bremen

'H' was laid down on 15 July 1939 and 'J' on 1 September 1939. 'K' was scheduled to be laid down on 15 September, but work was postponed because of the outbreak of war. A hold was also placed on construction of the two ships already started. At the time that construction was frozen, 'H' had 14,278 tonnes (14,055 tons) of material ordered, 5893 tonnes (5800 tons) delivered but only 778 tonnes (766 tons) worked into the keel. Less work had been carried out on 'J', for which 3587 tonnes (3531 tons) of material had been ordered but only 41 tonnes (40 tons) put into the keel. In 1940, it was decided to cancel the H-39 programme to free resources for U-boat construction – 'H' and 'J' were duly scrapped, but design studies into improved battleships continued.

H-40

Construction of the first of these battleships began in 1940, with an examination of potential improvements to the armour protection of the original H-39 design. Two solutions were considered, which were unofficially dubbed H-40A and H-40B. H-40A shipped a reduced main armament of three twin 40.6cm (16in) turrets to permit much thicker armour, without greatly increasing displacement, while H-40B retained the original four twin 40.6cm (16in) turrets, but was substantially enlarged to provide increased protection. As the increased weight required greater power to maintain the design speed of 59km/h (32 knots), it was decided to switch to a mixed powerplant of marine diesels supplemented by steam turbines, now driving four shafts instead of three. These were unofficial studies, and did not significantly influence later designs, from H-41 onwards.

H-41

In 1941, OKM started a formal series of studies into future battleships, specifying a top speed of at least 56km/h (30 knots) with armour heavy enough to match expected opposition. This resulted in the H-41 design which featured increased horizontal armour and deeper torpedo bulkhead protection together with the mixed propulsion system of

H-CLASS BATTLESHIPS ON THE DRAWING BOARD

Design	*Displacement/Length*	*Main Armament*	*Performance/Speed*
Tirpitz 	53,442 tonnes (52,600 tons)/ 251m (828ft)	8 x 38cm (15in)	163,000shp/ 57.5km/h (30.8 knots)
H-39 	63,497 tonnes (62,497 tons)/ 277.8m (917ft)	8 x 40.6cm (16in)	165,000shp/ 56km/h (30 knots)
H-40A 	66,650 tonnes (65,600 tons)/ 282.9m (933ft)	6 x 40.6cm (16in)	230,000shp/ 60.2km/h (32.2 knots)
H-40B 	71,120 tonnes (70,000 tons)/ 299.8m (989ft)	8 x 40.6cm (16in)	240,000shp/ 60.4km/h (32.3 knots)
H-41 	77,216 tonnes (76,000 tons)/ 300.4m (991ft)	8 x 40.6cm (16in)	165,000shp/ 53.9km/h (28.8 knots)
H-42 	99,568 tonnes (98,000 tons)/ 305.2m (1007ft)	8 x 40.6cm (16in)	270,000shp/ 60.2km/h (32.2 knots)
H-43 	121,920 tonnes (120,000 tons)/ 330.2m (1090ft)	8 x 50.8cm (20in)	270,000shp/ 58km/h (30.1 knots)
H-44 	143,764 tonnes (141,500 tons)/ 345.1m (1139ft)	8 x 50.8cm (20in)	165,000shp/ 58km/h (30.1 knots)
CVN *John C Stennis*, completed 1995 	103,632 tonnes (102,000 tons)/ 332.9m (1098ft)	none	280,000shp/ 56+km/h (30.0+knots)

the 1940 designs, but retained a three-shaft layout. The H-41 design was slightly larger than the Japanese *Yamato*-class, displacing nearly 77,216 tonnes (76,000 tons) full load with an overall length of just over 300m (990ft).

H-42

After the loss of the *Bismarck* in May 1941, the problem of vulnerability to air attack was re-examined. A new series of modifications to H-41 was drafted, which attempted to reduce the vulnerability of propellers and rudders to torpedo attack. The proposals also reflected the lessons learned from the damage inflicted on *Scharnhorst* by RAF bombing during 1941. Initially, amendments were worked into the existing plans for the H-41, but it soon became clear that a fresh start was required and a new design, designated H-42, was developed instead. It now used four shafts, with shrouding to protect the propeller skegs, and multiple rudders aligned with the shafts to provide manoeuvering redundancy in the event of damage to the steering gear. Increased displacement led to a deeper draft, which would have complicated the construction and

H-39, H-44, 'H-45', BRITISH *LION* CLASS, US *MONTANA* CLASS ARMAMENTS COMPARED

Ship	Main Armament	Secondary	AA	Torpedo
H-39 Battleship	8 x 40.6cm (16in) *Schnelladekanone* C/34	12 x 15cm (5.9in)	16 x 105mm (4.1in) 16 x 37mm (1.45in) 24 x 20mm (0.79in)	6 x 53.3cm (21in) torpedo tubes
H-44 Battleship	8 x 50.8cm (20in)	12 x 15cm (5.9in)	16 x 105mm (4.1in) 28 x 37mm (1.45in) 40 x 20mm (0.79in)	6 x 53.3cm (21in) torpedo tubes
'H-45' Battleship	8 x 80cm (31.5in)	12 x 24cm (9.5in) DP	24 x 128mm (5.04in) 55mm light AA gun 30mm light AA gun	
Lion Class	9 x 406mm (16in)	16 x 133mm (5.25in) DP	48 x 40mm (1.57in) 2pdr	
Montana Class	12 x 406mm (16in)	20 x 127mm (5in) DP	40 x 40mm (1.57in) Bofors 56 x 20mm (0.79in) Oerlikon	

'H-45' BATTLESHIP

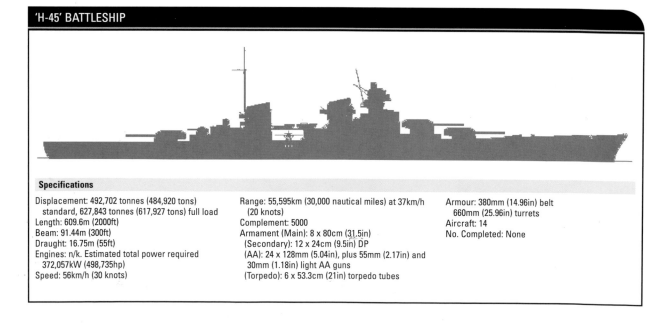

Specifications

Displacement: 492,702 tonnes (484,920 tons) standard, 627,843 tonnes (617,927 tons) full load
Length: 609.6m (2000ft)
Beam: 91.44m (300ft)
Draught: 16.75m (55ft)
Engines: n/k. Estimated total power required 372,057kW (498,735hp)
Speed: 56km/h (30 knots)
Range: 55,595km (30,000 nautical miles) at 37km/h (20 knots)
Complement: 5000
Armament (Main): 8 x 80cm (31.5in)
(Secondary): 12 x 24cm (9.5in) DP
(AA): 24 x 128mm (5.04in), plus 55mm (2.17in) and 30mm (1.18in) light AA guns
(Torpedo): 6 x 53.3cm (21in) torpedo tubes
Armour: 380mm (14.96in) belt 660mm (25.96in) turrets
Aircraft: 14
No. Completed: None

operation of these vessels. H-42 was already becoming a more massive ship than its predecessors; with improved armour and anti-torpedo protection it ended up 305m (1007ft) long with a beam of nearly 43m (142ft) and a full-load displacement of 99,568 tonnes (98,000 tons) – the size of a modern nuclear-powered supercarrier.

H-43 and H-44

After the H-42, designs became increasingly unrealistic – in order to defeat all possible opponents, the main armament was increased to eight 50.8cm (20in) guns, one of the largest calibres ever considered for seaborne use. However, there was no significant improvement to the secondary and heavy AA armament which had proved inadequate on *Bismarck*'s sole operational voyage. Only 37mm (1.45in) and 20mm (0.79in) weapons were augmented, but their effectiveness against air attack was quite limited. The H-43 was impractical – German yards would have been extremely hard-pressed to build the class and operating them in any confined waters would have been very hazardous. The design merely illustrated the possibilities, given no constraints, and resembled the US Navy's Tillman 'maximum battleship' studies of 1916.

The H-44 was the last serious large battleship study and incorporated elaborate protection, including multiple armoured decks which were intended to resist all but the heaviest armour-piercing bombs. The multiple anti-torpedo bulkheads had a total transverse depth of 11m (33ft) (twice that of *Bismarck*) and a triple bottom was proposed to minimise mine damage. The four-shaft mixed propulsion system was similar to those designed for the H-42 and H-43, but the increased size of the H-44 caused a slight reduction in speed, although endurance remained the same: 37,000km (20,000 nautical miles) at 35km/h (19 knots).

The main armament of the H-44 was identical to that of the H-43; eight 50.8cm (20in) guns in four twin turrets. Given the increasingly serious air threat, it is surprising that the heavy AA armament was still unchanged from that of the *Bismarck* and *Tirpitz*. Smaller AA guns were more numerous – a total of 28 x 37mm (1.45in) in twin mounts, plus 10 x 20mm (0.79in) quadruple *Flakvierling* mounts. The increased bulk of the H-44 allowed a larger hangar, with room for up to nine seaplanes.

The last word – 'H-45'

Although H-44 was the last proper battleship design study, there is a final twist to the story. In the aftermath of the loss of the *Bismarck*, Hitler pressed for the H-class designs

O-CLASS BATTLECRUISER

Specifications

Displacement: 32,818 tonnes (32,300 tons) standard, 38,813 tonnes (38,200 tons) full load
Length: 256m (840ft)
Beam: 30m (98ft)
Draught: 8.02m (26ft 3½in)
Engines: 8 x 24-cylinder diesel engines, plus Brown Boveri turbines totalling 131,243kW (176,000hp)
Speed: 65km/h (35 knots)
Range: 26,000km (14,000 nautical miles) at 35km/h (19 knots)
Complement: 1965
Armament (Main): 6 x 381mm (15in)
(Secondary): 6 x 150mm (5.9in)
(AA): 8 x 105mm (4.1in), 8 x 37mm (1.45in), 20 x 20mm (0.79in)
(Torpedo): 6 x 53.3cm (21in) torpedo tubes
Armour: 190mm (7.5in) belt, 210mm (8.3in) turrets
Aircraft: 4
No. completed: None

to be enlarged to allow a main armament of eight 80cm (31.5in) guns, derived from the *Gustav/Dora* railway guns. Had the idea been taken up, it would probably have resulted in an unwieldy leviathan. The design was designated 'H-45' for convenience – it would have far exceeded the tonnage of today's largest ship, the 564,763 tonne (555,843 ton) supertanker, *Knock Nevis*.

O-class battlecruiser

The O-class battlecruisers formed a key part of Plan Z, and were intended to operate against Allied convoys in conjunction with two task forces, each of which would be built around three H-class battleships and an aircraft carrier. The task forces would attack the convoy escorts, while the battlecruisers went for the merchant vessels. None were completed as U-boat construction took priority.

Linsen Explosive Motor-Boat (EMB)

Although the Imperial German Navy had pioneered the construction and use of Explosive Motor-Boats (EMBs) during World War I, the Kriegsmarine *was slow to develop the type, which was not deployed operationally until 1944.*

The first *Linsen* produced in early 1944 were derived from the contemporary Italian MTM EMBs but eventually evolved into rather more seaworthy craft. In theory, the *Linsen* operated at night in sections of three (two attack boats and one unarmed control boat). The approach to the target area was made at low speed, exploiting the near-silence of their engines at speeds below 14.8km/h (8 knots). When they had closed to within a few hundred metres of their target, the attack boats accelerated to full speed. At roughly 90m (100yd) range, their crews armed the warheads and jumped overboard to await rescue by the control boat.

The attack boats were then guided to their targets (primarily transports at anchor) by radio signals from an ultra-shortwave transmitter in the control boat – the operator simply had to align the attack boats' two shielded red and green recognition lights with the targets. If all went well, the attack boat's impact would compress a metal bumper framework around the bow, triggering a small charge that blew off the bow section and primed a seven-second delayed action fuse of the main, stern-mounted charge. The attack boat then sank and the 400kg (880lb) charge detonated with the effect of a ground mine. The controller could also detonate the main charge manually if he thought that the attack boats would 'near miss' the targets.

EXPLOSIVE MOTOR-BOATS (EMBs) COMPARED

Categories	*Linse*	*Boom Patrol Boat (British)*
Type	Explosive Motor-Boat	Explosive Motor-Boat
Crew	1	1
Displacement	1.83 tonnes (1.8 tons)	1.52 tonnes (1.5 tons)
Length	5.75m (18ft 10in)	5.5m (18ft)
Beam	1.75m (5ft 9in)	1.52m (5ft)
Draught	n/k	n/k
Engines	2 x 70.64kW (95hp) Ford V-8 petrol engines	1 x 104.4kW (140hp) Gray Fireball 12-cylinder petrol engine
Speed	65km/h (35 knots)	55.5km/h (30 knots)
Range	111km (60 nautical miles)	111km (60 nautical miles)
Warhead	400kg (880lb) HE	226kg (497lb) HE
No. Completed	1400	Prototype and trials vessels only

Commando raids

The first *Linsen* were used by Otto Skorzeny's SS special forces in unsuccessful attacks on Allied shipping off Anzio in April 1944 and by the *Kriegsmarine* in equally fruitless strikes against the invasion fleet off the Normandy coast in June. The fragility of these vessels led to a hasty redesign and the new boats were thrown into action from August 1944, operating initially in the Channel and Scheldt estuary. They suffered horrendous losses (often 50 per cent or more) from Allied light escort forces and scored very few confirmed 'kills' – probably no more than the minesweeping trawler HMS *Gairsay*, the fire-support landing craft LCG(L)(4)-764 and the Liberty ship *Samlong*. *Linsen* were also deployed in the Mediterranean and Adriatic seas, but suffered similar crippling losses and failed to sink or seriously damage a single Allied ship.

Two high-speed EMBs were designed, but never used operationally. The first, *Tornado*, was based on a pair of modified floats from the Junkers Ju 52 seaplane powered by an Argus 109-014 pulse-jet engine. A 700kg (1550lb) HE charge was carried, but the project was cancelled when it was found that the prototype could barely exceed 65km/h (35 knots) and showed an alarming tendency to capsize in anything other than calm weather. The second design, *Schlitten* (Sledge) was a one-man catamaran carrying a 1200kg (2650lb) warhead powered by a 447.42kW (600hp) engine, giving an estimated maximum speed of 120km/h (65 knots).

U-boats

Conventional U-boats came close to winning the Battle of the Atlantic in 1940–43, but were defeated by increasingly effective Allied counter-measures. In an attempt to regain the initiative, German naval yards produced highly sophisticated vessels which were to influence submarine design for the next 50 years.

Type XVII and XVIII U-boats

Hellmuth Walter patented an air-independent propulsion (AIP) system, in 1925. This used Perhydrol, an almost pure hydrogen-peroxide solution, in conjunction with a potassium permanganate catalyst to produce high pressure steam which powered a turbine. Although the system showed great promise when tested in the small experimental U-boat *V-80* in 1940, it also had a high rate of fuel consumption and there was a real risk of explosion if any impurities got into the system. In fact, a post-war British submarine, HMS *Explorer*, which used the same Walter design, suffered so many dangerous accidents that the Navy dubbed her 'HMS *Exploder*'. Despite the obvious drawbacks, orders were placed for Walter-powered coastal U-boats (Type XVII) and a larger, ocean-going class (Type XVIII). Three Type XVIIs were completed by the end of the war, but orders for the Type XVIII were cancelled in 1944 to free resources for the construction of Type XXI U-boats.

Type XXI and XXIII U-boats

The hulls of the revolutionary Type XXI and Type XXIII boats were derived from the design of the Walter U-boats, which had an enlarged double hull forming a figure-of-eight in section. The upper part housed the crew, engines and torpedoes while the lower section was completely filled with fuel tanks for the thirsty Walter system and diesel engines. As it became apparent that the Walter boats were pushing the technological boundaries too far, the design was adapted to take massive banks of batteries (tripling the battery capacity of the Type VIIC U-boats). With a streamlined hull, they gave exceptional submerged speed and endurance – the Type XXI could sustain 9km/h (5 knots) for over two days before recharging the batteries, which took less than five hours using the snorkel. The Type XXI and Type XXIII were also much quieter than the VIIC, making them much more difficult to detect when submerged.

The Type XXI was also much more habitable than earlier U-boats – a large freezer improved the rations

U-BOATS: TYPE XVIII, XXI, XXIII COMPARED

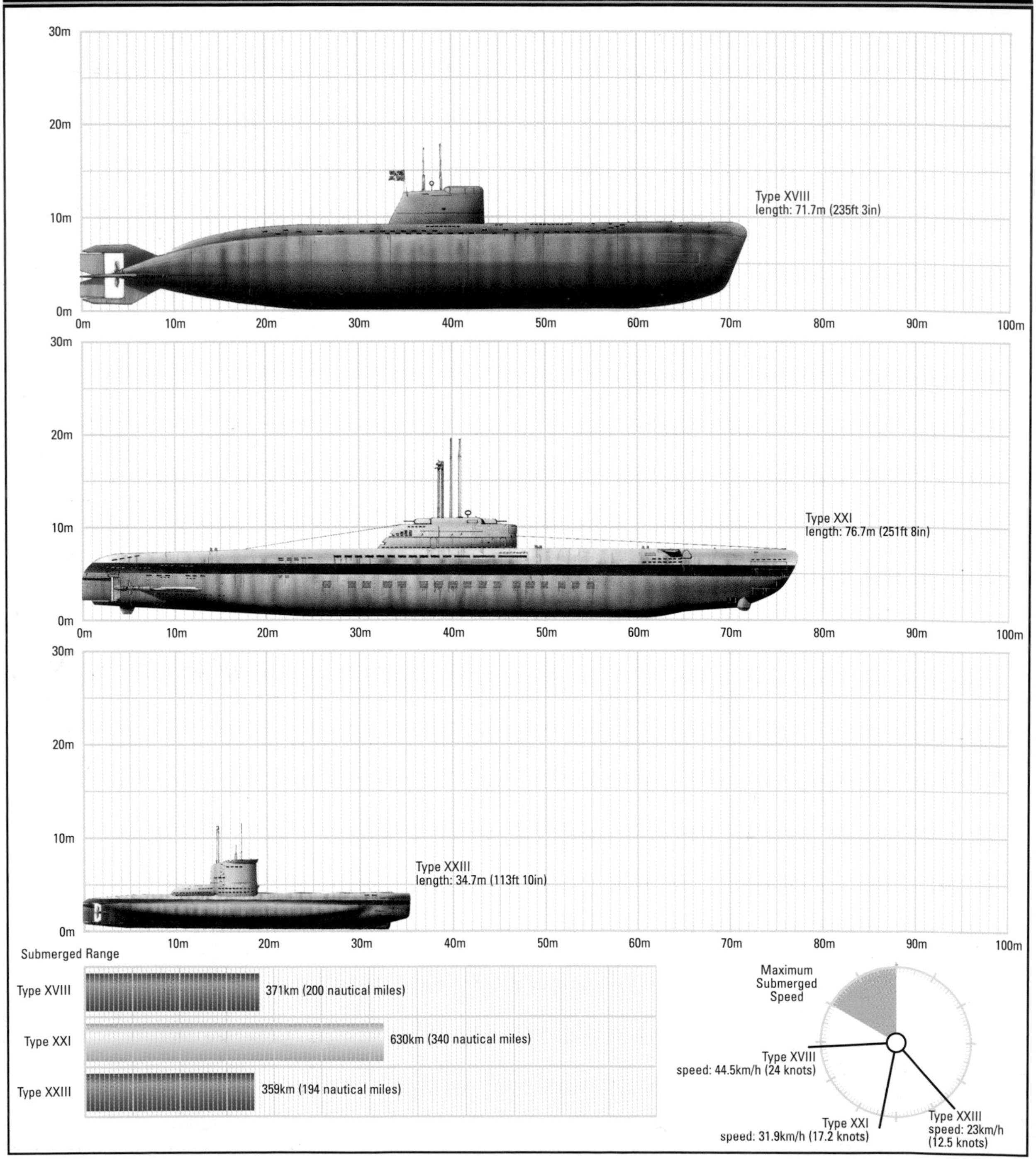
30m
20m
10m
0m
Type XVIII
length: 71.7m (235ft 3in)
Type XXI
length: 76.7m (251ft 8in)
Type XXIII
length: 34.7m (113ft 10in)
0m
10m
20m
30m
40m
50m
60m
70m
80m
90m
100m
Submerged Range
Type XVIII
371km (200 nautical miles)
Type XXI
630km (340 nautical miles)
Type XXIII
359km (194 nautical miles)
Maximum
Submerged
Speed
Type XVIII
speed: 44.5km/h (24 knots)
Type XXI
speed: 31.9km/h (17.2 knots)
Type XXIII
speed: 23km/h
(12.5 knots)

U-BOATS TYPE XVIII, XXI, XXIII: LENGTH, SPEED, AND SURFACE RANGE

U-boat Type	Length	Speed	Surface Range
XVIII Diesel	71.7m (235ft 3in)	33.8km/h (18.3 knots)	9637km (5200 nautical miles) at 22km/h (12 knots)
XXI Diesel	76.7m (251ft 8in)	28.9km/h (15.6 knots)	28,700km (15,500 nautical miles) at 19km/h (10 knots)
XXIII Diesel	34.7m (113ft 10in)	18km/h (9.7 knots)	4800km (2600 nautical miles) at 15km/h (8 knots)

that could be issued on long patrols. The installation of a shower and washbasins was an unprecedented luxury for crews who were accustomed to enduring weeks without shaving or bathing. Its operational effectiveness was enhanced by a hydraulic torpedo reloading system which could reload all six torpedo tubes more quickly than a Type VIIC could reload one. Three full salvoes, each of six torpedoes, could be fired within 20 minutes – these were generally aimed by data from the boat's active and passive sonar arrays to avoid the risk of coming up to periscope depth. A total of 23 torpedoes (or 17 torpedoes and 12 mines) could be carried.

Between 1943 and 1945, 118 Type XXI U-boats were assembled by Blohm und Voss (Hamburg), AG Weser (Bremen) and F Schichau (Danzig). The hulls were constructed from eight pre-fabricated sections with final assembly taking place at the shipyards. The system had been devised by Reich Minister Albert Speer in consultation with Otto Merker, who had considerable practical experience in mass production methods in the car industry and was based on the following assumptions:

- No prototypes would be completed before series production began
- Pre-fabricated sections would be manufactured in widely dispersed factories
- Sections to be transported to the shipyard by water (Type XXI) or rail (Type XXIII)
- Only the final assembly of sections would take place at the shipyard

The detailed building plan for the Type XXI consisted of the following stages:

- Stockpiling of raw materials and transport to steel works – 16 days
- Steel work – 40 days
- Transport to the section building plant – 5 days
- Section building – 50 days
- Transport to the yard – 4 days
- Assembly at the yard – 50 days
- Final work after launching – 6 days
- Total building time per boat – 171 days (6 months)

The system eliminated the bottleneck caused by limited shipyard resources. Instead of occupying a slip for the entire building process (18 months), the vessel now only occupied it for an average of 80 days of final completion work. Hence shipyard building efficiency was multiplied by a factor of almost seven, despite the disruption caused

TYPE XXI AND TYPE XXIII 'ELECTROBOATS': TIME LINE

Date	Event
November 1942	The birth of the 'Electroboat' idea
January 1943	Design calculations finished
June 1943	Designs completed
July 1943	Projects approved
September 1943	Conventional U-boat building programme limited
November 1943	Production orders placed
December 1943	Production planning completed
30 April 1944	First Type XXIII launched (U-2321)
12 May 1944	First Type XXI launched (U-2501)
12 June 1944	First Type XXIII commissioned (U-2321)
27 June 1944	First Type XXI commissioned (U-2501)
August 1944	First aerial mines laid in the Bay of Danzig training area
29 January 1945	First Type XXIII sailed on war patrol (U-2324)
February 1945	Trials and training transferred to the Bay of Lubeck
14 February 1945	First sinking by an Electroboat (U-2322)
30 April 1945	First Type XXI sailed on war patrol (U-2511)
7 May 1945	Last sinking by an Electroboat (U-2336)

TYPE XXI SERVICE RECORD

Boat	*Commissioned*	*Fate*
U-2501	27 Jun 1944	Scuttled 3 May 1945, Hamburg
U-2502	19 Jul 1944	Surrendered. Sunk off Ireland 2 Jan 1946
U-2503	1 Aug 1944	Scuttled off Horsens, Denmark, 4 May 1945. Thirteen crew killed after attack by RAF Beaufighters of 236 and 254 Sqdns
U-2504	12 Aug 1944	Scuttled Hamburg, 3 May 1945
U-2505	7 Nov 1944	Abandoned in 'Elbe II' U-boat bunker, Hamburg
U-2506	31 Aug 1944	Surrendered. Sunk off Ireland 5 Jan 1946
U-2507	8 Sept 1944	Scuttled 5 May 1945
U-2508	26 Sept 1944	Scuttled Kiel 3 May 1945
U-2509	21 Sept 1944	Sunk in bombing raid on shipyard 8 Apr 1945
U-2510	27 Sept 1944	Scuttled 2 May 1945
U-2511	29 Sept 1944	Surrendered, Berger, Norway. Scuttled off Ireland 7 Jan 1946
U-2512	10 Oct 1944	Scuttled 3 May 1945
U-2513	12 Oct 1944	Surrendered 8 May 1945. Transferred to US Navy Aug 1945. Sunk off Key West Florida in missile trials 7 Oct 1951
U-2514	17 Oct 1944	Sunk in bombing raid 8 Apr 1945
U-2515	19 Oct 1944	Sunk in bombing raid on Hamburg 17 Jan 1945
U-2516	24 Oct 1944	Sunk in bombing raid on Kiel 9 Apr 1945
U-2517	31 Oct 1944	Scuttled 5 May 1945
U-2518	4 Nov 1944	Surrendered 8 May 1945. Transferred to French Navy, 17 Feb 1945 as *Roland Morillot*, later renamed *0246* Decommissioned 17 Oct 1967. Scrapped 1969
U-2519	15 Nov 1944	Scuttled 3 May 1945 Kiel
U-2520	14 Nov 1944	Scuttled 3 May 1945
U-2521	21 Nov 1944	Sunk by RAF Liberator K/547, Kattegat, 5 May 1945
U-2522	22 Nov 1944	Scuttled 5 May 1945
U-2523	26 Dec 1944	Sunk in bombing raid on shipyard 17 Jan 1945
U-2524	16 Jan 1945	Sunk by RAF Beaufighters of 236 and 254 Sqdns 3 May 1945
U-2525	12 Dec 1944	Scuttled 5 May 1945
U-2526	15 Dec 1944	Scuttled 2 May 1945
U-2527	23 Dec 1944	Scuttled 2 May 1945
U-2528	19 Dec 1944	Scuttled 2 May 1945
U-2529	22 Feb 1944	Surrendered. Recommissioned in Royal Navy as *N28*. Transferred to Soviet Navy as *B28*, commissioning Feb 1946 Scrapped 1958
U-2530	30 Dec 1944	Sunk in bombing raid on Hamburg 31 Dec 1944. Raised and sunk again by RAF raid on Hamburg 17 Jan 1945
U-2531	18 Jan 1945	Scuttled 3 May 1945
U-2532	-	Never completed – sunk in raid on yard 31 Dec 1944
U-2533	18 Jan 1945	Scuttled 3 May 1945
U-2534	17 Jan 1945	Scuttled 3 May 1945
U-2535	28 Jan 1945	Scuttled 3 May 1945
U-2536	6 Feb 1945	Scuttled 3 May 1945
U-2537	-	Sunk in bombing raid on yard 31 Dec 1944. Never completed
U-2538	16 Feb 1945	Scuttled 8 May 1945
U-2539	21 Feb 1945	Scuttled 3 May 1945
U-2540	24 Feb 1945	Sunk by RAF Beaufighters in Kattegat, 4 May 1945. Raised in 1957 to become research boat *Withelm Bauer* 1960. Decommissioned 1982. Now on display at German Maritime Museum Bremerhaven.
U-2541	1 Mar 1945	Scuttled 5 May 1945
U-2542	5 Mar 1945	Sunk by bombs 3 Apr 1945
U-2543	7 Mar 1945	Scuttled 3 May 1945

TYPE XXI SERVICE RECORD

Boat	*Commissioned*	*Fate*
U-2544	10 Mar 1945	Scuttled 5 May 1945
U-2546	21 Mar 1945	Scuttled 3 May 1945
U-2547	-	Sunk in bombing raid 11 Mar 1945. Never completed
U-2548	9 Apr 1945	Scuttled 3 May 1945
U-2549	-	Sunk in bombing raid 11 Mar 1945. Never completed
U-2550	-	Sunk in bombing raid 11 Mar 1945. Never completed
U-2551	24 Apr 1945	Scuttled 5 May 1945
U-2552	21 Apr 1945	Scuttled 3 May 1945, Kiel
U-2553	-	Never completed. Broken up
U-2554	-	Never completed. Broken up
U-2555	-	Never completed. Broken up
U-2556	-	Never completed. Broken up
U-2557	-	Never completed. Broken up
U-2558	-	Never completed. Broken up
U-2559	-	Never completed. Broken up
U-2560	-	Never completed. Broken up
U-2561		Never completed. Broken up
U-2562	-	Never completed. Broken up
U-2563	-	Never completed. Broken up
U-2564	-	Never completed. Broken up
U-3001	20 Jul 1944	Scuttled 3 May 1945
U-3002	6 Aug 1944	Scuttled 2 May 1945
U-3003	22 Aug 1944	Sunk in bombing raid, Kiel, 4 Apr 1945
U-3004	30 Aug 1944	Abandoned in 'Elbe II' U-boat bunker, Hamburg
U-3005	20 Sept 1944	Scuttled 3 May 1945
U-3006	5 Oct 1944	Scuttled 1 May 1945
U-3007	22 Oct 1944	Sunk in bombing raid 24 Feb 1945
U-3008	19 Oct 1944	Transferred to US Navy, 1945 as trials boat. Scrapped Puerto Rico, 1955
U-3009	10 Nov 1944	Scuttled 1 May 1945
U-3010	11 Nov 1944	Scuttled 3 May 1945
U-3011	21 Dec 1944	Scuttled 3 May 1945
U-3012	4 Dec 1944	Scuttled 3 May 1945
U-3013	22 Nov 1944	Scuttled 3 May 1945
U-3014	17 Dec 1944	Scuttled 3 May 1945
U-3015	17 Dec 1944	Scuttled 5 May 1945
U-3016	5 Jan 1945	Scuttled 2 May 1945
U-3017	5 Jan 1945	Surrendered. Transferred to Royal Navy to become *N41* trials boat. Scrapped 1949
U-3018	7 Jan 1945	Scuttled 2 May 1945
U-3019	23 Dec 1944	Scuttled 2 May 1945
U-3020	23 Dec 1945	Scuttled 2 May 1945
U-3021	12 Feb 1945	Scuttled 2 May 1945
U-3022	22 Jan 1945	Scuttled 3 May 1945
U-3023	22 Jan 1945	Scuttled 3 May 1945
U-3024	13 Jan 1945	Scuttled 3 May 1945
U-3025	20 Jan 1945	Scuttled 3 May 1945

TYPE XXI SERVICE RECORD

Boat	*Commissioned*	*Fate*
U-3026	22 Jan 1945	Scuttled 3 May 1945
U-3027	25 Jan 1945	Scuttled 3 May 1945
U-3028	27 Jan 1945	Scuttled 3 May 1945
U-3029	5 Feb 1945	Scuttled 3 May 1945
U-3030	14 Feb 1945	Scuttled 8 May 1945
U-3031	28 Feb 1945	Scuttled 3 May 1945
U-3032	12 Feb 1945	Sunk by aircraft of 2nd Tactical Air Force in Kattegat, 3 May 1945
U-3033	27 Feb 1945	Scuttled 4 May 1945
U-3034	31 Mar 1945	Scuttled 4 May 1945
U-3035	1 Mar 1945	Surrendered Norway. Transferred to Royal Navy, 1945. Transferred to Soviet Navy, 1945 to become *B29*. Scrapped 1958
U-3036	-	Never completed. Broken up
U-3037	3 Mar 1945	Scuttled 3 May 1945
U-3038	4 Mar 1945	Scuttled 3 May 1945
U-3039	8 Mar 1945	Scuttled 3 May 1945
U-3040	8 Mar 1945	Scuttled 3 May 1945
U-3041	10 Mar 1945	Surrendered. Transferred to Royal Navy as *N29*, then transferred to Soviet Navy as *B30*. Scrapped 1959
U-3042	-	Damaged in air raid on yard, 22 Feb 1945. Never completed. Broken up
U-3043	-	Never completed. Broken up
U-3044	27 Mar 1945	Scuttled 5 May 1945
U-3045	-	Sunk in bombing raid on yard 30 Mar 1945
U-3501	29 Jul 1944	Scuttled 5 May 1945
U-3502	19 Aug 1944	Damaged by bomb attack May 1945
U-3503	9 Sept 1944	Sunk by RAF Liberator G/86 Kattegat
U-3504	23 Sept 1944	Scuttled 2 May 1945
U-3505	7 Oct 1945	Sunk in bombing raid 3 May 1945
U-3506	19 Oct 1944	Abandoned in 'Elbe II' U-boat bunker, Hamburg
U-3507	19 Oct 1944	Scuttled 3 May 1945
U-3508	2 Nov 1944	Sunk in bombing raid on Wilhelmshaven 4 Mar 1945
U-3509	29 Jan 1945	Scuttled 3 May 1945
U-3510	11 Nov 1944	Scuttled 5 May 1945
U-3511	18 Nov 1945	Scuttled 3 May 1945
U-3512	27 Nov 1944	Sunk in air raid on Kiel 8 Apr 1945
U-3513	2 Dec 1944	Scuttled 3 May 1945
U-3514	9 Dec 1944	Scuttled off north-west coast of Ireland 12 Feb 1946
U-3515	14 Dec 1944	Surrendered. Transferred to Royal Navy as *N30*. Transferred to Soviet Navy as *B28* Feb 1946
U-3516	18 Dec 1944	Scuttled 2 May 1945
U-3517	22 Dec 1944	Scuttled 2 May 1945
U-3518	29 Dec 1944	Scuttled 3 May 1945
U-3519	6 Jan 1945	Mined and sunk off Warnemunde Baltic 2 Mar 1945
U-3520	12 Jan 1945	Sunk in Baltic 31 Jan 1945
U-3521	14 Jan 1945	Scuttled 2 May 1945
U-3522	21 Jan 1945	Scuttled 2 May 1945
U-3523	23 Jan 1945	Sunk by depth charges dropped by RAF Liberator T/224 in Kattegat, 5 May 1945
U-3524	26 Jan 1945	Scuttled 5 May 1945
U-3525	31 Jan 1945	Scuttled 3 May 1945

TYPE XXI SERVICE RECORD

Boat	*Commissioned*	*Fate*
U-3526	22 Mar 1945	Scuttled 5 May 1945
U 3527	10 Mar 1945	Scuttled 5 May 1945
U-3528	18 Mar 1945	Scuttled 5 May 1945
U-3529	22 Mar 1945	Scuttled 5 May 1945
U-3530	22 Mar 1945	Scuttled 3 May 1945
U-3531	-	Never completed. Broken up
U-3532	-	Never completed. Broken up
U-3533	-	Never completed. Broken up
U-3534	-	Never completed. Broken up
U-3535	-	Never completed. Broken up
U-3536	-	Never completed. Broken up
U-3537	-	Never completed. Broken up
U-3546	-	Damaged in bombing raid on yard 30 Mar 1945. Never completed
U-3547	-	Never completed. Broken up
U-3548	-	Never completed. Broken up
U-3549	-	Never completed. Broken up
U-3550	-	Never completed. Broken up
U-3551	-	Never completed. Broken up
U-3552	-	Never completed. Broken up
U-3553	-	Never completed. Broken up
U-3554	-	Never completed. Broken up
U-3555	-	Never completed. Broken up
U-3556	-	Never completed. Broken up
U-3557	-	Never completed. Broken up
U-3558	-	Never completed. Broken up
U-3559	-	Never completed. Broken up
U-3560	-	Never completed. Broken up
U-3561	-	Never completed. Broken up
U-3562	-	Never completed. Broken up
U-3563	-	Never completed. Broken up

by increasingly effective Allied bombing campaigns.

The scheme was impressive in theory, but in practice all the U-boats were plagued with defects which were only rectified by extensive work after assembly. This was largely due to sub-contracting sections to inland companies who lacked experience of shipbuilding. The result was that of 118 assembled Type XXIs, only four were combat-ready before the end of the war.

The basic Type XXI was truly formidable, but two proposed developments, the Type XXIB with 12 torpedo tubes and the Type XXIC with 18, were potentially devastating and it was fortunate for the Allies that they never progressed beyond design studies.

Type XXIII U-boats

Development of the Type XXIII coastal U-boat began at the end of 1942 and, when finalized in mid-1943, the design strongly resembled a miniature Type XXI. In accordance with Admiral Dönitz's specifications, it was constructed in pre-fabricated sections which could be transported by rail and was fitted with standard 53.3cm (21in) torpedo tubes.

The Type XXIII had a streamlined outer casing and, apart from the relatively small conning tower and a fairing which housed the diesel exhaust silencer, it had an uncluttered upper deck. As with the

Type XXI, the lower section of the figure-of-eight hull was used to house a large 62-cell battery which gave exceptional submerged speed and endurance. The only significant limitations of the design were due to the size parameters imposed by the requirement for rail transportation.

As a result, habitability was poor, with very cramped crew accommodation. While this was not a major problem, given its short patrols, the restricted space seriously limited its armament. In fact, only two torpedo tubes could be fitted and there was no room for any reloads – the lack of space ruled out a conventional loading hatch and the submarine had to be trimmed down by the stern to lift the torpedo tubes clear of the water so that they could be loaded from a barge.

Type XXIII construction was concentrated at Germaniawerft (Kiel) and Deutsche Werft (Hamburg), Germaniawerft building 51 and Deutsche Werft 49. Of the 280 boats ordered, only 61 entered service, and only six carried out war patrols.

Operations record

All of the six operational Type XXIIIs – *U-2321, U-2322, U-2324, U-2326, U-2329* and *U-2336* – survived the Allied anti-submarine effort and sunk or damaged five vessels, totalling 14,835 tonnes (14,601 tons). The first war patrol of a Type XXIII was made by *U-2324*, which sailed from Kiel on 18 January 1945. Although she survives the war, she sank no Allied ships. The first Type XXIII to achieve combat success was *U-2322*, commanded by *Oberleutnant zur See* Fridtjof-Heckel. Sailing from Norway on 6 February 1945, she encountered a convoy off Berwick and sank the coaster *Egholm* on 25 February. *U-2321*, operating from the same base, sank the coaster *Gasray* on 5 April 1945 off St Abbs Head. *U-2336*, under the command of *Kapitänleutnant* Emil Klusmeier, sank the last Allied ships of the war in Europe on 7 May 1945, when she torpedoed the freighters *Sneland* and *Avondale Park* off the Isle of May inside the Firth of Forth.

TYPE XXIII SERVICE RECORD: KEY BOATS (*11. FLOTILLE*)

Boat	*Commissioned*	*Flotilla(s)*	*Patrols*	*Fate*
U-2321	12 Jun 1944	1 Feb 1945 – 8 May 1945	1 patrol. 1 ship sunk: total 1406 GRT	Surrendered at Kristiansand Süd, Norway. Taken to Loch Ryan 29 May 1945 for Operation Deadlight. Sunk 27 Nov 1945 by naval gunfire
U-2322	1 Jul 1944	1 Feb 1945 – 8 May 1945	2 patrols. 1 ship sunk: total 1317 GRT	Surrendered at Stavanger, Norway. Taken to Loch Ryan 31 May 1945 for Operation Deadlight. Sunk 27 Nov 1945 by naval gunfire
U-2324	25 Jul 1944	1 Feb 1945 – 8 May 1945	2 patrols	Surrendered at Stavanger, Norway. Taken to Loch Ryan 29 May 1945 for Operation Deadlight. Sunk 27 Nov 1945 by naval gunfire
U-2325	3 Aug 1944	1 Feb 1945 – 8 May 1945	No patrols	Surrendered at Kristiansand Süd, Norway. Taken to Loch Ryan 29 May 1945 for Operation Deadlight. Sunk 28 Nov by naval gunfire
U-2326	10 Aug 1944	1 Feb 1945 – 8 May 1945	2 patrols	Surrendered at Dundee, Scotland, 14 May 1945. Became the British submarine *N35*. Transferred to France in 1946. Sank 6 Dec 1946 at Toulon in an accident. Raised and broken up
U-2328	25 Aug 1944	1 Apr 1945 – 8 May 1945	No patrols	Surrendered at Bergen, Norway. Taken to Loch Ryan 30 May 1945 for Operation Deadlight. Took on water and sank while on tow to scuttling grounds 27 Nov 1945
U-2329	1 Sept 1944	15 Mar 1945 – 8 May 1945	1 patrol	Surrendered at Stavanger, Norway. Taken to Loch Ryan in Jun 1945 for Operation Deadlight. Sunk 28 Nov 1945 by naval gunfire
U-2330	7 Sept 1944	16 Mar 1945 – 3 May 1945	No patrols	Scuttled 3 May 1945 at Kiel
U-2334	21 Sept 1944	1 Apr 1945 – 8 May 1945	No patrols	Surrendered at Kristiansand Süd, Norway. Taken to Loch Ryan 29 May 1945 for Operation Deadlight. Sunk 28 Nov 1945 by naval gunfire
U-2335	27 Sept 1944	1 Apr 1945 – 8 May 1945	No patrols	Surrendered at Kristiansand Süd, Norway. Taken to Loch Ryan 29 May 1945 for Operation Deadlight. Sunk 28 Nov 1945 by naval gunfire

Midget Submarines

The Kriegsmarine *had almost ignored the potential of midget submarines until a British* Welman *craft was captured at Bergen, Norway, in 1943. The British vessel was used as a starting point for the development of the* Biber *(Beaver) midget submarine.*

Work began on the *Biber* prototype in February 1944 and the vessel was completed and was undergoing trials within a matter of six weeks. After an inspection by Admiral Dönitz, the *Biber* was formally accepted for service on 29 March 1944.

The submarine's general construction and finish was crude – the hull comprised three sections of 3mm (0.12in) thick steel surmounted by an aluminium alloy conning tower with armoured glass ports. These were the primary vision devices as the small periscope had a very limited field of view and was difficult to use whilst operating the main controls. Although the *Biber* was fitted with a 9.7kW (13hp) electric torpedo motor and two diving tanks, there were no trimming or compensating tanks which made it virtually impossible to keep the craft at periscope depth, or indeed to travel submerged for any significant distance. In practice, most *Bibers* operated on the surface where they

MIDGET SUBMARINES COMPARED

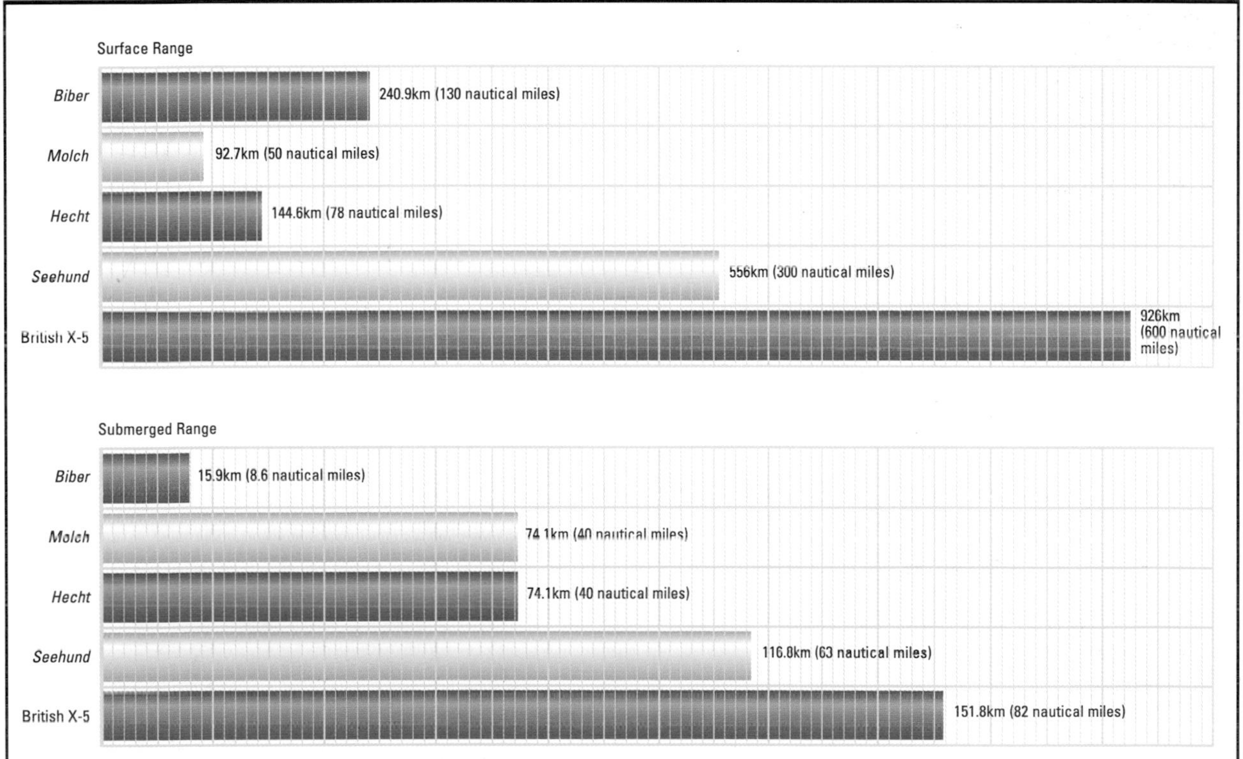

Surface Range
Biber
240.9km (130 nautical miles)
Molch
92.7km (50 nautical miles)
Hecht
144.6km (78 nautical miles)
Seehund
556km (300 nautical miles)
British X-5
926km (600 nautical miles)
Submerged Range
Biber
15.9km (8.6 nautical miles)
Molch
74.1km (40 nautical miles)
Hecht
74.1km (40 nautical miles)
Seehund
116.8km (63 nautical miles)
British X-5
151.8km (82 nautical miles)

MIDGET SUBMARINES COMBAT RECORD: SINKINGS

Date	Sub	Crew	Details
22 Dec 1944	*Biber*		Sank freighter *Alan-a-Dale*, 4702 grt, off Flushing
2 Jan 1945	*Seehund*	Paulsen/Huth	Sank trawler *Hayburn Wyke*, 329 tonnes (324 tons), off Ostend
12 Jan 1945	*Seehund*	Kiep/Palaschewski	Claimed to have sunk a collier estimated at 3,000 grt off Kentish Shoal
30 Jan 1945	*Seehund*	Ross/Vennemann	Claimed to have torpedoed a collier off Margate. Not confirmed officially
3 Feb 1945	*Seehund*	Wolter/Minetzke	Claimed to have sunk a ship estimated at 3,000 grt off Great Yarmouth (unconfirmed)
15 Feb 1945	*Seehund*	Ziepult/Reck	Damaged tanker *Liseta*, 2628 grt, off North Foreland
22 Feb 1945	*Seehund*	Gaffron/Köster	Claimed to have torpedoed a destroyer off Goodwin Sands (unconfirmed)
23 Feb 1945	*Seehund*	Sparbrodt/Jahnke	Sank the French destroyer *La Combattante* in the North Sea
22 Feb 1945	*Seehund*		Sank *LST 364*, 2750 grt, in convoy TAM 87, off North Foreland
24 Feb 1945	*Seehund*		Sank cable-layer *Alert*, 941 grt, with all hands off North Foreland
26 Feb 1945	*Seehund*		Sank freighter *Rampant*, convoy TAC, off North Foreland
26 Feb 1945	*Seehund*		Sank tanker *Nashaba*, convoy TAC, off North Foreland
11 Mar 1945	*Seehund*	Huber/Eckloff	Sunk freighter *Taber Park*, 2878 grt, from convoy FS 1753 off Southwold
12 Mar 1945	*Seehund*	Kugler/Schmidt	*U-5064* claimed to have sunk a steamer estimated at 3000 grt in the Thames Estuary
13 Mar 1945	*Seehund*	Fröhnert/Beltrami	Claimed to have sunk a steamer in the Thames Estuary
		Hauschel/Hessel	*U-5366* sunk a Liberty ship carrying munitions, off Lowestoft
		Küllmeyer/Raschke	Sank the steamer *Newlands*, 1556 grt, quadrant AN 7956
		Meyer/Schauerte	Probably sunk British escort *ML 466* off South Falls Bank
26 Mar 1945	*Seehund*		Destroyer HMS *Puffin* declared total loss after being rammed by *Seehund* which exploded, Buoy 4 North Foreland. German crew picked up
30 Mar 1945	*Seehund*		Coaster *Jim*, 833 grt, sunk off Orfordness
9 Apr 1945	*Seehund*		Sank tanker *Y17*, from convoy TAC 90, with all hands, off North Foreland
9 Apr 1945	*Seehund*	Buttman/Schmidt	Sank freighter *Samida*, 7219 grt, and damaged US freighter *Solomon Juneau*, 7116 grt, off Dungeness
9 Apr 1945	*Seehund*		A *Seehund* sank the cable-layer *Monarch*, 1150 grt, off Orfordness
10 Apr 1945	*Seehund*	Von Pander/Vogl	Claimed to have sunk tanker estimated at 1000 grt
11 Apr 1945	*Seehund*		*Seehund* damaged freighter *Port Wyndham*, 8580 grt, from convoy UC 63B off Dungeness
11 Apr 1945	*Seehund*	Markworth/Spallek	Claimed to have sunk a merchantman estimated at 3000–4000 grt off Dungeness
16 Apr 1945	*Seehund*		Tanker *Doldshell* from convoy TAM 40 off Ostend, sunk by *Seehund* or mine
23 Apr 1945	*Seehund*		Last comfirmed *Seehund* success, steamer *Svere Helmeren* sunk off South Falls
29 Apr 1945	*Seehund*		Steamer *Benjamin H Bristow* sunk off Walcheren either by mine or *Seehund*

were quite manoeuvrable, but their crewmen were at real risk of being poisoned by carbon monoxide fumes from the 24kW (32hp) Opel-Blitz petrol engine which had to be fitted due to dire shortages of suitable diesel engines. There was also a high risk of fires or the explosion of petrol fumes after minor fuel leaks and it is probable that these were responsible for a number of *Biber* losses.

The submarine could be armed with either two G7e T3 torpedoes, mines or a mixture of the two. *Bibers* also operated effectively as clandestine minelayers in the Scheldt estuary and would probably have had a greater impact on naval operations if they had been restricted to this role.

As well as their usual missions against Allied shipping, *Bibers* were used in attempts to destroy the road bridge across the river Waal at Nijmegen on the night of 12–13 January 1945. An earlier attack by German frogmen had damaged the Nijmegen railway bridge but had also prompted upgrading of the defences, which now included four net-and-boom barriers across the river upstream of the bridge. It was appreciated that extraordinary measures were required to crack these defences and an elaborate plan was set in motion. A total of 240 mines were floated downstream in four carefully timed waves in an attempt to break most, if not all of the barriers. These were followed up by 20 *Bibers* (camouflaged to resemble clumps of drifting foliage) that carried torpedoes to be launched against any remaining barriers. Finally, four more *Bibers* each towed a large tree trunk concealing a floating demolition

MIDGET SUBMARINE TYPES COMPARED

Type	*Displacement*	*Range*	*Complement*	*Armament*
Biber	6.4 tonnes (6.3 tons) surfaced 6.6 tonnes (6.5 tons) submerged	Surface, 240.9km (130 nautical miles) at 11.1km/h (6 knots) Submerged, 15.9km (8.6 nautical miles) at 9.3km/h (5 knots)	1	2 x 53.3cm (21in) hull mounted torpedoes in dropping gear or 2 x mines
Molch	11.2 tonnes (11 tons) submerged	Surface, 92.7km (50 nautical miles) at 7.4km/h (4 knots) Submerged, 74.1km (40 nautical miles) at 9.3km/h (5 knots)	1	2 x 53.3cm (21in) hull mounted torpedoes in dropping gear or 2 x mines
Hecht	12.2 tonnes (12 tons) submerged	Surface, 144.6km (78 nautical miles) at 5.6km/h (3 knots) Submerged, 74.1km (40 nautical miles) at 11.1km/h (6 knots)	3	1 x 53.3cm (21in) hull mounted torpedo in dropping gear or 1 x mine
Seehund	14.9 tonnes (14.7 tons)	Surface, 556km (300 nautical miles) at 25.2km/h (7 knots) Submerged, 116.8 km (63 nautical miles) at 11.1km/h (3 knots)	2	2 x 53.3cm (21in) hull mounted torpedoes in dropping gear or 2 x mines

charge of almost 3000kg (6600lb). These were to be launched at first light, so that photoelectric cells set into the tree trunks would detonate the charges as they drifted under the bridge. The explosions of the drifting mines alerted the defenders, who laid down a fierce barrage of fire which sank several *Bibers* and detonated all four demolition charges before they could reach the bridge.

Molch (Salamander)

Almost twice the tonnage of the *Biber* type, *Molch* was far safer for its crews, although it proved to be largely ineffective in combat. The greatly improved safety was due to the fact that its sole engine was a single-shaft electric torpedo motor, powered by large banks of batteries which occupied much of the hull. However, this dependence on a single, 9.7kW (13hp) engine restricted both speed and range, while an overly-complex system of trimming and diving tanks made the vessel very hard to control. The majority of the 363 completed were withdrawn from operational use in late 1944 and relegated to training.

Type XXVIIB *Seehund* (Seal)

The *Seehund* was derived from the unsuccessful Type XXVIIA *Hecht* (Pike) midget submarine. In contrast to its predecessor, it proved to be a highly effective design – as Admiral Sir Charles Little, British Commander-in-Chief Portsmouth said: 'Fortunately for us these damn things arrived too late in the war to do any damage.'

Seehund was, in effect, a miniature fleet submarine which handled well on the surface where its small size made it very hard to detect visually or on radar. Even when spotted, it had a good chance of survival – it could crash dive in less than five seconds. Once submerged, its small size and very quiet slow-speed running made it a very difficult sonar target, while it was light enough to 'ride' the shock-waves from exploding depth charges.

A total of 285 *Seehunde* were completed by the end of the war – besides sinking and damaging a significant number of Allied ships, they forced the deployment of an estimated 500 escort vessels and over 1000 aircraft to counter their operations. The last (and most unusual) *Seehund* sorties took place on 28 April and 2 May 1945, when two special missions were performed to resupply the isolated German garrison of Dunkirk. The submarines carried special food containers (nicknamed 'butter torpedoes') instead of torpedoes, and on the return voyage used the containers to carry mail from the garrison.

Prototypes and paper projects

At the end of the war, a large number of midget submarines were under development, including:

- *Seeteufel* (Sea Devil), a 20 tonne (19.7 ton) two-man tracked amphibious craft. The sole prototype was powered by an 60kW (80hp) petrol engine for land and surface use and an electric motor for use whilst submerged. The usual pair of under-slung torpedoes was supplemented by a machine gun and flamethrower for use on land.
- *Schwertal* (Grampus), a 14.7 tonne (14.5 ton) two-man submarine 'fighter' powered by a 597kW (800hp) Walter turbine with an estimated submerged speed of 56km/h (30 knots). The proposed armament was to be two under-slung torpedoes.

Manned Torpedoes

Italian special forces had demonstrated the potential of the manned torpedo in spectacular fashion as early as December 1941 when three Maiale *(Pig) human torpedoes penetrated Alexandria harbour and badly damaged the battleships HMS* Queen Elizabeth *and HMS* Valiant.

The Germans were slow to adopt the concept and their version was not ready for action until April 1944.

The *Neger*

The first German weapon was based on the standard G7e torpedo. It was designed by naval engineer Richard Mohr and developed at the torpedo trials establishment – *Torpedo Versuchs Anstalt* (TVA) – at Eckenforde near Kiel. Mohr not only designed the craft, but also played a big role in its development, including many hazardous test runs. Its unsavoury name, *Neger* (Nigger), was a pun on his surname, Mohr being an old German term for Moor.

The craft was very simple – the warhead was removed from a G7e torpedo and replaced by a small cockpit covered with a perspex dome for the single crewman. The craft was powered by an electric motor similar to that used in the conventional torpedo, but about 50 per cent of its battery capacity had to be removed to give sufficient buoyancy to support the weight of the sole armament, a single underslung G7e torpedo. As a result, the motor was fitted with a regulator which limited its speed to a maximum of 18.5km/h (10 knots) to give it an acceptable range.

NEGER: SERVICE RECORD

Date	*Location*	*Successes*
21 Apr 1944	Anzio, K-Flotilla 361	*Oberfähnrich* Voigt sank an escort vessel in the roadstead
		Oberfähnrich Potthast sank a steamer in the harbour
		Oberfernschreibmeister Berrer sank a troopship Subsequently Berrer transferred to *Linse* Flotilla 211 and sank another steamer. For these two sinkings he was awarded the Knights Cross
		Schreiberobergefreiter Walter Gerhold blew up a magazine below a gun battery on the harbour wall
		Matrose Herbert Berger, aged 17, torpedoed and destroyed a harbour installation. For this achievement he was awarded the Iron Cross 2nd Class and promoted to *Gefreiter*
6 Jul 1944	Normandy, K-Flotilla 361	0304 hrs *Schreiberobergefreiter* Walter Gerhold sank the frigate HMS *Trollope* and was subsequently awarded the Knights Cross
		0353 hrs A *Neger* sank the minesweeper HMS *Magic*
		c. 0430 hrs A *Neger* sank the minesweeper HMS *Cato*
		0545 hrs *Gefreiter* Horst Berger sank a 4064 tonne (4000 ton) steamer
7 Jul 1944	Normandy, K-Flotilla 361	0430 hrs *Oberfähnrich* Potthast sank the Polish cruiser *Dragon*
		0650 hrs A *Neger* sank the minesweeper HMS *Pylades*
		None of the 21 *Negers* returned to base. Four crewmen, including Potthast, were taken prisoner

Limited operational scope

Negers could not submerge and could only operate awash – buoyancy was so limited that the operator sat with his head and shoulders no more than 46cm (18in) above the waterline.

This could easily lead to him being blinded by oil slicks or floating debris – a situation made worse in early production examples in which the there was no internal release mechanism for the perspex dome covering the cockpit.

This was so dangerous that a quick-release system was hurriedly fitted, but solving one problem led to another as there was a high risk of the craft being swamped if the operator 'opened up' in anything other than a flat calm.

The *Neger* crewman was provided

■ **A *Neger* manned torpedo being launched by crane. The type was little more than a torpedo with a small cockpit replacing the warhead.**

with rudimentary controls: a wrist compass; a self-contained *Drager* breathing set and crude sighting arrangements consisting of a graduated scale marked on the Perspex dome and an aiming spike on the nose of the craft rather like a foresight on a rifle. However, given the craft's inherent instability and poor sights, the chances of hitting anything other than a stationary target at close range were almost non-existent. The torpedo itself had an alarming tendency to fail to release on firing, dragging the whole craft to destruction.

Unsurprisingly, *Negers* proved to be 'semi-suicidal' weapons, suffering losses of up to 80 per cent, possibly half of which were due to accidents rather than enemy action.

The *Marder* (Martin)

Attempts were made to produce a submersible *Neger*, but the craft was too small to take the necessary equipment without a dangerous loss of buoyancy. This prompted the development of a slightly 'stretched' version, dubbed the *Marder*, which incorporated a diving tank and could submerge to a depth of about 30m (100ft) for very short periods.

But the lack of a periscope meant *Marder* still had to attack while surfaced. Such attacks could only be made at close range as the very basic sighting arrangements were unchanged from those of the *Neger*.

MARDER: SERVICE RECORD

Date	*Location*	*Successes*
3 Aug 1944	Houlgate, Normandy, K-Flotilla 362* *Only 17 of the 58 *Marders* committed to this operation returned to base	*Marders* sank: – Naval trawler HMS *Gairsay* – Armed landing ship *LCT 764* – The Liberty ship *Samtucky*, 7335 tonnes (7219 tons) gross – Cruiser HMS *Durban*, declared a total loss after torpedo damage and sunk as part of a Mulberry Harbour breakwater *Marders* damaged: – Troopship *Fort Lac la Rouge* – Troopship *Samlong*
15 Aug 1944	Villers sur Mer, Normandy, K-Flotilla 363	A *Marder* sank an 8128 tonne (8000 ton) ammunition ship
16 Aug 1944	Mulberry Harbours, Normandy, K-Flotilla 363** **Only 17 of the 42 *Marders* committed to this operation returned to base	*Marders* sank: – Destroyer HMS *Isis* – A landing craft, either *LCF1*, *LCG 831* or *LCG 1062*, all 70 aboard lost – Freighter *Iddesleigh*, which had been damaged and beached on 9 Aug, a constructive total loss A *Marder* damaged: – Barrage balloon ship, HMS *Fratton*

K-Flotillas 363 and 364 (*Marders*) operated from the Italian Riviera in late 1944–45 but suffered heavy losses and achieved no successes.

MANNED TORPEDOES COMPARED

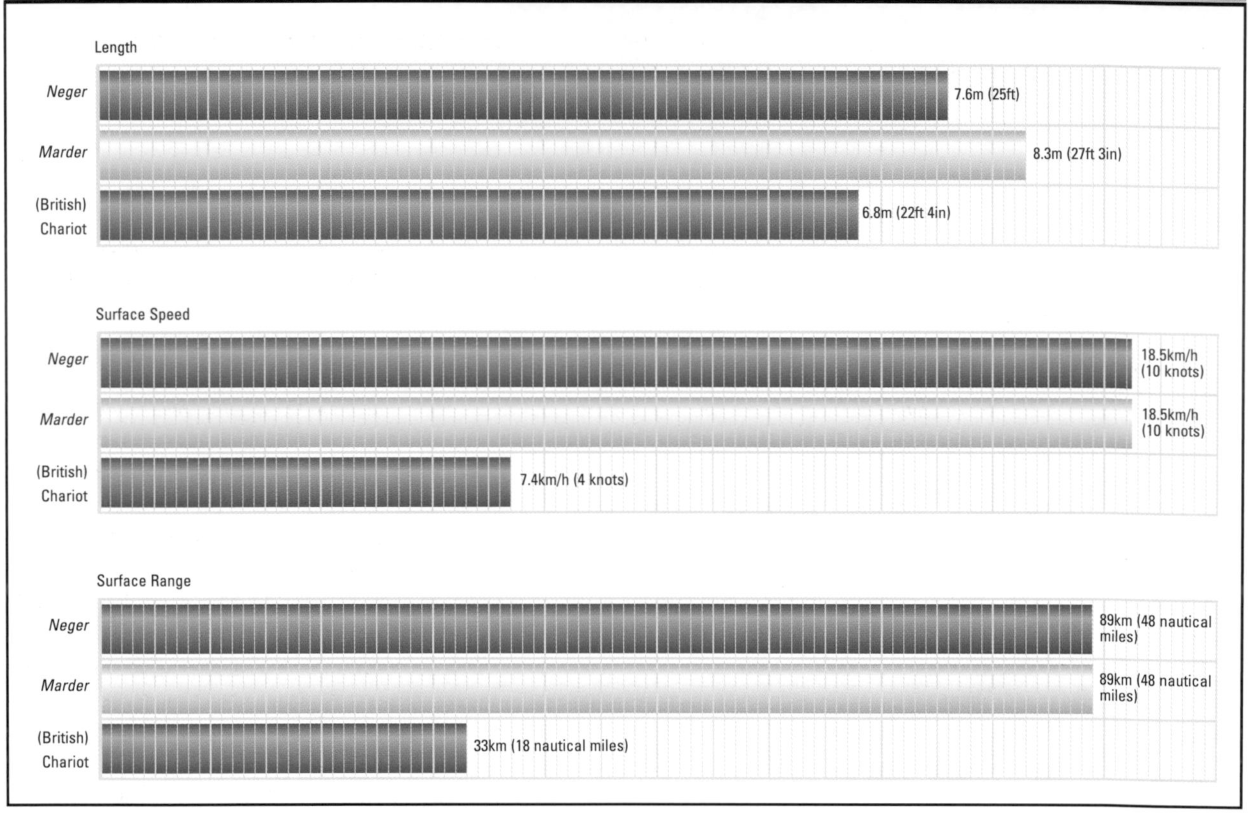
Length
Neger
7.6m (25ft)
Marder
8.3m (27ft 3in)
(British) Chariot
6.8m (22ft 4in)
Surface Speed
Neger
18.5km/h (10 knots)
Marder
18.5km/h (10 knots)
(British) Chariot
7.4km/h (4 knots)
Surface Range
Neger
89km (48 nautical miles)
Marder
89km (48 nautical miles)
(British) Chariot
33km (18 nautical miles)

MANNED TORPEDOES: FULL SPECIFICATIONS COMPARED

Categories	*Neger*	*Marder*
Type	Manned torpedo	Manned torpedo
Displacement	2.8 tonnes (2.7 tons)	3 tonnes (2.9 tons)
Length	7.6m (25ft)	8.3m (27ft 3in)
Beam	0.5m (1ft 7in)	0.5m (1ft 7in)
Draught	1.07m (3ft 6in)	1.07m (3ft 6in)
Engines	1 x 8.95kW (12hp) electric torpedo motor	1 x 8.9kW (12hp) electric torpedo motor
Surface Speed	18.5km/h (10 knots)	18.5km/h (10 knots)
Submerged Speed	n/a (*Negers* could not submerge)	n/k (*Marders* could submerge to a maximum depth of roughly 30m (100ft) to evade attack, but lacked the instrumentation to navigate whilst submerged)
Surface Range	89km (48 nautical miles) at 7.4km/h (4 knots)	89km (48 nautical miles) at 7.4 km/h (4 knots)
Submerged Range	–	–
Complement	1	1
Armament	1 x 53.3cm (21in) hull-mounted torpedo in dropping gear	1 x 53.3cm (21in) hull-mounted torpedo in dropping gear
No. completed	200 (estimated)	300 (estimated)

Torpedoes

Long before the outbreak of World War II, German designers put considerable effort into perfecting electric-powered torpedoes. These were very hard for defenders to spot as, unlike conventional types, they left no visible wake of bubbles.

G7e T3

This was the first of the electric-powered torpedoes to enter service in 1939 and remained unknown to Allied intelligence until parts were salvaged from Scapa Flow following the sinking of HMS *Royal Oak* by *U-47*, commanded by Gunther Prien.

The type was commonly referred to as the *Eto* and was powered by a 74.6kW (100hp) electric motor driving contra-rotating propellers. Maximum range was 7500m (8200yd) at 56km/h (30 knots), provided that the torpedo's batteries had been pre-heated to 30°C (86°F). If pre-heating was impossible, the range was reduced by about two-thirds. The type was fitted with a 300kg (660lb) HE warhead.

An important variant was the G7e T3d *Dackel* which was designed for long-range use against vessels in harbours or confined coastal waters. It could be programmed to circle at the end of a pre-set initial run to improve its chances of scoring a hit in a crowded anchorage.

A total of roughly 300 were produced in mid-1944, 80 or 90 of which were fired against Allied shipping off the Normandy beachhead. In order to achieve the remarkable maximum range of 57,000m (62,300yd), the torpedo's speed was drastically reduced to only 16.7km/h (9 knots)

G7e T4 *Falke* (Falcon)

This was the world's first acoustic homing torpedo which entered service in March 1943. It operated as a conventional torpedo for the first 400m (1320ft) of its run, after which its acoustic sensors were activated and began searching for a target. In order to minimize interference to the sensitive homing equipment, the *Falke's* speed was limited to 37km/h (20 knots). It had a maximum range of 7500m (8200yd) and carried a 200kg (440lb) HE warhead.

It seems likely that the type was only used operationally by three U-boats (*U-221, U-603* and *U-758*) against convoys HX-229 and SC-122 before being withdrawn in favour of the faster running and longer ranged G7e T5.

G7e T5 *Zaunkönig* (Wren)

The first 80 T5 *Zaunkönig* torpedoes (referred to in Allied reports as GNAT – German Naval Acoustic Torpedo) were delivered to the *Kriegsmarine* in August 1943 and superseded *Falke* in the autumn of that year. Initial production batches had a range of 5700m (6230yd) at 42.3km/h (25 knots) while the later G7e T5b improved this to 8000m (8750yd) at 40.7km/h (22 knots). Both versions carried a 200kg (440lb) HE warhead.

The torpedo operated in a similar fashion to *Falke*, homing onto the loudest source of sound after an initial 400m (1320ft) run. This could well be the U-boat itself and standing orders were given to dive immediately to a depth of 60m (198ft) after launch from a bow tube while a stern shot was followed by complete silence in the boat. Two U-boats were almost certainly lost when hit by one of their own T5 torpedoes, *U-972* in December 1943 and *U-377* in January 1944.

It has been estimated that a total of 640 T5 torpedoes were fired in combat, sinking 45 Allied ships. The success rate would have been far higher but for the rapid development of a simple Allied counter-measure, the Foxer noise-maker. This comprised a number of metal pipes with holes cut in them which were towed about 200m (660ft) astern of the boat. Water rushing through the holes and the pipes banging together created cavitation noise far greater than that coming from the ship's propeller. This was effective at drawing the torpedo away from the vessel, since the German homing torpedoes were tuned to home in on the loudest cavitation sound.

Despite the Foxer system, the U-boat crews were sufficiently impressed with *Zaunkönig's* successes against convoy escorts to dub it *Zerstörerknacker* (the Destroyer Cracker).

CHAPTER 3

AFVs and Self-Propelled Guns

German AFVs and self-propelled artillery were generally well-designed, well-built vehicles with superb firepower and high quality optical equipment which made their long range fire far more effective than that of their Allied counterparts. However, this excellence was achieved at a high cost – German tank manufacture involved much precision engineering which slowed down production.

Hitler's meddling with war production also had a negative effect as insufficient priority was given to the manufacture of spares. Guderian's advice that an adequate supply of spares would increase the Panzerwaffe's combat strength far more quickly and cheaply than building new AFVs went unheeded, largely because Hitler would not accept the 20 per cent reduction in AFV production that this would entail. His lack of interest in developing armoured recovery vehicles also caused many unnecessary tank losses until the Bergepanther *belatedly entered service in 1944.*

An abandoned Sturmtiger is examined by US forces at an unknown location in Belgium, winter 1944–45.

In Search of the Supertank

Between 1937 and mid-1941, Henschel and Porsche had been steadily developing a series of medium and heavy tank designs. Although the heavy British and French tanks encountered in 1940 had proved to be almost invulnerable to the fire of Panzer IIIs and IVs, there was little urgency among the Germans for getting new types into production.

On 26 May 1941, Hitler ordered Porsche and Henschel to produce prototypes of a new 45.7 tonne (45 ton) tank armed with the 88mm (3.5in) L/56. The threat posed by Soviet T-34s and KV-1s became apparent in the first weeks of Operation Barbarossa and gave the project a far greater sense of urgency. Porsche had an initial advantage in the race to win the production contract as his design studies were much more advanced than Henschel's, but chose to adopt a petrol-electric drive system. This comprised two air-cooled 238.6kW (320hp) Type 101/1 petrol engines driving generators, which in turn powered the two electric motors which actually drove the tracks.

Although it was a theoretically fuel-efficient system, it proved to be complex and unreliable, and used large quantities of scarce copper. Henschel wisely utilized a much more conventional Maybach petrol engine, which proved to be much less prone to breakdowns.

Both prototypes were fitted with almost identical Krupp turrets armed with the 88mm (3.5in) KwK 36 L/56 and a co-axial MG before being inspected by Hitler in April 1942. They then underwent competitive trials which ruthlessly exposed the Porsche design's inherent unreliability and poor cross-country performance. Accordingly, the Henschel design was ordered into production in August 1942, officially becoming the *Panzerkampfwagen Tiger Ausf. E*, although to most contemporaries, it was simply called the Tiger.

The Tiger

The loss of the contract was a financial blow to Porsche, who had unwisely started production and now had 90 apparently unusable tank hulls coming off his assembly lines. In early September 1942, it was proposed to complete these as gun tanks and issue them to two heavy tank battalions earmarked for deployment to North Africa. It seems likely that Dr Porsche's influential friends in the Nazi Party hierarchy were behind the move, which was justified on the grounds that the vehicles could be completed very rapidly and that their air-cooled engines were well-suited to North African conditions.

The Ferdinand

However, the type's mechanical unreliability was still obvious and within a matter of weeks the idea was dropped in favour of using the hulls as the basis for a new heavy tank destroyer mounting the 88mm (3.5in) PaK 43/2 L/71, also known as the StuK 43/1. The 90 tank hulls were moved to Alkett for conversion – Dr Porsche personally supervised the design work and the new vehicle was soon generally referred to as *Ferdinand*. The vehicle's official designation was *Panzerjäger Tiger (P) 'Ferdinand'* (SdKfz.184), although it was better known as the *Jagdpanzer Ferdinand*.

The unreliable air-cooled petrol engines of the original design were replaced with 223.7kW (300hp) Maybach HL120 water-cooled engines, although the electric drive system was retained. The powerplant was moved to the centre of the hull, freeing the rear for a large, fully enclosed fighting compartment for the limited traverse 88mm (3.5in) PaK 43/2. Armour protection was far greater than any that of any previous German AFV – 200mm (7.9in) frontal and 80mm (3.2in) over most of the sides and rear.

The *Ferdinand* had superb firepower and protection, but proved as unreliable as its predecessor and the crew had poor all-round visibility when the vehicle had to operate 'closed down'. One of the worst mistakes was the lack of effective secondary armament – a single MG 34 was carried in the fighting compartment, but there was no provision for firing it from the vehicle.

DR FERDINAND PORSCHE

■ **Dr Ferdinand Porsche, 1942. He designed a plethora of military vehicles, ranging from the tiny *Kubelwagen* to the enormous *Maus* super-heavy tank.**

Dr Ferdinand Porsche was a largely self-taught engineer who became involved in the construction of motor vehicles as early as 1898. He founded the Porsche motor company in 1930 and was instrumental in designing the classic Volkswagen Beetle.

BIRTH:	3 September 1875
DEATH:	30 January 1951
PLACE OF BIRTH:	Mattersdorf, Bohemia (now Liberec, Czech Republic)
FATHER:	Anton Porsche
MOTHER:	Anna Porsche
SIBLINGS:	None
PERSONAL RELATIONSHIPS:	Aloisia Johanna Kaes, married 1903 Two children, Ferdinand Anton Ernst (Ferry) and Louise
MILITARY SERVICE:	Austro-Hungarian Army (1902). Chauffeur to the Archduke Franz Ferdinand
EDUCATION:	Imperial Technical School, Mattersdorf
KEY POSITIONS:	Head of the Porsche motor company, supervised the design of the *Kubelwagen* and *Schwimmwagen* 'jeeps', the *Elefant* tank destroyer and the *Maus* super-heavy tank

Production Models: The Tiger I

When it began mass production of the Tiger I in August 1942, the Henschel factory at Kassel already had eight years experience of manufacturing AFVs, although the massive Tiger was very different to the tiny Panzer Is it had started building in 1934.

During the war years, the factory employed a total of 8000 workers in AFV production and operated around the clock, working two 12-hour shifts. Each six-hour stage in the manufacturing process was referred to as a *takt* and there were nine such *takte* in producing the Tiger I. The total time taken to complete a Tiger, including the various machining processes, was estimated to be 14 days. At any one time, between 18 and 22 tanks were on the hull assembly line with a further 10 tanks on the final assembly line. It has been estimated that the production of each Tiger took 300,000 man-hours.

Henschel did not have the capability to weld or bend the massive armour plates used in the Tiger and received the hull and turret

TIGER TANKS COMPARED

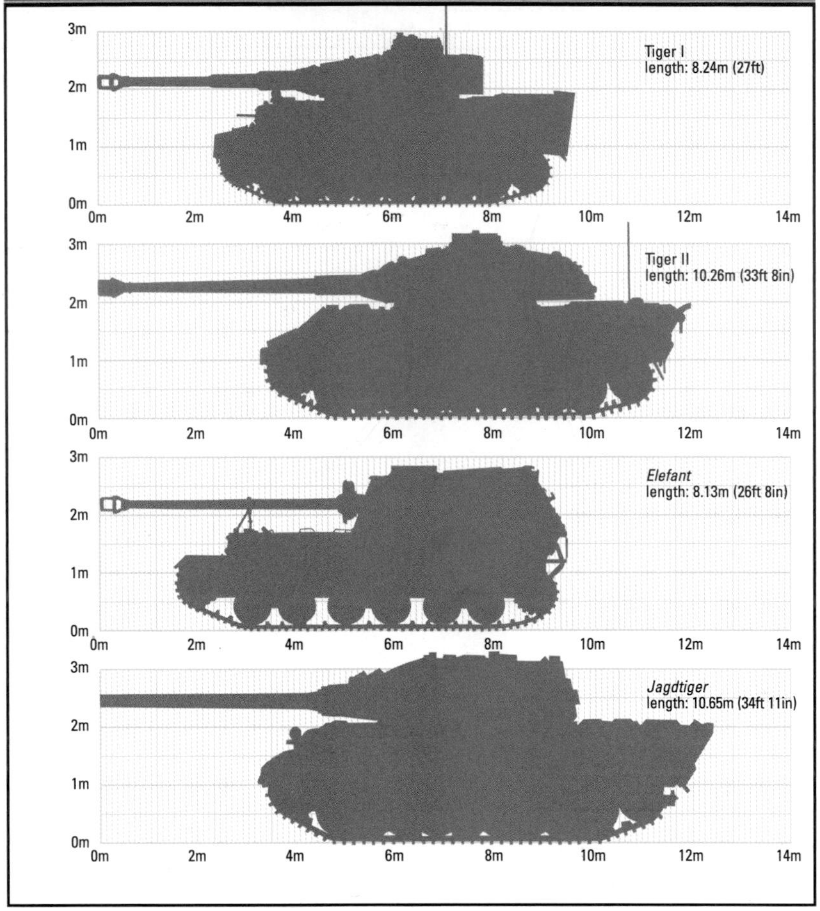
Tiger I
length: 8.24m (27ft)
Tiger II
length: 10.26m (33ft 8in)
Elefant
length: 8.13m (26ft 8in)
Jagdtiger
length: 10.65m (34ft 11in)
0m
1m
2m
3m
0m
2m
4m
6m
8m
10m
12m
14m

'shells' from other companies. The hulls were manufactured by two firms, Krupp and Dortmund-Hoerder Huettenverein, while the turrets were produced by Wegmann und Company that, like Henschel, was also based in Kassel.

Kassel was hit by at least 40 Allied air raids which disrupted Tiger production to varying degrees. One of the most serious was the attack on the night of 22–23 October 1943 when RAF bombing caused severe damage to the Henschel works.

In common with all other panzers, the Tiger I was continually modified throughout its production run. Problems caused by mud, ice and snow jamming the interleaved road wheels which were first encountered by Tiger units in Russia during the winter of 1942–43 were not solved until the introduction of the Tiger II. However, numerous improvements were made including:

- May 1943, the 522kW (700hp) Maybach HK 230 P45 engine with two air filters replaced the 485kW (650hp) Maybach HL 210 P45 and the transmission was improved
- July 1943, the turret was extensively redesigned. A new commander's cupola with periscopes and a 'lift and swing' hatch was installed. The cupola was later fitted with an AA mount for an MG 34 or MG 42. An improved spring counter-balance was fitted for the 88mm (3.5in) gun
- September 1943, *Zimmerit* anti-magnetic mine coating was applied at the factory to all surfaces within reach of enemy infantry
- January 1944, the *Nahverteidigungswaffe* (close defence weapon) for firing smoke bombs, fragmentation grenades and signal flares was mounted in the turret roof. Production of this breech-loading mortar was slow and most Tiger Is were not fitted with the weapon until March 1944
- February 1944, 'resilient rim' steel road wheels with internal rubber cushioning were fitted. These were similar to the road wheels adopted for the Tiger II

TIGER, *ELEFANT* AND *JAGDTIGER* PRODUCTION, 1942–45

Type	*Period*	*Number*
PzKpfw VI *Tiger Ausf E* (Tiger I)	1942–44	1355
Panzerjäger Tiger (P) Sd Kfz 184 *Ferdinand/Elefant*	1943	90
PzKpfw VI *Tiger Ausf B* (Tiger II)	1944–45	489
Panzerjäger Tiger Ausf B (Jagdtiger)	1944–45	85

PRODUCTION MODEL TIGERS

231

PzKpfw VI Tiger Ausf E (Tiger I)

Crew: 5
Weight: 55 tonnes (54.1 tons)
Length: 8.24m (27ft)
Width: 3.73m (12ft 3in)
Height: 2.86m (9ft $3\frac{1}{4}$in)
Powerplant: 1 x 522kW (700hp) Maybach HL 230 P 45 12-cylinder petrol engine
Speed: 38km/h (24mph)
Range: 195km (120 miles)
Armour: 110–25mm (4.3–0.98in)
Armament: 1 x 88mm (3.46in) KwK 36 L/56 gun, plus 2 or 3 x 7.92mm (0.31in) MG 34
Radio: FuG5 and FuG2

312

PzKpfw VI Tiger Ausf B (Tiger II)

Crew: 5
Weight: 69.7 tonnes (68.6 tons)
Length: 10.26m (33ft 8in)
Width: 3.75m (12ft $3\frac{1}{2}$in)
Height: 3.09m (10ft $1\frac{1}{2}$in)
Powerplant: 1 x 522kW (700hp) Maybach HL 230 P 30 12-cylinder petrol engine
Speed: 35km/h (22mph)
Range: 170km (105 miles)
Armour: 180–25mm (5.9–0.98in)
Armament: 1 x 88mm (3.5in) KwK 43 L/71 gun, plus 2 or 3 x 7.92mm (0.31in) MG 34
Radio: FuG5 and FuG2

Panzerjäger Tiger (P) Sd. Kfz. 184 Ferdinand/Elefant

Crew: 6
Weight: 65 tonnes (64 tons)
Length: 8.13m (26ft 8in)
Width: 3.38m (11ft 1in)
Height: 2.99m (9ft 10in)
Powerplant: 2 x 224kW (300hp) Maybach HL120TRM V-12 petrol engines
Speed: 30km/h (18.6mph)
Range: 150km (93.2 miles)
Armour: 200–25mm (7.9–0.98in)
Armament: 1 x 88mm (3.5in) Pak 43/2 L/71 gun, plus 2 x 7.92mm (0.31in) MG 34
Radio: FuG5 and FuG2

333

Panzerjäger Tiger Ausf B (Jagdtiger)

Crew: 6
Weight: 70.6 tonnes (69.5 tons)
Length: 10.65m (34ft $11\frac{1}{2}$in)
Width: 3.63m (11ft $10\frac{3}{4}$in)
Height: 2.95m (9ft 8in)
Powerplant: 1 x 522kW (700hp) Maybach HL 230 P 30 12-cylinder petrol engine
Speed: 34.6km/h (21.5mph)
Range: 170km (105 miles)
Armour: 250–40mm (9.8–1.57in)
Armament: 1 x 128mm (5.04in) PaK 44 L/55 gun, plus 2 x 7.92mm (0.31in) MG 34
Radio: FuG5 and FuG2

- March 1944, the 25mm (0.98in) roof plates were thickened to 40mm (1.6in), to improve protection. It also received the loader's hatch originally designed for the Tiger II
- April 1944, the superior monocular *Turmzielfernröhr 9c* sighting telescope replaced the originally specified binocular *Turmzielfernröhr 9b*

Production tapered off as resources were switched to the Tiger II during 1944 and the last Tiger Is left the Henschel factory for combat duty in August 1944.

In Combat

The first Tiger Is were issued to the 1st Company, 502nd Heavy Panzer Battalion in August 1942. The unit was attached to Army Group North for operations on the Leningrad sector of the front, where the terrain posed as many problems as the enemy.

Guderian later wrote scathingly of this deployment in his book *Panzer Leader*.

He [Hitler] was consumed by his desire to try his new weapon. He therefore ordered that the Tigers be committed in a quite secondary operation, in a limited attack carried out in terrain that was utterly unsuitable; for in the swampy forest near Leningrad heavy tanks could only move in single file along the forest tracks, which, of course, was exactly where the enemy anti-tank guns were posted, waiting for them. The results were not only heavy, unnecessary casualties, but also the loss of secrecy and of the element of surprise for future operations.

During this first attack in late August, all the Tigers sustained some damage and one was captured. Further attacks over the next month or so were equally unsuccessful. The Tiger's undoubted technical superiority to any contemporary AFV in the Red Army's inventory was

TIGER I ALLOCATION: HEER AND WAFFEN-SS UNITS

*Heer and Waffen-SS Heavy Tank Battalions (*Schwere Panzer Abteilungen*)*

- 501 Heavy Panzer Battalion
- 502 Heavy Panzer Battalion
- 503 Heavy Panzer Battalion
- 504 Heavy Panzer Battalion
- 505 Heavy Panzer Battalion
- 506 Heavy Panzer Battalion
- 507 Heavy Panzer Battalion
- 508 Heavy Panzer Battalion
- 509 Heavy Panzer Battalion
- 510 Heavy Panzer Battalion
- 3rd Battalion, *Grossdeutschland Division* (This Tiger unit was exceptional in that it was permanently assigned to a single division)

SS Heavy Panzer Battalions

- 101 SS Heavy Panzer Battalion (redesignated 501st SS Heavy Panzer Battalion in 1944 on re-equipping with the Tiger II), part of I SS Panzer Corps
- 102 SS Heavy Tank Battalion (redesignated 502nd SS Heavy Tank Battalion in 1944), part of II SS Panzer Corps
- 103 SS Heavy Panzer Battalion (redesignated 503rd SS Heavy Panzer Battalion in 1944), part of III (Germanic) SS Panzer Corps
- 104 SS Heavy Panzer Battalion was intended to be raised as a part of IV SS Panzer Corps in 1943, but was never formed

■ The first three Heavy Panzer Battalions (501, 502 and 503) were formed in 1942–43 and carried out extensive field trials of practically every possible combination of Panzer IIIs and Tigers within their company structures. The trials led to the adoption of an establishment of 10 Panzer IIIs in each of their two companies with a further six in the HQ company. These vehicles were Panzer III Ausf N, armed with the low-velocity 75mm (2.95in) L/24 close-support gun. These guns were particularly useful in tackling hostile anti-tank guns, allowing the Tigers to concentrate on destroying enemy AFVs.

The authorized strength of each battalion totalled 20 Tigers and 26 Panzer IIIs, but breakdowns and combat losses meant that units were rarely at full strength.

TIGER COMPANY, 1942–43

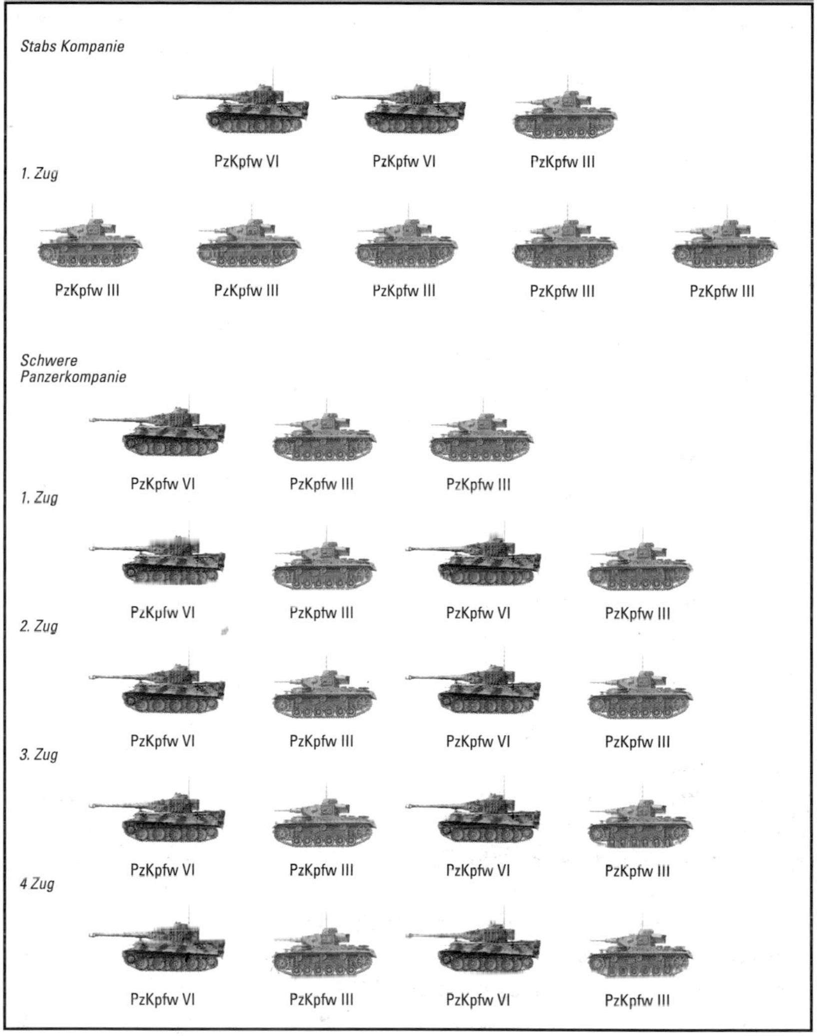
Stabs Kompanie
PzKpfw VI
PzKpfw VI
PzKpfw III
1. Zug
PzKpfw III
PzKpfw III
PzKpfw III
PzKpfw III
PzKpfw III
Schwere Panzerkompanie
PzKpfw VI
PzKpfw III
PzKpfw III
1. Zug
PzKpfw VI
PzKpfw III
PzKpfw VI
PzKpfw III
2. Zug
PzKpfw VI
PzKpfw III
PzKpfw VI
PzKpfw III
3. Zug
PzKpfw VI
PzKpfw III
PzKpfw VI
PzKpfw III
4 Zug
PzKpfw VI
PzKpfw III
PzKpfw VI
PzKpfw III

wasted in offensive operations in this setting, where all the advantages lay with well-camouflaged anti-tank guns deployed in depth to cover the few roads in the area. Although the Tigers' armour was virtually invulnerable to Soviet anti-tank guns, most of Tiger losses were 'mobility kills', where vehicles were immobilized by shots breaking tracks or damaging the running gear.

Defensive strength

When the Russians went on to the offensive in this sector early in 1943, the Tigers were in turn able exploit the swampy terrain which forced most Soviet AFVs to keep to the roads. During a period of less than three months (12 January to 31 March 1943) the company lost six Tigers, while destroying 160 Soviet tanks – a ratio of 26:1.

In common with most other heavy panzer battalions, the unit was plagued by inadequate recovery equipment and a constant shortage of spares. The unit never had more than four operational Tigers at any one time during the entire period. Three of the six Tigers lost were destroyed by their own crews to prevent capture; two of them after they had become stuck in swamps and one due to mechanical failure. The unit's war diary is filled with entries about retrieving 'bogged-down' Tigers.

After this unimpressive combat debut, things began to improve. Heavy Panzer Battalion 503 was sent

TIGER COMPANY , 1943–45

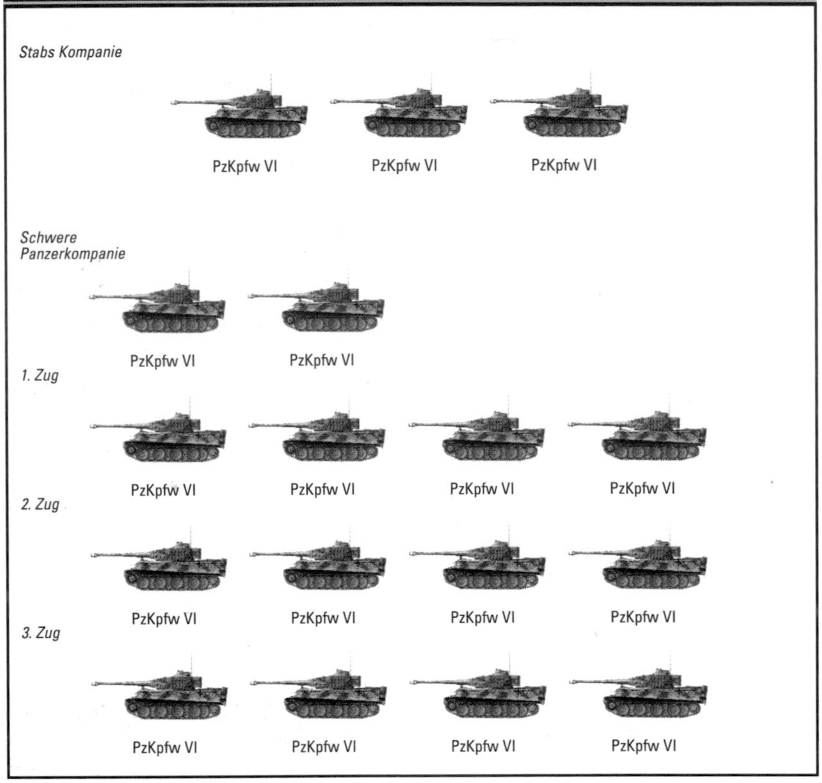
Stabs Kompanie
PzKpfw VI
PzKpfw VI
PzKpfw VI
Schwere Panzerkompanie
PzKpfw VI
PzKpfw VI
1. Zug
PzKpfw VI
PzKpfw VI
PzKpfw VI
PzKpfw VI
2. Zug
PzKpfw VI
PzKpfw VI
PzKpfw VI
PzKpfw VI
3. Zug
PzKpfw VI
PzKpfw VI
PzKpfw VI
PzKpfw VI

■ In March 1943, the decision was taken to change the battalion establishment to a total of 45 Tigers (3 x companies of 14, plus 3 Tigers in the HQ company). All the Panzer IIIs were replaced with Sd.Kfz.251 and 250 half-tracks to take on roles which were unsuitable for the Tigers, such as communications and reconnaissance duties.

to the Rostov area in January 1943. The open terrain of southern Russia allowed it to operate more freely than its counterparts in the Leningrad sector and to make use of the '88's' long-range anti-tank capability.

Experience showed that Tiger platoons could effectively open fire (concentrated platoon fire) against stationary targets at up to 3000m (3270yd). When firing against moving targets, it became general practice to open fire at between 1200m (1308yd) and 2000m (2180yd).

These early operations confirmed the effectiveness of the Tiger I's armour – in a matter of six hours one of the 503rd's vehicles took 227 hits from anti-tank rifles, 14 hits from 57mm (2.24in) anti-tank guns and a further 11 hits from 76mm (2.99in) anti-tank rounds. Despite this damage, the Tiger was still able to pull back 60km (37 miles) under its own power before being shipped back to Germany for major repairs. A slightly later action was the subject of a report by Panzer Regiment *Grossdeutschland's* Tiger company:

During a scouting patrol, two Tigers encountered about 20 Russian tanks on their front, while additional Russian tanks attacked from behind. A battle developed in which the armour and weapons of the Tiger were extraordinarily successful. Both Tigers were hit (mainly by 76.2mm (3in) armour-piercing shells) 10 or more times at ranges between 500 to 1000m (545 to 1090yd). The armour held up all round – not a single round penetrated the armour. Hits on the running gear, in which tore away the suspension arms, did not immobilize the Tigers ... The end result was 10 enemy tanks knocked out by two Tigers within 15 minutes.

Combat at Kursk

All 90 *Ferdinands* were issued to two heavy tank destroyer battalions (*schwere Heeres Panzerjager Abteilung* 653 and 654) for the Kursk Offensive. Their firepower and protection were outstanding – one platoon commander reported on 19 July 1943 that:

...crews of field and anti-tank guns run away after firing a few ineffective shots against our guns [Ferdinands]. In the first engagements, our battalion destroyed numerous artillery positions and bunkers as well as 120 enemy tanks ...

However, an attempt to use them in a breakthrough role exposed the shortcomings of the design – the lack

TIGER BATTALION COMBAT PERFORMANCE, 1942–45

Battalion	*Losses*	*Kills*
501st Heavy Panzer Battalion	120	450
502nd Heavy Panzer Battalion	107	1400
503rd Heavy Panzer Battalion	252	1700
504th Heavy Panzer Battalion	109	250
505th Heavy Panzer Battalion	126	900
506th Heavy Panzer Battalion	179	400
507th Heavy Panzer Battalion	104	600
508th Heavy Panzer Battalion	78	100
509th Heavy Panzer Battalion	120	500
510th Heavy Panzer Battalion	65	200
13th Coy, Panzer Regt *Grossdeutschland*	6	100
3rd Bn, Panzer Regt *Grossdeutschland*	98	500
13th (Heavy) Coy, 1st SS Panzer Regt	42	400
8th (Heavy) Coy, 2nd SS Panzer Regt	31	250
9th (Heavy) Coy, 3rd SS Panzer Regt	56	500
101st SS Heavy Panzer Battalion	107	500
102nd SS Heavy Panzer Battalion	76	600
103rd SS Heavy Panzer Battalion	39	500
TOTAL	**1715**	**9850**

of any effective secondary armament meant that crews either had to fire their single MG 34 down the barrel of the 88mm (3.5in) main gun or to attempt to break up Soviet infantry attacks with HE fire. Guderian memorably described the situation:

Once they had broken through into the enemy's infantry zone they literally had to go quail-shooting with cannon. They did not manage to neutralize, let alone destroy, the enemy's rifle and machine guns, so that our own infantry was unable to follow up behind them. By the time they reached the Soviet artillery they were on their own.

The crew's limited field of vision when operating 'closed down' made matters worse and unsurprisingly,

TIGER BATTALION KILL:LOSS RATIO, 1942–45

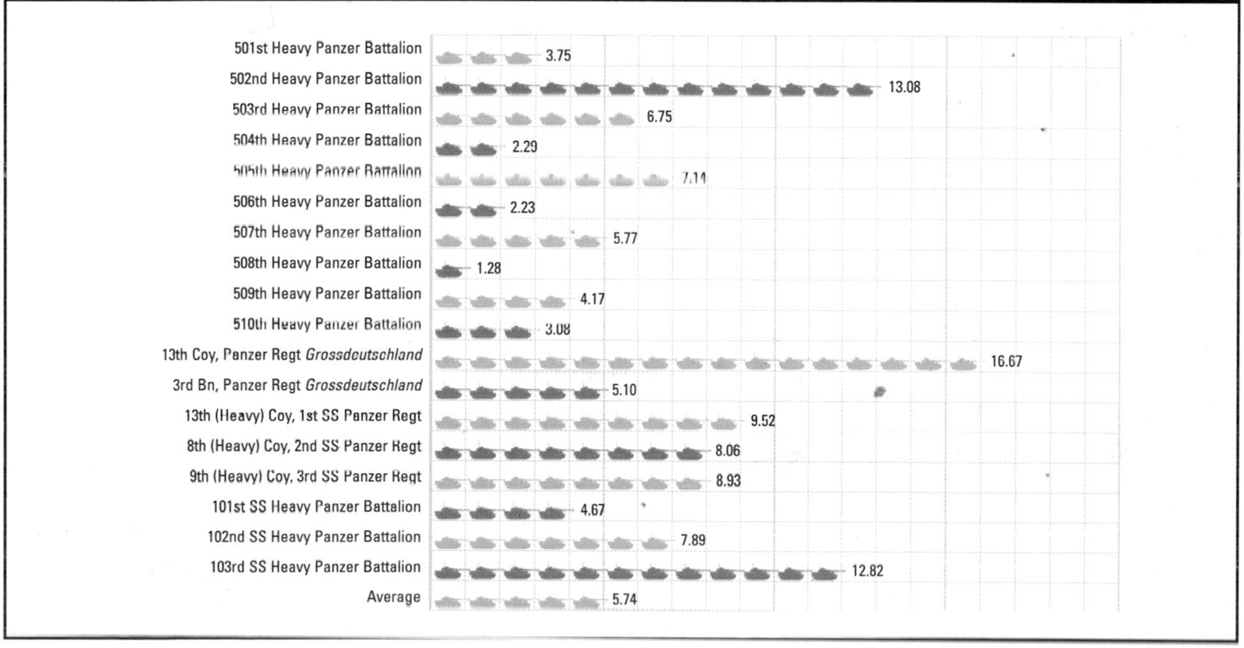
501st Heavy Panzer Battalion 3.75
502nd Heavy Panzer Battalion 13.08
503rd Heavy Panzer Battalion 6.75
504th Heavy Panzer Battalion 2.29
505th Heavy Panzer Battalion 7.11
506th Heavy Panzer Battalion 2.23
507th Heavy Panzer Battalion 5.77
508th Heavy Panzer Battalion 1.28
509th Heavy Panzer Battalion 4.17
510th Heavy Panzer Battalion 3.08
13th Coy, Panzer Regt Grossdeutschland 16.67
3rd Bn, Panzer Regt Grossdeutschland 5.10
13th (Heavy) Coy, 1st SS Panzer Regt 9.52
8th (Heavy) Coy, 2nd SS Panzer Regt 8.06
9th (Heavy) Coy, 3rd SS Panzer Regt 8.93
101st SS Heavy Panzer Battalion 4.67
102nd SS Heavy Panzer Battalion 7.89
103rd SS Heavy Panzer Battalion 12.82
Average 5.74

TIGER I: NUMBERS PRODUCED (APRIL 1942 – AUGUST 1944)

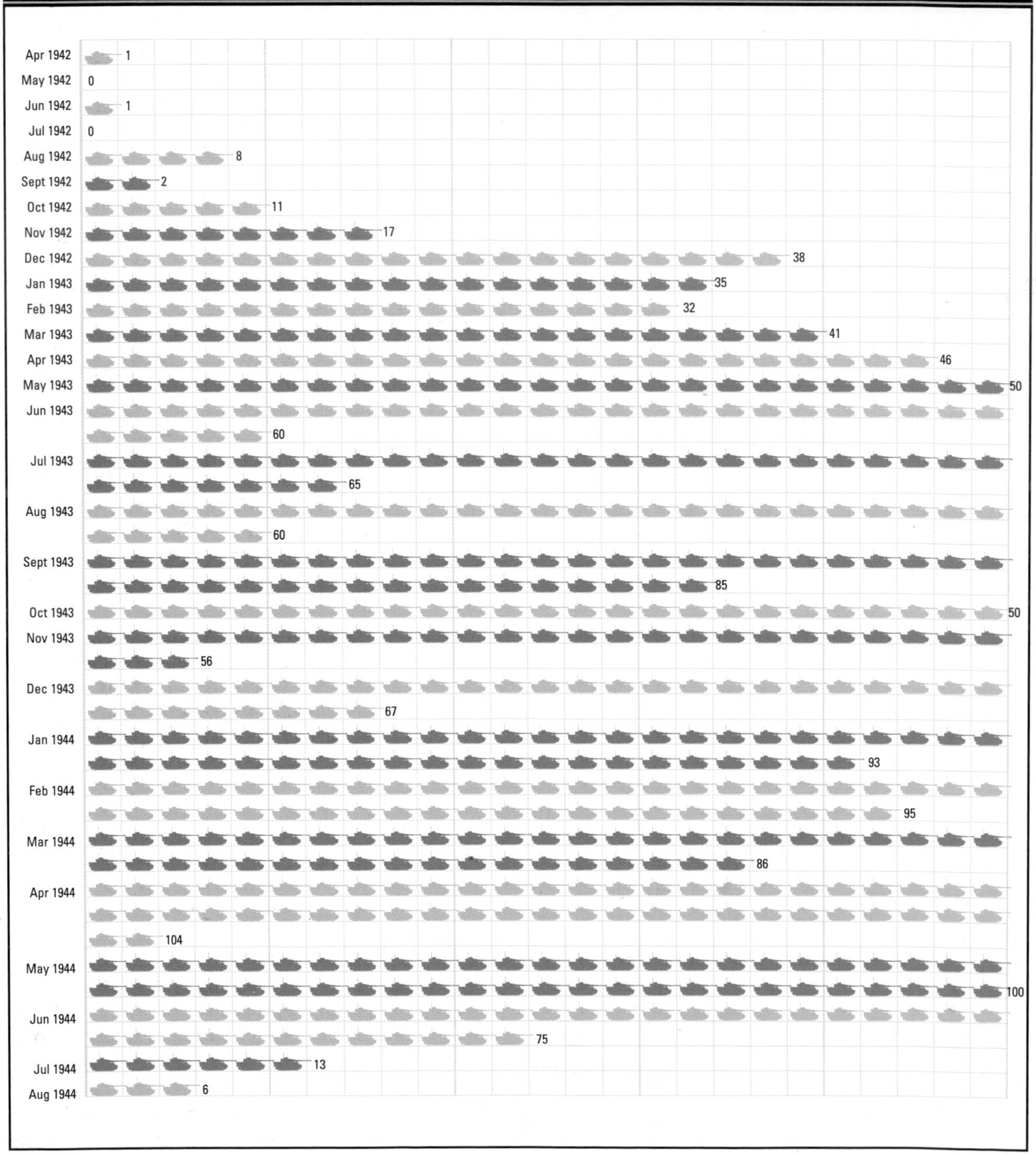
Apr 1942 1
May 1942 0
Jun 1942 1
Jul 1942 0
Aug 1942 8
Sept 1942 2
Oct 1942 11
Nov 1942 17
Dec 1942 38
Jan 1943 35
Feb 1943 32
Mar 1943 41
Apr 1943 46
May 1943 50
Jun 1943 60
Jul 1943 65
Aug 1943 60
Sept 1943 85
Oct 1943 50
Nov 1943 56
Dec 1943 67
Jan 1944 93
Feb 1944 95
Mar 1944 86
Apr 1944 104
May 1944 100
Jun 1944 75
Jul 1944 13
Aug 1944 6

Russian infantry disabled a significant number of Ferdinands by throwing demolition charges under the hull or on to the engine decks.

Losses

The majority of the losses were 'mobility kills', which temporarily disabled vehicles rather than totally destroyed them. While the Germans retained control of the battlefield, most of these vehicles could be recovered and repaired.The situation became more serious as soon as the Germans were forced to retreat when many such damaged vehicles could not be recovered and had to be destroyed to avoid capture.

TIGER I PRODUCTION TARGETS

Date	*Target*	*Notes*
April 1942	0	V1 prototype included; 1 delivered
May 1942	0	1 delivered
June 1942	5	0 delivered
July 1942	15	0 delivered
August 1942	10	9 delivered
September 1942	15	2 delivered
October 1942	16	V2 prototype included in number; 8 delivered
November 1942	18	14 delivered
December 1942	30	V3 prototype included in number; 35 delivered
January 1943	30	30 delivered (of which 1 was a rebuild vehicle)
February 1943	30	30 delivered (of which 3 were command vehicles)
March 1943	40	35 delivered (of which 4 were command vehicles)
April 1943	45	42 delivered (of which 5 were command vehicles)
May 1943	50	43 delivered (of which 4 were command vehicles)
June 1943	60	49 delivered (of which 6 were command vehicles)
July 1943	65	53 delivered (of which 4 were command vehicles)
August 1943	70	63 delivered (of which 11 were command vehicles)
September 1943	75	48 delivered (of which 7 were command vehicles)
October 1943	80	82 delivered (of which 3 were command vehicles)
November 1943	84	34 delivered (of which 2 were command vehicles)
December 1943	88	80 delivered
January 1944	93	78 delivered (of which 9 were command vehicles)
February 1944	95	96 delivered (of which 6 were command vehicles and 1 was a rebuild vehicle)
March 1944	95	84 delivered (of which 4 were command vehicles and 1 was a rebuild vehicle)
April 1944	95	88 delivered (of which 6 were command vehicles and 3 were rebuild vehicles)
May 1944	95	79 delivered (of which 6 were command vehicles and 5 were rebuild vehicles)
June 1944	75	100 delivered (of which 4 were command vehicles and 5 were rebuild vehicles)
July 1944	58	63 delivered (of which 2 were command vehicles and 8 were rebuild vehicles)
August 1944	9	13 delivered (of which 3 were command vehicles and 11 were rebuild vehicles)

The experience of the two Tiger battalions committed to the Kursk Offensive was in some respects similar to that of the *Ferdinands* – they often found themselves isolated after Soviet defences stripped away their supporting infantry and light armour. However, their turreted main armament and machine guns gave them a far better chance of fighting off infantry attacks and their losses were less serious. Both battalions also inflicted heavy casualties on Soviet armoured units, especially the 505th, which destroyed a total of 164 Russian AFVs for the loss of just five Tigers.

In the aftermath of Kursk, Tigers and the surviving *Ferdinands* (soon to be re-named *Elefants*) were largely committed to what has been described as a 'fire brigade role' rushing from one sector to another in attempts to contain Allied offensives.

Ferdinand to *Elefant*

In the autumn of 1943, the remaining 48 *Ferdinands* were sent back to Germany for overhaul and a number of modifications including:

- Fitting a commander's cupola similar to that already in production for the *StuG III Ausf G* assault gun.
- Installing a bow-mounted MG 34 machine gun to provide a degree of self-defence against infantry attack.

The modified vehicles were formally re-designated *Panzerjäger Tiger (P) 'Elefant'* in February 1944 and were reissued to *schwere Heeres Panzerjager Abteilung 653,* which was sent to Italy. Although they were once again highly effective

TIGER I AND ALLIED HEAVY TANKS COMPARED

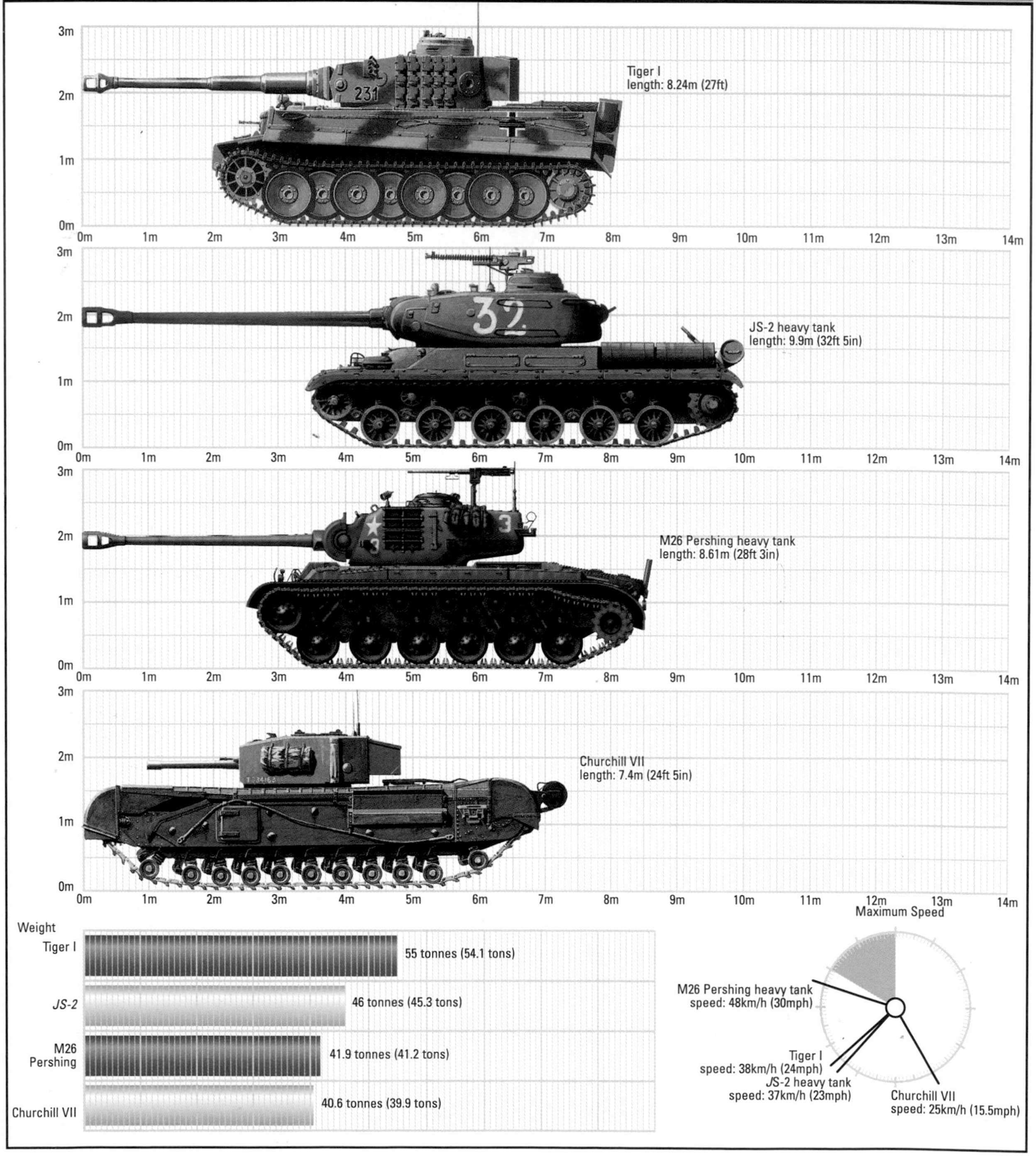
Tiger I
length: 8.24m (27ft)
JS-2 heavy tank
length: 9.9m (32ft 5in)
M26 Pershing heavy tank
length: 8.61m (28ft 3in)
Churchill VII
length: 7.4m (24ft 5in)
0m
1m
2m
3m
4m
5m
6m
7m
8m
9m
10m
11m
12m
13m
14m
Weight
Tiger I
55 tonnes (54.1 tons)
JS-2
46 tonnes (45.3 tons)
M26 Pershing
41.9 tonnes (41.2 tons)
Churchill VII
40.6 tonnes (39.9 tons)
Maximum Speed
M26 Pershing heavy tank
speed: 48km/h (30mph)
Tiger I
speed: 38km/h (24mph)
JS-2 heavy tank
speed: 37km/h (23mph)
Churchill VII
speed: 25km/h (15.5mph)

MICHAEL WITTMANN

■ **Wittmann seated on the barrel of the gun of his Tiger I – a propaganda photograph from May 1944.**

After transferring from the *Wehrmacht* to the *Leibstandarte SS Adolf Hitler* (LSSAH) in 1937, Wittmann served in armoured cars and assault guns, before being commissioned in 1942. In March 1943, he was transferred to *Leibstandarte's* Tiger I company and amassed a remarkable success rate against Soviet AFVs, which reached 100 hits by January 1944 and led to his award of the Knight's Cross with Oak Leaves. Subsequently posted to *schwere SS-Panzer-Abteilung 101* in France, in the Battle of Villers-Bocage, shortly after the Normandy landings, he destroyed a further 10 tanks, two anti-tank guns and 13 APCs, all in about 15 minutes. This achievement brought promotion and the award of the Swords to his Knights Cross with Oak Leaves. Wittmann was killed in action near St Aignan-de-Cramesnil, Normandy, on 8 August 1944.

Birth:	22 April 1914
Death:	8 August 1944
Place of birth:	Vogelthal, Bavaria
Father:	Johann Wittmann
Mother:	Ursula Wittmann
Siblings:	Johann, Franziska, Anni and Theresa
Personal relationships:	Hildegard Burmester, married 1 March 1944
Military Service:	19 Infantry Regiment, Freising, 1934–36 *Leibstandarte SS Adolf Hitler*, 1937–44
Key commands:	Commander Light Platoon, *4 Kompanie LSSAH,* 25 December 1942 Transferred to Tiger Company as commander of *3 Platoon, 4 Kompanie,* 31 March 1943 Commander of *2 Kompanie 101 Panzer battalion LSSAH,* 30 December 1943 Commander *101 Panzer battalion LSSAH,* 10 July 1944

when used in a defensive role as long-range tank destroyers, their bulk did not suit Italy's narrow roads and mountainous terrain. It is likely that the 14 surviving *Elefants* were moved to the Eastern Front in late 1944–early 1945 and the last vehicles may have fought as part of *Kampfgruppe Ritter* in defence of the *Zossen* sector during the Battle of Berlin.

Tigers fight on

Although production of the Tiger I ended in August 1944, surviving vehicles fought on until the end of the war. New Allied AFVs such as the Sherman Firefly, Pershing, JS-2 and JSU-122 were eroding the Tiger I's technical superiority, but it remained a formidable opponent when pitted against the T-34s and Shermans which still equipped most Allied tank units. On 8 August 1944, a single Tiger of 102 SS Heavy Panzer Battalion commanded by *SS-Unterscharfuehrer* Willi Fey, engaged a British tank column destroying 14 out of 15 Shermans. The battalion lost all its Tigers in Normandy but claimed the destruction of 227 Allied tanks in a matter of six weeks.

Late-War Production Models

The Tiger I had scarcely entered service before the German General Staff requested a bigger and better successor, with superior firepower and armour compared to any AFV that Soviet design teams were likely to produce.

German analysts calculated that armoured warfare was evolving so rapidly that the Tiger I's superiority might last for no more than about a year.

Tiger II

In January 1943, Hitler specified that that the new Tiger should have a new, long-barrelled 88mm (3.5in) gun based on Rheinmetall's 88mm (3.5in) Flak 41 and should also have sloped armour. Once again, Porsche and Henschel were asked for designs to meet this specification, whilst Krupp was awarded the contract to develop the 88mm (3.5in) KwK 43 L/71. Although the Rheinmetall Flak 41 gun provided a starting point, Krupp extensively modified the gun for tank use. In comparison with the Flak 41, the KwK 43 L/71 had shorter, fatter recoil cylinders to fit inside the confines of a turret and a new air blast system to evacuate fumes from the gun immediately after firing. The ammunition was also redesigned with shorter (but fatter) cartridge cases for easier handling and loading.

The Porsche designs were closely based on their previous proposals for the Tiger I contract and again used petrol-electric drive. This time, both conventional centre-mounted turret and rear-mounted turret configurations were offered, but the

TIGER II PRODUCTION (NOV 1943 – MARCH 1945)

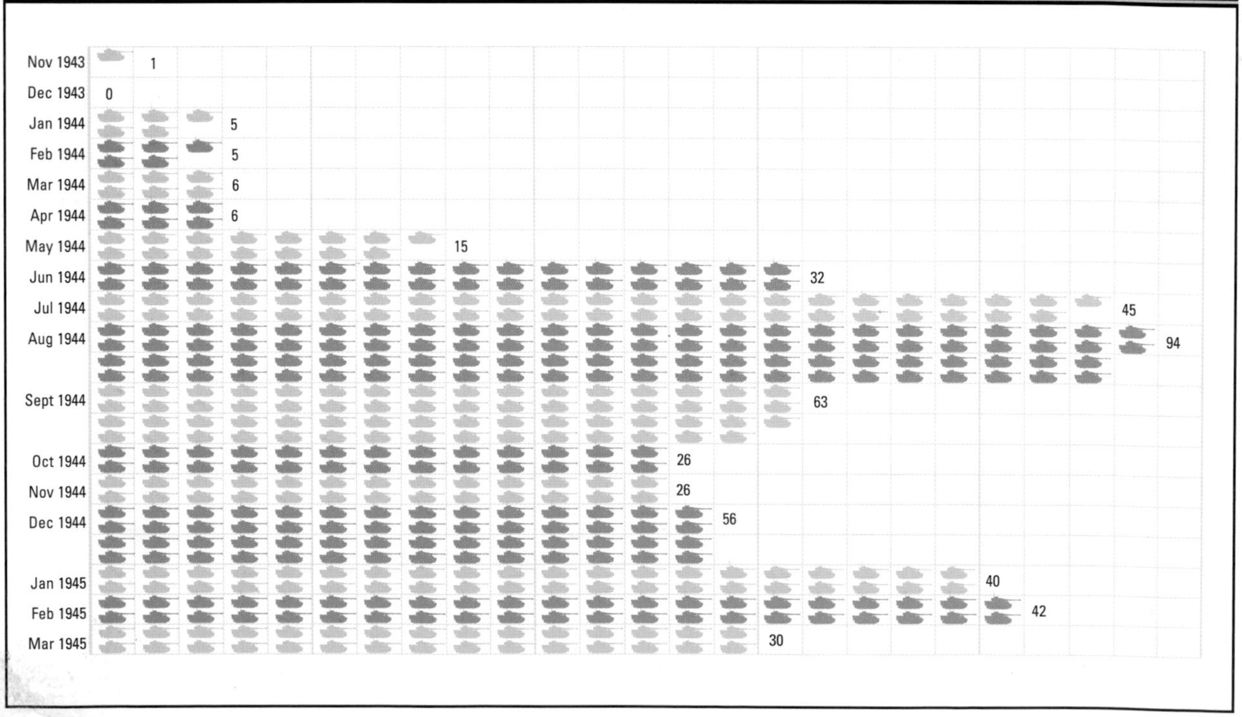
Nov 1943
1
Dec 1943
0
Jan 1944
5
Feb 1944
5
Mar 1944
6
Apr 1944
6
May 1944
15
Jun 1944
32
Jul 1944
45
Aug 1944
94
Sept 1944
63
Oct 1944
26
Nov 1944
26
Dec 1944
56
Jan 1945
40
Feb 1945
42
Mar 1945
30

Ferdinand/Elefant had been a stark warning of the inherent problems of petrol-electric drive systems. In the circumstances, it was not surprising that Henschel were again awarded the production contract for the Tiger II. An initial order for 176 vehicles was followed by more until Henschel had a total of over 1500 Tiger IIs on their books. Production was scheduled to increase steadily to a target figure of 50 vehicles per month by May 1944. The first prototype was completed in November 1943, with two further prototypes and the first three production Tiger IIs coming off the assembly lines in January 1944. The production run continued until the end of March 1945, when the Henschel factory completed work on the last 13 Tiger II tanks, which were handed over to 510 and 511 Heavy Panzer Battalions.

Despite disruption caused by heavy Allied bombing, Henschel always managed to have at least 60 vehicles moving along its tank assembly lines at any one time. However, the ever-worsening fuel shortage forced the modification of tank engines to run on bottled gas for factory testing as all available petrol was reserved for operational use.

Formidable record

The Tiger II's exceptional firepower and armour protection made it a formidable opponent for even the best Allied AFVs. During the Lake Balaton Offensive of March 1945 and its aftermath, the 501st SS and 509th Heavy Panzer Battalions demonstrated their advanced capabilities in a number of actions, notably:

TIGER IIs UNIT DEPLOYMENT

Dispatched	*Number*	*Unit*
14 Mar 1944	5	Pz.Kp.(FKL) 316/Pz.Lehr-Div
1 Apr 1944	3	*Ersatzheer*
11 May–24 Jun 1944	4	*Ersatzheer*
9 May–2 Jun 1944	6	*Wa.Prüf*
12 Jun 1944	12	s.H.Pz.Abt.503
24 Jun 1944	6	s.H.Pz.Abt.501
30 Jun 1944	4	*Ersatzheer*
3 Jul 1944	1	*Ersatzheer*
7–14 Jul 1944	25	s.H.Pz.Abt.501
26 Jul 1944	6	s.H.Pz.Abt.505
27–29 Jul 1944	14	s.H.Pz.Abt.503
28 Jul–1 Aug 1944	14	s.SS.Pz.Abt.101
4–7 Aug 1944	14	s.H.Pz.Abt.501
10–29 Aug 1944	39	s.H.Pz.Abt.505
10 Aug 1944	2	*Ersatzheer*
20 Aug–1 Sept 1944	17	s.H.Pz.Abt.506
3–12 Sept 1944	20	s.H.Pz.Abt.505
19–22 Sept 1944	43	s.H.Pz.Abt.503
28 Sept–3 Oct 1944	11	s.H.Pz.Abt.509 (Requisitioned by s.SS.Pz.Abt.501, for *Wacht am Rhein*)
17 Oct–11 Nov 1944	14	s.SS.Pz.Abt.501
19 Oct 1944	4	s.SS.Pz.Abt.503
26 Nov–3 Dec 1944	20	s.SS.Pz.Abt.501
8 Dec 1944	6	s.H.Pz.Abt.506
5–7 Dec 1944	9	s.H.Pz.Abt.509
8 Dec 1944–1 Jan 1945	36	s.H.Pz.Abt.509
13 Dec 1944	6	s.H.Pz.Abt.506
27 Dec 1944	6	s.SS.Pz.Abt.502 (Given to s.SS.Pz.Abt.503)
30 Jan 1945	3	*3.Kompanie*/s.H.Pz.Abt.502 (Given to s.H.Pz.Abt.507)
1 Feb 1945	3	*3.Kompanie*/s.H.Pz.Abt.510 (Given to s.H.Pz.Abt.507)
11–25 Jan 1945	29	s.SS.Pz.Abt.503
22 Jan 1945	6	s.SS.Pz.Abt.501
14 Feb–2 Mar 1945	27	s.SS.Pz.Abt.502
2–6 Mar 1945	4	s.SS.Pz.Abt.502
9–22 Mar 1945	15	s.H.Pz.Abt.507
11 Mar 1945	5	Pz.Div.*Feldhermhalle*
12 Mar 1945	13	s.H.Pz.Abt.506
31 Mar 1945	13	s.H.Pz.Abt.510 and 511

Delivery Totals	*Number*
schwere Heeres Panzer Abteilungen	319
schwere SS-Panzer-Abteilungen	124
Other units	30

- 13 March – Lead elements of III Panzer Corps encountered 24 dug-in SU-152s protected by a minefield. The 509th Heavy Panzer Batttalion attacked with the loss of 16 Tiger IIs (3 destroyed and 13 damaged). After lanes were cleared through the minefield, two Tiger IIs destroyed all the SU-152s.
- 20 March – A single Tiger II of the 501st SS Heavy Panzer Battalion destroyed 15 Soviet tanks near Varpalota, a town in western Hungary.
- 21 March – A single Tiger II from the same unit, supported by two Panthers, destroyed another 17 enemy tanks.

Jagdtiger

By 1943, it was becoming standard practice for German AFV design teams to develop a more heavily armed tank destroyer on the hull of each new tank type. It was clear that the Tiger II had the potential to carry an exceptionally heavy main armament in its *jagdpanzer* configuration and work began on the project in February 1943. A wooden mock-up was prepared for Hitler's inspection on 20 October 1943 and two prototypes, one with the eight-road-wheel Porsche suspension system and one with the Henschel nine-overlapping wheel suspension system were completed in February 1944. The type was first designated *Jagdpanzer VI*, but was subsequently named *Jagdtiger*. Series production was scheduled to start in December 1943 but did not begin until July 1944 as Panther production received priority. *Jagdtiger* production was slow and only 79 of the 150 vehicles ordered were completed.

The *Jagdtiger* was fitted with a boxy, fully enclosed fighting compartment on a slightly lengthened Tiger II chassis. Its very heavy armour and 128mm (5.04in) PaK 44 L/55 gun made it a daunting opponent as it was capable of destroying any Allied AFV at normal battle ranges. However, the PaK 44 had to use separate loading ammunition as the cased propelling charge weighed 15.3kg (33.7lb) and its armour piercing shell a further 28kg (62.4lb) which, even with the two loaders in the *Jagdtiger*'s crew, made for a slow rate of fire. The vehicle was also underpowered and its overloaded transmission gave its crews constant problems.

Only two heavy anti-tank battalions (*schwere Panzerjäger-Abteilung*), numbers 512 and 653, were equipped with *Jagdtigers*, with the first vehicles reaching the units in September 1944. Only about 20 per cent were lost in combat; far more succumbed to mechanical breakdowns or lack of fuel in the final weeks of the war.

It seems likely that all the *Jagdtigers* that actually saw combat were armed with the PaK 44, but a very few vehicles (probably no more than four) were fitted with the 88mm (3.5in) KwK 43 L/71. In November 1944, Krupp proposed re-arming *Jagdtigers* with a longer 128mm (5.04in) Pak L/66 gun. No such modifications were carried out, as the conversion would have entailed a major rebuild, principally extending the superstructure over the engine deck to allow for the gun's recoil. The performance of the L/66 would have been awe-inspiring, but the standard armament was very impressive – in US Army firing trials, a captured *Jagdtiger* penetrated the frontal armour of an M26 Pershing heavy tank at a range of 2100m (2297yd).

Sturmtiger

Analysis of the fighting at Stalingrad emphasized the need for a well-armoured assault gun mounting a heavy demolition weapon for urban warfare. At that time, the heaviest

AFV PURCHASE PRICES COMPARED

Weapon	*Price (Reichsmarks)*	*Notes*
Pz.Kpfw.I Ausf. B	Approx. 38,000	Without weapons
Pz.Kpfw.II Ausf B	52,640	
Pz.Kpfw.II Ausf F	49,228	Without weapons
15cm (5.9in) s.I.G. auf Fgst. Pz.Kpfw.II (Sf.)	53,000	
Pz.Kpfw.III Ausf.M	103,163	Without radio
Pz.Kpfw.IV Ausf.G	115,962	With 75mm (2.95in) Kw.K.40 L/43
Panther	117,100	Early, wihtout weapons
Tiger I	250,800	Without weapons or radio
	299,800	Fully equipped
	645,000	Export price for Japan
Tiger II	321,500	

available assault gun was the 150mm (5.9in) sIG 33B, but the loss of 12 of the 24 vehicles completed at Stalingrad indicated that greater firepower and protection were required to deal with the strongest enemy positions.

The original intention was to produce an entirely new vehicle based on the Tiger I hull and armed with a 21cm (8.3in) howitzer, but the howitzer was not available at the time and a heavy rocket launcher adapted from a naval depth-charge launcher was substituted. This was the 38cm (14.9in) *Raketen-Werfer* 61 L/5.4, a breech-loading weapon which fired two types of ammunition – the HE *Raketen Sprenggranate* 4581 containing 125kg (275lb) of explosives and the hollow-charge *Raketen Hohladungsgranate* 4582 which could penetrate up 2.5m (8ft) of reinforced concrete. Both types were roughly 1.5m (59in) in length and weighed 345–351kg (760–770lb). On firing, a normal propelling charge first accelerated the projectile to 45m/s (150ft/s) before the 40kg (88lb) of solid rocket fuel cut in to boost this to 250 m/s (820ft/s). The maximum range of the weapon was approximately 5650m (6180yd).

Only 13 rounds of the bulky ammunition could be carried – 12 in stowage racks, plus a further rocket loaded in the launcher. A hoist was fitted to the roof of the fighting compartment to lift the massive rounds from their racks onto the loading tray. Replenishing ammunition was even harder as it had to be passed through a roof hatch roughly 2.7m (9ft) above ground level. A hand-operated crane was fitted to the rear superstructure to lift the rounds to the loading hatch, but even so 'bombing-up' was a long job demanding back-breaking effort from the entire five-man crew. It was originally intended that each *Sturmtiger* would be accompanied by an ammunition carrier based on the Tiger I hull, but only one such carrier was completed.

The design of the rocket launcher caused some problems, as the hot rocket exhaust gasses could not be vented into the fighting compartment but neither could the barrel withstand the pressure if the gasses were not vented. The solution was to fit a

TANK PRODUCTION COSTS COMPARED (REICHMARKS)

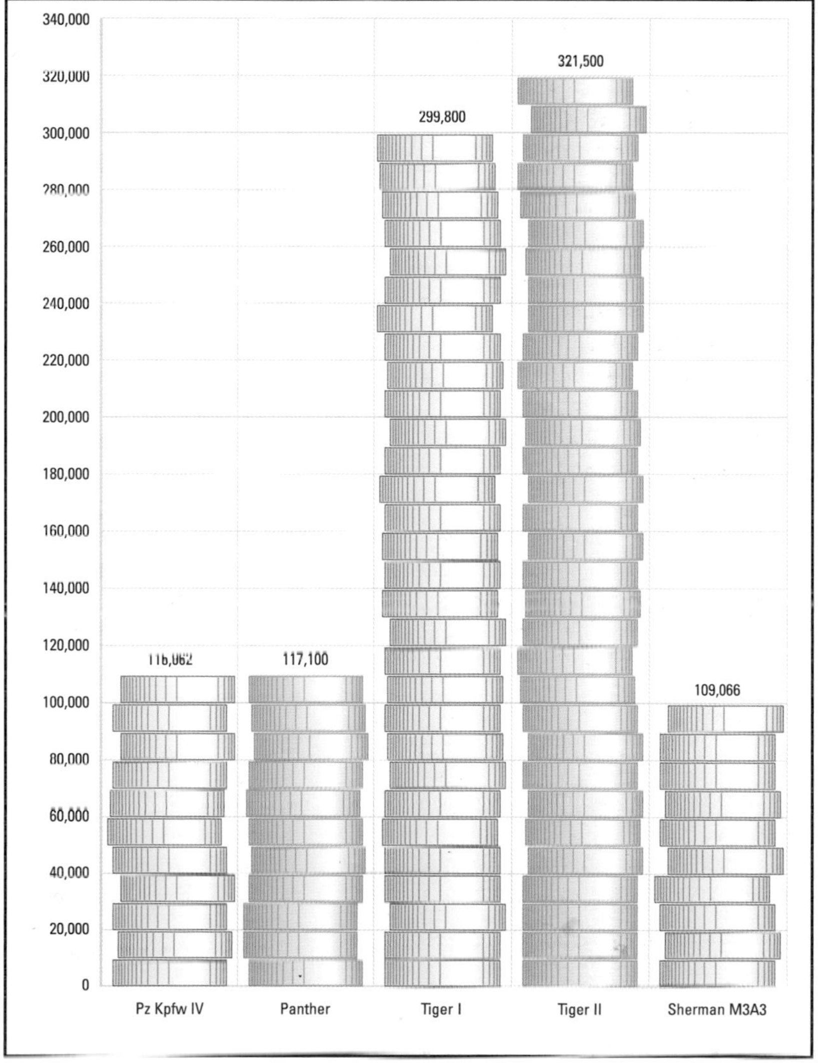
340,000
320,000
300,000
280,000
260,000
240,000
220,000
200,000
180,000
160,000
140,000
120,000
100,000
80,000
60,000
40,000
20,000
0
116,062
117,100
299,800
321,500
109,066
Pz Kpfw IV
Panther
Tiger I
Tiger II
Sherman M3A3

bypass valve in the breech which allowed the gasses to escape through a ring of small tubes which vented at the muzzle.

The prototype was demonstrated to Hitler in October 1943 and limited production began in 1944 – a total of 18 vehicles were completed by the time that production ended in December 1944. Three new Panzer companies were raised to operate the *Sturmtiger. Panzer Sturmmörser Kompanien* (PzStuMrKp) (Armoured Assault Howitzer Companies) 1000, 1001 and 1002. Each of these was originally intended to be equipped with 14 vehicles, but this figure was later reduced to four each, divided into two platoons. In January 1945, the authorised strength of each company was increased to six *Sturmtigers*, but it is doubtful that any company was ever brought up to this figure.

PzStuMrKp 1000 was formed on 13 August 1944 and one platoon (together with the prototype) supported the forces suppressing the Warsaw Uprising, which may have been the only time the *Sturmtiger* was used in its intended role. PzStuMrKp 1001 and 1002 followed in September and October. Both PzStuMrKp 1000 and 1001 served in the Ardennes Offensive, fielding a total of seven *Sturmtigers*. Accounts of its combat effectiveness are extremely rare, but in January 1945, three US Shermans taking cover in a village were reportedly destroyed by a single round from a PzStuMrKp 1001 Sturmtiger.

Rangefinders

Armoured combat in North Africa and Russia showed that there were situations where long-range tank gunnery could be a decisive factor. The ever-increasing armour-piercing performance of tank guns created a demand for more accurate range-finding so that effective fire could be brought to bear at ranges beyond the capabilities of conventional sights.

During 1944–45, optics company Zeiss attempted to develop a combined rangefinder and gun sight suitable for installation in future Panthers and Tiger IIs, but the technical problems were too complex and it was decided to concentrate efforts on a stereoscopic rangefinder. This would be fitted in a shock-absorbing mount in the turret roof so that its optics were not knocked out of alignment by the tank's movement or incoming rounds. Initial production models would automatically transfer ranges to the gun sights, while later versions were intended to be linked to stabilized periscopic gun sights, to allow aimed fire on the move.

The equipment could provide range data up to 20,000m (21,800yd) and had the potential to make German tank gunnery considerably more effective. It is possible that a tiny number of rangefinders were issued for troop trials, but series production was not scheduled to begin until July 1945.

IR equipment

German research into infrared (IR) night-fighting equipment had begun in the 1930s, but received little official backing until increasing Allied air superiority forced greater attention to be given to the problems of moving and fighting at night. Prototype IR equipment underwent troop trials in 1943–44 and led to the adoption of the 200mm (7.9in) FG1250 IR searchlight and viewer which was fitted to a small number of Panthers. The equipment was mounted on the commander's cupola and had an effective range of approximately 600m (656yd). These Panthers were intended to operate in conjunction with the SdKfz 251/20 *Uhu* half-track which mounted a 600mm (23.6in) Beobachtungs *Gerät 1251* IR searchlight that could illuminate targets at up to 1500m (1640yd).

TIGER AND JS-2 'FAMILY' PRODUCTION COMPARED

Type	*1942*	*1943*	*1944*	*1945*	*Total*
Tiger I	78	649	623	–	1350
Elefant	–	90	–	–	90
Sturmtiger	–	–	18	–	18
Tiger II	–	1	377	112	490
Jagdtiger	–	–	51	28	79
Total	78	740	1069	140	2027

Type	*1942*	*1943*	*1944*	*1945*	*Total*
JS-2	–	102	2252	1500	3854
JSU-122/152	–	35	2510	1530	4075
Total	–	137	4762	3030	7927

SELF-PROPELLED GUNS COMPARED

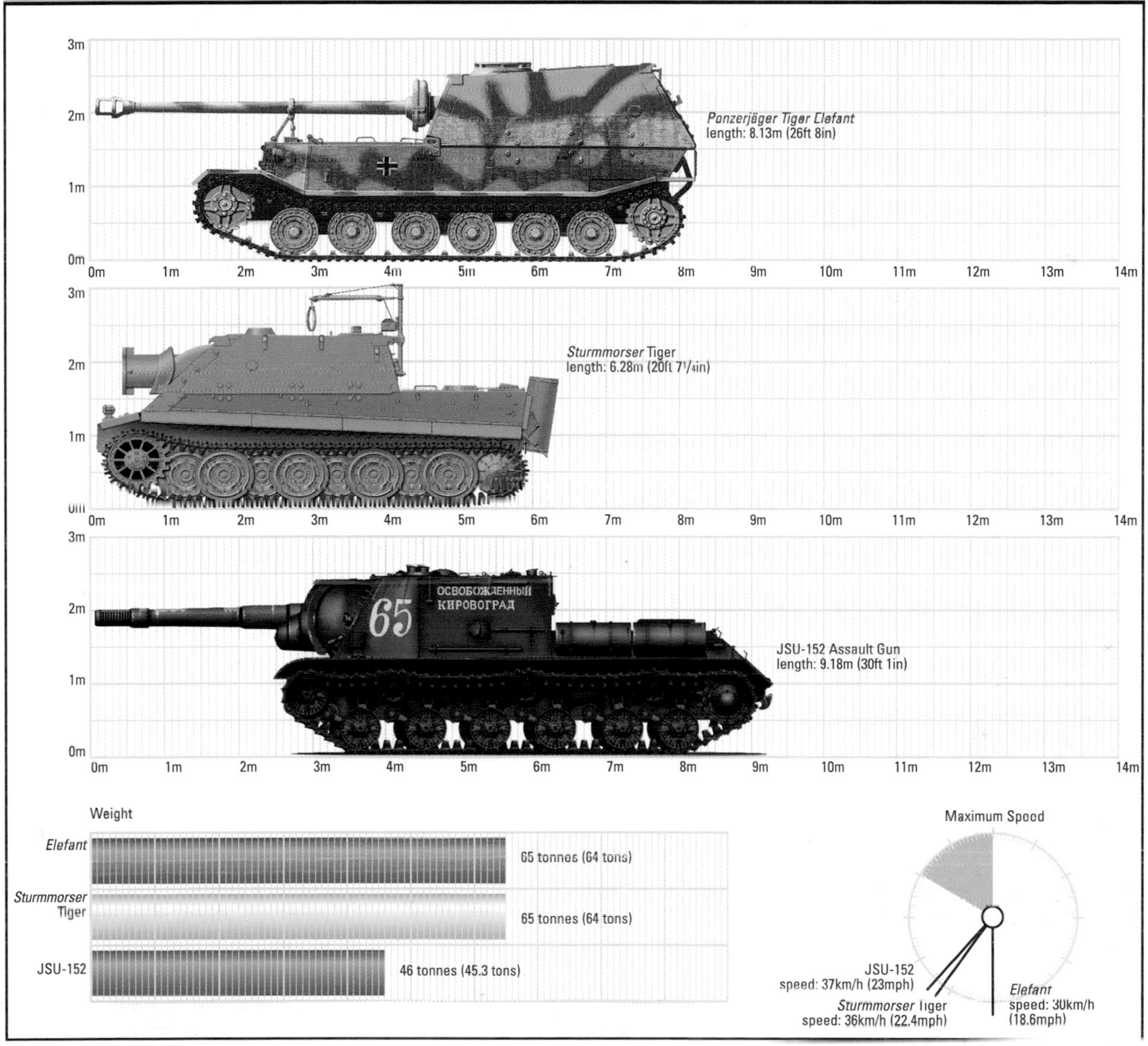
Panzerjäger Tiger Elefant
length: 8.13m (26ft 8in)
Sturmmorser Tiger
length: 6.28m (20ft 7¹/₄in)
ОСВОБОЖДЕННЫЙ
КИРОВОГРАД
65
JSU-152 Assault Gun
length: 9.18m (30ft 1in)
Weight
Elefant
65 tonnes (64 tons)
Sturmmorser Tiger
65 tonnes (64 tons)
JSU-152
46 tonnes (45.3 tons)
Maximum Speed
JSU-152
speed: 37km/h (23mph)
Sturmmorser Tiger
speed: 36km/h (22.4mph)
Elefant
speed: 30km/h
(18.6mph)

It was planned to support the tanks with infantry squads carried in *Falke* half-tracks – standard SdKfz 251s which were to be equipped with IR driving equipment. The infantry would be armed with StG44 assault rifles fitted with *Vampir* IR sights.

It is likely that a handful of IR-equipped tanks did get into action in the last days of the war:

- A Panther company of Panzer Division *Muncheberg* which reportedly fought on the Oder and in Berlin.
- A small Panther detachment of Panzer Division *Clausewitz* which allegedly overran a US anti-tank battery by Weser-Elbe Canal in a night attack and subsequently destroyed a troop of Comet tanks in another night action near Uelzen.

Self-Propelled Artillery

The origins of the spectacular Karl-Gerät *gun can be traced back to March 1936 when Rheinmetall proposed a super-heavy self-propelled howitzer capable of smashing the heaviest fortifications of the vaunted Maginot Line.*

Basic design work of the *Karl-Gerät* was completed by 1937 and extensive driving trials were undertaken in 1938–39 using the first *Neubaufahrzeug* tank prototype and a scale model. These showed that there were no insuperable problems with the high ground pressure and steering of such an enormous vehicle and the prototype began firing trials in June 1939. Full production was authorised following final trials at Unterlüss in May 1940, and the type was designated *Karl-Gerät* in honour of General Karl Becker, who had been in overall charge of the development programme of the weapon.

A total of seven *Karl-Gerät* howitzers were ultimately produced. The first six were given the nicknames 'Adam', 'Eva', 'Thor', 'Odin', 'Loki', and 'Ziu'; the seventh, the research and test weapon, *Versuchs-Gerät*, was never named. The six production vehicles were delivered between November 1940 and August 1941. As early as February 1941, research began into ways of increasing the range of the weapon and in May 1942, longer 54cm (21.3in) barrels (*Gerät 041*) were ordered for the six production vehicles. Only three of these barrels were actually completed and it was found that they increased the maximum range from 6440m (7040yd) to 10,060m (11,000yd).

The huge vehicles were really only designed to operate in the self-propelled mode for very short moves between firing positions. For slightly longer journeys, they were dismantled using a 35 tonne (34 ton) mobile crane and were moved in seven loads on specially designed road transporters. Long-distance moves were made by rail, with the entire vehicle suspended between two huge pedestal-mounted swivelling arms mounted on five-axle bogies.

As there was no room for on-board ammunition stowage, a total of 22 *Panzer IV Ausf. D, E* and *F* chassis were modified as *Munitionpanzer IVs*. Each could carry up to three 54/60cm (21.3/23.6in) shells and was fitted with a 3000kg (6600lb) capacity loading crane. Two or three of these *Munitionpanzers* were assigned to each howitzer.

Combat History

1941

The only significant action during the period for the *Karl-Gerät* was the bombardment of the Soviet fortress of Brest-Litovsk, where a battery of two howitzers from Heavy Artillery Battalion 833 fired a total of 31 rounds against the enemy.

1942

On 18 February, Heavy Artillery Battalion 833 was ordered to form a three-howitzer battery in preparation for the assault on Sevastopol. The

***KARL-GERAT* 040 AND 041 AMMUNITION**

Shell	*Calibre*	*Weight*	*Explosive*	*Muzzle Velocity*	*Max Range*	*Penetration*
Heavy concrete-piercing shell (*Schwere Betongranate*)	60cm (23.6in)	2170kg (4800lb)	289kg (640lb)	220m/s (720ft/s)	4320m (4720yd)	2.5m (8.2ft) + of concrete
Light concrete-piercing shell (*Leichte Betongranate*) 040	60cm (23.6in)	1700kg (3700lb)	220kg (490lb)	283m/s (930ft/s)	6440m (7040yd)	2.5m (8.2ft) + of concrete
Light concrete-piercing shell (*Leichte Betongranate*) 041	54cm (21.3in)	1250kg (2800lb)	no data	378m/s (1240ft/s)	10,060m (11,000yd)	3–3.5m (9.8–11ft) of concrete
High-explosive shell (*Sprenggranate*) 041	54cm (21.3in)	no data	no data	no data	no data	no data

battery was in position by late May and opened fire on 2 June as part of the 11th Army's general bombardment of the city's defences. It seems likely that about 200 rounds were fired by the battery before the siege ended on 4 July. Much of this fire was directed against the two twin 305mm (12in) gun turrets of the Maxim Gorky coast defence battery, although it had little effect apart from jamming one of the turrets and possibly knocking out their power supply. The guns inflicted more damage on the concrete bases supporting the turrets and the fire-control centre.

1944

Orders were issued on 13 August 1944 for the immediate formation of a battery with one 54cm (21.3in) *Karl-Gerät* for deployment with the 9th Army in suppressing the Warsaw Uprising. The next day, the Army Artillery Battery (Static) 638 (*Heeres-Artillerie Batterie (bodenständige))* was formed with the 60cm (23.6in) *Karl-Gerät Nr. VI* 'Ziu' since no 54cm (21.3in) weapon was available for use that time. It arrived at Warsaw on 17 August and went into action as soon as its ammunition train arrived the following morning.

On 24 August, OKH noted that it had been highly effective and ordered another *Karl-Gerät* to be sent to Warsaw. A second battery, numbered 428, was formed two days later, but didn't finally arrive until 7 September.

A third *Karl-Gerät* (040) was shipped to Warsaw on 10 September and incorporated into Battery 428. The gun nicknamed 'Ziu' was moved back to Germany on 22 September for repairs at Jüterbog. At an unrecorded time, a fourth *Karl-Gerät* was shipped to Warsaw and was reported as being operational on 25 September.

SELF-PROPELLED GUNS

Adam

Karl-Gerät 040

Crew: 21
Weight: 124 tonnes (122 tons)
Length: 11.15m (36ft 7 1/4in)
Width: 3.16m (10ft 5 3/4in)
Height: 4.38m (14ft 5 3/4in)
Powerplant: 1 x 432.5kW (580hp) Daimler-Benz MB 503A V-12 petrol engine or 1 x 432.5kw (580hp) Daimler-Benz MB 507C diesel engine
Speed: 10km/h (6.2mph)
Range: 42km (26.1 miles)
Armour: None
Armament: 1 x 60cm (23.6in) L/7 howitzer

Munitionpanzer IV

Crew: 4
Weight: 25 tonnes (24.6 tons)
Length: 5.41m (17ft 9in)
Width: 2.88m (9ft 5 1/2in)
Height: n/k
Powerplant: 1 x 223.7kw (300hp) Maybach HL 120 TRM petrol engine
Speed: 39.9km/h (24.8mph)
Range: 209km (130 miles)
Armour: 50–10mm (1.96–0.39in)
Armament: None
Load: 2–3 x 60cm (23.6in) or 54cm (21.3in) shells

GUN BARREL DIAMETERS COMPARED

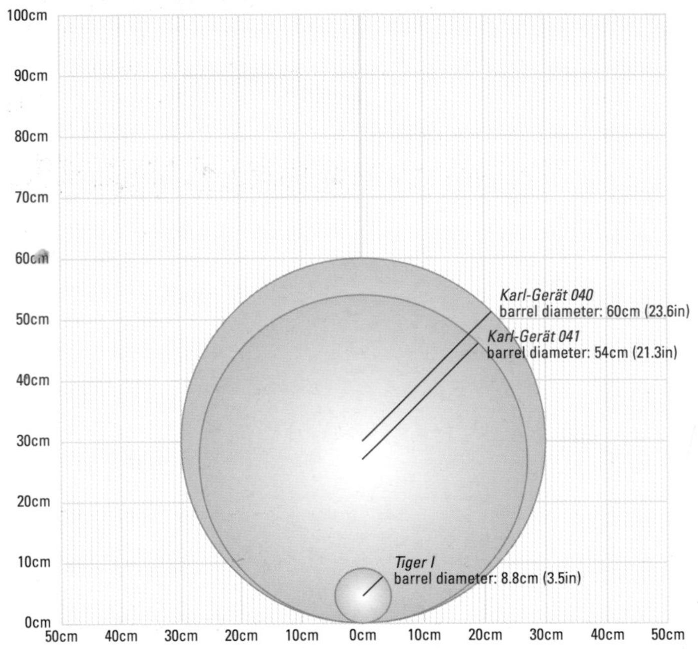
100cm
90cm
80cm
70cm
60cm
50cm
40cm
30cm
20cm
10cm
0cm
50cm 40cm 30cm 20cm 10cm 0cm 10cm 20cm 30cm 40cm 50cm
Karl-Gerät 040
barrel diameter: 60cm (23.6in)
Karl-Gerät 041
barrel diameter: 54cm (21.3in)
Tiger I
barrel diameter: 8.8cm (3.5in)

1945

Karl's last recorded action was fought in on 20 March 1945, when Battery 628 fired a total of 14 rounds at the Remagen bridgehead.

Sole Survivor

In March and April 1945, 'Eva' and 'Loki' were captured by US forces. The trials howitzer was found by the US Army in Hillersleben and shipped to Aberdeen Proving Grounds for examination, but was later scrapped. 'Ziu' was captured by the Red Army, probably when it overran Jüterbog on 20 April 1945.

This vehicle is now on display at Kubinka Tank Museum near Moscow, although marked as 'Adam'. 'Odin' was also captured by the Russians, but the fates of 'Adam' and 'Thor' are unknown. It is likely that both were seized by the Red Army, as they were stationed at Jüterbog in March 1945.

Supertanks on the Drawing Board

Throughout the war, German design teams were working on a bewildering variety of AFVs of all shapes and sizes. This section covers a sample of the fascinating projects which never achieved series production.

Panzer VII *Löwe* (Lion) VK 7201

In 1941, Krupp began design studies for a new heavy tank to combat the Soviet KVs which had proved almost invulnerable to the armament of contemporary panzers in the first weeks of Operation Barbarossa. In early 1942, a specification was issued for a 91.4 tonne (90 ton) heavy tank with armour of up to 140mm (5.5in) which Krupp designated *Löwe* (VK 7201). Provision was made for a turreted main armament of either a 105mm (4.1in) L/70 or a 150mm (5.9in) L/37 and the design was to utilize the maximum number of components from the Tiger II to simplify production.

Heavy 91.4 tonne (90 ton) and light 77.2 tonne (76 ton) versions of the design were proposed, differing only in the maximum thickness of their armour and the position of the turret. Both were to be armed with the 105mm (4.1in) L/70 gun and a co-axial machine gun.

Hitler himself ordered that work should be concentrated on the heavy version, which was to be modified to mount the larger 150mm (5.9in) KwK 44 L/38 gun. In late 1942, the project was cancelled in favour of *Maus*, although Krupp proposed a redesigned version armed with the 88mm (3.5in) KwK L/71 or the 128mm (5.04in) L/60 which would be the eventual replacement for the Tiger II.

Porsche Typ 205, Panzer VIII *Maus*

The Panzer VIII *Maus* (Sd.Kfz 205) was the heaviest tank to reach the prototype stage during World War II. Dr Porsche obtained Hitler's approval of the basic design concept in June 1942 after which work began in earnest on the project which was designated as VK7001/Porsche Type 205. The first prototype was scheduled to be completed during

SUPERTANKS COMPARED

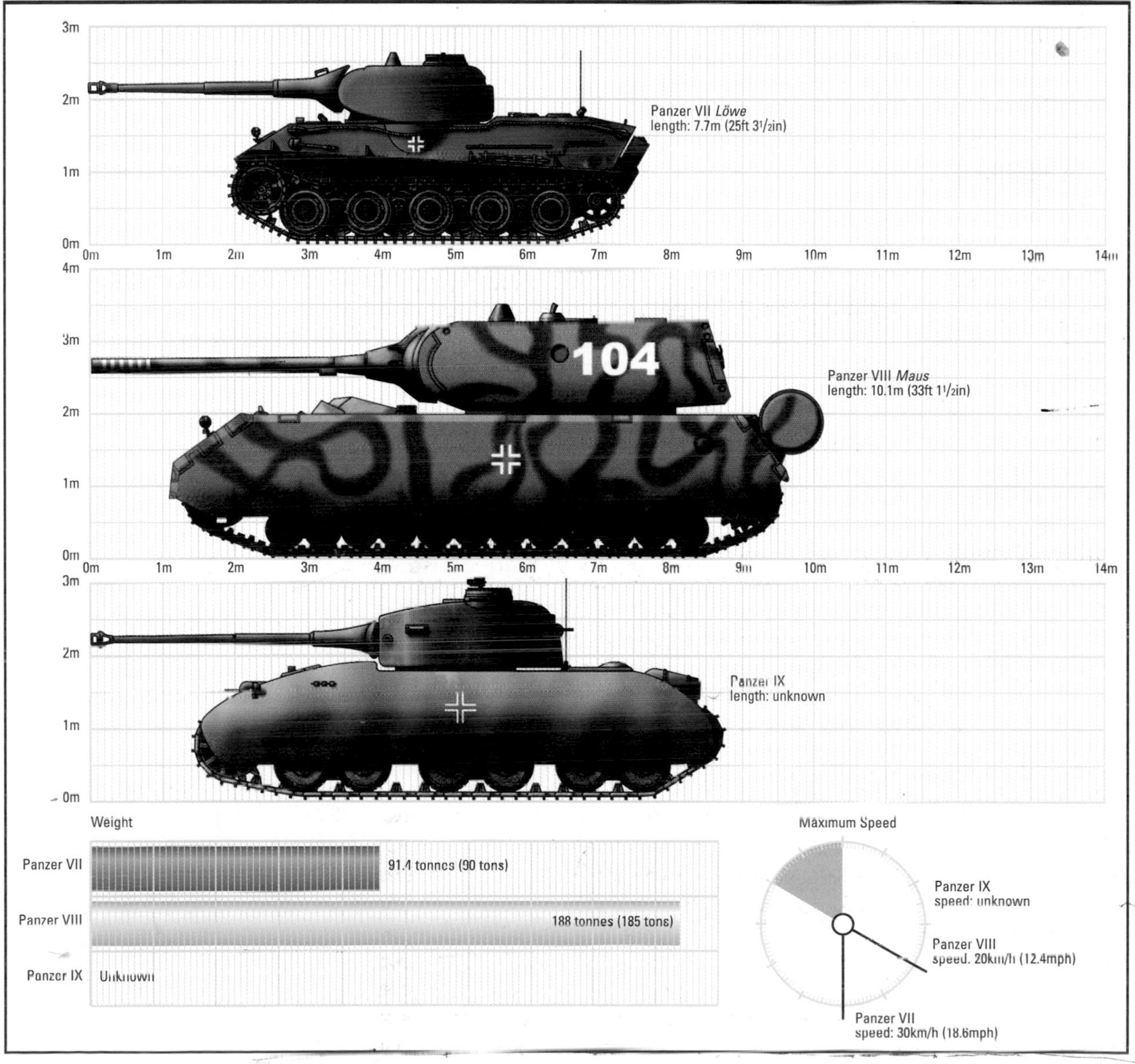
Panzer VII *Löwe*
length: 7.7m (25ft 3 1/2in)
104
Panzer VIII *Maus*
length: 10.1m (33ft 1 1/2in)
Panzer IX
length: unknown
Weight
Panzer VII
91.4 tonnes (90 tons)
Panzer VIII
188 tonnes (185 tons)
Panzer IX
Unknown
Maximum Speed
Panzer IX
speed: unknown
Panzer VIII
speed: 20km/h (12.4mph)
Panzer VII
speed: 30km/h (18.6mph)

MAUS VERSUS ALLIED HEAVY TANKS: TORTOISE AND T-29 COMPARED

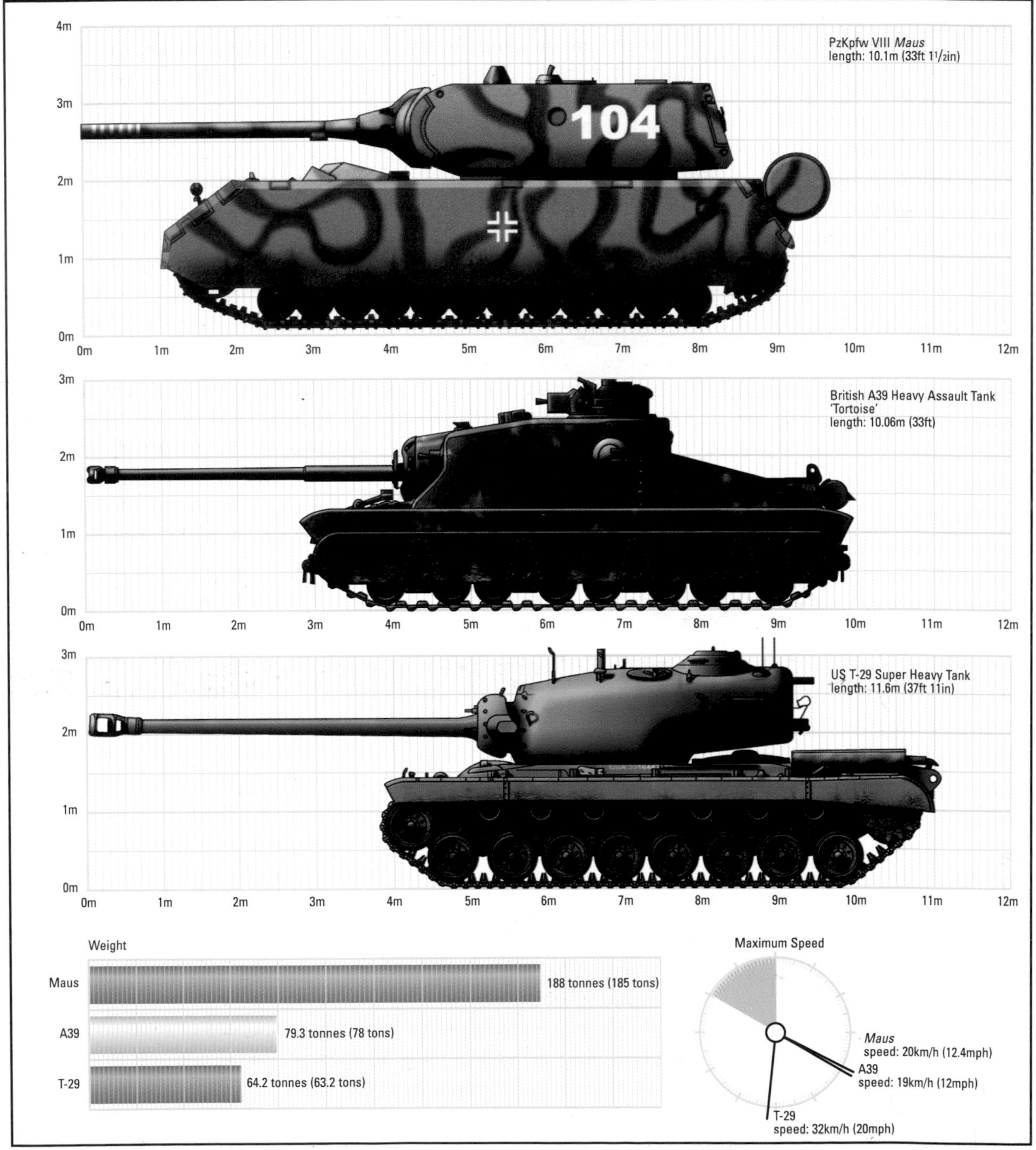
PzKpfw VIII *Maus*
length: 10.1m (33ft 1 1/2in)
104
British A39 Heavy Assault Tank
'Tortoise'
length: 10.06m (33ft)
US T-29 Super Heavy Tank
length: 11.6m (37ft 11in)
0m
1m
2m
3m
4m
5m
6m
7m
8m
9m
10m
11m
12m
Weight
Maus
188 tonnes (185 tons)
A39
79.3 tonnes (78 tons)
T-29
64.2 tonnes (63.2 tons)
Maximum Speed
Maus
speed: 20km/h (12.4mph)
A39
speed: 19km/h (12mph)
T-29
speed: 32km/h (20mph)

1943 and was initially referred to as *Mammut* (Mammoth). The name was changed to *Mäuschen* (Mousie) in December 1942 and finally *Maus* (Mouse) in February 1943.

In January 1943, Hitler ordered that the type should have turret-mounted co-axial 128mm (5.04in) and 75mm (2.95in) guns, with provision for later production models to be armed with a turreted 150mm (5.9in) KwK 44 L/38 or 170mm (6.7in) KwK 44 gun. Initial ammunition stowage specifications were never met and were further decreased by later modifications.

In May 1943, a wooden mock-up of *Maus* was presented to Hitler, who approved it for service, ordering an initial production run of 150 vehicles. The work was to be divided between Krupp, which would produce the chassis, armament and turret, and Alkett, which would be responsible for final assembly. It is possible that these tanks were intended to be fitted with the 150mm (5.9in) gun – the story goes that this was the result of Hitler's comment that the size of the tank made the 128mm (5.04in) weapon look like a 'toy gun'.

In October 1943, Hitler cancelled the production order followed by an ordered to halt to any further development of the type. Permission was, however, given for the completion of the prototypes which were already under construction. The hull of the first of these, designated V1, was completed in December 1943. It was fitted with a dummy turret, ballasted to match the weight of the production model before being put through extensive automotive trials. It was powered by Dr Porsche's petrol-electric drive with the generator driven by a modified Daimler-Benz MB 509 (developed from the DB 603 aircraft engine). However, it consistently failed to meet its design speed of 20km/h (12.4mph), managing at best only 13km/h (8mph).

The sheer weight of the vehicle also posed problems – the suspension had to be modified in order to cope with the unprecedented load and it was realized that few bridges could safely support its 188 tonne (185 ton) weight. Its size allowed it to ford many streams, but for deeper ones it could submerge and drive across the river bed. The solution required tanks to be paired up, with one *Maus* supplying electrical power to the crossing vehicle via a cable until it reached the other side. While submerged, the tank would draw air through a large 'snorkel', which could operate at depths of up to 8m (26ft).

The second prototype (V2) was finally completed in June 1944. This was fitted with a Krupp turret mounting a 128mm (5.04in) KwK 44

PANZER VIII *MAUS*

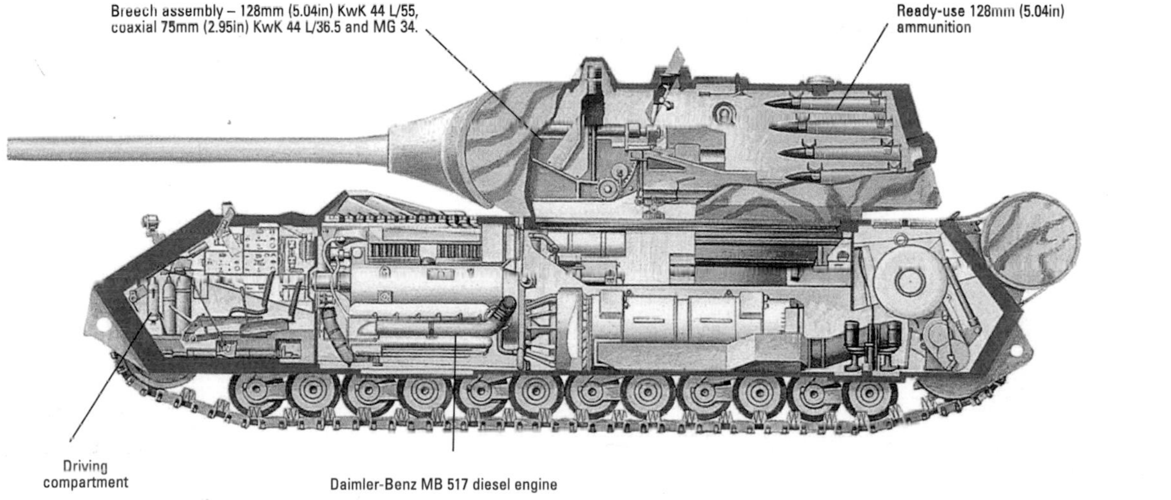
Breech assembly – 128mm (5.04in) KwK 44 L/55, coaxial 75mm (2.95in) KwK 44 L/36.5 and MG 34.
Ready-use 128mm (5.04in) ammunition
Driving compartment
Daimler-Benz MB 517 diesel engine

L/55 with a coaxial 75mm (2.95in) KwK 44 L/36.5 and a 7.92mm (0.31in) MG 34. It was also intended to fit a Zeiss stereoscopic rangefinder which would allow accurate 128mm (5.04in) fire against enemy AFVs at up to 4000m (4360yd).

The first prototype was scheduled to be fitted with Krupp's second turret but this was never delivered and it retained the weighted dummy turret. On 25 July 1944, Krupp reported that four more hulls were nearing completion, but it was subsequently ordered to scrap them and stop all further work on the project.

In September 1944, the second prototype began a series of trials with a diesel-electric drive using a Daimler-Benz MB 517 diesel engine and an advanced electric steering system. These offered only slight improvements. It was also fitted with revised running gear and 110cm (43.3in) wide tracks, both designed by Skoda. Incredibly, given that the *Maus* project had been cancelled, at least one example of a special 14-axle rail transporter (*Verladewagon*) was produced by Graz-Simmering-Pauker Works in Vienna.

In the last weeks of the war V1, still with its dummy turret, was seized by Soviet forces near the Kummersdorf artillery ranges, where V2 was also captured after its hull had been thoroughly sabotaged. The Red Army were determined to carry out its own trials and ordered that the hull of V1 was to be mated with the turret of V2. The composite vehicle was completed in Germany and sent back to Russia for further testing in May 1946. On completion of these trials the vehicle was handed over to the Kubinka Tank Museum near Moscow where it is now on display.

E-series

By 1942, it was apparent that AFV production was being hampered by the increasing number of vehicle types entering service, all of which were competing for factory space. The position regarding spares was even worse and many vehicles had to be abandoned or remained inoperable due to a lack of components.

In May 1942, General Kniekamp, the chief engineer of the weapons test establishment *Waffenprufamt 6* (*WaPruAmt 6*) began work on a development (*Entwicklung*, or *E*) programme to investigate tank design. His proposals to rationalize AFV production by replacing all existing types with six categories of vehicles were accepted by the *Heereswaffenamt* (Army Weapons Office) in April 1943.

Each vehicle category was intended to use standardized components to simplify production and maintenance. In addition, some basic principles were to be applied across the board, from E5 to E100. These included:

- The use of bolted-on external suspension units rather than the more complex torsion bar suspension
- The substitution of 'resilient rimmed' metal-tyred road wheels for the conventional rubber-tyred type
- The replacement of ball and roller bearings by plain bearings whenever possible
- All main armament was to be stabilized in order to give a degree of fire-on-the-move capability and also to alleviate trunnion loads as the tank moved cross country.

The E-series vehicles were formidable and highly advanced AFVs, some of which were close to coming into production at the end of the war. Prototypes of an E25 *Jagdpanzer* armed with an updated version of the Panther's 75mm (2.95in) L/70 gun were being readied for trials in early 1945. The most spectacular of this family of vehicles, E100, had been officially cancelled following a decision in late 1944 to cease all super-heavy tank development. However, work continued at a low priority on the hull of the prototype which was almost complete by April 1945. Krupp never managed to supply the turret, which would have mounted a 150mm (5.9in) KwK44 L/38, a co-axial 75mm (2.95in) KwK44 L/36.5 and an MG 34.

E SERIES

Name	*Class in Tons*	*Vehicle Type*
E5	5–10	All light AFVs
E10	10–25	Heavier armoured cars, light *jagdpanzers* and SP artillery
E25	25–50	Reconnaissance tanks, medium *jagdpanzers* and heavy SP artillery
E50	50–75	Medium tanks to replace the Panther, Tiger I and their derivatives
E75	75–100	Heavy tanks to replace the Tiger II and *Jagdtiger*
E100	100 or more	Super-heavy tanks such as *Maus* and E100

■ **The E50 was intended as the successor to the Panther, which it closely resembled. A greatly simplified suspension system would have been fitted, together with a new, smaller turret. The modernized 75mm (2.95in) L/70 main armament was intended to be fully stabilized and to have a semi-automatic loading system. The fire-control system would have incorporated a stereoscopic rangefinder.**

■ **The E75 was to be the new heavy tank, replacing the Tiger II. The design was very similar to that of E50, but had thicker armour and a heavier main armament. Early production vehicles would probably have been armed with the 88mm (3.5in) KwK 44 L/71, a development of the 88mm (3.5in) KwK 43 L/71. This was redesigned to chamber new ammunition with a shorter, fatter cartridge to ease handling in the confines of a relatively small turret.**

E-SERIES SUPER TANKS

E50

Specifications not known

E75

Specifications not known

E100

Crew: 6
Weight: 140 tonnes (137.8 tons)
Length: 10.27m (33ft 8in)
Width: 4.48m (14ft 8in)
Height: 3.29m (10ft $9^{1}/2$in)
Powerplant: 1 x 894.8kW (1200hp) Maybach HL234 V-12 petrol engine
Speed: 40km/h (24.9mph)
Range: 120km (74.6 miles)
Armour: 240–40mm (9.5–1.57in)
Armament: 1 x 150mm (5.9in) KwK 44 L/38, or 1 x 170mm (6.7in) KwK 44 gun, plus 1 x co-axial 75mm (2.95in) Kwk 44 L/36.5 gun and 1 x 7.92mm (0.31in) MG 34
Radio: FuG5

P-Series Land Cruisers

The concept of gigantic 'land battleships' dates back to at least 1903 when H. G. Wells wrote about the war-winning potential of such AFVs in a short story called The Land Ironclads. *By the 1930s, it seemed that technology might have advanced far enough to make such designs something more than science fiction.*

There are reports that a German engineer, Grotte, who worked for the OKMO design bureau in Leningrad in the early 1930s masterminded an abortive project to produce a Soviet 'Land Cruiser', designated the 'Bolshevik Tank'. Few details are available, but weight was assessed at approximately 1000 tonnes (984 tons) and the main armament was probably intended to be twin 203mm (7.99in) naval guns. Multiple engines were to provide a total of 17,897kW (24,000hp) and the vehicle would have required a total crew of 60. The authenticity of this project has been questioned, but it would have been entirely in keeping with Stalin's love of 'prestige weapons' such as the *Sovietsky Soyuz* class battleships.)

Landkreuzer P1000 'Ratte'

Slightly more is known about the *Landkreuzer P1000* project which

P1000 *RATTE*

Specifications

Crew: n/k
Weight: 1800 tonnes (1771.6 tons)
Length: 35m (114ft 10in)
Width: 14m (45ft 11in)
Height: 11m (36ft 1in)
Powerplant: 8 x 1491.4kW (2000hp) Daimler-Benz MB501 diesel engines
Speed: 40km/h (24.9mph)
Range: n/k
Armour: 360–150mm (14.2–5.9in)
Armament: 2 x 280mm (11in) SK C/34 L/54.4 guns, 1 x 128mm (5.04in) KwK 44 L/55 gun, 8 x 20mm (0.79in) Flak 38 AA guns plus 2 x 15mm (0.59in) Mauser MG 151/15 cannon
Radio: n/k

seems to have originated with Krupp's 1941 review of Soviet heavy tanks. This came to the attention of Grotte, who was then working for Krupp on U-boat related studies. In June 1942, he sent Hitler an outline proposal for a 1000 tonne (984 ton) tank, the *Landkreuzer*. Hitler was impressed with the concept and ordered Krupp to undertake further design studies. By December 1942, the firm had produced a series of drawings for what was dubbed *Ratte* (Rat). Speer never shared Hitler's enthusiasm for the design and was able to cancel the project in early 1943 before construction work began.

Despite its nominal 1000 tonne (984 ton) design weight, it seems likely that *Ratte* would have been much heavier. Its main turret was to mount two 28cm (11in) guns of the type that armed the *Scharnhorst* class battlecruisers and would probably have weighed at least 650 tonnes (640 tons) alone, even allowing for the weight saved by eliminating one of the three guns of the naval turret. The stowage of even a modest number of main armament rounds would have added to the problem as every 28cm (11in) AP shell and its propelling charge totalled 454kg (1000lb). The situation was further worsened by the significant cumulative weight of the 128mm (5.04in) secondary armament, AA guns and their ammunition.

(E100 for size comparison)

Special equipment

To compensate for its immense weight, the *Ratte* would have been fitted with three 1.2m (3.9ft) wide tracks on each side with a total track width of 7.2m (23.6in). This would help stability and ground pressure, but the vehicle's sheer mass would have destroyed roads and rendered bridge crossings completely impractical. The vehicle's bulk would have had the advantage of making it possible to ford many rivers without preparation, although deep-wading equipment, such as snorkel air intakes, was to be carried.

Other special equipment included a vehicle bay large enough to hold two BMW R12 motorcycles for scouting, besides several smaller storage compartments, a compact infirmary area, and a self-contained lavatory system.

Two powerplants were proposed for the *Ratte*:

- 2 x MAN V12Z32/44 24-cylinder marine diesel engines of 6338.5kW (8500hp) each similar to those used in U-boats
- 8 x Daimler-Benz MB 501 20-cylinder marine diesel engines of 1491.4Kw (2000hp) each as used in E-boats.

It seems likely that the simpler and well-proven MB 501 would have been selected to give a theoretical top speed of 40km/h (24.9mph), although in practice its speed was likely to be significantly less to minimize the inevitable transmission and suspension problems.

Even by the most optimistic assessment, *Ratte* was never going to be a practical proposition – the vehicle was so huge that no tank factory could cope with the assembly work and naval construction techniques would have been required. It is quite possible that a single prototype would have absorbed much of the resources of a naval shipbuilding yard for several months. Its firepower was amazing – the 28cm (11in) gun was capable of penetrating more than 450mm (17.7in) of armour at its maximum effective direct-fire range of roughly 5km (3.1 miles). At a maximum elevation of 40 degrees, the gun's range was almost 41km (25.6 miles). However, bringing this firepower to bear was another matter entirely – its mobility would have been strictly limited, while dealing with a breakdown would have been a major engineering operation. It is probable that at least one other *Ratte* would have been needed to tow it.

Finally, there was the problem that each vehicle represented an enormous slow-moving target – its armour was proof against many ground-fired weapons, but Allied air supremacy would have ensured that it was subjected to repeated air attacks. Not even *Ratte's* turret and hull-roof armour could cope with heavy armour-piercing bombs.

P1500 *MONSTER*

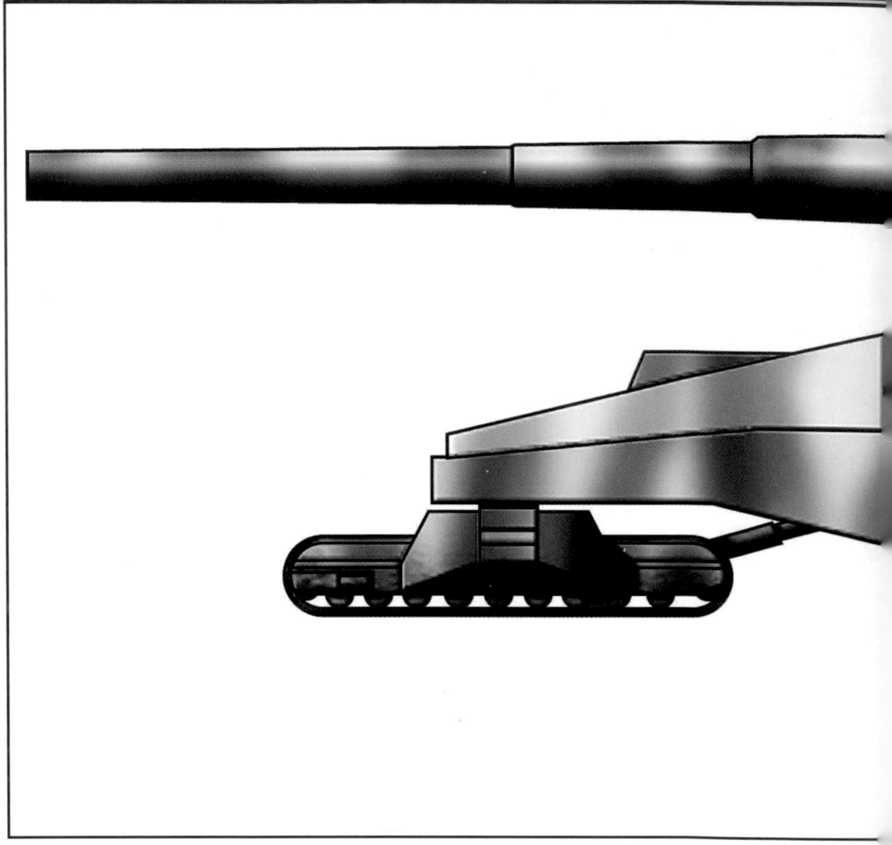

Landkreuzer P1500 'Monster'

The *Monster* was a further development of *Ratte*, which had an even more ephemeral existence – it seems to have originated with an outline proposal by Krupp in December 1942, which was followed by a few design studies before the project was cancelled by Albert Speer in early 1943.

The problems posed by *Ratte*'s size and weight were even more acute in *Monster*'s case. It seems likely that some form of articulated hull would have been needed in order to allow the vehicle to steer at all. Diesel-electric drive, with each of the four diesel engines powering a separate generator might have provided enough power to reach the design speed of 10km/h (6.2mph). However, careful surveys of all routes would have been essential as there would have been a real risk of the top-heavy weight of the huge gun causing *Monster* to keel over on anything more than a very slight side slope.

The configuration of the vehicle is strange and seems to have been the result of some rather muddled thinking. The 800mm (31.5in) Dora/Schwerer Gustav main armament had a maximum range of 48km (29.8 miles) and was hardly a practical direct fire weapon, given its rate of fire of perhaps two rounds per hour. This would have restricted

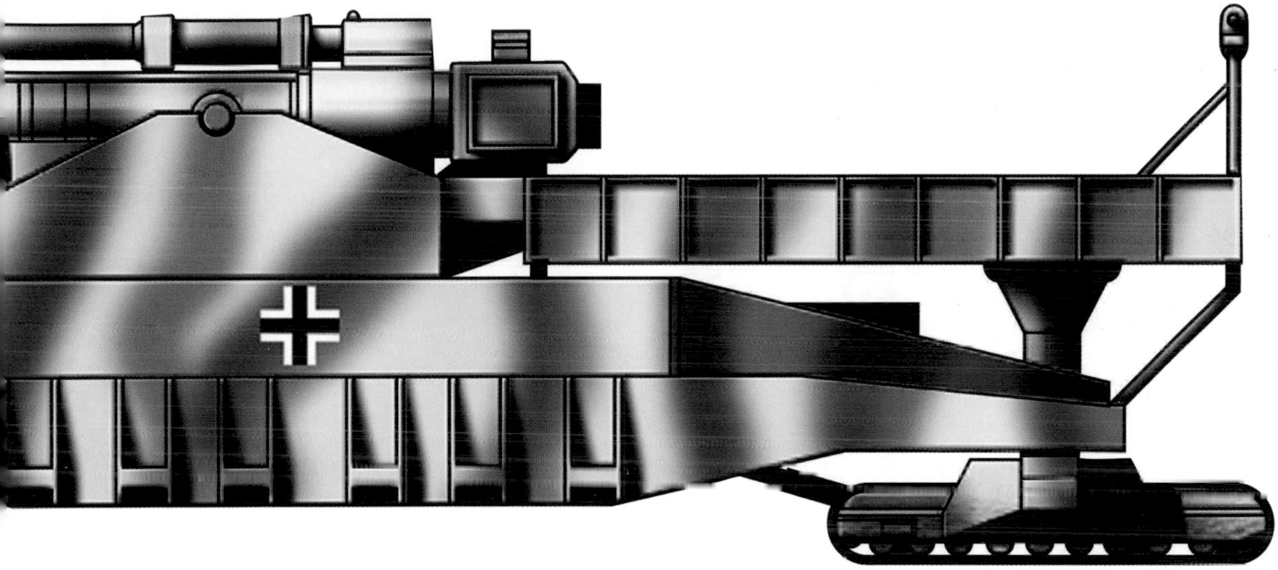

Specifications

Crew: over 100
Weight: 2500 tonnes (2460.5 tons)
Length: 42m (138ft)
Width: n/k
Height: n/k

Powerplant: 4 x 1640.54Kw (2200hp) MAN M6V 40/46 diesel engines
Speed: 10km/h (6.2mph)
Range: n/k
Armour: 250mm (9.84in) maximum

Armament: 1 x 800mm (31.5in) Dora/Schwerer Gustav K (E) gun, plus 2 x 150mm (5.9in) SFH 18/1 L/30 howitzers and multiple 15mm (0.59in) MG 151/15 cannon
Radio: n/k

Monster to operating well behind the front line as a giant self-propelled gun and yet it was supposed to have 250mm (9.84in) of armour, which would have been totally unnecessary if it was to be used for long-range, indirect fire. The inclusion of two 150mm (5.9in) howitzers is also odd – their maximum range was only 13.25km (8.2 miles), so to bring them into action, the vehicle would have had to be deployed relatively close to front and within range of enemy medium artillery. As stability considerations would have prevented fitting any overhead armoured protection, *Monster* would have been particularly vulnerable to counter-battery fire.

Even if it survived the attentions of hostile artillery and aircraft, *P1500* would have been difficult to keep in action. There would have been little, if any, stowage space for main armament ammunition as each of the 800mm (31.5in) HE shells was 3.5m (11.5ft) long and weighed 4.8 tonnes (4.7 tons), while the propelling charge added another 2.24 tonnes (2.2 tons). The 'standard' railway gun version was simply supplied with ammunition by rail, but *Monster* would have needed dedicated and highly specialized ammunition supply vehicles. The likeliest solution would have been adaptations of *Munitionpanzer IV* design used to supply the Karl batteries. Each *Munitionpanzer* would probably have been limited to carrying a single round and its propelling charge.

Monster had all of *Ratte's* problems, but on an even greater scale due to its increased size and weight. As an engineering design study it was a fascinating theoretical exercise, but it could never have been a practical weapon.

CHAPTER 4

Superguns and Railway Guns

Superguns have existed in various forms for centuries – the giant siege bombards of the fifteenth century fired stone shot of up to 700kg (1540lb). The mobility of such artillery was always very limited until the introduction of railway guns in the American Civil War and artillery tractors in the early 1900s.

Germany developed formidable, mobile super-heavy artillery in the years before World War I to smash the French and Belgian frontier fortresses, in accordance with the Schlieffen Plan for the rapid defeat of France. The prolonged trench warfare of the Western Front convinced the Germans of the importance of super-heavy artillery and development continued during the inter-war years.

Although aircraft increasingly took over the role of long-range bombardment, highly sophisticated superguns formed an important part of the armoury of Hitler's Third Reich.

Precursor of the Third Reich's superguns, the 38cm (14.9in) SK L/45 *Lange Max* supergun in action, 1918.

Railway Guns and the V-3

Railway artillery 'came of age' during World War I when increasingly heavy guns were developed by both sides in their attempts to break the deadlock imposed by trench warfare. By 1939, railway artillery was approaching the peak of its capabilities, but other highly unconventional guns were also under development.

21cm (8.3in) *Kanone 12 in Eisenbahnlafette* (21cm/8.3in) K12 (E)

The Paris Gun of World War I could fire up to 130km (81 miles) but at the expense of such rapid bore wear that barrels had to be replaced after firing only 65 rounds. K12 avoided this problem by the use of deeply rifled barrels and ribbed ammunition. The shells were made with carefully machined curved ribs which slotted into the rifling on loading. When fired, the ribs rode smoothly up the rifling and greatly reduced barrel wear.

There was some doubt about the practicality of this system which was tested using a few 105mm (4.1in) barrels and experimental ammunition. After these successful firing trials work began on the challenging task of producing the full-size gun. In common with the Paris Gun, the barrel had to be braced to prevent it bending under its own weight. The 33.3m (109ft) long barrel posed other problems – it was at first thought to be impossible to devise a balancing mechanism which could cope with its full weight and the trunnions were set well forward to give the maximum possible weight at the breech. This meant that the breech was liable to hit the track at full recoil and the only solution was to fit the carriage with hydraulic jacks which lifted it 1m (3.3ft) above the bogies for firing. This had to be repeated for every shot as the gun could not be loaded when the mounting was raised.

The gun was completed in 1938 and was formally accepted for service in March 1939. While its performance fully met the Army's

SUPERGUN SHELLS COMPARED

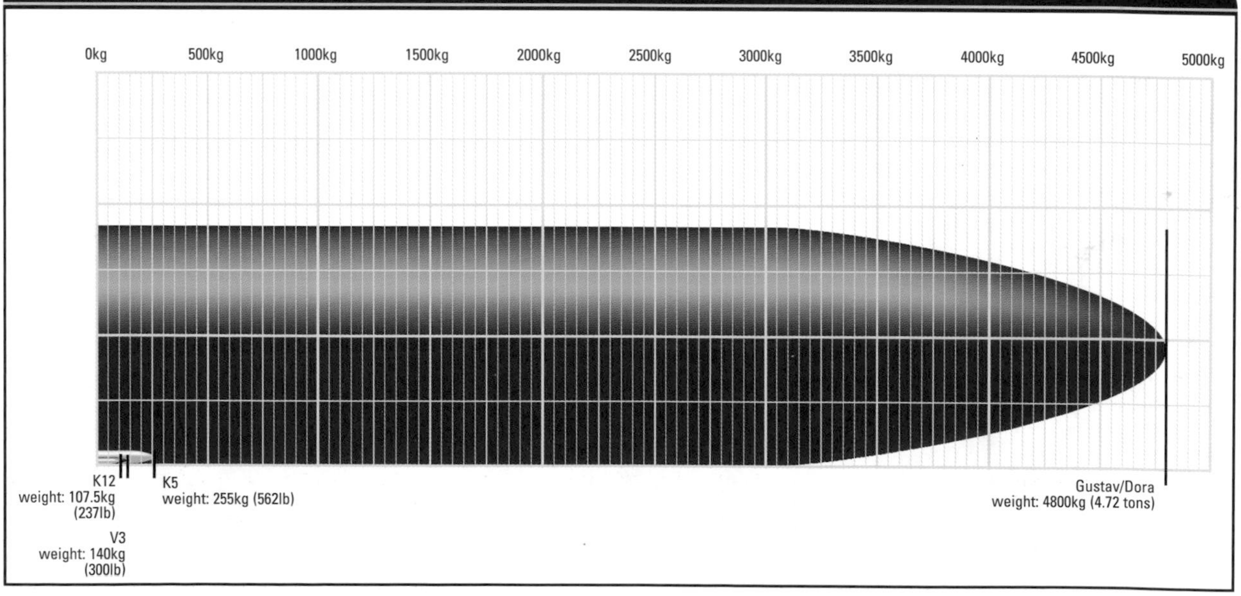

0kg
500kg
1000kg
1500kg
2000kg
2500kg
3000kg
3500kg
4000kg
4500kg
5000kg
K12
weight: 107.5kg (237lb)
V3
weight: 140kg (300lb)
K5
weight: 255kg (562lb)
Gustav/Dora
weight: 4800kg (4.72 tons)

requirements, there was a lack of enthusiasm for the awkward procedure of jacking it up and down between shots. Krupp re-examined the problem and managed to devise hydro-pneumatic balancing gear which could bear the gun's weight and dispense with the hydraulic jacks. This was incorporated in a second gun which was completed in mid-1940 and was far more popular with its users. In order to clearly identify each gun, the original gun was designated K12V whilst the second was officially K12N.

Both guns were issued to *Artillerie-Batterie* 701 (E) which spent most of the war on the French coast firing cross-Channel bombardments, reaching the Chatham area at a range of about 88km (55 miles).

These were the only two guns to be built as it seems that there was tacit recognition of their minimal military value. In fact, the Krupp design team were said to have commented that they were a waste of time as practical weapons, but that as a research project they were 'worth every Pfennig' of the 1.5 million Reichsmarks spent on them.

28cm (11in) *Kanone 5 in Eisenbahnlafette* (28cm/11in) K5 (E)

Krupp began development of the K5 in 1934 and the first gun was test-fired in 1937. In common with the K12, ribbed ammunition was used to minimize barrel wear. By 1940, eight guns were in service and apparently operating successfully when there was a sudden spate of accidents as barrels split on firing. An investigation was unable to establish any definite reasons for the problem, but there were suspicions about the rifling and it was decided to try the effect of reducing the depth of the rifling grooves from 10mm (0.39in) to 7mm (0.28in). This worked surprisingly well and the modified guns proved to be highly reliable – a total of 25 were completed by 1945.

Although the standard 255.5kg (562.1lb) ammunition had a very respectable range of 62.2km (38.6 miles), there were constant attempts to extend this range. One of the first proposed the use of a rocket-assisted shell and this was adopted as the *Raketen Granate 4331* (R Gr 4331). A solid-fuel rocket motor was fitted in

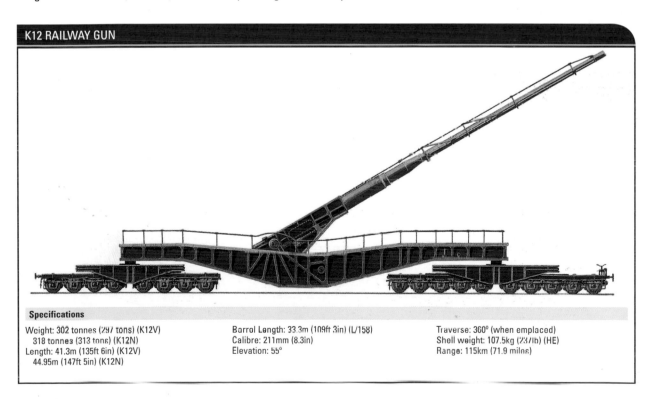

K12 RAILWAY GUN

Specifications

Weight: 302 tonnes (297 tons) (K12V)
318 tonnes (313 tons) (K12N)
Length: 41.3m (135ft 6in) (K12V)
44.95m (147ft 5in) (K12N)
Barrel Length: 33.3m (109ft 3in) (L/158)
Calibre: 211mm (8.3in)
Elevation: 55°
Traverse: 360° (when emplaced)
Shell weight: 107.5kg (237lb) (HE)
Range: 115km (71.9 miles)

K5 RAILWAY GUN

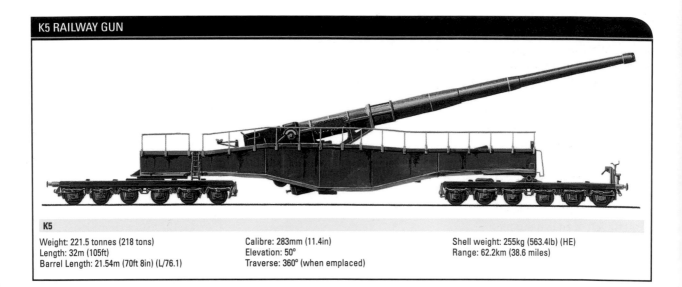

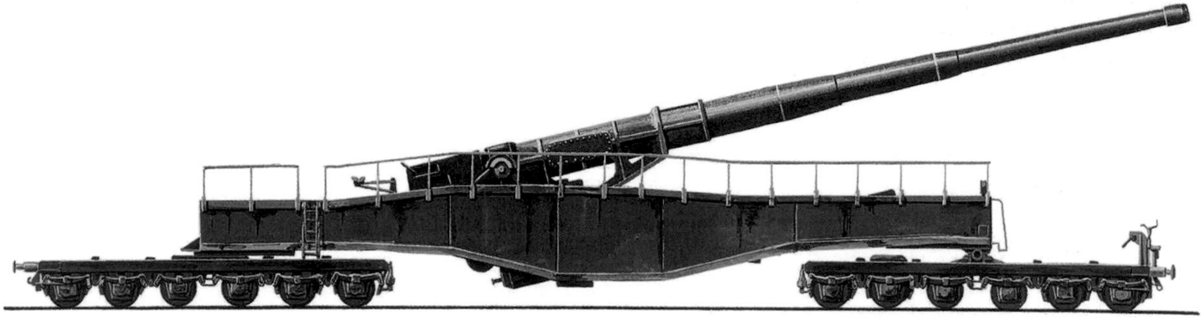

K5

Weight: 221.5 tonnes (218 tons)
Length: 32m (105ft)
Barrel Length: 21.54m (70ft 8in) (L/76.1)
Calibre: 283mm (11.4in)
Elevation: 50°
Traverse: 360° (when emplaced)
Shell weight: 255kg (563.4lb) (HE)
Range: 62.2km (38.6 miles)

the shell's nose which was fired by a time fuse 19 seconds into the shell's flight. The rocket exhaust vented down a central blast tube and out of the base of the shell. Range was increased to 86.5 kilometres (53.8 miles), but the space filled by the rocket cut the HE filling from 30.5kg (67.3lb) to 14kg (30.9lb).

The most spectacular boost to the K5's range came with the development of the adoption of the *Peenemünder Pfeilgeschosse* (*Peenemünde* arrow shells). These were long, 120mm (4.7in), fin-stabilized shells fired by K5s fitted with new, smooth-bore 31cm (12.2in) barrels. The shells were fitted with a 31cm (12.2in) ring sabot and four rear-mounted fins. On firing, the three-piece sabot broke up as it left the muzzle and the dart-like shell flew on to a maximum range of 151km (94.3 miles).

As a bonus, the *Peenemünder Pfeilgeschosse* had an HE filling of 25kg (55lb) a significant improvement on that of the R Gr 4331. Fortunately for the Allies, only two K5s were modified to fire these shells, which entered service in small numbers in 1944, too late to have any real effect on the outcome of the war.

V-3 (15cm/5.9in) *Hochdruckpumpe/Fleissige Lisel/Der Tausendfussler*

The concept of an ultra-high velocity gun using multiple propelling charges was first considered in the nineteenth century. Although patents were granted in the 1860s, the first attempt to produce a working gun on this principle was made in the 1880s by two US inventors, James Haskell and Azel Lyman. Their Lyman-Haskell 'multi-charge gun' closely resembled the V-3 – it had a long barrel with multiple pairs of propellant chambers set into it which were angled back at 45 degrees, forming a 'herring-bone pattern'. The whole assembly was mounted on a long inclined ramp and was test fired at the Frankfort Arsenal, Philadelphia. The gun proved to have a muzzle velocity of only 335m/s (1100ft/s), worse than conventional artillery of the same period. Investigations established that that flash from the main propellant charge bypassed the shell and detonated the supplementary charges before the shell reached them. Instead of boosting the muzzle velocity, the additional propelling charges were actually having a braking effect, but the technology of the time could not provide a solution and the project was abandoned.

The idea was revived at various times – the British Ordnance Board rejected a proposal in 1941, noting that it was the third time that such a design had been submitted since 1918. At about the same time, August Cönders, who was the chief engineer of Röchling Eisen-und Stahlwerke proposed a similar 15cm (5.9in) gun, with a barrel length of 150m (492ft) which he claimed would be capable of bombarding London from sites along the French coast. The success of one of Cönders' other projects, the Röchling anti-concrete shell, convinced the company to fund the construction of a 20mm (0.79in) prototype to test the feasibility of the project. This worked quite well and its potential was reported to Albert Speer, the Reich Minister of Armaments and War Production. He briefed Hitler, who was fascinated by the concept and ordered the construction of an underground battery of 50 full-sized guns at Marquise-Mimoyecques near Calais.

Unfortunately, the prototype 15cm (5.9in) gun completed in 1943 was plagued with faults – initial attempts to electrically fire the propelling charges in sequence failed and the simpler option of letting the flash from the main charge do the work led to the same problems which had defeated Lyman and Haskell. Although these were eventually overcome, sections of the barrel were prone to bursting, the shells were unstable in flight and the muzzle velocity was totally inadequate to achieve the promised range of 153km (96 miles).

Cönders had insisted on keeping total control of the project, without the usual supervision of the *Heereswaffenamt* (HWA), the Army Ordnance Department, but by early 1944, the lack of progress and the problems encountered forced him to agree to their involvement.

The HWA were able to solve some of the problems, but even by May 1944, the best range achieved was no more than 88.5 kilometres (55 miles). However, if the muzzle velocity could be boosted to the promised 1524m/s (5000ft/s) there seemed to be a good chance that the promised range could indeed be reached. Work on the heavily fortified battery at Marquise-Mimoyecques was by now well advanced, but in July 1944 the installation was thoroughly wrecked by the RAF's 617 Squadron which scored four hits with 5443kg (12,000lb) 'Tallboy' bombs. Shortly afterwards, the Allied armies broke out of the Normandy beachhead and captured the badly damaged site, ending any possibility that the guns could ever be deployed in their intended role.

Despite these major setbacks, the development programme continued under the supervision of the SS and two shorter guns approximately 50m (164ft) long each with 12 side chambers were completed. They were assigned to the army artillery unit, *Artillerie Abteilung 705,* under the command of Captain Patzig and were sited in a wooded ravine at Lampaden near Trier. Between 30 December 1944 and 22 February 1945, they bombarded the city of Luxembourg at a range of roughly 43 km (27 miles), firing a total of 183 rounds. Their fire caused only minor damage and total casualties were 10 dead and 35 wounded. The guns were hastily dismantled and withdrawn as Allied forces approached the battery position in late February 1945 and were never used again.

SUPERGUN CALIBRES COMPARED

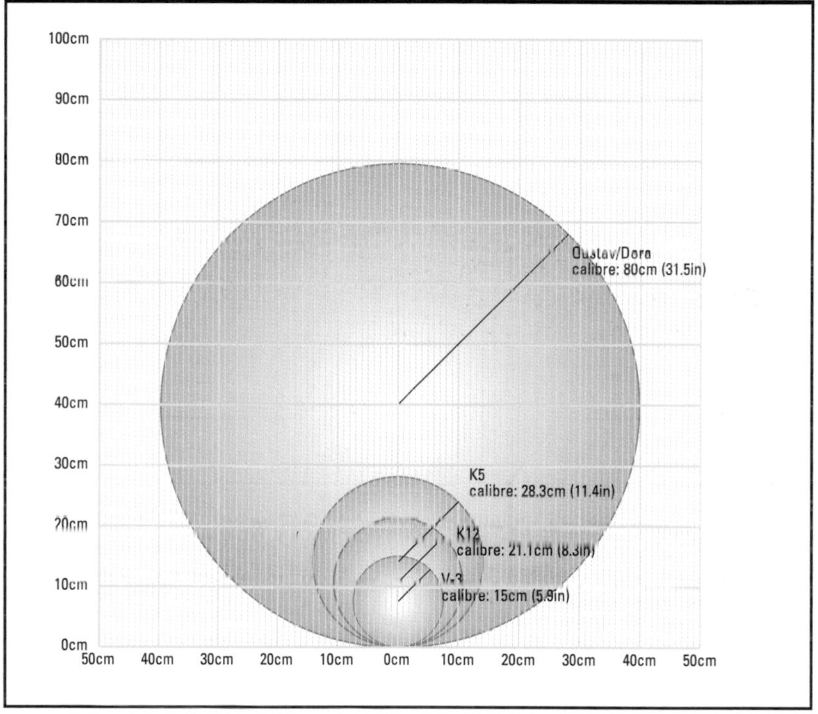
100cm
90cm
80cm
70cm
60cm
50cm
40cm
30cm
20cm
10cm
0cm
50cm 40cm 30cm 20cm 10cm 0cm 10cm 20cm 30cm 40cm 50cm
Gustav/Dora
calibre: 80cm (31.5in)
K5
calibre: 28.3cm (11.4in)
K12
calibre: 21.1cm (8.3in)
V-3
calibre: 15cm (5.9in)

SUPERGUN RANGES COMPARED

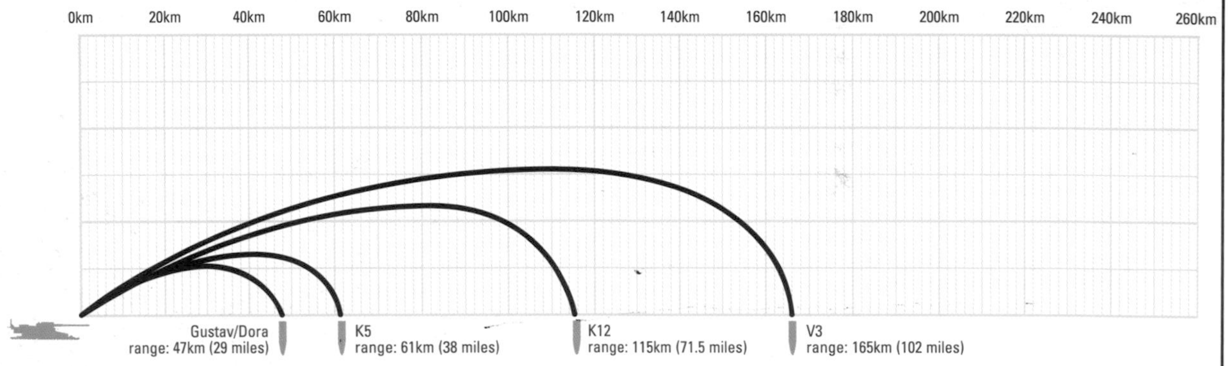
0km
20km
40km
60km
80km
100km
120km
140km
160km
180km
200km
220km
240km
260km
Gustav/Dora range: 47km (29 miles)
K5 range: 61km (38 miles)
K12 range: 115km (71.5 miles)
V3 range: 165km (102 miles)

80cm (31.5in) Kanone Gustav Gerät

In 1935, the Heereswaffenamt *(HWA) requested Krupp's assessment of the artillery required to destroy the largest forts of the Maginot Line. Krupp's design staff carried out a series of studies and submitted a report containing ballistic data on three possible guns of 70cm (27.5in), 80cm (31.5in) and 100cm (39.4in) calibre.*

The report was filed away and no further action was taken until Hitler asked the same question during a visit to the Krupp factory in March 1936. He was given a copy of the report and queried the feasibility of producing such huge weapons, but was assured that, although manufacture would be difficult, it was certainly not impossible. Sensing Hitler's weakness for spectacular weapons, Gustav Krupp von Bohlen und Halbach, the head of the Krupp consortium, ordered detailed design studies to be prepared for the 80cm (31.5in) gun.

As anticipated, an order for the gun was placed in 1937 and work began under the supervision of Dr Ing. Erich Müller. The entire programme was run under the strictest possible secrecy which succeeded in ensuring that Allied Intelligence never learned of this new weapon.

Despite the best efforts of a highly skilled design team, progress was slow. This was unsurprising as the gun had to meet some extremely demanding specifications – its concrete piercing shell had to penetrate 1m (3.3ft) of armour, plus 7m (23ft) of reinforced concrete and 30m (98ft) of compacted earth. This sort of performance could only be achieved by a truly massive gun and indeed, its sheer size caused endless problems – it was clear that it could only be moved by rail and that it would have to be dismantled to meet rail loading gauge limits. The barrel and breech assembly had to be constructed so that it could be broken down into four separate components for transport. Designing such an assembly that would be capable of withstanding the enormous pressures generated by every shot was far from simple and the barrel was not ready for test-firing from an improvised mounting until early 1941.

The ammunition was just as impressive as the gun itself – the HE shell weighed 4800kg (4.73 tons) and

contained 400kg (882lb) of explosives, producing craters with an average depth and diameter of 12m (39.4ft). The concrete-piercing shell weighed 7100kg (6.99 tons) including a bursting charge of 200kg (441lb). Propelling charges were equally enormous – the total charge used to fire each anti-concrete round weighed 2100kg (2.07 tons), while the charge for each HE shell weighed 2240kg (2.2 tons).

As soon as the test-firings had been completed, work began on the carriage and the complete weapon was moved to the artillery ranges at Rugenwalde where it was demonstrated to Hitler in early 1942. This was almost two years later than scheduled and Hitler had become increasingly impatient with the seemingly interminable delays, but he was deeply impressed by the spectacular sight of the gun firing and the results of trial shots against 'hard' targets which fully met the specified penetration figures.

Doubtless with an eye on future lucrative contracts, Gustav Krupp von Bohlen und Halbach formally presented the gun, now designated Gustav Gerät in his honour, to Hitler as the company's gift to the Reich's war effort. There is considerable disagreement about the number of guns actually completed – many sources claim that a second gun nicknamed 'Dora', was also operational. However, it seems likely that 'Dora' was actually the German gunners' nickname for Gustav, which gave the impression that there were two guns.

There was some difficulty in finding suitable targets for the gun – at various times it had been earmarked for use against the Maginot Line and the fortifications of Gibraltar, but these plans had been overtaken by the unexpectedly rapid defeat of France and General Franco's refusal to abandon Spanish neutrality. This only left Soviet targets and

■ A fallen giant – a damaged 'Gustav' barrel found by US forces at the *Wehrmacht*'s Grafenwoehr training area in Bavaria. This was probably one of the essential spare barrels – each had to be replaced after firing no more than 300 rounds.)

Sevastopol was chosen as it was appreciated that the heaviest possible firepower would be needed to breakthrough the city's elaborate defences without incurring massive German casualties.

Siege of Sevastopol

Gustav was duly dismantled and sent on the long journey to the Crimea – a total of 28 special wagons, including a gantry crane for assembly, plus two diesel locomotives for haulage on site. The gun reached the Perekop Isthmus in early March 1942, where it was held until early April. A special railway spur line was built from the Simferopol-Sevastopol railway to

RAILWAY GUN BATTERIES: DEPLOYMENT

Battery	*Type of Gun*	*Number of Guns*	*Posting*
Battery 717	17cm (6.7in) KE	3	Artillery regiment 676, Aug 1944
Battery 718	17cm (6.7in) KE	3	Artillery regiment 676, Aug 1944
Battery 701	21cm (8.3in) K12 V	1	Qty 1 in 1941, Qty 2 in 1943–44 Artillery regiment 655, Aug 1944
Battery 686	28cm (11in) K5 + 40cm (15.8in) 752 (f)	2 + 4	Artillery regiment 679, Aug 1944
Battery 688	28cm (11in) K5	2	
Battery 689	28cm (11in) *Schwere Bruno* L/42	2	
Battery 710	28cm (11in) K5	2	Artillery regiment 655, Aug 1944
Battery 711	37cm (14.6in) (f) MIS	2	Captured gun (no longer a unit in 1941 forward)
Battery 712	28cm (11in) K5	2	Artillery regiment 646, Aug 1944
Battery 697	28cm (11in) K5	2	Velocity measuring troop
Battery 713	28cm (11in) K5	2	
Batteries 765 and 617	28cm (11in) K5	2	Velocity measuring troop
Detachment 100	28cm (11in) K5	2	Training and replacement
Battery 690	28cm (11in) *Kurze Bruno*	2	(Qty 2: 1941, Qty 4: Jan 1944) Coastal Artillery regiment 676, Aug 1944
Battery 694	28cm (11in) *Kurze Bruno*	2	1941, no longer a unit in 1943–44
Battery 695	28cm (11in) *Kurze Bruno*	2	(Qty 1: 1941, +32cm (f) 1943–44) Artillery regiment 679, Aug 1944
Battery 696	28cm (11in) *Kurze Bruno*	2	Artillery regiment 676, Aug 1944
Battery 721	28cm (11in) *Kurze Bruno*	2	(Qty 1 in 1940, Qty 2 in 1943–44) Artillery regiment 780, combined with regiment 640 in Aug 1944
Battery 692	27.4cm (10.8in) 592 (f)	3	Artillery regiment 640 combined with regiment 780 in Aug 1944
Battery 691	24cm (9.4in) 651 (f)	3	Artillery regiment 646, Aug 1944
Battery 722	24cm (9.4in) *Th. Bruno*	4	Coastal
Battery 674	24cm (9.4in) *Th. Bruno*	2	Artillery regiment 780 combined with regiment 640 in Aug 1944
Battery 664	24cm (9.4in) *Kurze Th. Bruno*	2	Artillery regiment 780 combined with regiment 640 in Aug 1944
Battery 749	28cm (11in) K5	2	Artillery regiment 640 combined with regiment 780 in Aug 1944
Battery 725	28cm (11in) K5 + 28cm (11in) *N.Bruno*	2 + 2	Artillery regiment 646, *N.Bruno* split off Aug 1944
Battery 459	37cm (14.6in) 651 (f)	3	Artillery regiment 646, Aug 1944
Battery 693	40cm (15.8in) 752 (f)	4	Artillery regiment 646, Aug 1944
Battery 698	38cm (14.9in) *Siegfried*	2	(Qty 1: in 1944 with 1 *Siegfried* going to 679) Artillery regiment 640 combined with regiment 780 in Aug 1944

(Courtesy of www.one35th.com)

Bakhchisaray, 16km (10 miles) north of the target, at the end of which four semi-circular tracks were built for Gustav to traverse. Outer tracks were laid for the 112 tonne (110 ton) gantry crane needed to assemble Gustav and a small marshalling yard was constructed to accommodate the support equipment. An 8m (26.2ft) deep cutting was dug to shelter the gun from Soviet air attacks and counter-battery fire and a dummy gun position was built a few kilometres away. Finally, two light flak batteries were moved up to provide close-range AA protection for the complex.

Despite Krupp's ingenuity in designing the gun's components, its assembly was far from easy, especially the stage when the second half of the 102 tonne (100 ton) barrel had to be lined up and secured to the first whilst dangling from the gantry crane. The whole process took three weeks using a force totalling 1720 men under the command of a Major General, before Gustav finally opened fire on 5 June. Its maximum rate of fire was about four rounds per hour as the size and weight of the ammunition made loading a slow business, even with power assistance. In addition, a mass of data was required for each shot, including muzzle velocity, time of flight, powder mass and temperature, firing chamber pressure, range, atmospheric conditions and wear of firing chamber and rifling.

During the siege, it fired a total of 48 rounds at a variety of targets, primarily:

- 5 June: Coast defence batteries were engaged at a range of 25km (15.6 miles) with fire corrected by Gustav's own spotter aircraft. The targets were destroyed by a total of eight rounds. Fire was then directed against Fort Stalin, which was wrecked by six concrete-piercing rounds.
- 6 June: The day's first target was Fort Molotov which was knocked

out by seven rounds. Gustav then bombarded what was perhaps the most heavily protected installation in Sevastopol, the White Cliff. This was a magazine 30m (98ft) beneath Severnaya Bay protected by at least 10m (33ft) of ferro-concrete. Nine rounds were fired and the final shot caused a spectacular ammunition explosion, totally destroying the target
- 11 June: Five rounds were fired against Fort Siberia
- 17 June: Gustav fired its last five rounds of the siege against Fort Maxim Gorky I, a heavily armoured position armed with two twin 305mm (12in) guns.

After Sevastopol's surrender on 4 July, Gustav was sent back to Germany to have its worn-out barrel relined. It was intended for use against both Stalingrad and Leningrad, but it seems likely that it never saw action again, although there are unconfirmed reports that it fired a few rounds during the 1944 Warsaw Uprising.

A number of developments of the basic design were proposed, including a 52cm (20.5in) gun to fit the standard Gustav carriage. This would fire a 1420kg (1.39 ton) shell to a range of 110km (68 miles). Alternative ammunition was to have included a 52/38cm (20.5/14.9in) sabot shell with a maximum range of 150km (93 miles) or A 52/38cm (20.5/14.9in) rocket-assisted shell which was intended to reach 190km (118 miles). It was recognized that these were all projects that would take years of work, so as an interim measure, it was decided to extend the range by fitting a smooth-bore liner to the standard 80cm (31.5in) barrel to allow the use of *Peenemünde* arrow shells. Two shell designs were proposed, an 80/35cm (31.5/13.8in) with a maximum range of 140km (87 miles) and an 80/30.5cm (31.5/12in) which would reach 160km (99.5 miles). None of these developments came close to entering service, although work began on a prototype 52cm (20.5in) gun which was never completed after being badly damaged by one of the many RAF bombing raids on Essen.

Gustav's demise

There are a number of conflicting accounts regarding Gustav's fate, but it is probable that it was scrapped towards the end of 1944. Gustav was never a practical weapon as it was incredibly expensive, costing about seven million Reichsmarks, excluding support equipment. This was the equivalent of at least 21 Tiger IIs at 321,500 Reichsmarks each!

In addition, the gun absorbed enormous manpower resources – many of the 1720 men involved in its operation were highly-skilled, notably the 20 scientists and engineers who calculated the firing data for each round.

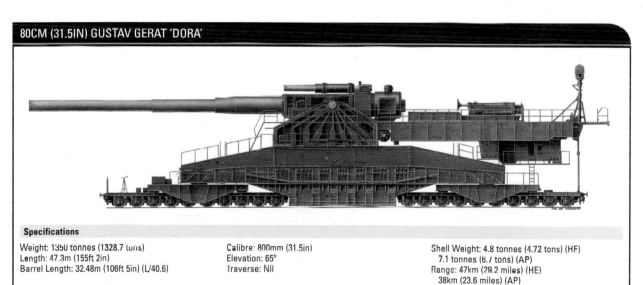

80CM (31.5IN) GUSTAV GERAT 'DORA'

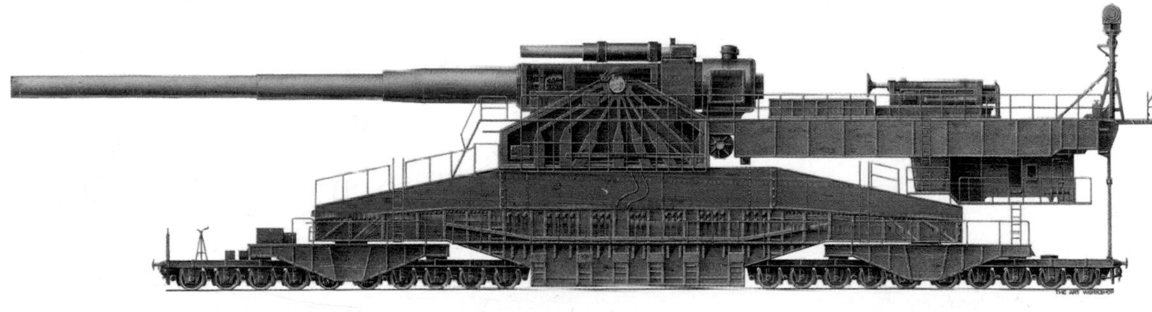

Specifications

Weight: 1350 tonnes (1328.7 tons)
Length: 47.3m (155ft 2in)
Barrel Length: 32.48m (106ft 5in) (L/40.6)

Calibre: 800mm (31.5in)
Elevation: 65°
Traverse: Nil

Shell Weight: 4.8 tonnes (4.72 tons) (HE)
7.1 tonnes (6.7 tons) (AP)
Range: 47km (29.2 miles) (HE)
38km (23.6 miles) (AP)

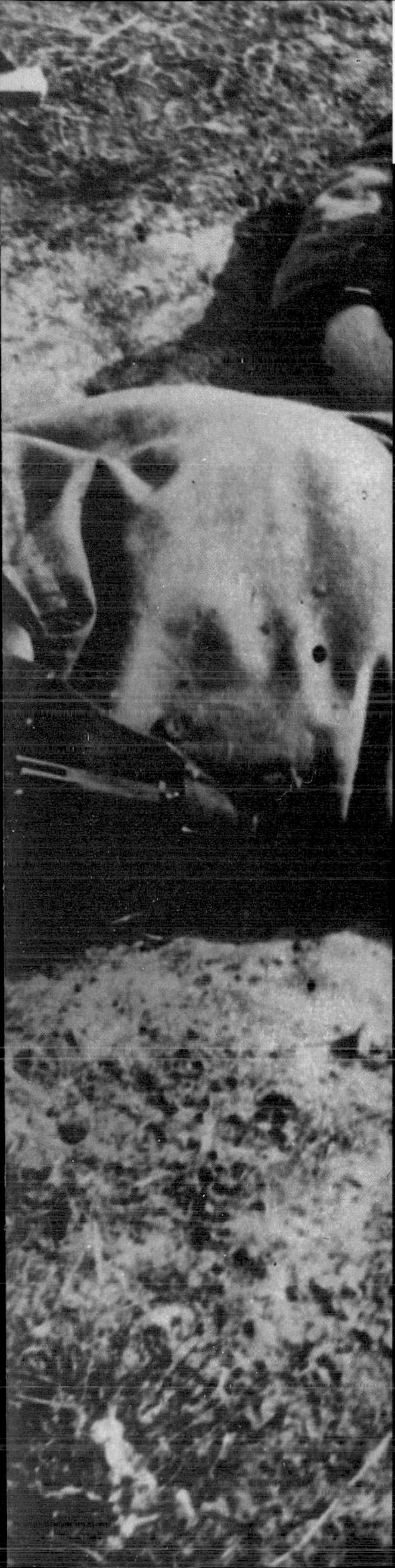

CHAPTER 5

Infantry Weapons

Within a few years of the end of World War I, the tiny German army permitted by the Treaty of Versailles was being restructured in accordance with wartime experience. This was carried out so well that the basic infantry division structure devised in 1921 underwent remarkably few changes until well into World War II.

The Wehrmacht's *first-line infantry units of 1939 were extremely well-trained formations with exceptionally good firepower by the standards of the time. Each infantry regiment fielded six 75mm (2.95in) and two 150mm (5.9in) infantry guns, plus 18 8cm (3.15in) mortars and 12 37mm (1.45in) anti-tank guns.*

However, the rapidly changing demands of warfare would force the pace of innovation and drastically alter many infantry weapons by 1945.

An infantryman trains with the RPzB 54 *Panzerschrek* tank killer on the firing range.

Weapons Development

In 1939, the German infantry went to war with beautifully made, expensively produced machine guns and bolt-action rifles, supported by a small range of anti-tank weapons, infantry guns and mortars. By 1945, it fought with assault rifles, panzerschrecks *and* panzerfausts *and was on the point of fielding shoulder-fired AA rockets.*

Well before 1939, it was recognized that the standard German machine gun, the MG 34, was too expensive, too labour-intensive to produce and too prone to malfunction in extreme battlefield conditions. The new design, the MG 42, required considerably less tooling and its construction was much simpler – each gun took only 75 man-hours to complete, compared to 150 man-hours for the MG 34. Production costs were also drastically reduced from 327 to 250 Reichsmarks per gun.

The first MG 42s entered service in 1942 and shocked Allied troops with their unprecedented rate of fire (1200rpm). US troops promptly dubbed it 'Hitler's Buzz Saw' and over 40,000 were produced by 1945. The basic design was so effective that a modernized version, the MG 3, is still in service in Germany and many other countries.

Fallschirmjägergewehr 42 (FG 42)

Early in the war, it became apparent that the German infantry needed greater firepower – the basic design of their *Karabiner 98k* rifles dated back to the 1890s. Although reliable and accurate, these bolt-action weapons had a magazine capacity of only five rounds and could not produce the volume of fire needed in modern warfare. The MP 38 and MP 40 submachine guns were a partial answer with rates of fire of over 500rpm, but their weak 9mm (0.35in) pistol ammunition was ineffective beyond 200m (218yd).

The MG 34 and its successor, the MG 42, were fine general purpose machine guns, but they were crew-served support weapons rather than personal weapons and there could never be enough of them. The ideal infantry weapon would combine the best features of each, but this proved to be a demanding requirement. The first serious attempt to solve the problem was made in 1941, when the *Luftwaffe* requested a selective fire weapon for its paratroopers which would replace the bolt-action rifle, submachine gun, and light machine gun in the air assault role. The LC-6 specification issued on 14 December, 1941 included stipulations that the weapon should:

- Fire standard 7.92mm (0.31in) ammunition
- Not exceed 1m (39.4in) in length
- Not be significantly heavier than the *Kar 98k* rifle
- Fire single shots from a closed bolt
- Fire fully-automatic from an open bolt
- Use detachable 10- or 20-round magazines
- Be able to fire rifle grenades

Unsurprisingly, it proved extremely difficult to design a serviceable rifle incorporating all these requirements and the new weapon, designated *Fallschirmjägergewehr 42* (FG 42), did not enter service until well into 1943. It equipped the paratroop detachment which rescued Mussolini in September 1943, but its first combat use was in the little-known Dodecanese campaign of September–November 1943. Good as it was, the FG 42 had its problems, especially when firing in the fully-automatic mode – it was not heavy enough for any real accuracy when firing at over 750rpm and the relatively light barrel overheated very quickly. It was also expensive to manufacture and no more than 7000 were produced by the end of the war.

Sturmgewehr 44 (StG 44)

The definitive solution to the problem began to emerge in the late 1930s when Polte-Werke Munition Fabriken modified the standard 7.92mm (0.31in) service ammunition. The 57mm (2.24in) long cartridge case was shortened to 33mm (1.29in), halving the propellant load, and was fitted with a shorter, lighter 7.92mm (0.31in) bullet. This new round performed well and could be produced with only minor alterations to existing factory machinery.

At first, development of the ammunition and compatible weapons had a relatively low priority, but the situation changed dramatically following the *Wehrmacht*'s encounters with the Red Army following the invasion of the Soviet Union in June 1941. Many Russian infantry companies were armed with the PPSh-41 submachine gun and there was a need for the outnumbered German forces to match their immense close-range firepower. The first service weapon produced was the *Maschinenkarabiner 42(H)* (MKb 42(H)), nearly 12,000 of which were issued for troop trials in 1943. These were enthusiastically received and full-scale production began of a slightly simplified version designated *Maschinenpistole 43* (MP 43). This was renamed *Sturmgewehr 44* (StG 44) on Hitler's orders in mid-1944 and proved to be so effective that it was intended to replace all bolt-action rifles and submachine guns in infantry units by late 1945. Despite the disruption caused by Allied bombing, almost 426,000 StG 44s were completed by the end of the war, although probably just a third of these reached front-line units.

The StG 44 formed the basis for the development of what was to become one of the world's most important post-war infantry weapons, the Soviet AK-47 Kalashnikov assault rifle. Another derivative was the Spanish CETME assault rifle, which went into licence production for the *Bundeswehr* in 1959 as the G3 and was adopted by over 50 countries.

BERTHOLD KONRAD HERMANN ALBERT SPEER

■ Albert Speer became Reich Minister of Armaments and War Production in February 1942, after his predecessor had died in an air crash. Speer put the German economy on a full wartime footing, maximizing output.

Speer was unexpectedly appointed Reich Minister of Armaments and War Production in February 1942 following the death of the previous Minister in an air crash. He proved to be an exceptionally able administrator who massively increased the output of all types of weapons despite ever-increasing Allied bombing.

Birth:	19 March 1905
Death:	1 September 1981
Place of birth:	Mannheim, Baden
Father:	Albert Speer
Mother:	Luise Speer
Siblings:	n/k
Personal relationships:	Margarete Weber, married 28 August 1928. Six children – Albert, Hilde, Fritz, Margaret, Arnold and Ernst
Military service:	n/a
Education:	Karlsruhe Institute of Technology Technical University of Munich Technical University of Berlin
Key pre-war positions:	NSDAP member (1931) Commissioner for Artistic and Technical Presentation of Party Rallies and Demonstrations (1933) General Building Inspector for the Reich Capital (1937) Architect of the new Reich Chancellery (1938)
Key wartime positions:	Reich Minister of Armaments and War Production (1942)

Anti-Tank Weapons

In common with most other armies at the beginning of the war, German infantry relied on a variety of anti-tank rifles for close-range defence against enemy AFVs. These were effective against armoured cars and light tanks, but were useless when pitted against the better-protected Allied tanks encountered from 1940 onwards.

The first infantry anti-tank weapons to show real promise of being able to deal with most AFVs were the 'shaped charge' – now generally referred to as High Explosive Anti-Tank (HEAT) – rifle grenades which were introduced in 1940. These used the 'Monroe Effect', which had been discovered in the 1880s, but only began to be developed for military use in the late 1930s. The front of the explosive charge of the shell, rocket or grenade is hollowed out to form a cone which is lined with copper or other metal. On hitting the target, a fuse detonates the charge, which collapses the cone, forming a jet of molten metal and explosive gases travelling at roughly 10,000m/s (32,800 ft/s). This readily penetrates armour or any other hard target, such as reinforced concrete.

The characteristic which made HEAT warheads especially suitable for infantry anti-tank weapons was that their effect was independent of range and velocity – it did not matter if they hit their target at 50m (54yd) or 500m (545yd) and they would work just as well in a grenade as in a high-velocity shell.

The early rifle grenades, designated GG/P40, had a maximum range of roughly 100m (109yd) and could penetrate 40mm (1.57in) of armour. The basic design was gradually improved – by 1942 versions were in service with a similar range, but which could penetrate up to 120mm (4.7in) of armour. While this was far better than anything an anti-tank rifle could manage, rifle grenades were not the complete answer to the problem of effective close-range defence against tanks, since they were still not good enough to deal with increasingly well-armoured Allied AFVs.

8.8cm (3.5in) *Raketenwerfer 43* '*Puppchen*'

By 1943, a small HEAT anti-tank rocket had been developed with a formidable performance – it could penetrate up to 200mm (7.9in) of armour. The launcher, the 8.8cm (3.5in) *Raketenwerfer 43*, more generally dubbed '*Puppchen*' (Dolly) closely resembled a small

PANZERFAUST ANATOMY

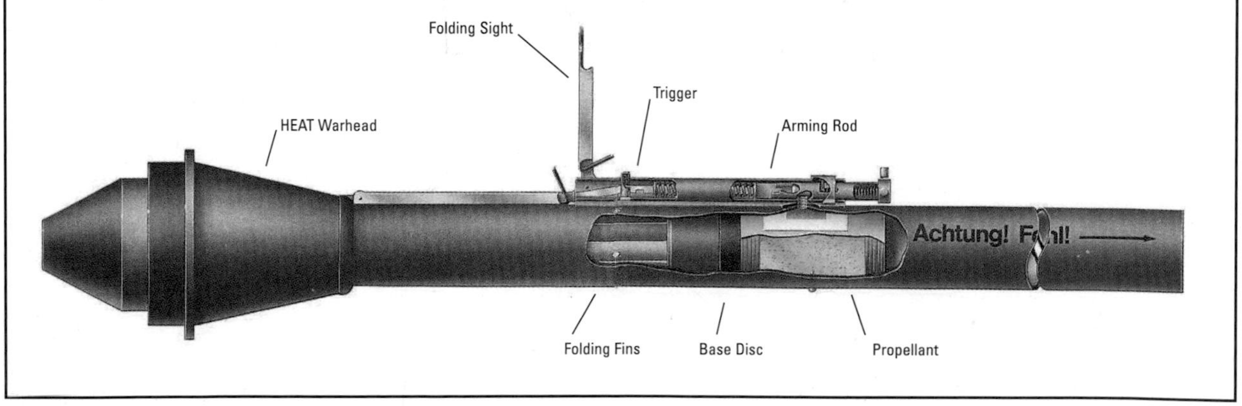
Folding Sight
Trigger
HEAT Warhead
Arming Rod
Folding Fins
Base Disc
Propellant

PANZERFAUST TYPES COMPARED

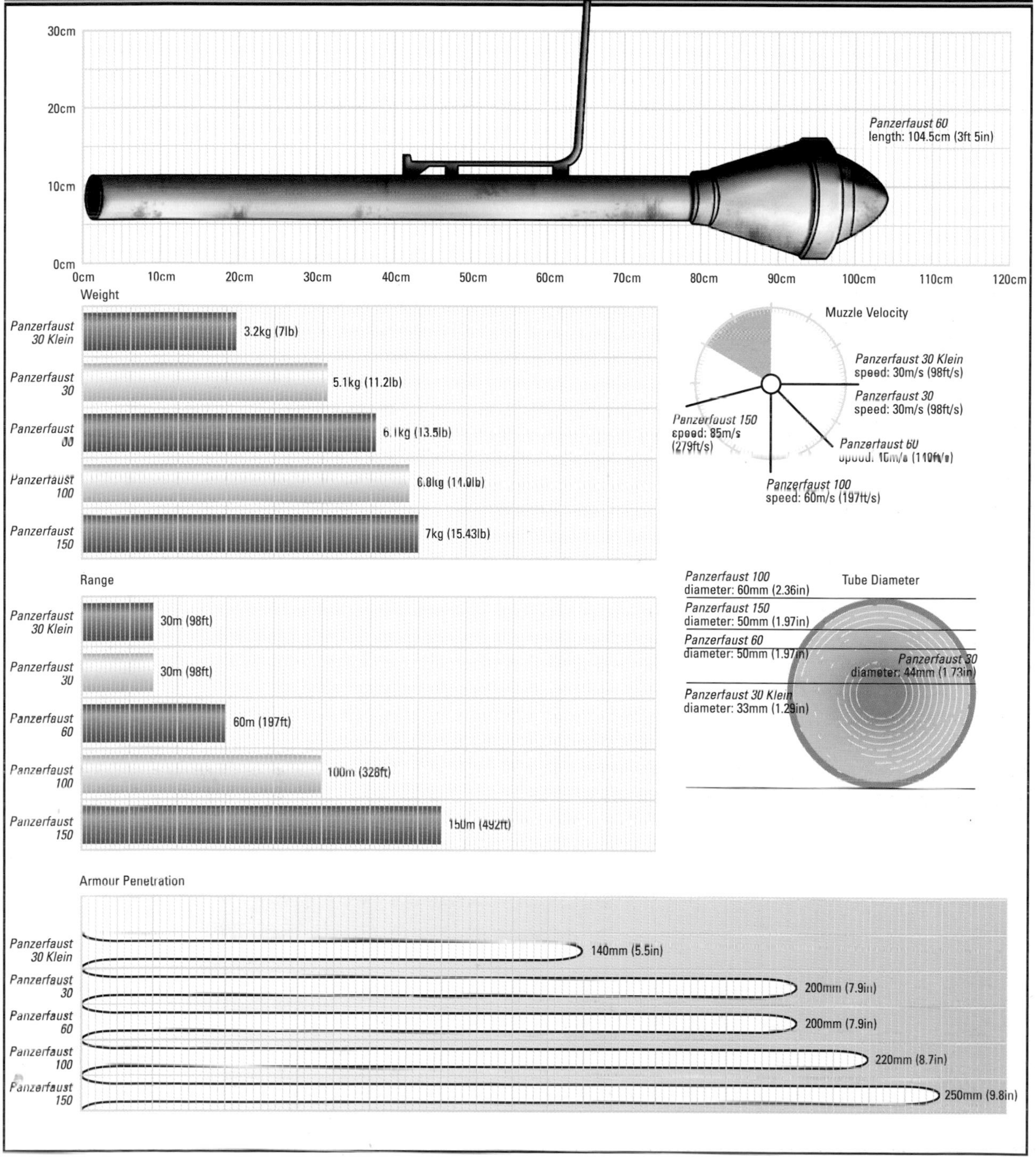
30cm
20cm
10cm
0cm
0cm 10cm 20cm 30cm 40cm 50cm 60cm 70cm 80cm 90cm 100cm 110cm 120cm
Panzerfaust 60
length: 104.5cm (3ft 5in)
Weight
Panzerfaust 30 Klein 3.2kg (7lb)
Panzerfaust 30 5.1kg (11.2lb)
Panzerfaust 6.1kg (13.5lb)
Panzerfaust 100
Panzerfaust 150 7kg (15.43lb)
Muzzle Velocity
Panzerfaust 30 Klein
speed: 30m/s (98ft/s)
Panzerfaust 30
speed: 30m/s (98ft/s)
Panzerfaust 150
speed: 85m/s
(279ft/s)
Panzerfaust 100
speed: 60m/s (197ft/s)
Range
Panzerfaust 30 Klein 30m (98ft)
Panzerfaust 30 30m (98ft)
Panzerfaust 60 60m (197ft)
Panzerfaust 100 100m (328ft)
Panzerfaust 150 150m (492ft)
Tube Diameter
Panzerfaust 100
diameter: 60mm (2.36in)
Panzerfaust 150
diameter: 50mm (1.97in)
Panzerfaust 60
diameter: 50mm (1.97in)
Panzerfaust 30
diameter: 44mm (1.73in)
Panzerfaust 30 Klein
diameter: 33mm (1.29in)
Armour Penetration
Panzerfaust 30 Klein 140mm (5.5in)
Panzerfaust 30 200mm (7.9in)
Panzerfaust 60 200mm (7.9in)
Panzerfaust 100 220mm (8.7in)
Panzerfaust 150 250mm (9.8in)

PANZERSCHRECK TYPES COMPARED

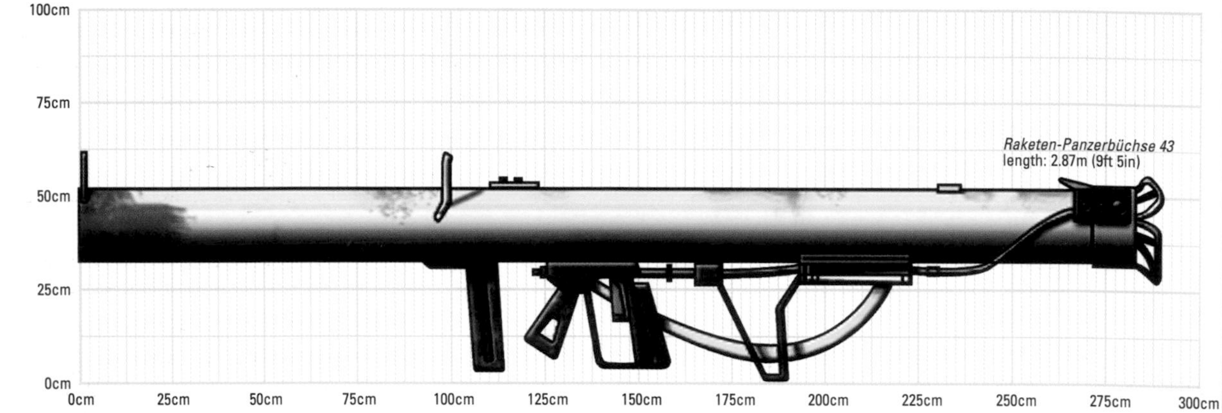
100cm
75cm
50cm
25cm
0cm
Raketen-Panzerbüchse 43
length: 2.87m (9ft 5in)
0cm
25cm
50cm
75cm
100cm
125cm
150cm
175cm
200cm
225cm
250cm
275cm
300cm

Range

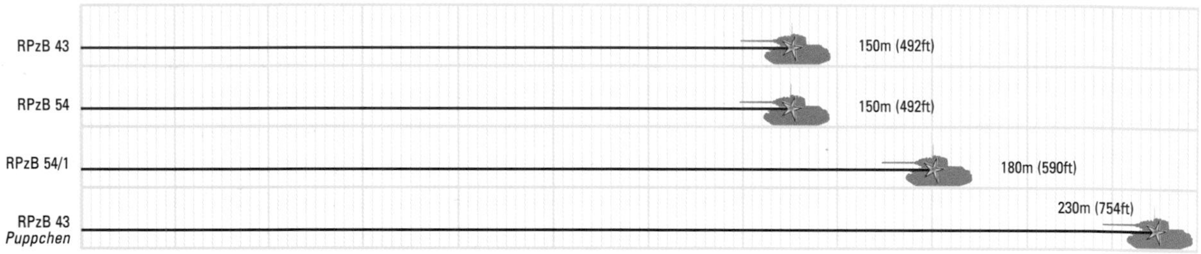
RPzB 43
150m (492ft)
RPzB 54
150m (492ft)
RPzB 54/1
180m (590ft)
RPzB 43 Puppchen
230m (754ft)

Length

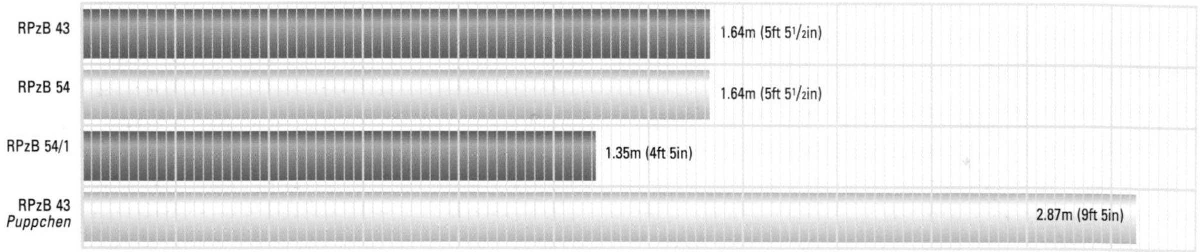
RPzB 43
1.64m (5ft 5½in)
RPzB 54
1.64m (5ft 5½in)
RPzB 54/1
1.35m (4ft 5in)
RPzB 43 Puppchen
2.87m (9ft 5in)

Weight

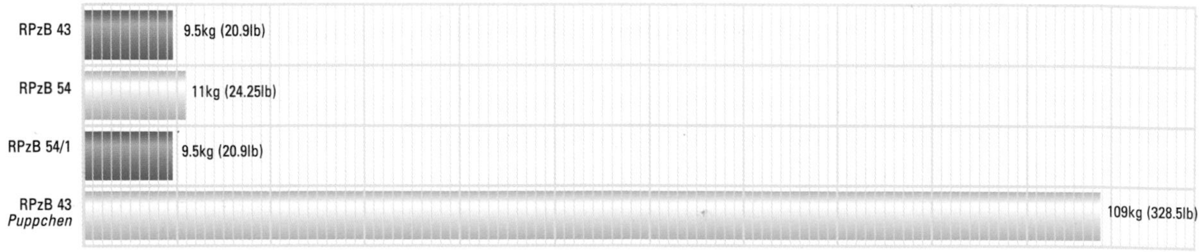
RPzB 43
9.5kg (20.9lb)
RPzB 54
11kg (24.25lb)
RPzB 54/1
9.5kg (20.9lb)
RPzB 43 Puppchen
109kg (328.5lb)

conventional anti-tank gun. When operating in its primary anti-tank role, it had an effective range of 230m (252yd), but it could be used at ranges up to 700m (766yd) against bunkers and field defences.

Although rapidly superseded in production by the far simpler *Panzerschreck*, those which had been completed were issued to infantry anti-tank units (primarily in Italy) and remained in service throughout the war.

Raketen-Panzerbüchse 43 and *54* (*Panzerschreck*)

Examination of bazookas captured in North Africa led to the cancellation of *Puppchen* production in favour of a 'bazooka equivalent' which entered service in mid-1943 as the *Raketen-Panzerbüchse 43*, or *Panzerschreck* (Tank Terror). To many front-line troops, it was also known simply as the *Ofenrohr* (Stove pipe).

The first model was the RPzB 43, which was 164cm (5ft 5in) long and weighed 9.25kg (20.4lb) while empty. The rocket was very similar to that fired by the *Puppchen*, but the relatively short launch tube meant that the propellant was still burning as it left the tube, forcing the firer to wear a flame-proof poncho and gas mask to avoid serious burns. The maximum effective range against AFVs was about 150m (164yd) and firing positions had to be carefully chosen to allow for the large danger area to the rear caused by the weapon's considerable back blast.

In October 1943, it was succeeded by the heavier RPzB 54 which was fitted with a blast shield to protect the operator who no longer had to wear cumbersome protective clothing. This was followed by the RPzB 54/1 with a shorter launch tube and an improved rocket with an effective range of 180m (196yd).

Total *Panzerschreck* production exceeded 315,000 – each weapon cost 70 Reichsmarks and took no more than 10 man-hours to complete.

Panzerfaust

The *Panzerfaust* was essentially a disposable recoilless gun which could be issued to infantrymen as a highly effective personal anti-tank weapon. The first version, generally known as the *Faustpatrone*, was issued in August 1943 and by the end of World War II, total production of all models exceeded six million units.

The main models were:

- *Panzerfaust 30 klein (Faustpatrone)*
  This fired a 100mm (3.94in) bomb, which could penetrate 140mm (5.5in) of armour, to a maximum range of 30m (98ft).
- *Panzerfaust 30*
  This was an improved version which also entered service in August 1943. An enlarged warhead boosted armour penetration to 200mm (7.9in), but the maximum range was unchanged.
- *Panzerfaust 60*
  This was the most common version, which entered service in September 1944. Armour penetration was still 200mm (7.9in), but it had a range of 60m (66yd).
- *Panzerfaust 100*
  This was the final version to be produced in quantity from November 1944 onwards. It had a larger propelling charge which extended the nominal maximum range to 100m (109yd). Armour penetration was also improved to 220mm (8.7in).

***PANZERFAUST* AND *PANZERSCHRECK* PRODUCTION FIGURES**

Type	*1943*	*1944*	*1945 (Jan–Mar)*	*Total*
Faustpatrone	123,900	1,418,300	12,000	1,554,200
Panzerfaust 30, 60, 100, 150	227,800	4,120,500	2,351,800	6,700,000
Panzerschreck RPzB.54 (Dec 1944) and RPzB.54/1 (1945)	50,835	238,316	25,744	289,151
Panzerschreck ammunition (RPzB.Gr.4322 and 4992)	173,000	1,805,400	240,000	2,218,400

EASTERN FRONT 1944: REPORTED TANK KILLS

Kills	*January*	*February*	*March*	*April*	*Total*
Total no. of kills	4727	2273	2663	2878	12,541
Cause known	3670	1905	1031	1524	8130
By *Faustpatrone/Panzerfaust*	58	45	51	110	262
By *Panzerschreck*	9	24	29	26	88
By *Hafthohlladung* antitank grenade	21	13	14	19	67
By hand grenade	6	5	5	6	22
By *Tellermine*	20	4	43	11	78

- *Panzerfaust 150*
  This entered production in March 1945 and was deployed in small numbers in the last weeks of the war, but too late to have any real impact on the battlefield. Range was again extended, this time to 150m (164yd) and a redesigned warhead improved armour penetration to 250mm (9.8in). The reinforced firing tube was reusable for up to ten shots before being discarded.

Anti-Tank Guns

German design teams pioneered both recoilless and taper-bore guns which seemed to offer potential solutions to the problem of providing lightweight but effective anti-tank guns for infantry and airborne forces.

The first practical recoilless guns were developed by Commander Cleland Davis, US Navy, and were test-fired from a variety of Allied aircraft during World War I. The Davis gun had a breech that was open to the rear and fired a counter-weight (normally lead shot) to the rear which was equal to the

RECOILLESS GUNS COMPARED

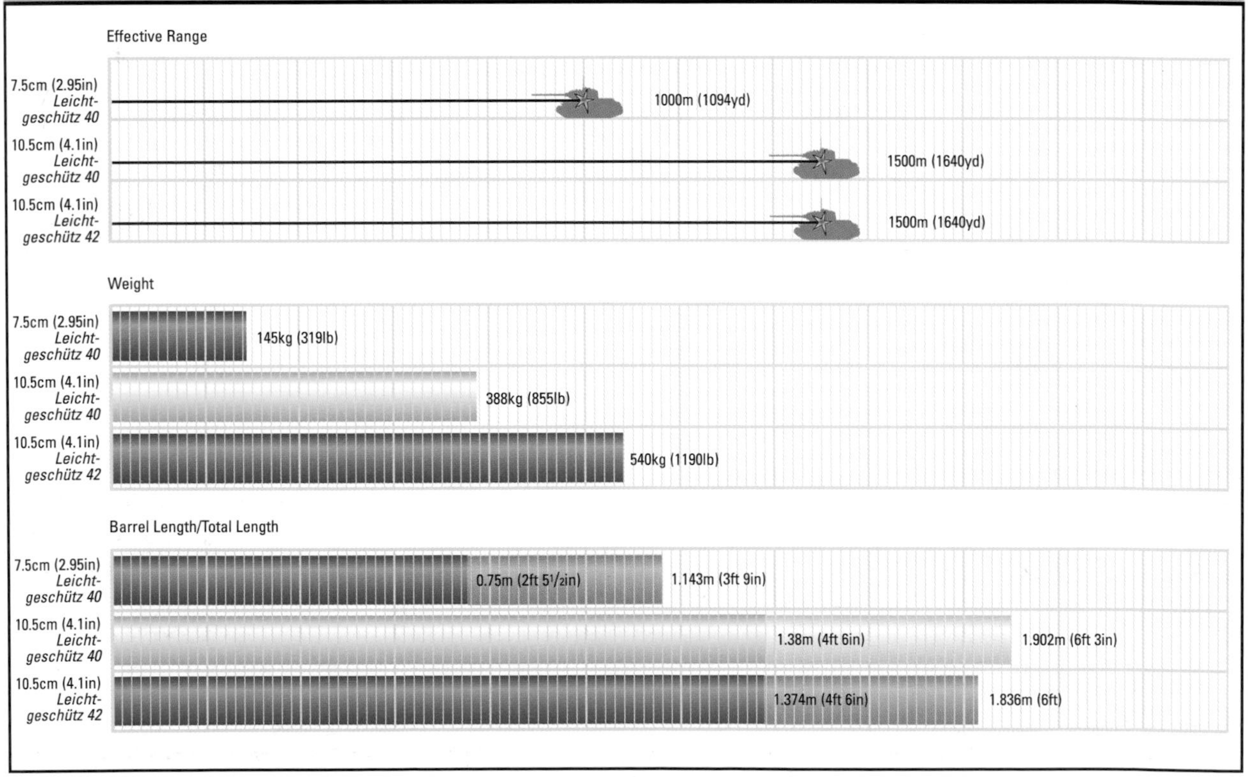
Effective Range
7.5cm (2.95in) Leicht-geschütz 40
1000m (1094yd)
10.5cm (4.1in) Leicht-geschütz 40
1500m (1640yd)
10.5cm (4.1in) Leicht-geschütz 42
1500m (1640yd)
Weight
7.5cm (2.95in) Leicht-geschütz 40
145kg (319lb)
10.5cm (4.1in) Leicht-geschütz 40
388kg (855lb)
10.5cm (4.1in) Leicht-geschütz 42
540kg (1190lb)
Barrel Length/Total Length
7.5cm (2.95in) Leicht-geschütz 40
0.75m (2ft 5½in)
1.143m (3ft 9in)
10.5cm (4.1in) Leicht-geschütz 40
1.38m (4ft 6in)
1.902m (6ft 3in)
10.5cm (4.1in) Leicht-geschütz 42
1.374m (4ft 6in)
1.836m (6ft)

TAPER-BORE ANTI-TANK GUNS COMPARED

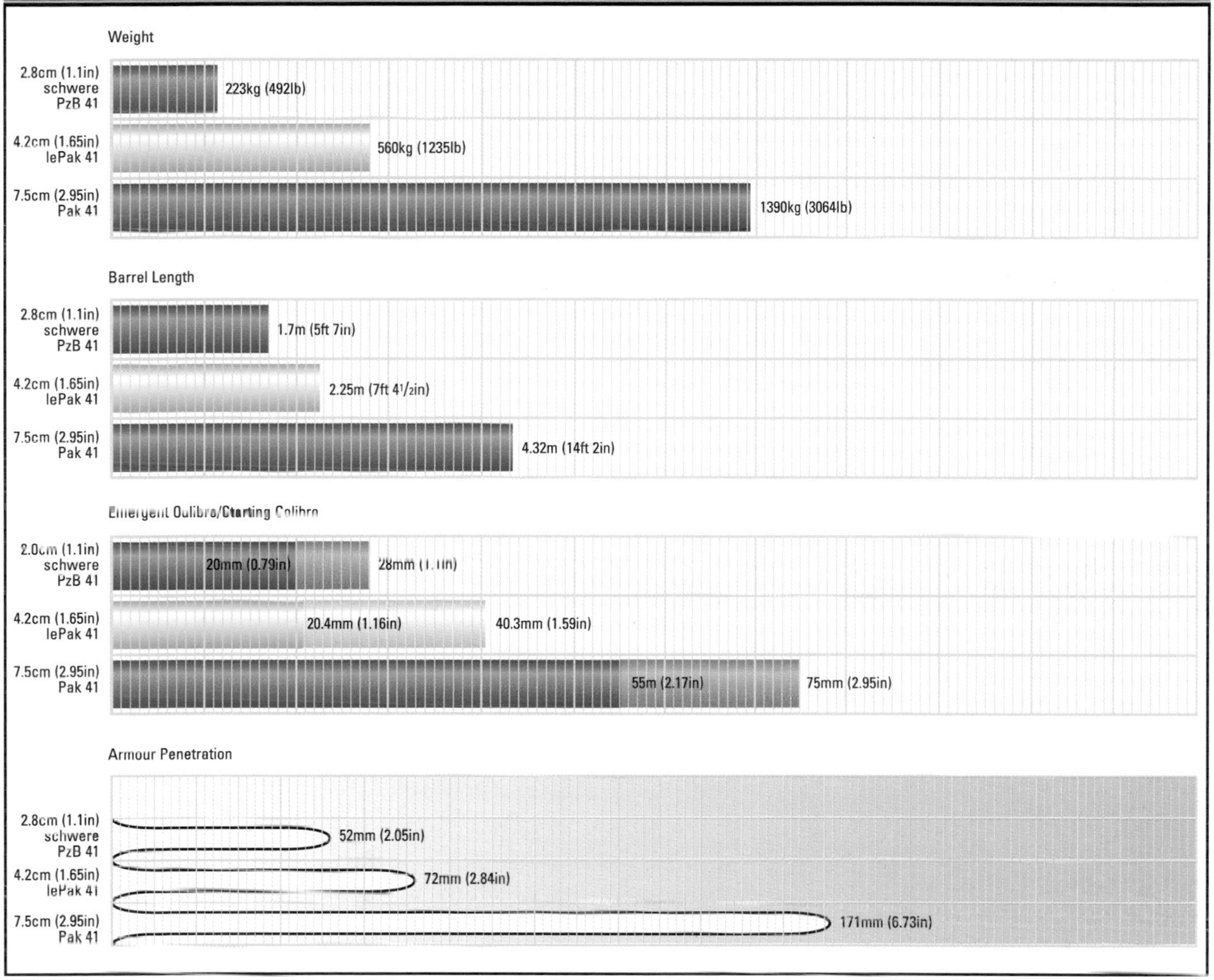
Weight
2.8cm (1.1in) schwere PzB 41
223kg (492lb)
4.2cm (1.65in) lePak 41
560kg (1235lb)
7.5cm (2.95in) Pak 41
1390kg (3064lb)
Barrel Length
2.8cm (1.1in) schwere PzB 41
1.7m (5ft 7in)
4.2cm (1.65in) lePak 41
2.25m (7ft 4½in)
7.5cm (2.95in) Pak 41
4.32m (14ft 2in)
Emergent Calibre/Starting Calibre
2.0cm (1.1in) schwere PzB 41
20mm (0.79in)
28mm (1.1in)
4.2cm (1.65in) lePak 41
20.4mm (1.16in)
40.3mm (1.59in)
7.5cm (2.95in) Pak 41
55m (2.17in)
75mm (2.95in)
Armour Penetration
2.8cm (1.1in) schwere PzB 41
52mm (2.05in)
4.2cm (1.65in) lePak 41
72mm (2.84in)
7.5cm (2.95in) Pak 41
171mm (6.73in)

projectile weight, cancelling out the recoil. During the 1930s, it was realized that the counter-weight would be unnecessary if the gun could be designed to 'fire' a very high velocity stream of gas rearwards from the propelling charge.

The first weapon to enter service was the 7.5cm (2.95in) *Leicht Geschutz 40*, which was soon supplemented by 10.5cm (4.1in) guns. All were used primarily by German airborne forces as both anti-tank guns firing HEAT rounds and as close support weapons.

Taper-bore anti-tank guns

The taper-bore principle was patented in 1903 and was developed during the inter-war years by German engineer Hermann Gerlich, who produced an experimental ultra-high velocity 7mm (0.26in) anti-tank rifle. This was so promising that work began on a more powerful version, which entered service in 1941 as the 2.8cm (1.1in) *schwere Panzerbusche 41* (PzB 41). In common with all subsequent German taper-bore designs, it used tungsten-cored solid shot, fitted with soft metal flanges that were 'squeezed' flat as the round travelled down the narrowing barrel.

This gave extremely high muzzle velocity and exceptional armour penetration for such a light gun.

The success of the PzB 41 led to the rapid development of larger 4.2cm (1.65in) and 7.5cm (2.95in) guns, but all three relied on tungsten-cored ammunition. Tungsten was essential for machine-tool production in a range of vital war industries and was in increasingly short supply. By 1942, it had become necessary to reserve supplies for industrial use and the guns were scrapped after existing ammunition stocks were exhausted.

High-low pressure guns

The enforced scrapping of the taper-bore guns forced German design teams to examine radical alternative systems for lightweight anti-tank guns. In late 1943, Rheinmetall-Borsig proposed their high-low pressure system which used a heavy-duty breech and a lightweight smooth-bore barrel to fire fin-stabilized HEAT ammunition. The projectile was based on the standard 8cm (3.15in) mortar bomb and was attached to a heavy iron plate which fitted into the cartridge case. On firing, the high pressure generated by the propellant gradually passed through a ring of holes in the plate until it built up sufficiently to blast the bomb up the barrel of the gun.

The weapon was highly successful, but problems with the carriage design delayed series production until December 1944 and no more than 260 of the type were completed under the designation 8cm (3.15in) *Panzerabwehrwerfer 600.* A similar though larger design, the 10cm (3.94in) PWK 10H64, never reached the prototype stage.

HIGH-LOW PRESSURE GUNS COMPARED

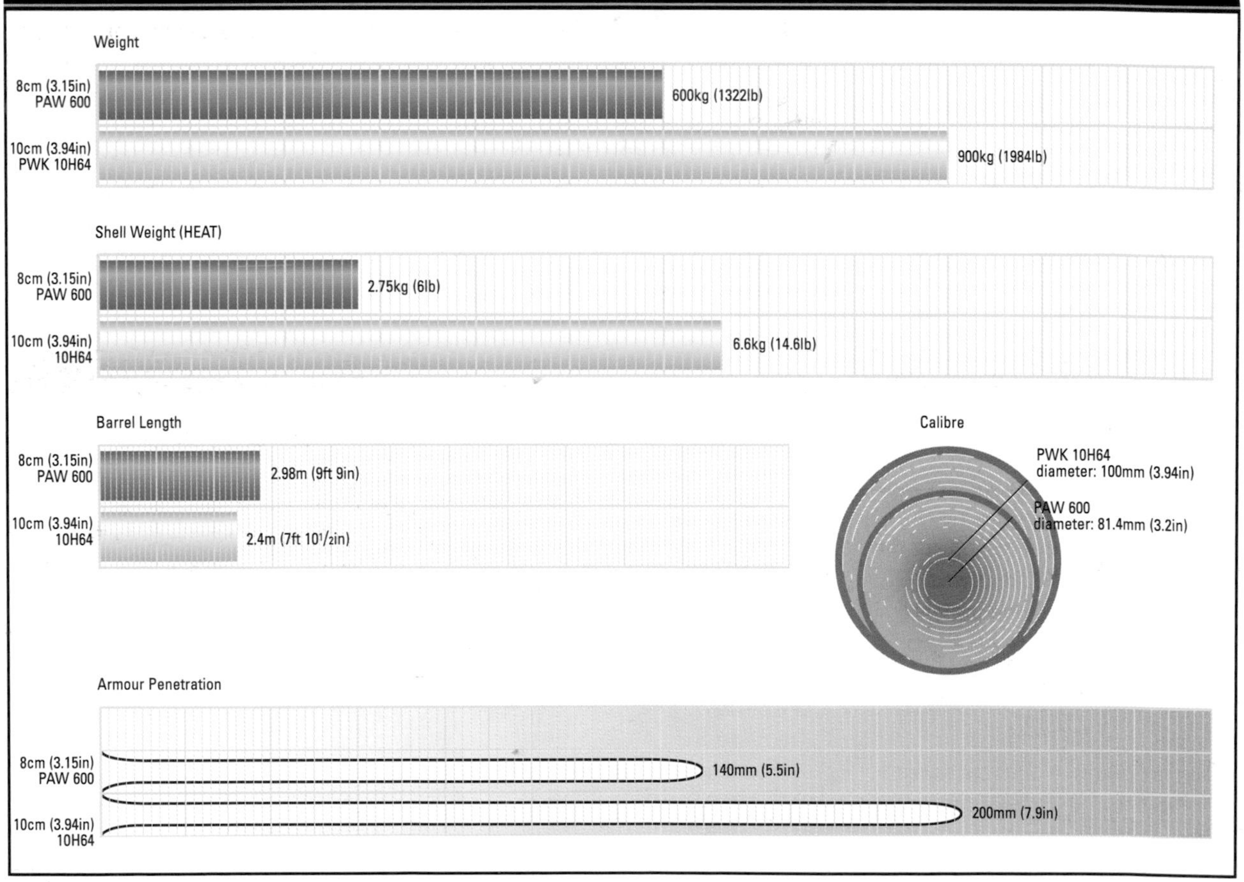
Weight
8cm (3.15in) PAW 600
600kg (1322lb)
10cm (3.94in) PWK 10H64
900kg (1984lb)
Shell Weight (HEAT)
8cm (3.15in) PAW 600
2.75kg (6lb)
10cm (3.94in) 10H64
6.6kg (14.6lb)
Barrel Length
8cm (3.15in) PAW 600
2.98m (9ft 9in)
10cm (3.94in) 10H64
2.4m (7ft 10½in)
Calibre
PWK 10H64
diameter: 100mm (3.94in)
PAW 600
diameter: 81.4mm (3.2in)
Armour Penetration
8cm (3.15in) PAW 600
140mm (5.5in)
10cm (3.94in) 10H64
200mm (7.9in)

Anti-Aircraft Weapons

By 1945 German forces were on the point of fielding a range of weapons that could have significantly reduced the effects of Allied air superiority. One of the most remarkable of these was the Luftfaust, *a shoulder-fired AA rocket system.*

The *Luftfaust* was cheap and simple, but potentially highly effective. This AA rocket projector comprised eight steel tubes mounted in a circle surrounding a ninth central tube, held in place by four plates.

Luftfaust was trigger-fired with the aid of a folding shoulder rest and two hand grips. Its ammunition was issued in clips, which were breech-loaded directly into the projector. The warhead of each spin-stabilized solid-fuel rocket was a standard impact-fused HE 20mm (0.79in) cannon shell. These rockets were fired in two groups, with delay pellets in the initiators of the second group, giving a 0.2 second gap between salvoes.

Production of *Luftfaust* began early in 1945, mainly in small workshops, using unskilled labour. Despite this, some 10,000 units were completed by the time of the German surrender, although few, if any, were issued and there are no reliable accounts of any being fired in action.

The *Fliegerfaust* was a proposed development of *Luftfaust* which comprised six 30mm (1.18in) barrels. The rockets were to be slightly enlarged versions of those used by *Luftfaust*, fitted with standard 30mm (1.18in) MK 108 cannon shells. This was a promising project that would have had significantly better firepower than *Luftfaust*, but it never got beyond the design study stage.

Fliegerschreck

This was another ingenious system that was being readied for service trials in the final weeks of the war. It was a new form of ammunition which effectively converted the *Panzerschreck* into an AA weapon. The new time-fused warhead, containing a bursting charge and 144 small incendiary sub-munitions, was fitted to the standard rocket motor. A new AA sight was included, which was similar to those already in production for the MG 42.

Development of the warhead was completed in January 1945 and a pre-production batch of 500 rockets was completed, but they were never issued to front-line units.

LUFTFAUST

Specifications

Launcher Weight: 6.6kg (14.6lb)
Launcher Length: 1.3m (4ft 3¼in)
Launcher Diameter: 135mm (5.31in)
Rocket Calibre: 20mm (0.79in)
Effective Range: 210–500m (230–547yd)

CHAPTER 6

Aircraft Secret Weapons Programme

The entire Luftwaffe *began its existence as a 'secret weapon'. German military aviation was banned by the Treaty of Versailles, but clandestine aircraft development and flying training resumed in the early 1920s. Much of this took place in Russia under secret treaty arrangements with the Soviet government – between 1924 and 1933, a German flying school operated at Lipetsk. As many as 1200 German airmen attended its courses on military flying and air warfare tactics.*

In January 1934, Hitler authorized a major military aircraft construction programme. A total of 4021 aircraft were ordered, including no fewer than 1760 training machines. Initially, all military types were flown in the liveries of civilian organizations, but the pretence was abandoned on 1 March 1935 when Hitler felt sufficiently confident to formally announce the existence of the Luftwaffe.

Heinkel He 162s on an assembly line in the Seegrotte Caves at Hinterbrühl, Austria.

The Production War

By 1935 Germany had produced more military aircraft than any other country. The 3,183 machines completed were predominantly trainers rather than combat types, reflecting the priorities of the rapidly expanding Luftwaffe.

By 1939, production more than doubled to bring the total to 7350 aircraft, most of which were combat types. During the next four years, output increased to more than 40,000.

Fortunately for Germany's future enemies, the determination shown by Göring in building up a numerically impressive *Luftwaffe* was not matched by a real appreciation of the rapid changes in military aviation technology. However, innovation flourished, nurtured by the Condor Legion's combat experience in the Spanish Civil War, where 200 aircraft were deployed, dropping bombs totalling 16,953,700kg (3,7298,140lb) and expending 4,327,949 rounds of ammunition. However, the development of heavy bombers, naval and long-range maritime reconnaissance aircraft, which could have had a major impact on the course of World War II, was side-lined in favour of fighters, dive-bombers and medium bombers. The chosen types demanded far fewer of Germany's limited resources and allowed the *Luftwaffe* to field a total of roughly 4000 modern combat aircraft by 1939. While these were highly effective, both as propaganda and as a component of *blitzkrieg*, the *Luftwaffe* ultimately proved to be unequal to the demands of a prolonged war of attrition.

Indeed, attrition was an ever-present factor in eroding aircraft numbers, even in the pre-war years when training accidents took a steady toll. Block obsolescence of early production types also occured as biplanes were supplanted by all-metal monoplanes in the late 1930s. As soon as the war began, combat losses added to the problem – the *Luftwaffe* lost an estimated 3860 aircraft in the first year's fighting alone. Under the circumstances, it is unsurprising that the decision was taken to concentrate production on well-established types such as the Messerschmitt Bf 109, Heinkel He 111 and Junkers Ju 88, but many of these were kept in production for too long. Many promising development programmes were blighted by Hitler's over-confidence in 1940, which led him to order a halt to all projects that could not be guaranteed to reach operational status within 12 months.

Even when it came to the output of well-established aircraft types, the Germans were less successful in expanding production than the Allies. Although German production in 1939 was over 25 per cent higher than that of Britain, by 1941 British factories had caught up and remained ahead for the remainder of the war. US production, which stood at half the German total in 1939, also rapidly caught up and grew at a much higher rate until 1945. Germany's failure to match Allied production figures severely hampered its war effort and was a major factor in its final defeat.

Another problem was the uncontrolled flood of new types under development in 1944–45. The obvious and urgent need to combat the increasingly effective Allied bombing campaign led to a bewildering array of proposals for piston-engined, jet and rocket-propelled interceptors, many of which never progressed beyond preliminary design studies. Much of this effort was wasted on designs which stood no chance of reaching squadron service and diverted resources from types such as the Messerschmitt Me 262 and Arado Ar 234 that could have had a real impact on the air war.

AIRCRAFT PRODUCTION BY COUNTRY, ALL TYPES (1939–45)

Country	*Strength*
United States	324,750
United Kingdom	131,549
Soviet Union	157,261
Germany	119,307
Japan	76,320
Canada	16,431
Italy	11,122
France (Sept 1939–Jun 1940)	4016
Other Commonwealth countries	3081
Hungary	1046
Romania	1000

HANNA REITSCH

■ **Hanna Reitsch, one of the most able test-pilots of all time.**

Hanna Reitsch's father pressured her to take up a career in medicine, but her overriding love of flying drove her to abandon her medical training in 1933 to become a full-time gliding instructor. In 1937, she began test-flying for the *Luftwaffe* and by the end of World War II had flown most types of aircraft in its inventory, including the Messerschmitt Me 163 rocket-propelled fighter and the giant Messerschmitt Me 321 transport glider.

BIRTH:	29 March 1912
DEATH:	24 August 1979
PLACE OF BIRTH:	Hirschberg, Silesia (now Jelenia Gora, Poland)
FATHER:	Dr Willi Reitsch
MOTHER:	Emy Reitsch
SIBLINGS:	Kurt Reitsch (born 1910) and Heidi Reitsch (born 1914)
PERSONAL RELATIONSHIPS:	Never married, but was the lover of *Luftwaffe* General Ritter von Greim, who was appointed Commander-in-Cheif of the *Luftwaffe* in April 1945
KEY PRE-WAR AND WARTIME POSITIONS:	*Luftwaffe* test pilot 1937–45

New Fighter Types

From its inception, the Luftwaffe *was designed for the offensive, with little thought given to its role as protector of German airspace, apart from the creation of a strong AA* (Flak) *force, which was an integral part of the* Luftwaffe.

Even as the Allied air forces began sustained offensives in 1943, the *Luftwaffe* refused to give priority to the production of urgently needed fighters over that of bombers, many of which were obsolescent, if not actually obsolete.

It was not shaken out of its complacency until the USAAF raids of Operation Big Week in February 1944 inflicted massive damage on German aircraft factories. This led to the creation of a new administrative body, the *Jagerstab* (Fighter Staff) to ensure that fighter production was given priority in a network of new, widely dispersed factories.

The final official recognition of the dire need for new fighter types came in July 1944, with the establishment of the *Jägernotprogramm* (Emergency Fighter Programme). This halted all production of conventional bombers and shifted resources to fighters, with priority given to advanced piston-engined fighters, such as the Dornier Do 335, and rocket-propelled aircraft and jets, especially the Messerschmitt Me 163 and Me 262. A key part of the programme was the Emergency Fighter Competition, which was intended to develop new jet aircraft superior to the known 'first generation' Allied jet aircraft, such as the Meteor and P 80.

FIGHTER PRODUCTION

Type	*1939*	*1940*	*1941*	*1942*	*1943*	*1944*	*1945*	*Total*
Dornier Do 335	–	–	–	–	–	23	19	42
Focke-Wulf Ta 152	–	–	–	–	–	34	46	80
Focke-Wulf Ta 154	–	–	–	–	–	8	–	8
Heinkel He 162	–	–	–	–	–	–	116	116
Heinkel He 219	–	–	–	–	11	195	62	268
Messerschmitt Me 163	–	–	–	–	–	327	37	364
Messerschmitt Me 262	–	–	–	–	–	564	730	1294
Messerschmitt Me 410	–	–	–	–	271	629	–	910

FIGHTER AIRCRAFT PRODUCTION BY COUNTRY

Country	*Strength*
United States	99,950
Soviet Union	63,087
Germany	55,727
United Kingdom	49,422
Japan	30,447
Italy	4510
France (Sept 1939–Jun 1940)	1597

Even at this critical stage in the war, there was an inability to focus resources on a few key types – exemplified by the acrimonious dispute within the *Luftwaffe* regarding jet fighters. One group, led by *General der Jagdflieger* (General of Fighters) Adolf Galland, believed that Allied numerical superiority had to be countered with superior technology, and demanded that an all-out effort should be put into increasing production of the Me 262, even if it was at the expense of other aircraft types.

Their opponents pointed out that this would be unlikely to solve the problem as the Me 262's engines were notoriously unreliable and Germany's chronic logistics problems would mean there would merely be more of them on the ground waiting for parts or fuel that would never arrive. Instead, they advocated a new design, one so simple and inexpensive that if damaged or unserviceable, it could simply be discarded – a 'disposable fighter'.

Single-engined jet fighter

Galland and other *Luftwaffe* '*experten*' were vehemently opposed to this concept, which was strongly supported by *Reichsmarschall* Hermann Göring and Armaments Minister Albert Speer. Göring and Speer got their way, and an official requirement was issued on 10 September for a single-engined jet fighter that was optimized for rapid mass production under the name *Volksjäger* (People's Fighter). After a hurried design competition involving almost all German aircraft companies, Heinkel's lightweight 'Sparrow' jet fighter proposal – the He 162 *Volksjäger* – was selected.

Even allowing for the preliminary design studies which Heinkel had undertaken throughout 1944, it was a remarkable technical achievement. The first prototype flew on 6 December 1944 and about 320 aircraft were completed by May 1945.

GROUND-ATTACK AIRCRAFT PRODUCTION BY COUNTRY

Country	*Strength*
Soviet Union	37,549
Germany	12,539
France (Sept 1939–Jun 1940)	280

The *Miniaturjagerprogramm* (Miniature Fighter Programme) was a further dissipation of resources. It was launched at the end of 1944 with the aim of swiftly developing and mass-producing a very small interceptor at minimum cost. It was stipulated that the *Miniaturjager* must be powered by a pulse jet, which required far fewer construction man-hours than a turbojet. Little interest was shown in this new project by the *Luftwaffe* or most German aircraft designers, largely due to the fact that the Heinkel He 162 programme was already absorbing the bulk of what was left of the country's aircraft production capacity. It was also well-known by this time that pulse jets were unsuitable as engines for manned aircraft due to their severe vibration.

Three designs were proposed to meet the requirement, Heinkel's pulse-jet powered He 162, Blohm & Voss' angular BV P.213 and Junkers' EF126 'Elli'. It was calculated that the cost of a completed Ju EF126 aircraft would be 30,000 Reichsmarks, compared to 74,000 for a completed Heinkel He 162 jet fighter or 150,000 Reichsmarks for a Messerschmitt Me 262. Although the 'Elli' was adopted for the ground-attack role, it never progressed beyond the mock-up stage.

Piston-Engined Fighters

The Messerschmitt Bf 109 first flew in 1935 and remained in service until the end of the war. Although it was continually updated, with total production exceeding 33,000, it was clear that a successor was needed to counter increasingly formidable Allied fighters.

The only major fighter type to enter *Luftwaffe* service after the outbreak of war was the Focke-Wulf Fw 190. Although it was a superb low altitude fighter, it was not the complete answer to the *Luftwaffe*'s needs.

Messerschmitt Me 609

A series of designs for a successor to the Bf 109 culminated with the twin-fuselage Me 609. It was intended to be produced as both a heavy fighter and high-speed bomber – both were 'single-seaters', with the pilot in the port fuselage and the starboard cockpit faired over. The fighter version was to be armed with four 30mm (1.18in) cannon – two MK 108s and two MK 103s, with provision for two additional MK 108s which could be supplemented by under-wing bombs. The bomber version would have a lighter armament of only two MK 108s and an increased bomb load. Despite its heavy armament and a projected speed of 760km/h (472mph), the Me 609 could not match the performance of the Me 262 and the project was stopped in 1944.

Heinkel He 219

The He 219 *Uhu* (Eagle Owl) was the most advanced piston-engined night fighter to see combat service with the *Luftwaffe*. The prototype first flew in November 1942. A few pre-production aircraft entered service in mid-1943 and proved to be highly successful against the RAF's night bombers. On the night of 11 June 1943, Major Werner Streib shot down five British Lancasters in a single sortie.

Unfortunately for the *Luftwaffe*, *Generalfeldmarschall* Milch was a strong opponent of the He 219 and engineered the cancellation of the project in May 1944.

Despite this, a number of variants were unofficially completed and total production may well have totalled 300 aircraft.

GERMAN AND ALLIED FIGHTERS COMPARED

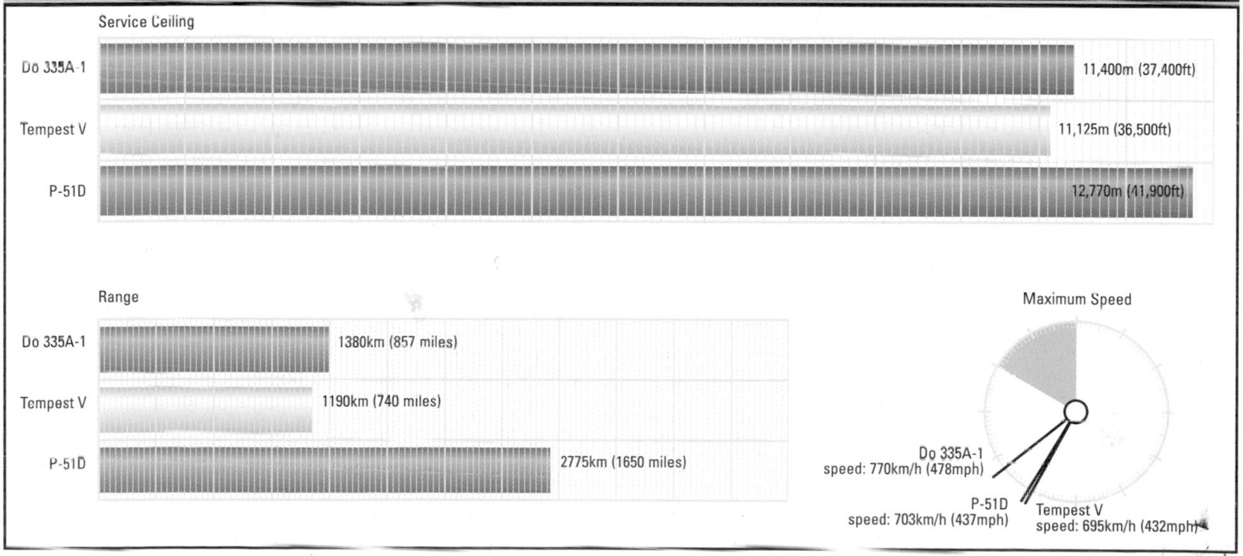
Service Ceiling
Do 335A-1
11,400m (37,400ft)
Tempest V
11,125m (36,500ft)
P-51D
12,770m (41,900ft)
Range
Do 335A-1
1380km (857 miles)
Tempest V
1190km (740 miles)
P-51D
2775km (1650 miles)
Maximum Speed
Do 335A-1
speed: 770km/h (478mph)
P-51D
speed: 703km/h (437mph)
Tempest V
speed: 695km/h (432mph)

PISTON-ENGINED FIGHTERS COMPARED

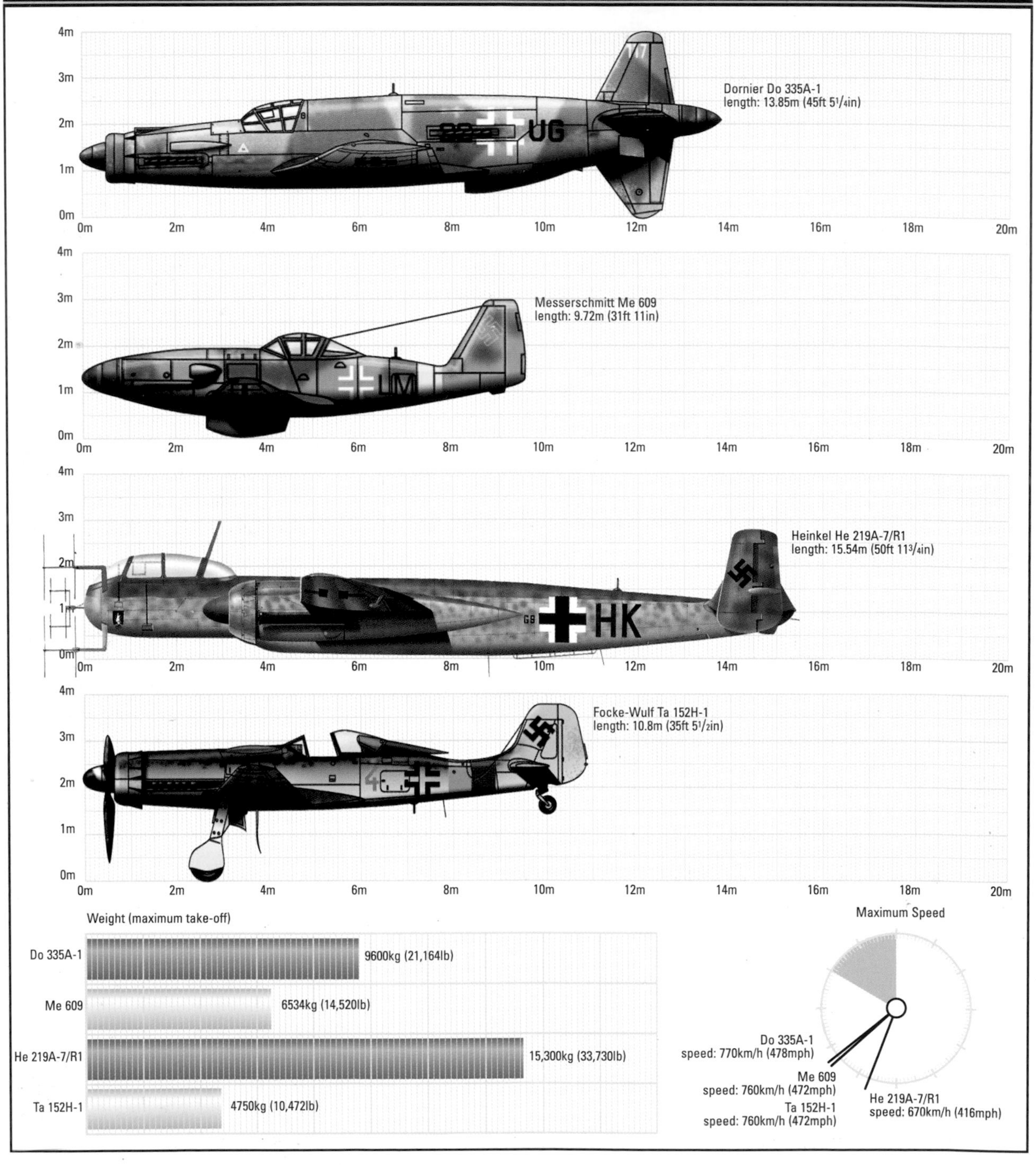
Dornier Do 335A-1
length: 13.85m (45ft 5¼in)
Messerschmitt Me 609
length: 9.72m (31ft 11in)
Heinkel He 219A-7/R1
length: 15.54m (50ft 11¾in)
Focke-Wulf Ta 152H-1
length: 10.8m (35ft 5½in)
Weight (maximum take-off)
Do 335A-1
9600kg (21,164lb)
Me 609
6534kg (14,520lb)
He 219A-7/R1
15,300kg (33,730lb)
Ta 152H-1
4750kg (10,472lb)
Maximum Speed
Do 335A-1
speed: 770km/h (478mph)
Me 609
speed: 760km/h (472mph)
Ta 152H-1
speed: 760km/h (472mph)
He 219A-7/R1
speed: 670km/h (416mph)

DRNIER DO 335 – PRODUCTION FIGURES

Version	*Quantity*	*Assembly Location*	*Period*
Do 335V1 to V14	13+1*	Friedrichshafen	mid-1943–mid-1944
Do 335A-0	10	Oberpfaffenhofen	July–Oct 1944
Do 335A-1	11+9*	Oberpfaffenhofen	Nov 1944–Apr 1945
Do 335A-4	4*	Oberpfaffenhofen	Jan–Feb 1945
Do 335A-6	none	Heinkel, Vienna-Swechat	–
Do 335A-10	1+1*	Oberpfaffenhofen	Oct 1944–Apr 1945
Do 335A 12	2+2*	Oberpfaffenhofen	Nov 1944–Apr 1945
Do 335B-1	1	Oberpfaffenhofen	Jan–Feb 1945
Do 335B-2	2	Oberpfaffenhofen	Feb–Mar 1945
Do 335B-3	1*	Oberpfaffenhofen	Feb–Apr 1945
Do 335B-6	2	Oberpfaffenhofen	Jan–Feb 1945
Do 335B-7	1*	Oberpfaffenhofen	Feb–Apr 1945
Do 335B-8	2*	Oberpfaffenhofen	Feb–Apr 1945
Total:	42+21*		

** not completed*

Focke-Wulf Ta 152

The Ta 152 was a development of the Focke-Wulf Fw 190, but the prefix was changed from 'Fw' to 'Ta' in recognition of Kurt Tank who headed the design team. It was intended to be produced in at least three versions – the Ta 152H *Höhenjäger* high-altitude fighter, the Ta 152C, which was optimized for low-altitude operations and ground-attack, and the Ta 152E fighter-reconnaissance aircraft. Service trials began in late 1944 and the first production Ta 152H aircraft armed with a 30mm (1.18in) MK 108 and two 20mm (0.79in) MG 151 cannon entered service in January 1945.

Dornier Do 335

In May 1942, Dornier submitted a proposal for a tandem-engine aircraft in response to a requirement for a single-seat high-speed bomber. This Do P.231 was a modified version of a fighter design and was put into development under the designation Do 335. In late 1942, the requirement was altered to one for a heavy fighter and work was delayed while the plans were revised. The first prototype, Do 335 V1, flew in October 1943, surprising test pilots with its speed, acceleration, and general handling – it was a heavy fighter that flew like a light interceptor. The only criticisms concerned the poor rearward visibility and weak landing gear.

Under the *Jägernotprogramm* directive, the Do 335 was one of the types awarded production priority. Pre-production and A-series aircraft were fighter-bombers armed with a 30mm (1.18in) MK103 cannon and two 15mm (0.59in) MG 151 cannon, but the armament of the definitive B-series was increased to three MK 103 and two 20mm (0.79in) MG 151. A few prototypes equipped an operational trials unit, EK 335, but Allied bombing disrupted production and no more than 42 aircraft were completed.

Jet Fighters

The increasingly urgent need to counter the Allied bombing campaign spurred German designers to produce fighters that were technologically far ahead of their time, but they were too few in number and too late to affect the outcome of the air war.

Heinkel He 280

In late 1939, Heinkel began the He 280 project on its own initiative after the world's first practical jet, the He 178, had failed to attract official support. The first prototype was completed in the summer of 1940, but delays in the development of its HeS 8 engine confined it to flight trials in glider configuration. It was not until 30 March 1941 that the second prototype made its first powered flight, but failed to impress General Ernst Udet, head of the Air Ministry's development wing.

Heinkel continued to develop the type despite the lack of official backing and arranged for trials that pitted it against the Focke-Wulf Fw 190, the best contemporary German fighter. In one trial, the He 280 completed four laps of an oval course before the Fw 190 could complete three, while in a later mock combat, it convincingly out-fought the Focke-Wulf. This was sufficient to win an order for 20 pre-production aircraft, to be followed by an initial production run of 300 machines, which were intended to be armed with three 20mm (0.79in) MG 151 cannon.

Chronic engine problems continued to plague the project and a range of alternatives were tried, including the Argus As 014 pulse jet of the V1, which quickly proved to be impractical for use in manned aircraft. This search for viable alternatives delayed the programme so badly that it was cancelled in March 1943 as its development was overtaken by the Me 262.

Messerschmitt Me 262

The Me 262 originated with a 1938 contract awarded to Messerschmitt to design an airframe around axial-flow turbojets that were under development by BMW. As with almost all German jet engines of the period, these suffered constant problems and the prototype Me 262 first flew on 18 April 1941 powered only by a nose-mounted Jumo 210G piston engine. When the BMW engines did arrive, the Jumo was retained as a safety measure – one which proved essential as both jet engines failed soon after take-off. After further trials, it was decided to replace the malfunctioning BMW engines with the more promising Junkers Jumo 004A turbojets and the first flight with these engines was made on 18 July 1942.

However, the development of the Jumo turbojets was also proving difficult and the programme languished until General Adolf Galland flew one of the prototypes in spring 1943. He was deeply impressed, writing that: '... when asked what it felt like, I said, "It was as though angels were pushing"'. His backing helped to revive official interest in the project, but when the type was demonstrated to Hitler in November 1943, he ordered its development as a high-speed bomber. While his interference was probably not critical, it certainly slowed the process of turning the Me 262 into an effective operational fighter. The delay caused bitter frustration. Galland wrote that:

> *In the last four months [January–April 1944] our day fighters have lost 1000 pilots ... we are numerically inferior and will always remain so ... I believe that a great deal can be achieved with a small number of technically and far superior aircraft such as the [Me] 262 and [Me] 163 ... I would at this moment rather have one Me 262 in action rather than five Bf 109s. I used to say three 109s, but the situation develops and changes.*

Entering service

Nearly eight months after Hitler first saw the aircraft, the first production models finally entered service in July 1944 and proved to be highly effective against USAAF daylight raids once suitable tactics had been devised for

MESSERSCHMITT ME 262 VARIANTS

Type	*Description*
Me 262A-1a *Schwalbe*	The main production version, built as both a fighter and fighter/bomber
Me 262A-1a/R-1	Modified to carry R4M air-to-air rockets
Me 262A-1a/U1	A single prototype fitted with six nose-mounted cannon – two 20 mm (0.79in) MG 151/20, two 30mm (1.18in) MK 103 and two 30mm (1.18in) MK 108
Me 262A-1a/U2	A single night-fighter prototype equipped with FuG 220 Lichtenstein SN-2 radar
Me 262A-1a/U3	An unarmed reconnaissance version produced in small numbers, with two Reihenbilder RB 50/30 cameras mounted in the nose
Me 262A-1a/U4	An experimental bomber destroyer version fitted with a single nose-mounted 50mm (1.97in) MK 214 (or *Bordkanone* BK 5) anti-tank gun
Me 262A-1a/U5	A bomber destroyer armed with six 30mm (1.18in) MK 108 cannon
Me 262A-2a *Sturmvogel*	The definitive bomber version fitted with two 30mm (1.18in) MK 108 and external racks for one 500kg (1100lb) or two 250kg (550lb) bombs
Me 262A-2a/U2	Two prototypes with glazed nose position for a bomb aimer
Me 262A-5a	The definitive reconnaissance version, small numbers of which were in service by the end of the war
Me 262B-1a	A two-seat advanced trainer
Me 262B-1a/U1	Me 262 B-1a trainers converted as interim night fighters, equipped with FuG 218 *Neptun* radar

JET FIGHTERS COMPARED

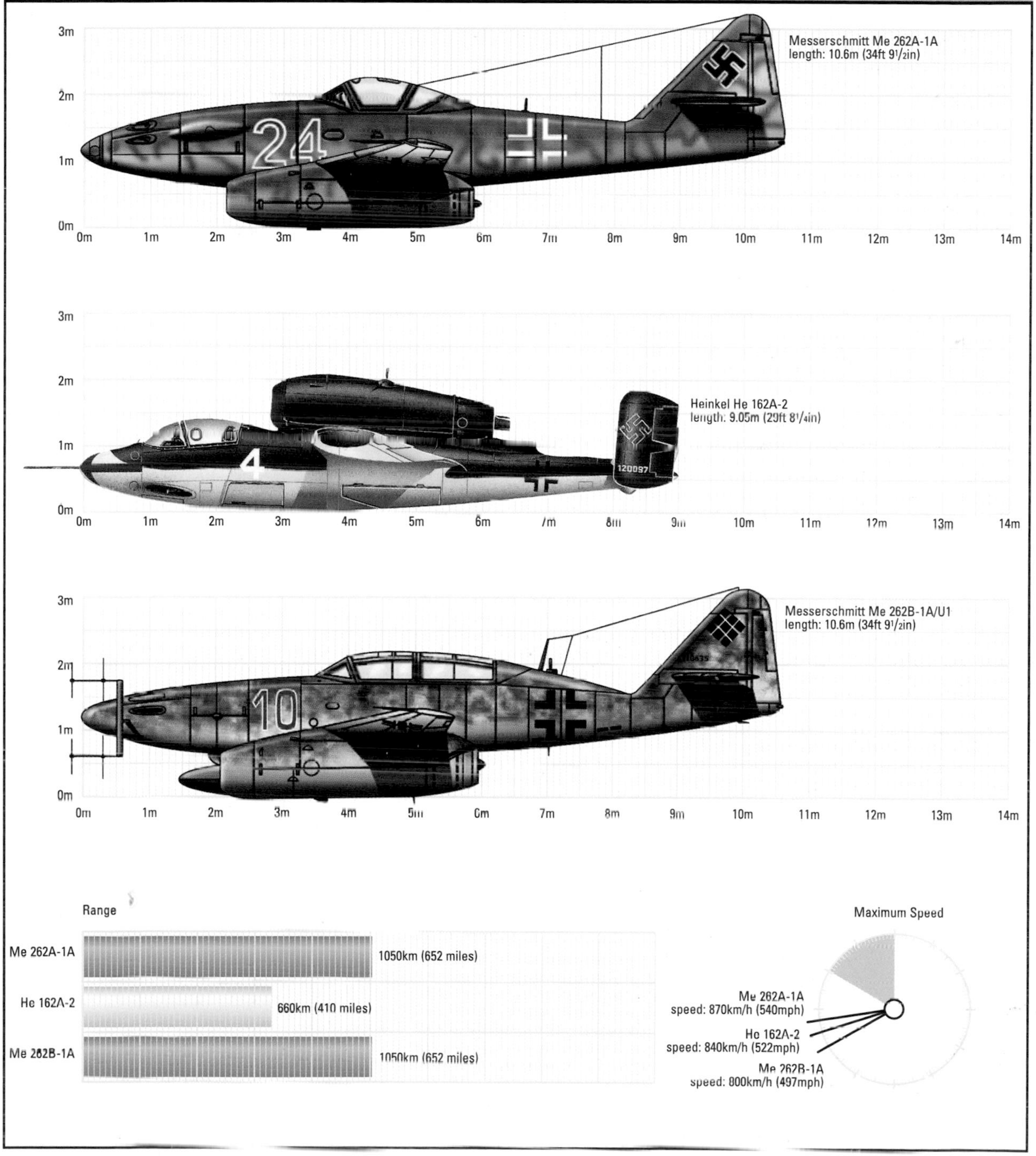
Messerschmitt Me 262A-1A
length: 10.6m (34ft 9¹/₂in)
Heinkel He 162A-2
length: 9.05m (29ft 8¹/₄in)
Messerschmitt Me 262B-1A/U1
length: 10.6m (34ft 9¹/₂in)
Range
Me 262A-1A
1050km (652 miles)
He 162A-2
660km (410 miles)
Me 262B-1A
1050km (652 miles)
Maximum Speed
Me 262A-1A
speed: 870km/h (540mph)
He 162A-2
speed: 840km/h (522mph)
Me 262B-1A
speed: 800km/h (497mph)

JET FIGHTERS COMPARED (CONTINUED)

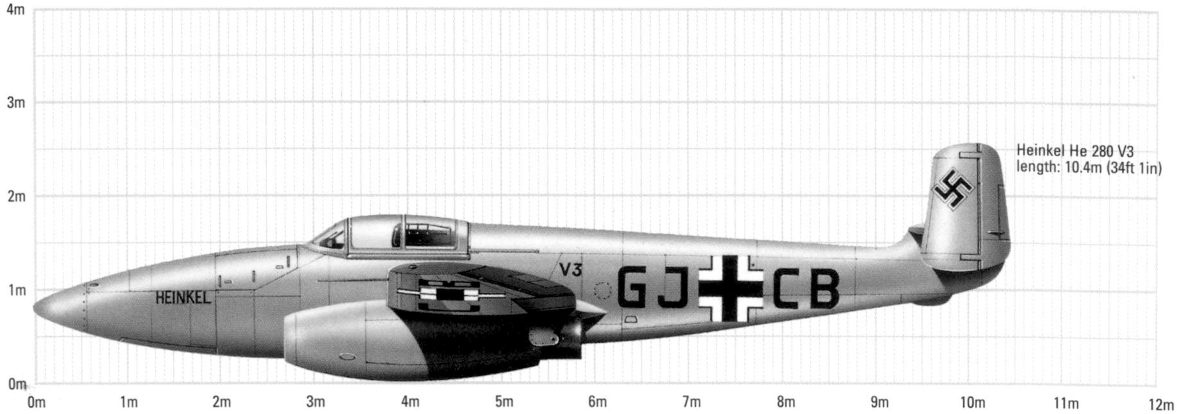
4m
3m
2m
1m
0m
0m
1m
2m
3m
4m
5m
6m
7m
8m
9m
10m
11m
12m
HEINKEL
V3
GJ CB
Heinkel He 280 V3
length: 10.4m (34ft 1in)

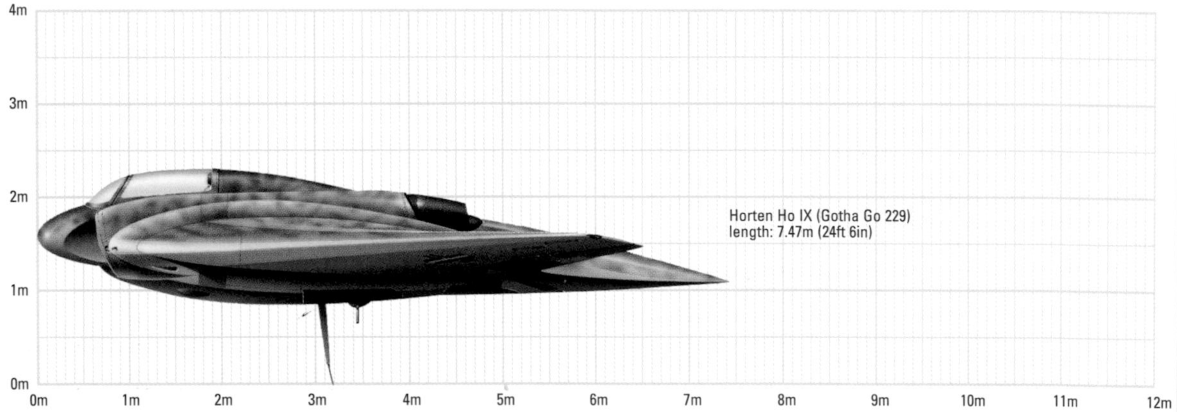
4m
3m
2m
1m
0m
0m
1m
2m
3m
4m
5m
6m
7m
8m
9m
10m
11m
12m
Horten Ho IX (Gotha Go 229)
length: 7.47m (24ft 6in)

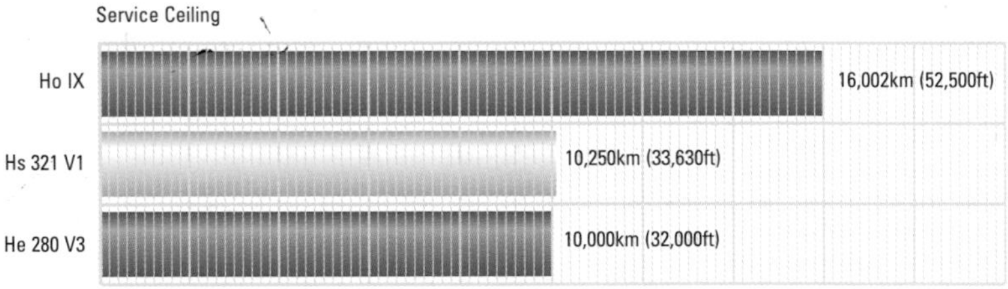
Service Ceiling
Ho IX
16,002km (52,500ft)
Hs 321 V1
10,250km (33,630ft)
He 280 V3
10,000km (32,000ft)

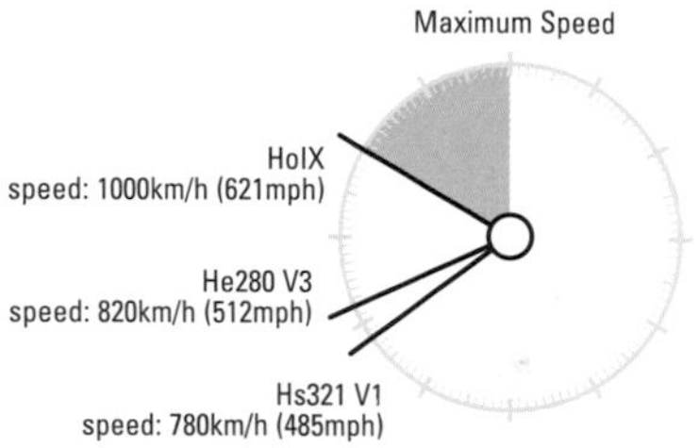
Maximum Speed
HoIX
speed: 1000km/h (621mph)
He280 V3
speed: 820km/h (512mph)
Hs321 V1
speed: 780km/h (485mph)

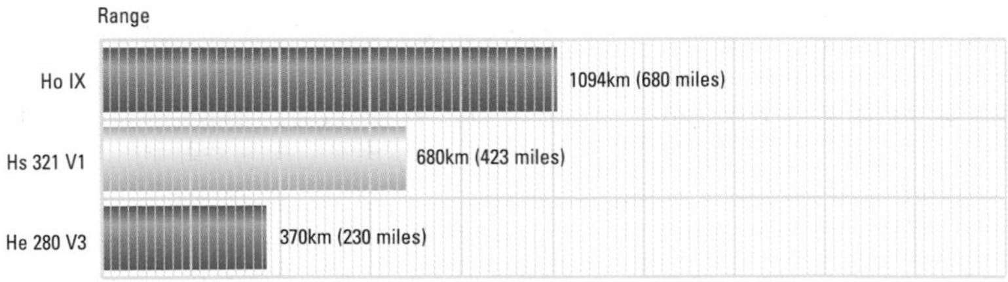
Range
Ho IX
1094km (680 miles)
Hs 321 V1
680km (423 miles)
He 280 V3
370km (230 miles)

HEINKEL HE 162

He 162A-2

4
120097

He 162D

10

Specifications: He 162A-2

Type: Single-seat jet fighter
Powerplant: 1 x BMW 003A-1 800kg (1764lb) thrust turbojet engine
Speed: 840km/h (522mph) at 6000m (19,685ft)
Service Ceiling: 12,040m (39,500ft)
Range: 660km (410 miles)
Weight: 2050kg (4520lb) (empty)
2695kg (5941lb) (maximum take-off weight)
Length: 9.05m (29ft 8¼in)
Height: 2.55m (8ft 4½in)
Span: 7.2m (23ft 7½in)
Armament: 2 x 20mm (0.79in) MG151/20 cannon
No. completed: 116 (including prototypes)

their deployment, but they were still plagued by unreliable engines and majority of the 1294 aircraft produced never saw combat.

Heinkel He 162

Heinkel's little He 162 was a product of desperate times – the outcome of a specification issued on 4 September 1944. The prototype made its first flight on 6 December 1944, which was marred by the loss of one of the plywood undercarriage doors, due to defective bonding. The test pilot, *Flugkapitän* Gotthard Peter, was able to land safely, but was killed on his second test flight when the aircraft crashed after the acidic substitute glue caused a disastrous structural failure of the wooden wings.

Hastily modified second and third prototypes flew in January 1945 and the type entered production the same month. The initial production version was the He 162A-1, which was armed with two 30mm (1.18in) MK 108 cannon whose recoil was found to be too powerful for the lightweight fuselage. As a result, production quickly switched to the He 162A-2, which used two of the lighter 20mm (0.79in) MG 151 cannon. A total of 116 He 162s were completed and over 800 more were under construction at the time of the German surrender. Although it was inadequately developed when it was rushed into service, it had the potential to become a very good interceptor – one *Luftwaffe* fighter pilot described it as '...a first-class combat aircraft'.

Horten Ho IX/Gotha Go 229

The Horten Ho IX fighter-bomber was one of a number of flying wings designed by the Horten brothers. An unpowered prototype flew in March 1944 and Gotha then took over development of a powered version which made its first flight in February 1945. The flight trials were promising and more prototypes were under construction at the end of the war.

Henschel Hs 132 V1

The Hs 132 was developed as a dive-bomber. Its general appearance closely resembled that of the Heinkel He 162, but the pilot lay prone in the cockpit to minimize the effects of the high G-forces involved in dive-bombing attacks. Construction of the first prototype began in March 1945, but it was still incomplete when it was captured by Soviet forces in May 1945.

In Combat

By March 1944, the Luftwaffe's *fighter arm was suffering from the effects of prolonged attrition of both aircraft and aircrew.*

Adolf Galland had to appeal for volunteers to fill the gaps in the ranks of the fighter squadrons:

The strained manpower situation in units operating in defence of the Reich demands urgently the further transfer of experienced flying personnel from other arms of the service, in particular … tried pilots of the ground attack and bomber units.

Although the number of newly-qualified fighter pilots had risen from 1662 in 1942 to 3276 in 1943, this was barely adequate to make up for the 2870 lost in the same period. In order to achieve these figures, flying hours at the training schools had been cut to less than half those of their British and US counterparts. By 1944–45, declining standards had created a 'two-tier' *Luftwaffe* – a small number of *experten* and a far larger number of pilots who could not survive for long in combat. Significantly, only eight of the 107 German pilots with scores of 100 or more victories joined their squadrons after mid-1942.

The Allied attacks on German synthetic fuel plants in early 1944 created such dire fuel shortages that training flights had to be further restricted, leading to Adolf Galland's appeal for volunteers from bomber and ground-attack units who could convert to fighters. However, even the best bomber aircrew would need time to become good fighter pilots, time that the Allied air forces had no intention of giving them, as an Ultra decrypt of a report from *Luftflotte Reich* on 24 March 1944 indicated:

LUFTFLOTTE REICH, GROUND-ATTACK AIRCRAFT (JAN 1945)

Luftwaffe *Unit*	*Type*	*Strength*	*Serviceable*
NSGr. 1	Ju 87D	8	1
NSGr. 2	Ju 87D	5	5
NSGr. 20	Fw 190	27	11
I/KG 200	Various	n/k	n/k
II/KG 200	*Mistel*	Ju 188	Ju 188
Ju 88			
Ju 188			
III/KG 200	Fw 190	31	21
KG 200	total	ca. 100	ca. 60

KG 76 JET BASES (JUN 1944–APR 1945)

Unit	*Date*	*Base*
Stab	Jun 1944	Alt-Lönnewitz
	Feb 1945	Achmer
	Mar 1945	Karstädt
II/KG 76	Aug 1944	Burg
	Mar 1945	Scheppern
III/KG 76	Jun 1944	Alt-Lönnewitz
	Dec 1944	Burg, Münster-Handorf
	Jan 1945	Achmer
	Mar 1945	Marx
	Apr 1945	Kalternkirchen
IV/KG 76	Oct 1944	Alt-Lönnewitz

LUFTFLOTTE REICH, DAY FIGHTERS (JAN 1945)			
Luftwaffe *Unit*	*Type*	*Strength*	*Serviceable*
I/JG 2	Fw 190	5	3
II/JG 2	Fw 190	8	4
III/JG 2	Fw 190	12	9
Stab/JG 4	Fw 190	6	4
II/JG 4	Fw 190	50	34
III/JG 4	Bf 109	61	56
Stab/JG 7	Me 262A-1	5	4
I/JG 7	Me 262A-1	41	36
II/JG 7	Me 262A-1	30	23
Stab/JG 26	Fw 190	4	3
I/JG 26	Fw 190	44	16
II/JG 26	Fw 190	57	29
III/JG 26	Fw 190	35	15
I/JG 27	Bf 109	29	13
II/JG 27	Bf 109	48	27
III/JG 27	Bf 109	19	15
I (J.)/KG 54	Me 262A-1	37	21
Stab/JG 301	Ta 152H	3	2
I/JG 301	Fw 190	35	24
II/JG 301	Fw 190	32	15
II/JG 400	Me 163A	38	22
JGr. 10	Fw 190	15	9
Jagdverband 44	Me 262A-1	c.30	c.15

During flights into the home war zone, enemy fighters have repeatedly carried out attacks on aircraft which were landing or on the airfields themselves. In doing so, they imitate the landing procedure of German fighters or effect surprise by approaching the airfield in fast and level flight. The difficulty in distinguishing friend from foe often makes it impossible for flak to fire on them.

New units

In April 1944, *Erprobungskommando 262* was formed at Lechfeld in Bavaria as a trials unit (*Jäger Erprobungskommando Thierfelder*) to introduce the Messerschmitt Me 262 into service and train a cadre of pilots on the aircraft. On 25 July 1944, *Leutnant* Alfred Schreiber scored the world's first jet victory when he damaged a Mosquito reconnaissance aircraft of No. 544 Squadron, which was destroyed in a crash landing at an air base in Italy.

Major Walter Nowotny took over command after the death of Werner Thierfelder in July 1944, and the unit was redesignated as *Kommando Nowotny*. Initial operational missions in August 1944 allegedly shot down 19 Allied aircraft for the loss of six Me 262s, although these claims have never been verified.

Nowotny was killed in action on 8 November 1944 and the *Kommando* was then withdrawn for further training in revised combat tactics to exploit the Me 262's strengths.

In January 1945, *Jagdgeschwader 7* (JG 7) was formed as a jet fighter unit, although it would be several weeks before it was operational. In the meantime, a bomber unit – *I Gruppe, Kampfgeschwader 54* (KG 54) – re-equipped with the Me 262A-2a fighter-bomber for the ground-attack role, but the unit had minimal success and lost 12 jets in action in only two weeks.

JV 44

The elite *Jagdverband 44* (JV 44) was another Me 262 fighter unit formed in February 1945 by Lieutenant General

LUFTWAFFENKOMMANDO WEST, DAY FIGHTER AND BOMBERS (JAN 1945)			
Luftwaffe *Unit*	*Type*	*Strength*	*Serviceable*
Stab/JG 53	Bf 109	1	1
II/JG 53	Bf 109	39	24
III/JG 53	Bf 109	40	24
IV/JG 53	Bf 109	54	27
I/KG 51	Me 262A-2	15	11
II/KG 51	Me 262A-2	6	2
Stab/KG 76	Ar 234B	2	2
II/KG 76	Ar 234B	5	1
III/KG 76	Ar 234B	5	1

Adolf Galland, who had recently been dismissed as Inspector of Fighters after arguments with Hermann Göring over *Luftwaffe* operational policies. Galland was able to recruit many of the most experienced and decorated *Luftwaffe* fighter pilots from other units grounded by lack of fuel.

Records suggest the unit shot down about 47 Allied aircraft between April and May 1945. *Oberstleutnant* Heinz Bär was the unit's top scorer with 16 kills, while *Hauptmann* Georg-Peter Eder scored at least 12 victories. Galland himself claimed seven kills before being wounded in action.

During March 1945, jet fighter units began attacks on Allied bomber formations. On 18 March, 37 Me 262s of JG 7 intercepted a force of 1221 bombers and 632 escorting fighters, shooting down 12 bombers and one fighter for the loss of three Me 262s. Although this 4:1 ratio was what the

JET ACES OF THE *LUFTWAFFE*

Name	*Rank*	*Victories*	*Unit*	*Total*	*Notes*
Kurt Welter	*Oberleutnant*	20+[(a)]	*Kdo Welter*, 10./NJG 11	63	Possibly the all-time leading jet ace
Heinrich Bar	*Oberstleutnant*	16	EJG 2, JV 44	220	
Franz Schall*	*Hauptmann*	14	*Kdo Nowotny*, JG 7	137	Killed in flying accident 10 April 1945
Hermann Buchner	*Oberfeldwebel*	12	*Kdo Nowotny*, JG 7	58	
Georg-Peter Eder	Major	12	*Kdo Nowotny*, JG 7	78	Wounded 16 February 1945
Erich Rudorffer	Major	12	JG 7	222	
Karl Schnörrer	*Leutnant*	11	EKdo 262, *Kdo Nowotny*, JG 7	46	Wounded 30 March 1945
Erich Büttner*	*Oberfeldwebel*	8	EKdo 262, *Kdo Nowotny*, JG 7	8	Killed in action 20 March 1945
Helmut Lennartz	*Feldwebel*	8	EKdo 262, *Kdo Nowotny*, JG 7	13	First aerial victory over a B-17 Flying Fortress by a jet fighter on 15 August 1944
Rudolf Rademacher	*Leutnant*	8	JG 7	126	
Walther Schuck	*Oberleutnant*	8	JG 7	206	
Günther Wegmann	*Oberleutnant*	8	EKdo 262, JG 7	14	Wounded 18 March 1945
Hans-Dieter Weihs	*Leutnant*	8	JG 7	8	Midair collision with Hans Waldmann on 18 March 1945, killing Waldmann
Theodor Weissenberger	Major	8	JG 7	208	
Alfred Ambs	*Leutnant*	7	JG 7	7	
Heinz Arnold*	*Oberfeldwebel*	7	JG 7	49	Killed in action 17 April 1945. Arnold's Me 262 A-1a W.Nr.500491 'Yellow 7' of II./JG 7 bearing his personal victory marks is now on display at the Smithsonian Institution, Washington, D.C., USA.
Karl-Heinz Becker	*Feldwebel*	7	10./NJG 11	7	
Adolf Galland	*Generalleutnant*	7	JV 44	104	Wounded 26 April 1945
Franz Köster	*Unteroffizier*	7	EJG 2, JG 7, JV 44	7	
Fritz Muller	*Leutnant*	6	JG 7	22	
Johannes Steinhoff	*Oberst*	6	JG 7, JV 44	176	Wounded 18 April 1945
Helmut Baudach*	*Oberfeldwebel*	5	*Kdo Nowotny*, JG 7	20	Killed in action 22 February 1945
Heinrich Ehrler*	Major	5	JG 7	206	Killed in action 4 April 1945
Hans Grünberg	*Oberleutnant*	5	JG 7, JV 44	82	
Joseph Heim*	*Gefreiter*	5	JG 7	5	Killed in action 10 April 1945
Klaus Neumann	*Leutnant*	5	JG 7, JV 44	37	
Alfred Schreiber*	*Leutnant*	5	*Kdo Nowotny*, JG 7	5	First jet ace in aviation history. Killed in flying accident 26 November 1944
Wolfgang Späte	Major	5	(JG 400), JV 44	99	

Footnotes:
(a) Kurt Welter is credited in excess of 20 aerial victories while flying the Me 262, but the exact number is disputed.
** Killed in action or in a flying accident*

ADOLF 'DOLFO' JOSEPH FERDINAND GALLAND

■ Despite his eventual promotion to General der Jagdflieger, Adolf Galland always remained a flamboyant fighter pilot at heart.

Galland joined the still-secret *Luftwaffe* in 1933. He flew ground-attack missions with the Condor Legion during the Spanish Civil War and transferred to fighters in 1940, scoring an official total of 94 victories before being appointed *General der Jagdflieger*, the head of the *Luftwaffe's* fighter arm. He test-flew prototypes of the Me 262 jet fighter and pressed for its urgent introduction to service before being demoted in early 1945 after violent disagreements with Göring about the command of the *Luftwaffe*. In the last months of the war, he commanded the elite *Jagdverband 44* equipped with Me 262s, scoring a further seven victories by the end of the war.

BIRTH:	19 March 1912
DEATH:	9 February 1996
PLACE OF BIRTH:	Westerholt, Lower Saxony
FATHER:	Adolf Galland
MOTHER:	Anne Galland
SIBLINGS:	Fritz Galland, Paul Galland and Wilhelm-Ferdinand Galland
PERSONAL RELATIONSHIPS:	Sylvinia, Countess von Donhoff, married 12 February 1954. Hannelies, married 1963. Two children, Andreas-Hubertus (1966) and Alexandra-Isabella (1969) Heidi Horn, married 1984
EDUCATION:	Hindenburg High School, Buer
KEY PRE-WAR AND WARTIME POSITIONS:	*Staffelkaptan 3. Staffel J/88*, Condor Legion, flying approximately 300 ground-attack missions (1937–39). Transferred from ground-attack unit to the fighter arm (1940). Steadily promoted, scoring 94 confirmed aerial victories (1940–41). Appointed *General der Jagdflieger* (November 1941). Demoted to command *Jagdverband 44* (March–May 1945)

Luftwaffe needed to make an impact on the air war, this was a minor success, as it represented only one per cent of the attacking force. In 1943–44, the USAAF had been able to maintain its bombing offensive despite losses of 5 per cent or more. The Me 262s were simply too few to matter.

Several two-seat Me 262 trainers were adapted as night fighters and served with *10 Staffel, Nachtjagdgeschwader 11*. This handful of aircraft (together with a few single-seat Me 262s) accounted for most of the 13 Mosquitoes lost over Berlin in the first three months of 1945. However, most of these kills were made using *Wilde Sau* methods, rather than AI radar-controlled interception.

Anti-bomber tactics

The Me 262's high speed dictated a different approach against bomber formations to the head-on attacks often used by piston-engined fighters. The most effective manoeuvre proved to be for the Me 262s to close in from above and astern the bombers, then dive below their formation to gain speed before climbing again and

LUFTWAFFE AND ALLIED JET FIGHTERS COMPARED

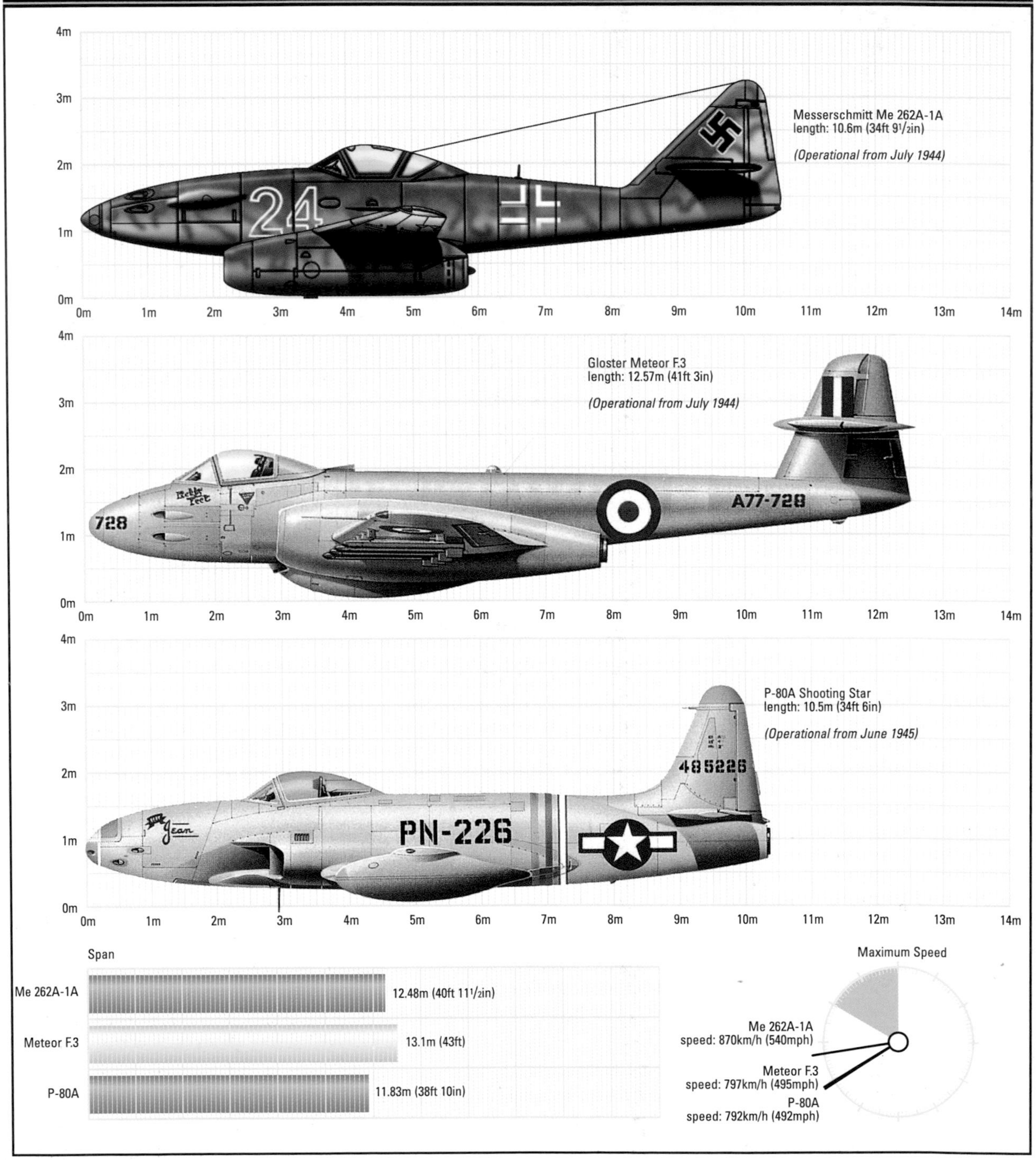
Messerschmitt Me 262A-1A
length: 10.6m (34ft 9½in)
(Operational from July 1944)
Gloster Meteor F.3
length: 12.57m (41ft 3in)
(Operational from July 1944)
P-80A Shooting Star
length: 10.5m (34ft 6in)
(Operational from June 1945)
Span
Me 262A-1A
12.48m (40ft 11½in)
Meteor F.3
13.1m (43ft)
P-80A
11.83m (38ft 10in)
Maximum Speed
Me 262A-1A
speed: 870km/h (540mph)
Meteor F.3
speed: 797km/h (495mph)
P-80A
speed: 792km/h (492mph)

opening fire. The gunners of Allied bombers found that their fire was largely ineffective as powered turrets had problems in tracking jets closing in at high speeds.

The introduction of the R4M rocket and EZ 42 gyro gunsight dramatically increased the Me 262's effectiveness, allowing attacks from beyond the effective range of the bombers' defensive fire and it was fortunate for the Allies that this equipment only entered service in very small numbers in the last weeks of the war.

The obvious threat posed by the Me 262 drove the Allied air forces to develop urgent counter-measures. Allied escort fighters flew high above the bombers, ready to dive on attacking jets – the acceleration gained in their dives dramatically cut the jets' speed advantage. The Me 262 was less manoeuverable than conventional fighters, which could deal with any jet whose pilot was unwise enough to engage in a dogfight rather than exploiting his speed advantage by fighting on the dive and the climb.

However, it was soon found that the only reliable way of dealing with the jets and rocket fighters was to attack them on the ground and during take-off and landing. Their airfields were subjected to repeated bombing and Allied fighters patrolled the area waiting to attack jets trying to land. The *Luftwaffe* countered by setting up flak alleys along the main flight paths to protect the Me 262s and providing top cover with conventional fighters (mainly Fw 190s and Ta 152s) during take-off and landing.

Nevertheless, throughout March and April 1945, Allied fighter patrols over the airfields inflicted serious losses and considerably reduced the effectiveness of the *Luftwaffe*'s jets.

Rocket Fighters

Rocket-propelled fighters seemed to be the answer to the problem of defending key industrial and military targets against Allied bombing. Unfortunately, the technology of the period could only produce aircraft with extremely limited range, whose highly volatile fuels made them more dangerous to their pilots than to the enemy.

Messerschmitt Me 163 *Komet*

The prototype Me 163 first flew as a glider in early 1941, followed by powered flights in August of the same year. These demonstrated both the type's amazing performance and its dire problems. Although speeds of up to 885km/h (533mph) were regularly attained, the liquid rocket fuels were dangerously unstable and highly corrosive. Fuel consumption was also far higher than predicted and these problems were to persist throughout the service life of the aircraft.

Essential modifications were not completed until mid-1943 when the definitive Me 163B began powered flight trials. Even in its final form, the Me 163B1a had considerable problems – the fuels of its Walter HWK 509A-2 rocket motor were only slightly less dangerous than those of the prototypes and the lack of a conventional undercarriage caused innumerable problems. Take-off was made on a two-wheeled dolly, which was jettisoned immediately afterwards. The aircraft landed on a retractable skid beneath the forward fuselage and the tail wheel.

The first production aircraft began to equip *Jagdgeschwader 400* (JG 400), commanded by Major Wolfgang Späte in May 1944. The unit soon found that the Me 163 posed some unique problems. One of these became apparent during the type's first combat on 28 July when five *Komets* unsuccessfully attacked a USAAF bomber formation near Merseburg. They closed in at about 900km/h (559mph) on bombers cruising at roughly 402km/h (250mph) which gave time for no more than a three-second burst from the fighters' two 30mm (1.18in) MK 108 cannon before they had to break away to avoid collision.

Only a few exceptionally skilled pilots were able to get lethal hits on

ROCKET FIGHTERS COMPARED

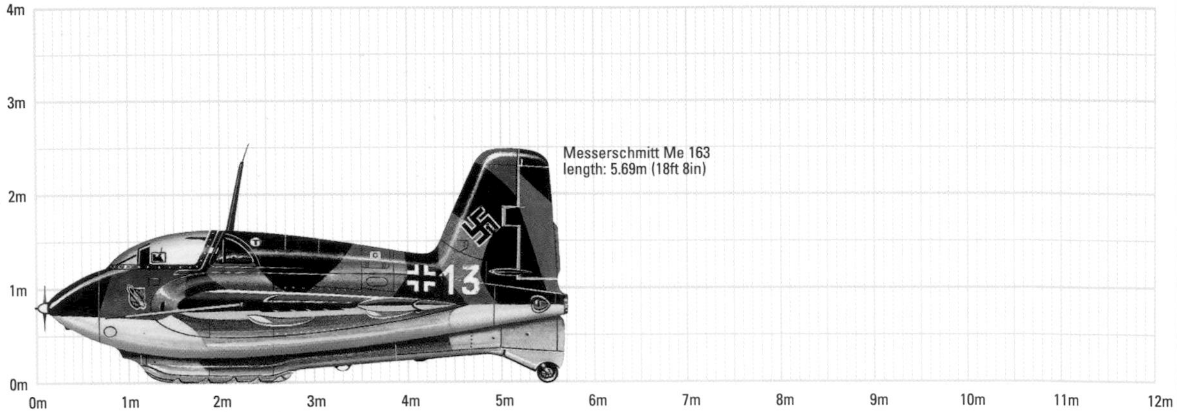
Messerschmitt Me 163
length: 5.69m (18ft 8in)
4m
3m
2m
1m
0m
0m
1m
2m
3m
4m
5m
6m
7m
8m
9m
10m
11m
12m

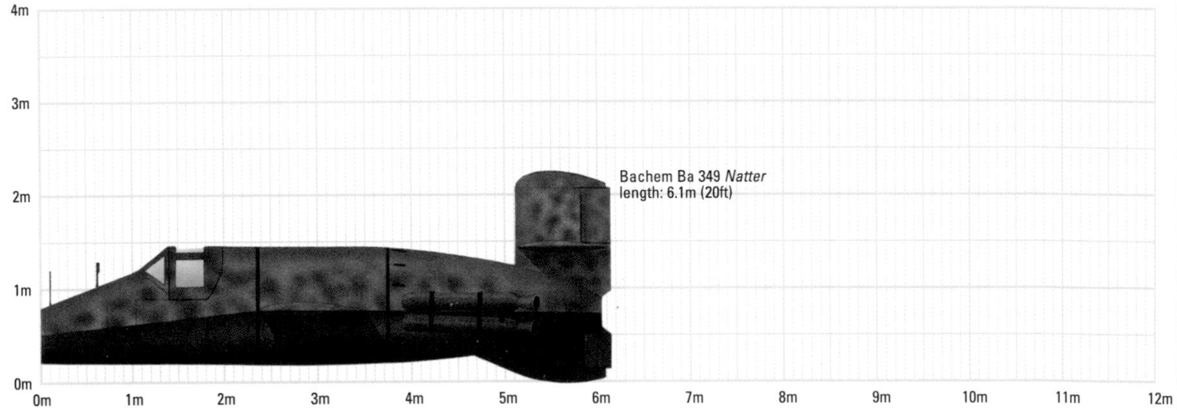
Bachem Ba 349 *Natter*
length: 6.1m (20ft)
4m
3m
2m
1m
0m
0m
1m
2m
3m
4m
5m
6m
7m
8m
9m
10m
11m
12m

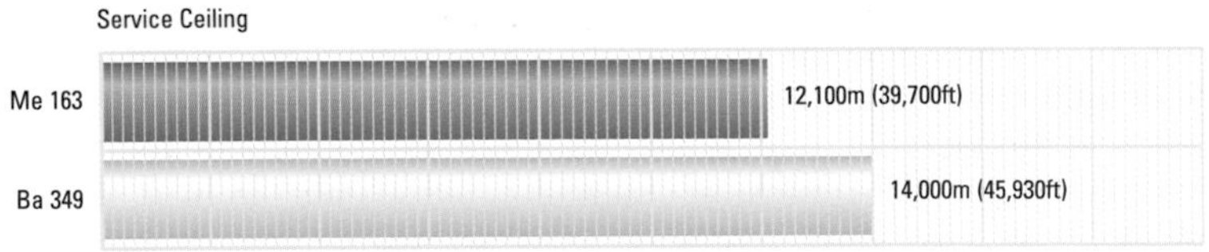
Service Ceiling
Me 163
12,100m (39,700ft)
Ba 349
14,000m (45,930ft)

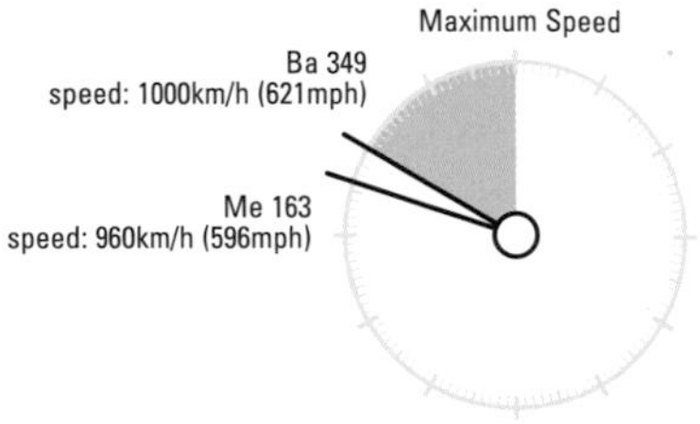
Maximum Speed
Ba 349
speed: 1000km/h (621mph)
Me 163
speed: 960km/h (596mph)

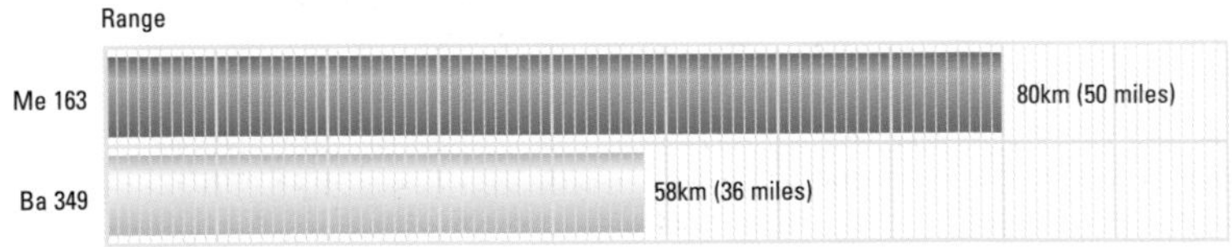
Range
Me 163
80km (50 miles)
Ba 349
58km (36 miles)

LUFTWAFFE JET AND ROCKET UNITS: SERVICE HISTORY

Aircraft Type	*Unit*	*Date*	*Movements*
Heinkel He 162	JG1 *Stab* (Staff Flight)	8 April 1945	Re-equipped with the He 162A at Ludwigslust airfield, Mecklenburg-Schwerin
		30 April 1945	Transferred to Leck air base, Schleswig-Holstein
		8 May 1945	Surrendered to British forces
	I/JG1	9 February 1945	Began training on the He 162 at Parchim, Mecklenburg-Vorpommern
		9 April 1945	Moved to Ludwigslust airfield, Mecklenburg-Schwerin
		15 April 1945	Withdrew to Leck airbase, Schleswig-Holstein
		8 May 1945	Surrendered to British forces
	II/JG1	7 April 1945	Re-equipped with the He 162 at Warnemünde, Mecklenburg Vorpommern
		30 April 1945	Transferred to Leck airbase, Schleswig-Holstein
		8 May 1945	Surrendered to British forces
Messerschmitt Me 262	*Kommando Nowotny*	26 September 1944	Formed at Achmer and Hesepe
		3 October 1944	Attained operational status with about 40 Me 262A-1a interceptors
		19 November 1944	Redesignated as III/JG7
	JG 7 *'NowotnyStab*	December 1944	Re-equipped with the Me 262 at Brandenburg-Briest, west of Berlin
		11 April 1945	Withdrew to Saatz, Sudetenland
		8 May 1945	Surrendered to Allied forces
	I/JG7	1 December 1944	Began converting to the Me 262 at Unterschlauersbach/Lechfeld, Bavaria
		8 January 1945	Transferred to Brandenburg-Briest
		9 February 1945	Moved to Kaltenkirchen
		1 April 1945	Returned to Brandenburg-Briest
		11 April 1945	Transferred to Brandis, near Leipzig
		17 April 1945	Withdrew to Prague-Rusin and Saatz
		8 May 1945	Surrendered to Allied forces
	II/JG7	7 February 1945	Re-equipped with the Me 262 at Brandenburg-Briest
		10 April 1945	Moved to Parchim, Mecklenburg Vorpommern
		20 April 1945	Withdrew to Prague-Rusin and Saat
		8 May 1945	Surrendered to Allied forces
	III/JG7	19 November 1944	Formed at Lechfeld, near Augsburg, with the Me 262s and personnel of *Kommando Nowotny*
		10 December 1944	Moved to Brandenburg-Briest
		20 February 1945	Transferred to Parchim, Mecklenburg Vorpommern
		11 April 1945	Withdrew to Brandis, near Leipzig
		20 April 1945	Evacuated to Prague-Rusin
		7 May 1945	Surrendered to Allied forces
	IV/JG7	3 May 1945	Formed at Salzburg-Maxglam, Austria with the Me 262s and personnel from JV44
		8 May 1945	Surrendered to Allied forces
	Jagdverband 44	10 January 1945	Formed at Brandenburg-Briest with 60 Me 262A and many elite pilots
		3 April 1945	Transferred to München-Riem, near Munich
		29 April 1945	Withdrew to Salzburg-Maxglan, Austria
		3 May 1945	Became III/JG7
	III/NJG11	28 January 1945	Formed at Burg bei Magdeburg from the operational trials unit *Sonderkommando Welter*, a unit testing the standard Me 262A-1a as a *'Wilde Sau'* night fighter
		12 April 1945	Transferred to Lübeck
		21 April 1945	Withdrew to Reinfeld
		7 May 1945	Evacuated to Schleswig-Jagel
		8 May 1945	Surrendered

LUFTWAFFE JET AND ROCKET UNITS: SERVICE HISTORY (CONTINUED)

Aircraft Type	*Unit*	*Date*	*Movements*
Messerschmitt Me 262	*Sonderkommando Braunegg*	November 1944	Formed at Münster-Handorf with Me 262A-1a/U3 reconnaissance aircraft, serving under *Versuchsverband OKL*
		6 February 1945	Became *Stab* and 2/NAGr.6
	KG 6 *Stab*	January 1945	Began converting to the Me 262A at Prague-Rusin
		April 1945	Withdrew to Graz, Austria
	III/KG6	October 1944	Began converting to the Me 262A at Prague-Rusin
		9 April 1945	Withdrew to Graz
		5 May 1945	Surrendered
	KG 51 *'Edelweiss' Stab*	August 1944	Began converting to the Me 262A at Landsberg/Lech
		November 1944	Transferred to Rheine/ Hörstel/Hopsten
		20 March 1945	Moved to Giebelstadt
		30 March 1945	Withdrew to Leipheim
		21 April 1945	Evacuated to Memmingen
		24 April 1945	Moved to Holzkirchen
		30 April 1945	Disbanded
	I/KG51	23 May 1944	Began converting to the Me 262A from the Me 410 at Lechfeld/ Leipheim
		20 July 1944	Transferred to Chateaudun
		12 August 1944	Transferred to Etampes
		15 August 1944	Moved to Creil
		27 Aug–5 Sept 1944	Withdrawn to Rheine/Hörstel/Hopsten
		20 March 1945	Transferred to Giebelstadt
		30 March 1945	Moved to Leipheim
		21 April 1945	Withdrew to Memmingen
		24 April 1945	A further withdrawal to München-Riem
		30 April 1945	Evacuated to Prague-Rusin
		6 May 1945	Transferred to Saaz
		8 May 1945	Surrendered
	II/KG51	15 August 1944	Began converting to the Me 262A from the Me 410 at Schwäbisch-Hall
		31 December 1944	Transferred to Achmer
		10 January 1945	Moved to Essen-Mülheim
		21 March 1945	Withdrew to Schwäbisch-Hall
		30 March 1945	Evacuated to Fürth and Linz/Hörsching
	KG 54 *'Totenkopf'* Stab	22 August 1944	Converted to the Me 262A from Ju 88s at Giebelstadt
	I/KG54	22 August 1944	Converted to the Me 262A from Ju 88s at Giebelstadt
		28 March 1945	Transferred to Zerbst
		14 April 1945	Withdrew to Prague-Rusin
		7 May 1945	Evacuated to Saaz
		8 May 1945	Surrendered
	II/KG54	5 January 1945	Became operational with the Me 262A at Gardelegen
		13 January 1945	Transferred to Kitzingen
		28 March 1945	Moved to Fürstenfeldbruck
		21 April 1945	Withdrew to Waltersdorf-Miesbach
		30 April 1945	Evacuated to Fischbachau-Schliersee
		3 May 1945	Surrendered

Aircraft Type	*Unit*	*Date*	*Movements*
Messerschmitt Me 262	III/KG54	6 September 1944	Converted to the Me 262 from Ju 88s at Neuburg/Donau
		21 April 1945	Transferred to Erding
		1 May 1945	Withdrew to Prien/Chiemsee
		3 May 194	Surrendered
Messerschmitt Me 163	JG 400 *Stab*	December 1944	Formed at Brandis, near Leipzig
		7 March 1945	Disbanded
	I/JG400	July 1944	Began equipping with the Me 163 at Venlo, Holland
		August 1944	Transferred to Brandis
		19 April 1945	Disbanded
	II/JG400	November 1944	Formed at Stargard-Klutzow, Mecklenburg Vorpommern
		December 1944	Transferred to Brandis
		February 1945	Moved to Salzwedel, Saxony-Anhalt
		April 1945	Evacuated to Nordholz, near Cuxhaven
		May 1945	Withdrew to Husum, Schleswig-Holstein
	III/JG400	21 July 1944	Formed at Brandis as *Erg.Staffel/JG400* from *Ausb.Kdo./Erprobungskommando 16*
		September 1944	Transferred to Udetfeld, Poland
		March 1945	Withdrew to Brandis
Arado Ar 234	*Sonderkommando Götz*	September 1944	Formed at Rheine with four Ar 234B-1 reconnaissance aircraft, with crews drawn from *1/Versuchsverband OKL*. Its primary role was to undertake strategic reconnaissance missions over Britain
		January 1945	Disbanded
	Sonderkommando Hecht/ Sonderkommando Sommer	November 1944	Formed at Udine, Italy as *Sonderkommando Hecht* with four Ar 234B-1 reconnaissance aircraft
		February 1945	Redesignated *Sonderkommando Sommer* on the transfer of command to Olt. Erich Sommer. The three remaining serviceable Arados continued to operate from Udine until the end of the war
	Sonderkommando Sperling	November 1944	Formed at Rheine with Ar 234B reconnaissance aircraft, with crews drawn from *1/Versuchskommando OKL*
		January 1945	Disbanded and absorbed by 1(F)/Aufkl.Gr.100
	KG 76 *Stab*	10 June 1944	Began converting from Ju 88s to Ar 234s at Alt-Lönnewitz
		13 February 1945	Transferred to Achmer
		March 1945	Withdrew to Karstädt
	II/KG76	August 1944	Converted from Ju 88s to Ar 234s at Burg
		March 1945	Withdrew to Scheppern
	III/KG76	10 June 1944	Began converting from Ju 88s to Ar 234s at Alt-Lönnewitz
		December 1944	Transferred to Burg
		23 January 1945	Moved to Achmer
		March 1945	Withdrew to Marx
		April 1945	Kaltenkirchen
	IV/KG76	August 1944	Converted from Ju 88s to Ar 234s at Alt-Lönnewitz
		31 December 1944	Disbanded

their targets in such circumstances and research urgently began into more effective alternative armament. It is likely that a few aircraft were fitted with R4M air-to-air rockets and at least one *Komet* seems to have been flown with the SG 500 *Jagdfaust*. This comprised a bank of five upward-firing 50mm (1.97in) recoilless guns in each wing root, salvo-fired by a photo-electric mechanism as the aircraft flew beneath a bomber formation. Reports indicate at least one kill, a Halifax of No. 6 (RCAF) Group, which was destroyed during a daylight raid on Leipzig on 10 April 1945.

Between May 1944 and the end of the war, it is estimated that only about 100 of the 400 *Komets* completed were issued to fighter units. They destroyed no more than 16 Allied aircraft for the loss of 15 Me 163s. *Feldwebel* Siegfried Schubert was the most successful pilot with three bombers to his credit.

Bachem Ba 349 *Natter*

Eric Bachem's *Natter* was developed under the Emergency Fighter Programme (*Jägernotprogramm*) after Bachem managed to secure the support of *Reichsfuhrer* SS Heinrich Himmler.

The tiny point-defence interceptor was largely of laminated wood construction and was powered by a Walter 509A-2 rocket motor. It took off vertically from a 15m (49ft) launch tower, with four jettisonable solid-fuel Scmidding rocket boosters blasting it to 700km/h (435mph) in 10 seconds. As G-forces could cause the pilot to temporarily black-out on take-off, the *Natter* was launched on auto-pilot.

The pilot would take control on reaching a position above and ahead of the bombers and jettison the plastic nose cone covering the battery of 24 x 73mm (2.87in) Fohn rockets or 33 x 55mm (2.17in) R4M rockets. These were aimed by a simple ring sight and fired in a single salvo at close range as the *Natter* dived towards the bombers. It was originally intended that the aircraft would then be set on a ramming course before the pilot bailed out, but this near-suicidal requirement was dropped.

Bailing out was in any case quite hazardous enough – the pilot unfastened his harness, then released catches which freed the entire fuselage forward of his seat. The aircraft then broke apart, with the pilot and rear fuselage landing under separate parachutes – the idea being to re-use the Walter rocket motor.

Trials

Several prototypes were used in manned and unmanned gliding trials between November 1944 and February 1945 when the SS insisted on a fully powered test flight to assess the aircraft's real performance. This took place on

PARASITE FIGHTERS FULL SPECIFICATIONS COMPARED

	Arado Ar E.381 I	*Arado Ar E.381 II*	*Arado Ar E.381 III*
Type	Single-seat parasite miniature rocket interceptor	Single-seat parasite miniature rocket interceptor	Single-seat parasite miniature rocket interceptor
Powerplant	1 x 2000kg (4410lb) thrust Walter 509B liquid-fuel rocket engine	1 x 2000 kg (4410lb) thrust Walter 509B liquid-fuel rocket engine	1 x 2000 kg (4410lb) thrust Walter 509B liquid-fuel rocket engine
Speed	900km/h (559mph)	885km/h (550mph)	895km/h (556mph)
Range	100km (63 miles) after release at an altitude of 7000m (22,695ft)	100km (63 miles) after release at an altitude of 7000m (22,695ft)	100km (63 miles) after release at an altitude of 7000m (22,695ft)
Loaded Weight	1200kg (2646lb)	1265kg (2789lb)	1500kg (3307lb)
Length	4.69m (15ft 4in)	4.95m (16ft 3in)	5.7m (18ft 8in)
Height	1.29m (4ft 3in)	1.15m (3ft 9in)	1.51m (4ft 11in)
Span	4.43m (14ft 6in)	5m (16ft 5in)	5.05m (16ft 7in)
Armament	1 x 30mm (1.18in) MK 108 cannon	1 x 30mm (1.18in) MK 108 cannon	6 x 73mm (2.87in) Fohn rockets

■ **Several variants of the Ar E.381 began development in late 1944. All were intended to be air-launched by Ar 234C-3 jet bombers against US bomber formations. The theory was that the E. 381 would be released 1000 metres (3281ft) above the target formation, making an initial gliding attack in a shallow high-speed dive, before using its Walter 509B rocket motor for a second attack. It would then break away and begin a long diving glide back to its base, landing on a retractable skid. A single mock-up of the design had been completed when the project was cancelled at the beginning of 1945.**

1 March, but the test pilot, Lothar Sieber, was killed when the aircraft went out of control and crashed after one of the rockets failed to release.

Despite the design's obvious shortcomings, 10 of the 36 *Natters* completed were deployed for operational trials near Stuttgart in April 1945, but were eventually destroyed by the Germans to prevent their capture by rapidly advancing Allied forces.

Bombers, Recon Aircraft and Transports

The Luftwaffe*'s first Chief of Staff, General Wever, was a firm believer in strategic bombing and initiated the Ural Bomber project, which led to the production of two prototype four-engined bombers – the Dornier Do 19 and the Junkers Ju 89.*

Development of both these promising aircraft stopped a year after Wever's death in 1936 and the wartime *Luftwaffe* was left with a series of unsatisfactory improvizations which never adequately filled this long-range capability gap.

Junkers Ju 90/Ju 290/Ju 390 series

Although the Ju 89 bomber project was cancelled in 1937, the design served as the basis for development of the Ju 90 airliner, a small number of which were operated by the *Lufthansa* commercial airline in 1937–39. At the outbreak of war, these were taken over by the *Luftwaffe* to help meet an urgent need for heavy transport aircraft. Only 18 Ju 90s were completed, but their success belatedly convinced the *Luftwaffe* of the need for long-range transports and the type's obvious potential as a bomber and reconnaissance aircraft led to the urgent development of a successor, the Ju 290. The Junkers 290V1 prototype first flew on 16 July 1942 and strongly resembled the Ju 90, but had a lengthened fuselage, more powerful engines, and a *'Trapoklappe'* hydraulic-operated rear loading ramp. Both the V1 and the first eight A-1 production aircraft were unarmed transports that were pressed into service as soon as they were completed. Subsequent

LUFTHANSA
WÜRTTEMBERG

■ Early in 1939, the Junkers Ju 90V-5 Württemberg (left) airliner was withdrawn from service with *Lufthansa* and completely rebuilt as the first stage in the development of the Ju 290 programme.

LUFTWAFFE RECONNAISSANCE AIRCRAFT PRODUCTION

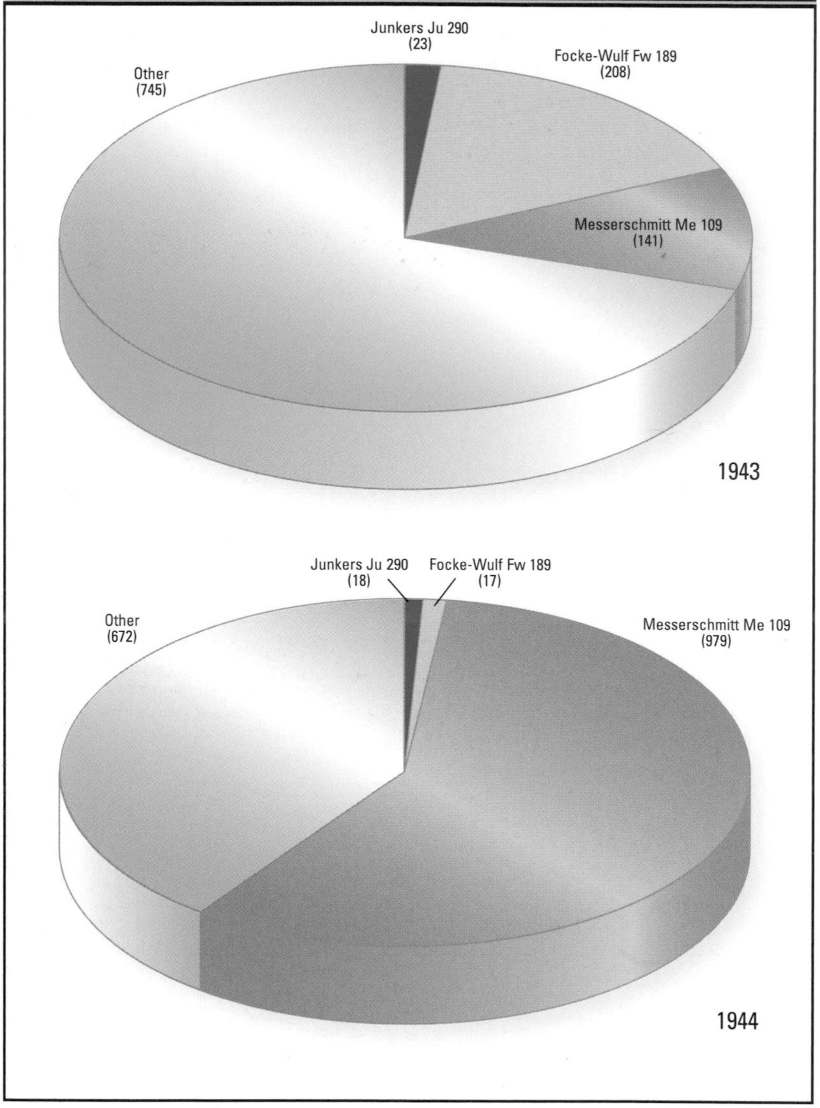
Junkers Ju 290
(23)
Focke-Wulf Fw 189
(208)
Other
(745)
Messerschmitt Me 109
(141)
1943
Junkers Ju 290
(18)
Focke-Wulf Fw 189
(17)
Other
(672)
Messerschmitt Me 109
(979)
1944

transport versions were fitted with a variety of armament after three of these aircraft were lost to Allied fire in early 1943.

The urgent need for Ju 290s in the long-range maritime reconnaissance role led to the development of the Ju 290A-2. Three A-1 aircraft were converted to A-2 specification on the assembly line. The A-2 was fitted with FuG 200 *Hohentwiel* search radar which was capable of locating Allied convoys at ranges of up to 80km (50 miles) from an altitude of 499m (1640ft), or 100km (62 miles) from an altitude of 999m (3280ft). It allowed convoys to be tracked while remaining well out of range of their AA fire.

Ju 290A-3 model

The A-3 version followed shortly after with added navigational equipment and one of the heaviest defensive armaments carried by any World War II aircraft; it was fitted with two hydraulically-powered HDL 151 dorsal turrets, each armed with a single 20mm (0.79in) MG 151 cannon, with a further 20mm (0.79in) MG 151 and a 13mm (0.51in) MG 131 machine gun in a gondola beneath the nose, and another 20mm (0.79in) MG 151 in the tail. Two more 13mm (0.51in) MG 131s were also fitted in waist positions. Both the A-2 and A-3 were fitted with large auxiliary fuel tanks in the fuselage and retained the rear loading ramp so that they could be used as transports when necessary.

Together with small numbers of the later A-4, A-5 and A-7 variants, these aircraft mainly served with a special long-range maritime reconnaissance group, FAGr 5 (*Fernaufklärungsgruppe 5*), which had been formed on 1 July 1943. During the late summer of 1943, three new Ju 290 A-2s were delivered to its *1st Staffel*, which became operational at Mont-de-Marsan near Bordeaux on 15 October. They began combat missions in November 1943, which could last up to 18 hours, shadowing Allied convoys in support of U-boat wolf packs.

In November 1943, a second *Staffel* was activated and, with a range of over 6100km (3790 miles) the Ju 290s flew out to the mid-Atlantic, relaying sightings of Allied convoys to U-boats. They proved so effective that towards the end of 1943, Admiral Dönitz demanded that the entire output of Ju 290s be made available to support his U-boats. However, a mere 20 machines were assigned to this role before all orders for the Ju 290 were cancelled in 1944 to free resources for fighter production.

After the loss of their French bases following the Normandy landings, most of the surviving aircraft were transferred to KG 200 for use in a range of clandestine operations.

The final development of the series was the Ju 390. This was basically an enlarged Ju 290 powered by six 1268kW (1700hp) BMW 801D engines. Only two prototypes were completed in 1943 before orders for transport, bomber and maritime patrol versions were cancelled in 1944.

Messerschmitt 321 and 323

The Me 321 and 323 originated with a 1940 requirement for a large assault glider in preparation for Operation Sealion, the projected invasion of Britain. Although Operation Sealion had been effectively cancelled by the time that the requirement was issued in October 1940, there was still an urgent need for this sort of heavy air transport capability as attention was now focussed on the forthcoming Operation Barbarossa, the invasion of the Soviet Union.

On 18 October 1940, Junkers and Messerschmitt were given 14 days to submit proposals for a large transport glider capable of lifting loads including an 88mm (3.5in) gun and its half-track tractor, or a Panzer IV medium tank. The Junkers Ju 322 *Mammut* prototype was quickly eliminated as it failed to meet the load-carrying requirement and the Messerschmitt design was ordered into production as the Me 321.

The type's worst fault was its sheer weight – fully loaded aircraft could only just be towed by three Bf 110s and required rocket-assisted

LUFTWAFFE BOMBER AIRCRAFT PRODUCTION

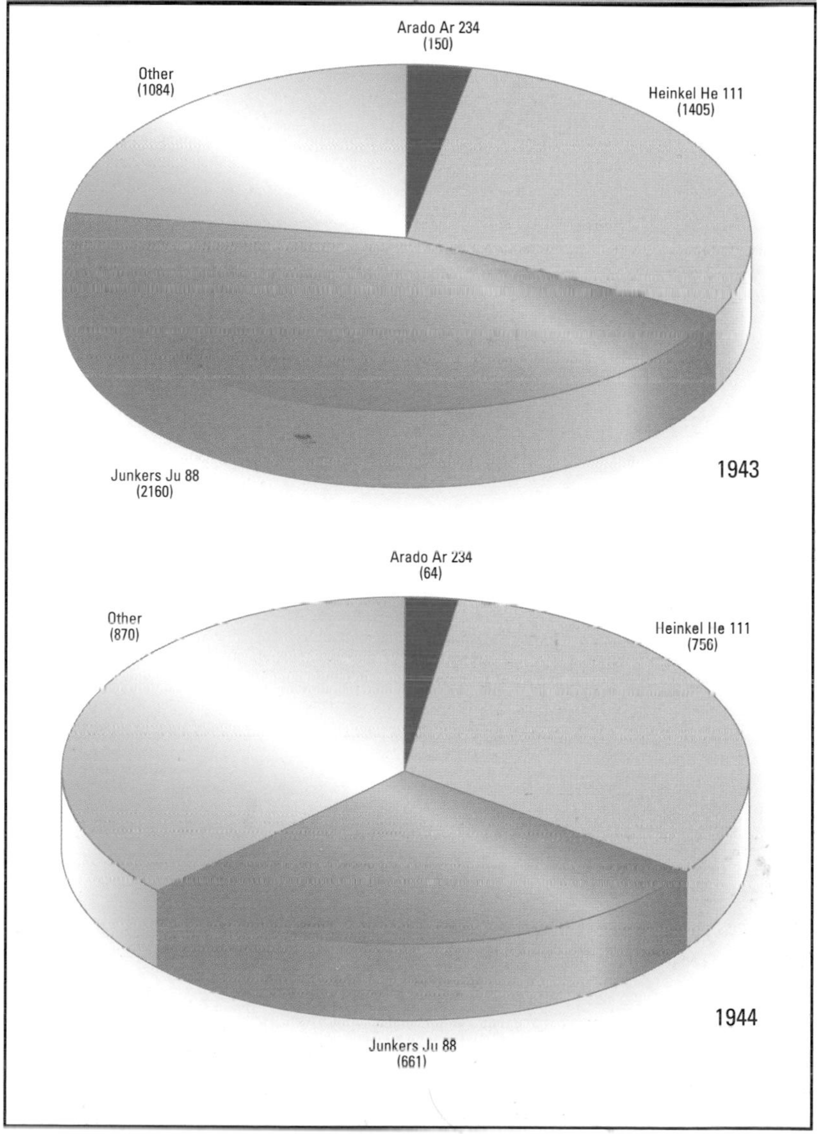
Arado Ar 234
(150)
Other
(1084)
Heinkel He 111
(1405)
Junkers Ju 88
(2160)
1943
Arado Ar 234
(64)
Other
(870)
Heinkel He 111
(756)
Junkers Ju 88
(661)
1944

take-off (RATO) packs to get into the air. Although about 200 Me 321s were completed before production ended in 1942, it was clear that something better was needed.

The solution adopted was to develop a powered version of the Me 321, which was designated as the Me 323. It was decided to use French Gnome-Rhone GR14N radial engines to reduce the burden on Germany's overstrained industry. Both four- and six-engine versions were tested, but the four-engine prototype was quickly rejected as it still had to be towed into the air.

BOMBER AND TRANSPORT AIRCRAFT PRODUCTION BY COUNTRY

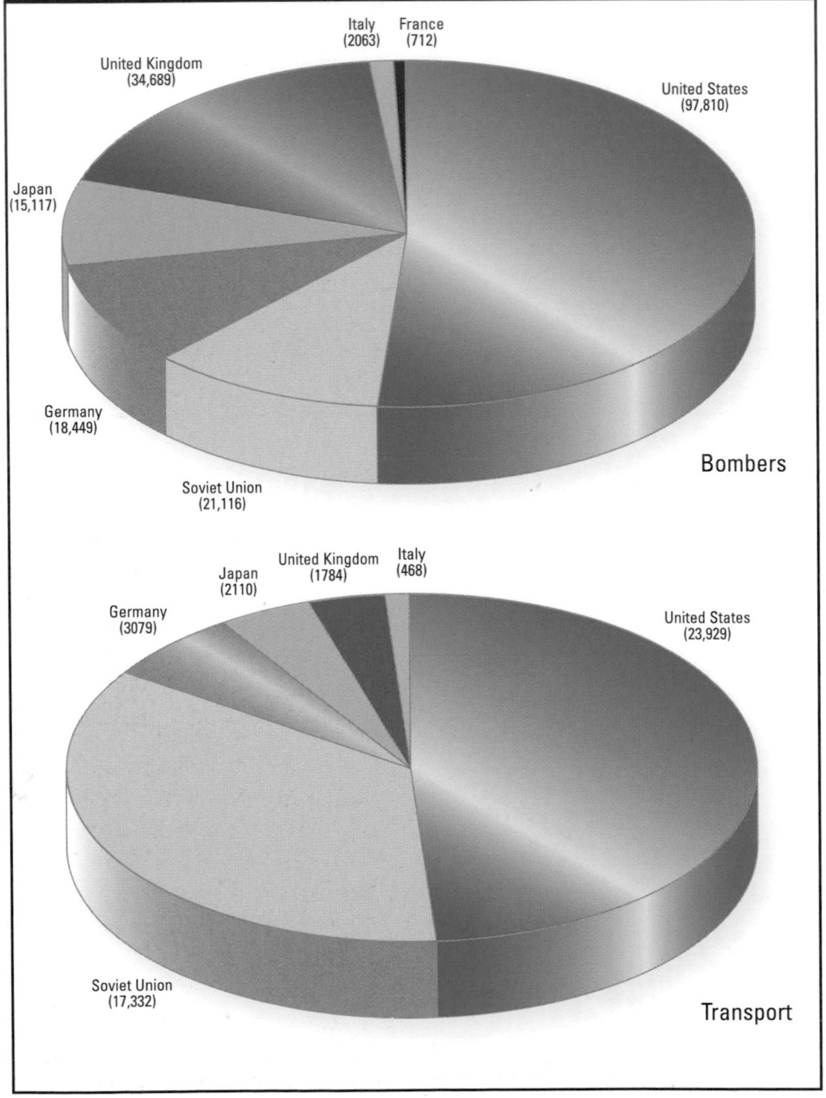
Italy (2063)
France (712)
United Kingdom (34,689)
United States (97,810)
Japan (15,117)
Germany (18,449)
Soviet Union (21,116)
Bombers
United Kingdom (1784)
Italy (468)
Japan (2110)
Germany (3079)
United States (23,929)
Soviet Union (17,332)
Transport

The six-engine version proved to be capable of taking off under its own power (although it still required RATO packs when fully loaded) and was accepted for service as the Me 323D.

A total of 198 Me 323s were completed before production ended in April 1944. Although very slow and vulnerable to Allied fighters, they had a remarkable lifting capacity for their time and played a particularly important role in supplying Axis forces on the Russian front. Typical loads included 120 fully equipped troops, 60 stretcher cases with medical attendants, or 9750kg (21,495lb) of general stores.

Blohm und Voss Bv 222 and Bv 238

The Bv 222 was the largest flying boat to reach operational service during the war. The design originated with a 1937 *Lufthansa* requirement for an aircraft capable of carrying 16 passengers from Berlin to New York in 20 hours. *Lufthansa* ordered three Bv 222s in September 1937, but the prototype did not make its first flight until 7 September 1940.

The type's military potential was obvious and it was quickly modified for the long range transport role. No more than 30 examples (including several prototypes) were completed, but all saw extensive service as armed transports capable of carrying up to 76 fully equipped troops or as maritime reconnaissance aircraft.

The Bv 222 was so useful that in early 1941 an official requirement was issued for a larger flying boat, which resulted in the Bv 238. The

PISTON-ENGINED BOMBERS AND TRANSPORT AIRCRAFT COMPARED

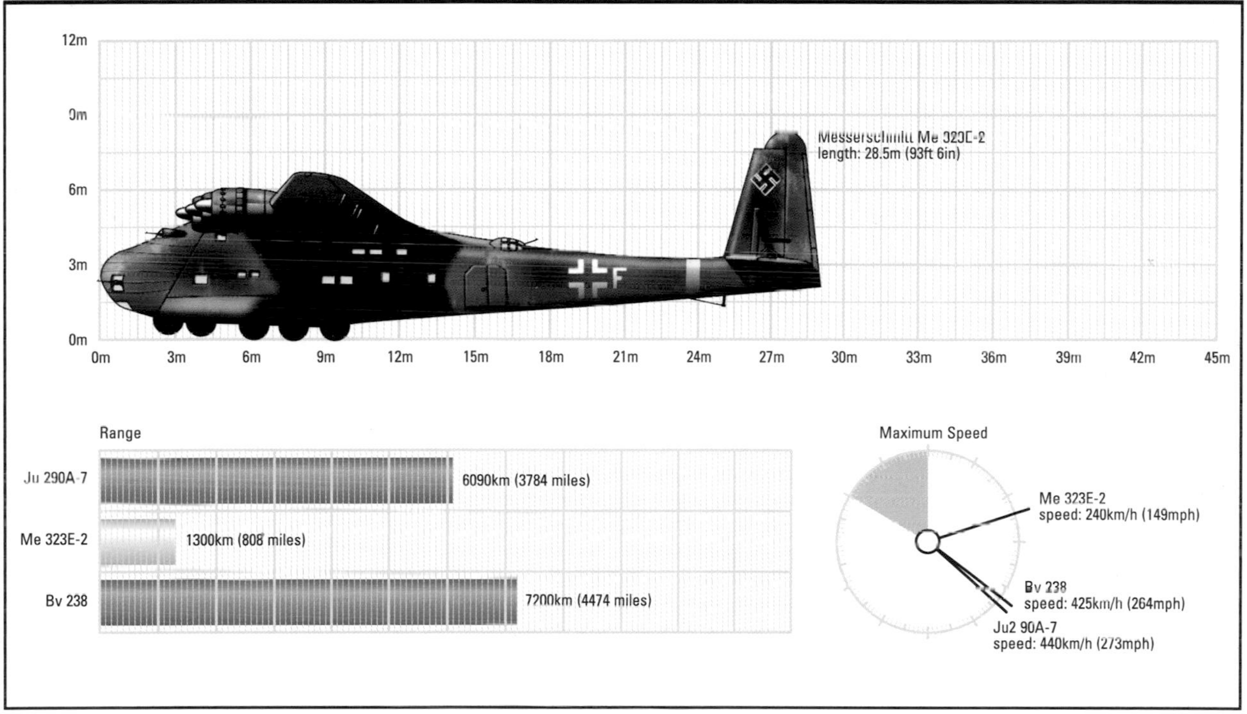
12m
9m
6m
3m
0m
length: 28.5m (93ft 6in)
0m
3m
6m
9m
12m
15m
18m
21m
24m
27m
30m
33m
36m
39m
42m
45m
Range
Ju 290A-7
6090km (3784 miles)
Me 323E-2
1300km (808 miles)
Bv 238
7200km (4474 miles)
Maximum Speed
Me 323E-2
speed: 240km/h (149mph)
Bv 238
speed: 425km/h (264mph)
Ju2 90A-7
speed: 440km/h (273mph)

LUFTWAFFE TRANSPORT AIRCRAFT PRODUCTION

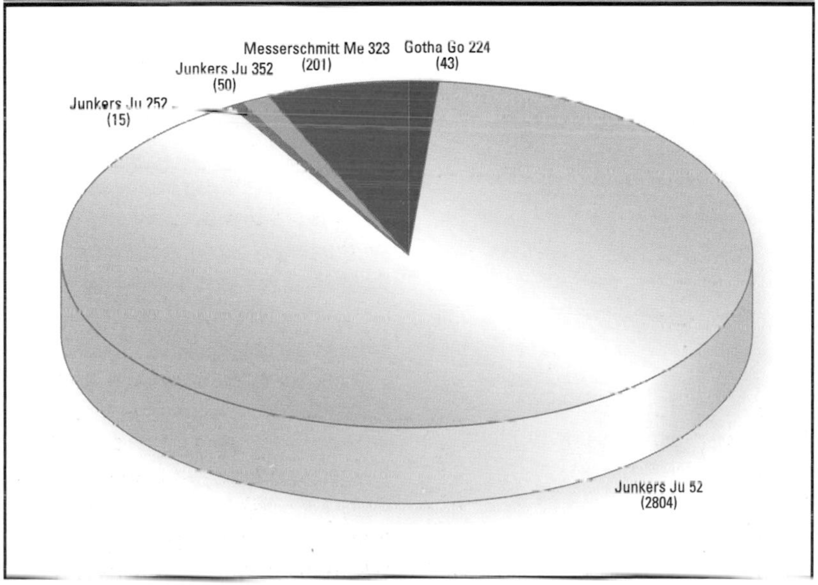
Messerschmitt Me 323 (201)
Gotha Go 224 (43)
Junkers Ju 352 (50)
Junkers Ju 252 (15)
Junkers Ju 52 (2804)

prototype was the world's heaviest aircraft at the time of its first flight on 11 March 1944, and had a truly remarkable performance, with the ability to carry a 20,000kg (44,080lb) payload for a distance of 3750km (2329 miles). However, the sole prototype was sunk at its moorings on Lake Schaal near Hamburg by USAAF P-51 Mustang fighters.

Blohm und Voss were convinced of the potential of the Bv 238 so they carried out detailed design studies for a land-based version, designated Bv 250. This would have been powered by six 1454kW (1950hp) engines and was intended to carry 45 tonnes (44.3 tons) of bombs up to 2500km (1552 miles), or a 20 tonne (19.7 ton) bomb load over 7000km (4347 miles).

Jet Bombers

By the end of the war, the Luftwaffe *had a plethora of highly sophisticated jet bomber designs under development, but almost all never got beyond the drawing board stage. The obvious potential of the few which did take to the air demonstrated that jet engines would dramatically transform the performance of future bombers.*

Arado Ar 234 *'Blitz'*

In late 1940, the German Air Ministry issued a requirement for a high-speed reconnaissance aircraft. Arado were the only manufacturer to respond with a proposal for a twin-jet aircraft, designated E.370. This evolved into the single-seat Ar 234, which first flew on 15 June 1943.

The sixth and eighth prototypes were powered by four BMW 003 jet engines instead of two Jumo 004s, the sixth having four engines housed in individual nacelles, and the eighth flown with two pairs of BMW 003s fitted in 'twinned' nacelles underneath each wing.

In order to reduce weight and maximize internal fuel capacity, Arado did not use a conventional undercarriage – each of the eight prototypes took off from a jettisonable three-wheeled trolley and landed on three retractable skids, one under the fuselage and one under each engine nacelle.

Schnellbomber

In July 1943, Arado was requested to supply two prototypes of a *schnellbomber* (fast bomber) version as the Ar 234B. There was no room in the slender fuselage for an internal bomb bay and the bomb load had to be carried on external racks. The bombs' added weight and drag reduced speed from 742km/h (461mph) at 6000m (19,700ft), to 668km/h (415 mph). Two fixed rearward firing 20mm (0.79in) MG 151 cannon were also fitted. These were aimed by a periscopic sight, but the system was generally considered useless and many pilots had the guns removed to save weight.

The external bomb load and the vulnerability of immobile aircraft littering the airfield after landing made the skid-landing system impractical and the Ar 234B was modified to incorporate a tricycle undercarriage. The first Ar 234B flew on 10 March 1944 and although slightly slower than earlier versions, still had an impressive performance. A total of 20 B-0 pre-production aircraft were delivered by the end of June, but series production was delayed by Allied bombing.

Recon aircraft

As a stop-gap measure, several prototypes were flown on high-priority reconnaissance missions, the first of which was undertaken by the V7 prototype on 2 August 1944. In many cases, these aircraft were never detected, as they cruised at about 740km/h (460mph) at over 9100m (29,900ft).

A few Ar 234Bs entered service in the autumn of 1944 and impressed their pilots with their speed and manoeuvrability. Their normal bomb load comprised two 500kg (1100lb) bombs hung beneath the engines, or a single 1000kg (2200lb) bomb semi-recessed in the underside of the fuselage, with a maximum bomb load of 1500kg (3310lb).

The Ar 234s' long take-off and landing runs led to several accidents; improved training and RATO (rocket-assisted take-off) packs helped, although the problem was never entirely eliminated. Their Jumo 004B engines were always the real problem as they suffered repeated flameouts and needed overhaul or replacement after about 10 hours of operation. A few bombing attacks were made in support of the Ardennes Offensive, the first being launched on Christmas Eve 1944, when nine Ar-234Bs, each carrying a single 500kg (1100lb) bomb, attacked Liège. Similar raids continued until early January, when bad winter weather prevented operational flying.

Bridge assault

The most notable use of the Ar 234 in the bomber role were the attempts to destroy the Ludendorff Bridge across the Rhine at Remagen. Between 7 March 1945, when it was captured by the US 9th Armored Division, and 17 March, when it finally collapsed,

JET BOMBERS AND RECONNAISSANCE AIRCRAFT COMPARED

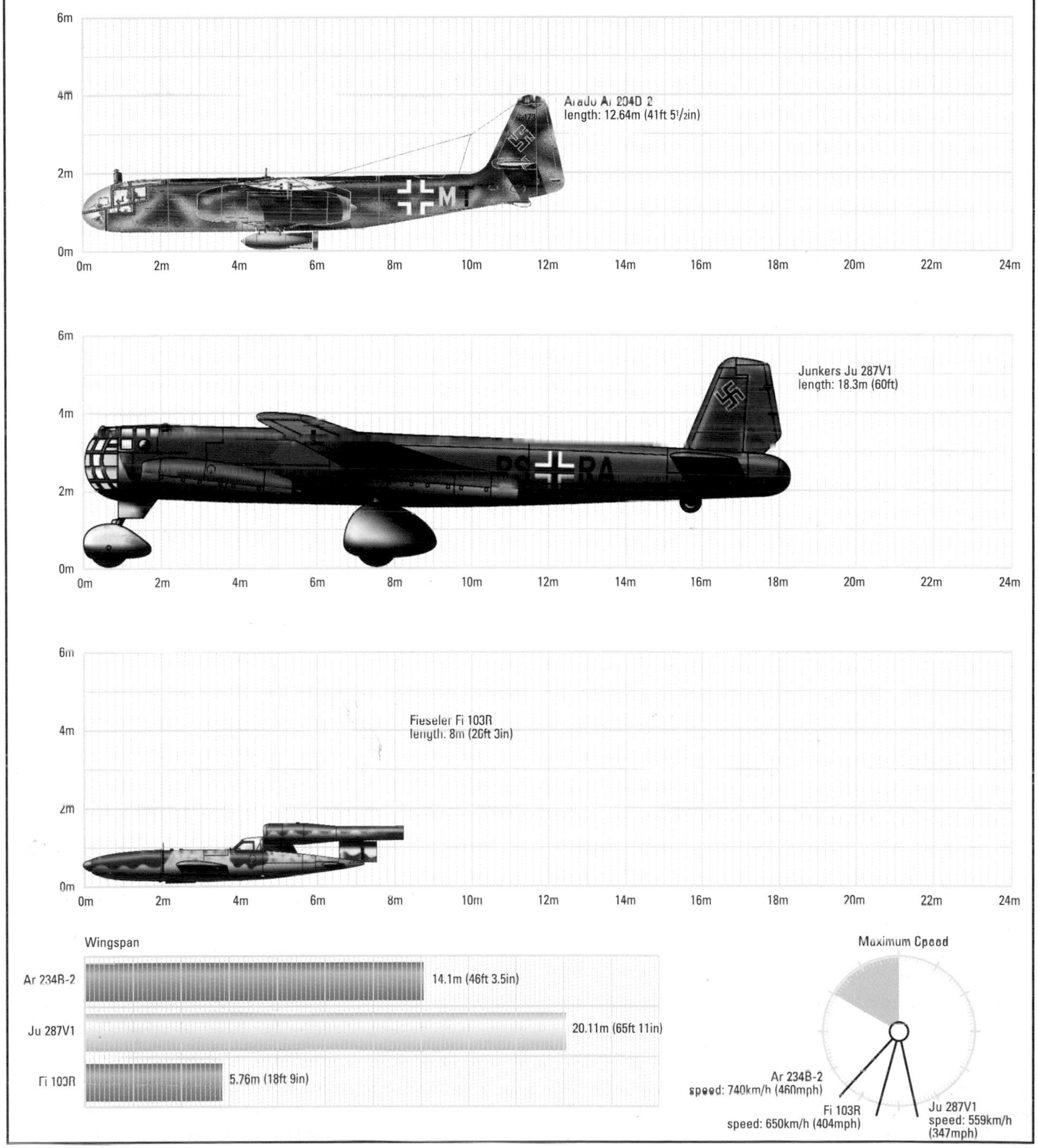
Arado Ar 234D-2
length: 12.64m (41ft 5½in)
Junkers Ju 287V1
length: 18.3m (60ft)
Fieseler Fi 103R
length: 8m (26ft 3in)
0m
2m
4m
6m
8m
10m
12m
14m
16m
18m
20m
22m
24m
Wingspan
Ar 234B-2
14.1m (46ft 3.5in)
Ju 287V1
20.11m (65ft 11in)
Fi 103R
5.76m (18ft 9in)
Maximum Speed
Ar 234B-2
speed: 740km/h (460mph)
Fi 103R
speed: 650km/h (404mph)
Ju 287V1
speed: 559km/h (347mph)

ARADO AR 234 – PRINCIPAL VARIANTS

Type	*Description*
Ar 234B-0	20 pre-production aircraft
Ar 234B-1	Reconnaissance version, equipped with two Rb 50/30 or Rb 75/30 cameras
Ar 234B-2	Bomber version, with a maximum bomb load of 2000kg (4410lb)
Ar 234C	The Ar 234C was powered by four BMW 003A engines, mounted in a pair of twin-engine nacelles. The primary reason for this change was to release Junkers Jumo 004s needed for the Me 262, but the lighter BMW engines also improved overall performance. Airspeed was found to be about 20 per cent higher than that of the B-series and range was increased due to the faster climb to altitude. Although 14 Ar 234C prototypes, including the C-1 and C-2, were completed, the type did not become operational before the end of the war
Ar 234C-1	Four-engined version of the Ar 234B-1
Ar 234C-2	Four-engined version of the Ar 234B-2
Ar 234C-3	Multi-purposed version, armed with two 20mm (0.79in) MG 151 cannon.
Ar 234C-3/N	Proposed two-seat night fighter version, armed with two 20 mm (0.79in) MG 151 and two 30mm (1.18in) MK 108 cannon, equipped with FuG 218 Neptun V radar
Ar 234C-4	Armed reconnaissance version, fitted with two cameras, armed with four 20mm (0.79in) MG 151 cannon
Ar 234C-5	Proposed two-seat version with side-by-side crew seating. The 28th prototype was converted to this configuration
Ar 234C-6	Proposed two-seat reconnaissance aircraft converted from the 29th prototype
Ar 234C-7	Two-seat night fighter, with side-by-side seating for the crew, fitted with an enhanced FuG 245 Bremen radar
Ar 234C-8	Proposed single-seat bomber, powered by two 1080kg (2380lb) thrust Jumo 004D turbojet engines
Ar 234D	This was intended to be a two-seat aircraft based on the B-series fuselage, powered by a pair of Heinkel HeS 011 turbojet engines, but never reached the prototype stage
Ar 234D-1	Proposed reconnaissance version
Ar 234D-2	Proposed bomber version
Ar 234P	This was to be a two-seat night fighter, capable of accepting a range of engines and radars, which never progressed beyond design studies
	(Although a total of 210 aircraft were completed by the end of the war, it was rare for more than 40 to be operational at any one time.)

the bridge was continually attacked by Ar 234s of III/KG 76 carrying 1000kg (2200lb) bombs.

Junkers Ju 287

Apart from the Ar 234, the Ju 287 was the only German jet bomber to fly before the end of the war. Junkers had started work on the project in 1943, and following concerns about low-speed handling characteristics, altered the original design – which was to have had wings swept back at 25 degrees – to a forward-swept wing configuration. Wind tunnel tests confirmed the advantages of this layout and a prototype was completed, which first flew in August 1944. In order to speed construction, assemblies from a variety of aircraft were used, including the nose of a Heinkel He 177 and the tail of a Ju 188. To allow the use of readily available components, a fixed undercarriage was fitted that included components from a captured USAAF B-24 Liberator.

Test flights began on 16 August 1944 and were very promising – the definitive 'service version' was expected to have a top speed of about 885km/h (550mph) and a range of 14,430km (8960 miles) with a 4000kg (8816lb) bomb load. A production order was placed but no further examples were completed by the end of the war.

Fieseler Fi 103R *Reichenburg*

The idea of a piloted version of the V-1 flying bomb was first raised in late 1943, but was rejected in favour of the Messerschmitt Me 328 piloted glider bomb. When the Messerschmitt project was cancelled in mid-1944, the concept was reconsidered and adopted after vigorous lobbying by influential figures including Hanna Reitsch and Otto Skorzeny.

The V-1 was converted by fitting ailerons to the wings and installing a small cockpit with basic flight instruments immediately in front of the pulse-jet's intake. The single-piece, awkward side-hinged canopy incorporated an armoured glass windscreen with engraved lines marking various diving angles. The operational R-IV version would have been armed with a 850kg (1870lb) HE warhead and carried to within range of its target by a Heinkel He 111 bomber. It was calculated that a launch at an altitude of 2500m (8200ft) would give the R-IV a maximum range of 330km (205 miles).

JET BOMBER PAYLOADS COMPARED

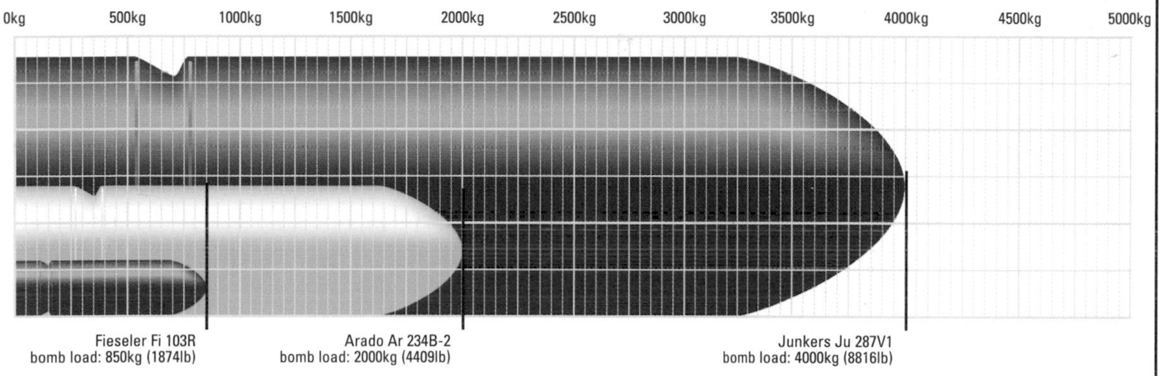
0kg
500kg
1000kg
1500kg
2000kg
2500kg
3000kg
3500kg
4000kg
4500kg
5000kg
Fieseler Fi 103R
bomb load: 850kg (1874lb)
Arado Ar 234B-2
bomb load: 2000kg (4409lb)
Junkers Ju 287V1
bomb load: 4000kg (8816lb)

On reaching the target, the pilot was to arm the warhead and make his terminal dive at a speed of up to 850km/h (530mph) before bailing out. In practice, there would have been almost no chance of survival – even if he did manage to release the awkward canopy and get out of the cockpit, the pilot would almost certainly have been thrown into the pulse-jet. After a succession of fatal accidents in unpowered training versions of the *Reichenburg*, the project was abandoned in March 1945.

Long-Range Bombers

Although German designers submitted numerous proposals for multi-engine long-range bombers, none were produced in significant numbers. In addition to these relatively conventional designs, there were some highly unusual projects.

Junkers Ju 88 *Mistel* composites

The *Mistel* (Mistletoe), also known as *Beethoven-Gerät* (Beethoven Device) and *Vati und Sohn* (Daddy and Son), was based on a Ju 88 with the entire crew compartment replaced by a large hollow-charge (HEAT) warhead. The Ju 88 was controlled by the pilot of a fighter mounted on a set of struts above the bomber's centre section. After take-off, the fighter would draw fuel from the bomber to top up its tanks for the return flight and on sighting the target, the pilot aimed the composite using his standard gun sight. He then fired explosive bolts to release the bomber which flew on to the target.

First contact

The first such composite, with a Bf 109F-4 as the control aircraft, flew in July 1943 and was promising enough for the design to be adopted for service. The 3800kg (8378lb) HEAT warhead was designed for use against targets such as battleships, and these were the primary targets of initial attacks against the Allied invasion fleet off Normandy by KG 101. The *Mistel* pilots claimed some unconfirmed successes and it is probable that hits were scored on the old French battleship *Courbet*, which had been scuttled in the shallows as a block ship to protect Sword Beach.

MISTEL COMPOSITES

An operational Mistel 1. The Ju 88's 3800kg (8378lb) HEAT warhead could defeat 7m (23ft) of armour or 18m (60ft) of concrete.

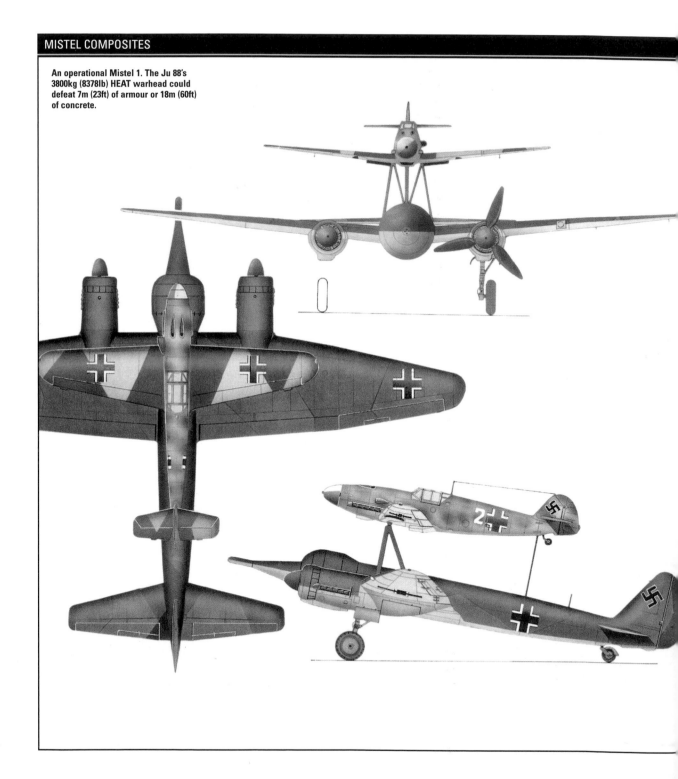

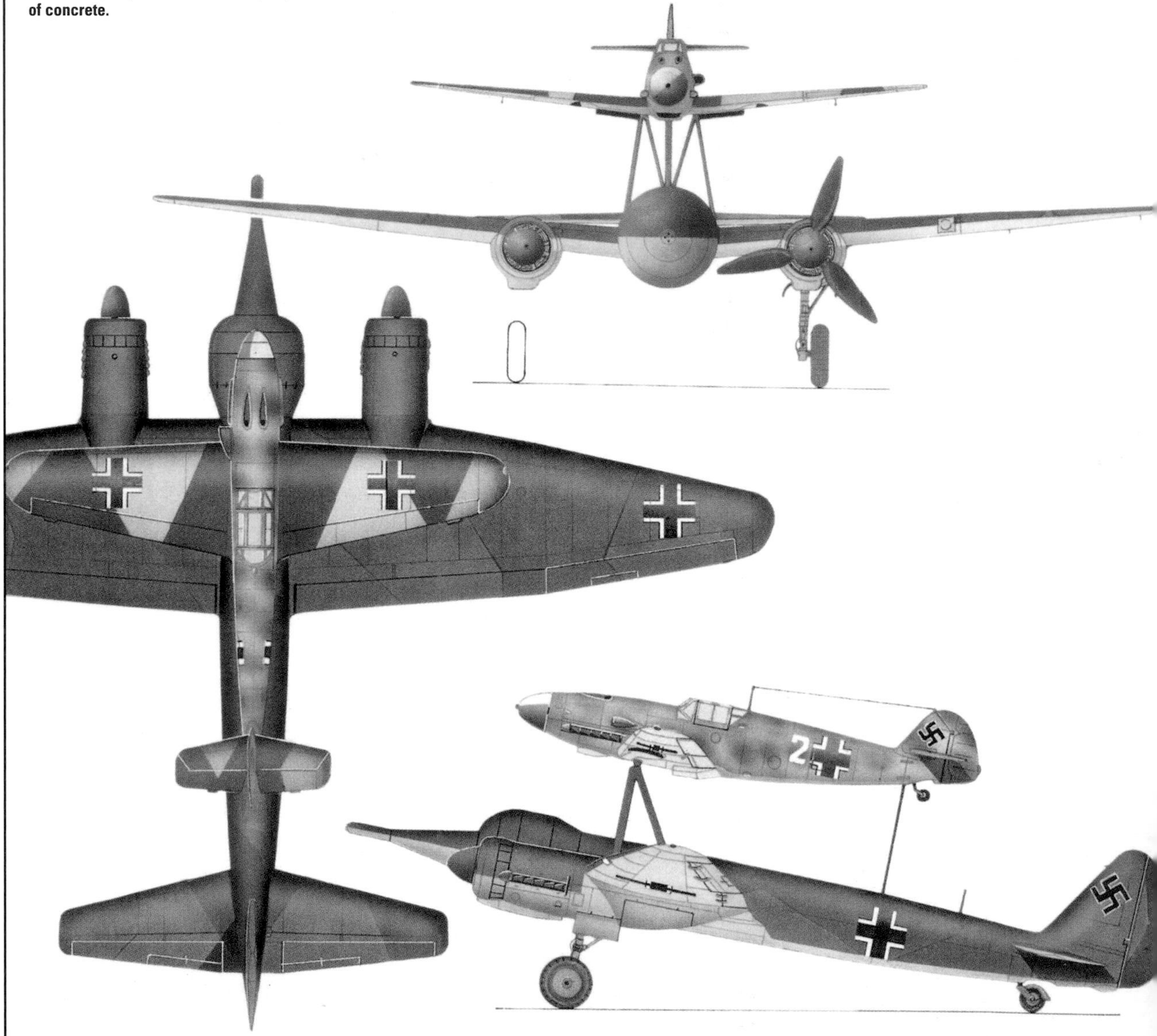

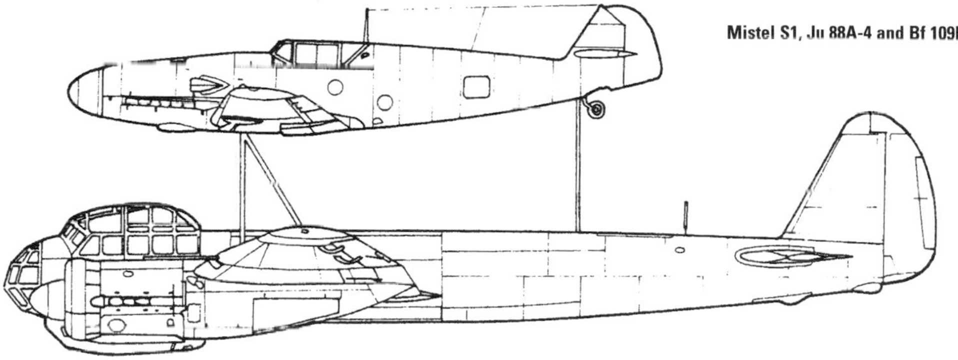

Mistel S1, Ju 88A-4 and Bf 109F-4

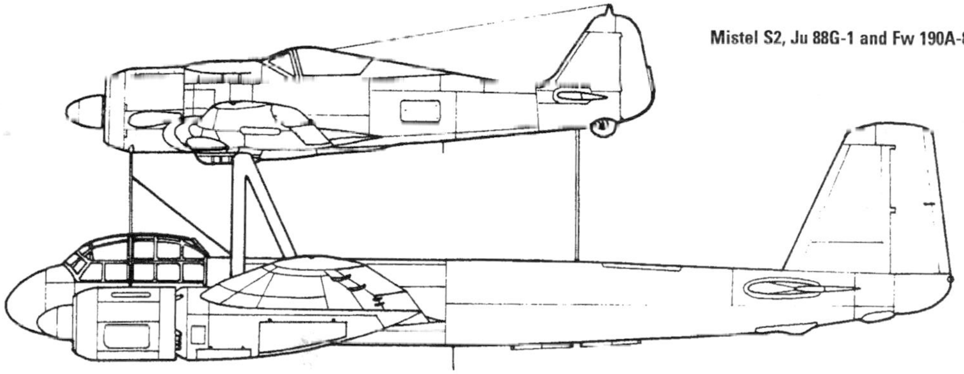

Mistel S2, Ju 88G-1 and Fw 190A-8

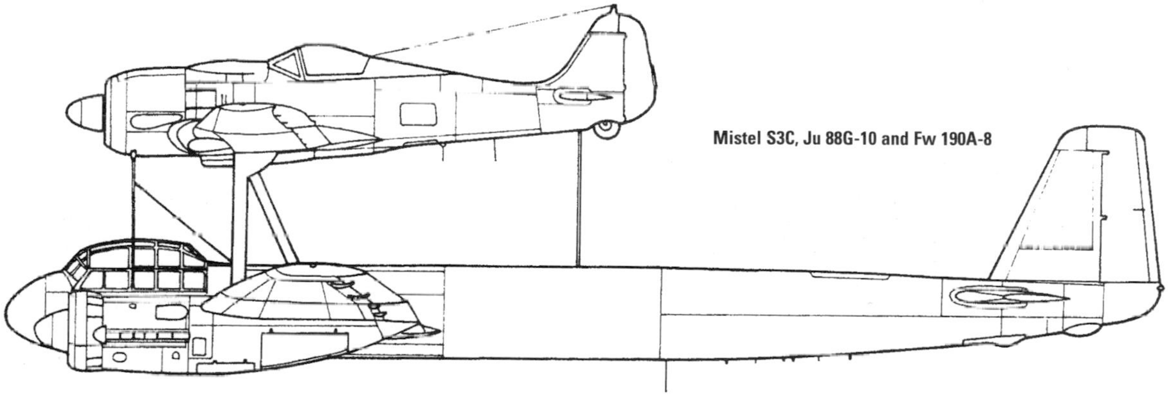

Mistel S3C, Ju 88G-10 and Fw 190A-8

MISTEL COMPOSITES

Type	*Aircraft*
Mistel Prototype	Ju 88A-4 and Bf 109F-4
Mistel 1	Ju 88A-4 and Bf 109F-4
Mistel S1	Trainer version of *Mistel 1*
Mistel 2	Ju 88G-I and Fw 190A-8 or F-8
Mistel S2	Trainer version of *Mistel 2*
Mistel 3A	Ju 88A-4 and Fw 190A-8
Mistel S3A	Trainer version of *Mistel 3A*
Mistel 3B	Ju 88H-4 and Fw 190A-8
Mistel 3C	Ju 88G-10 and Fw 190F-8
Mistel S3C	Trainer version of *Mistel 3C*
Mistel Führungsmaschine	Ju 88 A-4/H-4 and Fw 190 A-8
Mistel 4	Ju 287 and Me 262
Mistel 5	Arado E.377A and He 162

In late 1944, an earlier proposal for an attack on the battleships and aircraft carriers of the Home Fleet at Scapa Flow was revived. A total of 60 *Mistels* were assembled on Danish airfields for the operation, which was cancelled after a prolonged spell of bad weather in December 1944 when it was apparent that most of the intended targets were being redeployed to the Far East.

SANGAR *AMERIKA* BOMBER

	Specification
Type	Proposed rocket orbital bomber
Powerplant	1 x 101.6 tonnes (100 tons) thrust liquid-fuel rocket engine
Speed	22,100km/h (13,724mph)
Service Ceiling	280km (174 miles)
Range	23,500km (14,594 miles)
Weight (empty)	9979kg (22,000lb)
Length	27.98m (91ft 10in)
Height	–
Span	15m (49ft 2in)
Armament	Bomb load of 3629 kg (8000lb), almost certainly the German atomic bomb

Eastern targets

Research into suitable alternative targets led to the reactivation of another raid – Operation Iron Hammer – which intended to attack key Soviet power stations around Moscow and Gorky. Originally planned in late 1943, the operation had been cancelled when the Red Army's advance overran the *Luftwaffe* airfields earmarked for the attack. The *Mistels'* greater endurance meant that the attacks were now feasible again, although the targets were at the extreme limit of their range.

Preparations were in hand for the attacks to be launched in late March 1945, but the Russian seizure of bridgeheads across the Oder, less than 56km (35 miles) from Berlin forced a rapid change of plans. The majority of the 80 or so serviceable *Mistels* were expended in attacks on the Oder bridges but these had little effect beyond imposing a slight delay on the Soviet build-up for the assault on Berlin.

Total *Mistel* production seems likely to have been approximately 250. The majority of those used operationally were *Mistel 1s*, but these may have been supplemented by a very small number of *Mistel 2s* and *3s*. Later variants never progressed beyond the design stage.

Sänger Silbervogel (Silverbird) Orbital Bomber

The *Sänger Silbervogel* (Silverbird) (also known as the Antipodal Bomber or Atmosphere Skipper) was designed as an intercontinental supersonic bomber. It had a flattened fuselage to help augment the lift of its small wings and tail and was powered by a 'regeneratively cooled' 109 tonne (100 ton) thrust rocket motor supplemented by two auxiliary rocket engines. The pilot sat in a pressurized cockpit in the forward fuselage, and a tricycle undercarriage was fitted for a gliding landing. A central weapons bay held a single 3629kg (8000lb) free-fall bomb (almost certainly intended to be the German atomic bomb).

The *Silbervogel* was to be launched from a 3km (1.9 mile) long monorail track by a rocket-powered sled, accelerating it to 1850km/h (1149mph) at an altitude of 1500m (5100ft). The main rocket engine would then be fired for eight minutes, boosting the *Silbervogel* to a maximum speed of 22,100km/h (13,724mph) and an altitude of over 145km (90 miles). As the aircraft descended under the pull of gravity, it would hit the denser atmosphere at about 40km (25 miles) and 'skip' back up like a stone skips across the surface of a pond.

The 'skips' would gradually decrease but it was still calculated that the *Silbervogel* could cross the Atlantic and bomb a US target such as New York before landing at an airfield somewhere in the Japanese held Pacific, after covering 19,000–24,000km (12,000–15,000 miles).

This highly ambitious project was cancelled in 1941, but Sanger's research was incorporated in the abortive post-war US X-20 Dyna-Soar project, which in turn yielded valuable data for NASA's Space Shuttle programme.

Helicopters and other Rotary Wing Designs

German research into rotary wing aircraft was well advanced by 1939. Hanna Reitsch had flown an early helicopter, the Focke-Wulf Fw 61, inside the Deutschlandhalle *during the 1938 Berlin Motor Show and more sophisticated designs were being developed.*

Flettner Fl 282 *Kolibri* (Hummingbird)

The single-seat Fl 282 *Kolibri* was developed from the Flettner Fl 265 that underwent service trials in 1940 and had the same intermeshing rotor configuration as the earlier helicopter. The airframe was largely fabric-covered tubular steel with a fixed undercarriage.

The *Kolibri* was extensively test-flown in the ship-borne reconnaissance role throughout 1941, operating from a small helicopter pad on the light cruiser *Köln*. The *Kreigsmarine* were impressed by its performance, ordering 15 prototypes and 30 production machines.

By 1943, over 20 *Kolibris* were serving with naval units in the Baltic, Mediterranean and Aegean. Their success prompted the *Luftwaffe* to consider converting the Fl 282 for battlefield use. The design was modified by the addition of a second seat for an observer and 1000 examples of this version were ordered in 1944. Only 24 were completed before production was halted when the factory was destroyed in an air raid.

They were useful artillery spotting aircraft and an observation unit was established in 1944 with three Fl 282 and three Fa 223 helicopters. It is probable that some additional machines also operated from Berlin-Rangsdorf in this role in the last months of the war.

Focke Achgelis Fa 223 *Drache* (Dragon)

The *Drache* had its origins in a design for a civilian helicopter capable of carrying six passengers on *Lufthansa*'s short-haul routes. The first twin-rotor prototype began ground trials in September 1939, but incorporated much new technology that needed prolonged refining and delayed the first flight until August 1940. Service trials led to orders for versions optimized for several different roles, including anti-submarine, reconnaissance, air-sea rescue, transport and training duties.

It was soon decided to switch production to a single multi-purpose type that could satisfactorily fulfil all the required roles, and series production began at the Focke-Achgelis factory in Delmenhorst in mid 1942.

Shortly afterwards, the factory was destroyed in an Allied air raid, together with two prototypes and the first seven pre-production machines undergoing final assembly.

Attempts were made to resume production but were abandoned in 1943 after producing eight *Draches*, and a new plant was set up at Laupheim, near Stuttgart.

Only seven machines were completed at Laupheim before another air raid in July 1944 destroyed the factory. This led to a decision to cancel the entire programme, which was rescinded within weeks when the company was ordered to set up a new factory at Berlin's Templehof airport.

The scheme to produce 400 machines a month was totally impractical in the increasing chaos and destruction of the final stages of the war and no further examples were completed. It seems likely that a total of only a dozen or so *Draches* ever flew.

Focke-Achgelis Fa 284 Sky Crane

This was the most ambitious of the wartime helicopter projects. As a 'flying crane', it was larger than anything produced until the 1950s. It was designed to have two contra-rotating rotors mounted on outriggers, one each side of the fuselage. A 1193.12kW (1600hp) or 1491.4kW (2000hp) engine was mounted at the base of each outrigger, giving the machine the ability to lift loads of up to seven tonnes (6.9 tons).

Although design work was completed by the end of 1942 and some components were produced, no prototype was ever completed.

Focke Achgelis Fa 225

German glider-borne assaults in the early years of the war had demonstrated the limitations of conventional gliders, which required extensive unobstructed landing zones. It was believed that a rotary-wing glider would have far greater tactical flexibility as it could exploit the very steep descents possible under auto-rotation.

In 1942, the Fa 225 project was initiated to convert standard DFS 230 gliders to rotary-wing configuration. The wings were replaced with an Fa 223 rotor and a substantial fixed undercarriage was fitted to absorb the increased forces associated with near-vertical landings. A prototype was test-flown under tow by a Heinkel He 45 during 1943 and had a landing run of as little as 18m (59ft). Although the design fully met its requirements, it was not adopted for service use.

Focke Achgelis Fa 330 *Bachstelze* (Wagtail)

This was an ultra-light rotary wing glider designed for submarine use, which was stowed in two metal tubes built into the U-boat's conning tower. They were towed behind German U-boats to allow a lookout to see farther, giving the submarines a better chance of escape when threatened by Allied aircraft.

Assembly by four crewmen took only three minutes in calm conditions. Launch procedure was simple – a deckhand hauled on a rope wrapped around a drum on the rotor hub to spin the rotor for take-off from a small platform attached to the aft railing of the conning tower. The towline extended from an electric winch to a quick-release coupling on the glider.

The pilot was linked to the submarine by telephone with the cable wrapped around the towline. Normal landings simply involved winching in the glider. At touchdown, the pilot applied a brake to stop the rotor blades.

Dismantling time was not much greater than that required for assembly. If the U-boat came under attack and had to crash dive, the pilot pulled a lever above his seat. The towline disconnected from the aircraft, allowing the U-boat to dive while the spinning rotor simultaneously departed from the airframe rotor mast. As the rotors flew up and away, they pulled a cable that deployed the pilot's parachute. The pilot then released his seat harness and the remainder of the glider fell into the sea. After the submarine evaded the threat, it could return to the surface to pick up the pilot.

Only the Type IX U-boat could tow the Fa 330 fast enough for flight in low wind conditions using the standard 300m (984ft) steel cable. At a maximum airspeed of 80km/h (50mph), it could climb to 220m (722ft), at which altitude the pilot could spot a ship up to 53km (33 miles) away in clear conditions.

By the time that the type entered service, increasing numbers of Allied escort vessels and aircraft made its use against the Atlantic convoys too hazardous. However, in the Indian Ocean, merchantmen still sailed independently without the benefit of convoy protection and the Fa 330 was used by Type IX U-boats in that theatre from early 1943.

A powered version of the design was proposed for use from surface vessels. This would have been a true microlight helicopter with a 45kW (60hp) engine, but the concept never left the drawing board.

Focke-Wulf *Triebflugel*

In complete contrast to other rotary-wing designs, this was a high-performance VTOL ramjet-powered interceptor. The three wings were mounted on a rotating ring just behind the cockpit, each powered by a Pabst ramjet, which was boosted to operating speed by a small solid-fuel rocket.

At take-off and landing the wings acted as helicopter rotor blades, while in level flight they functioned as an oversized propeller. The *Triebflugel* was a 'tail-sitter' and was fitted with a single central tail wheel and four stabilizing outrigger wheels, one at the end of each tail fin. In flight, each wheel was covered by streamlined clamshell doors.

Focke-Wulf completed the design in September 1944 and tested a wind-tunnel model at speeds of up to Mach 0.9, but no prototype was ever built.

GERMAN HELICOPTERS COMPARED

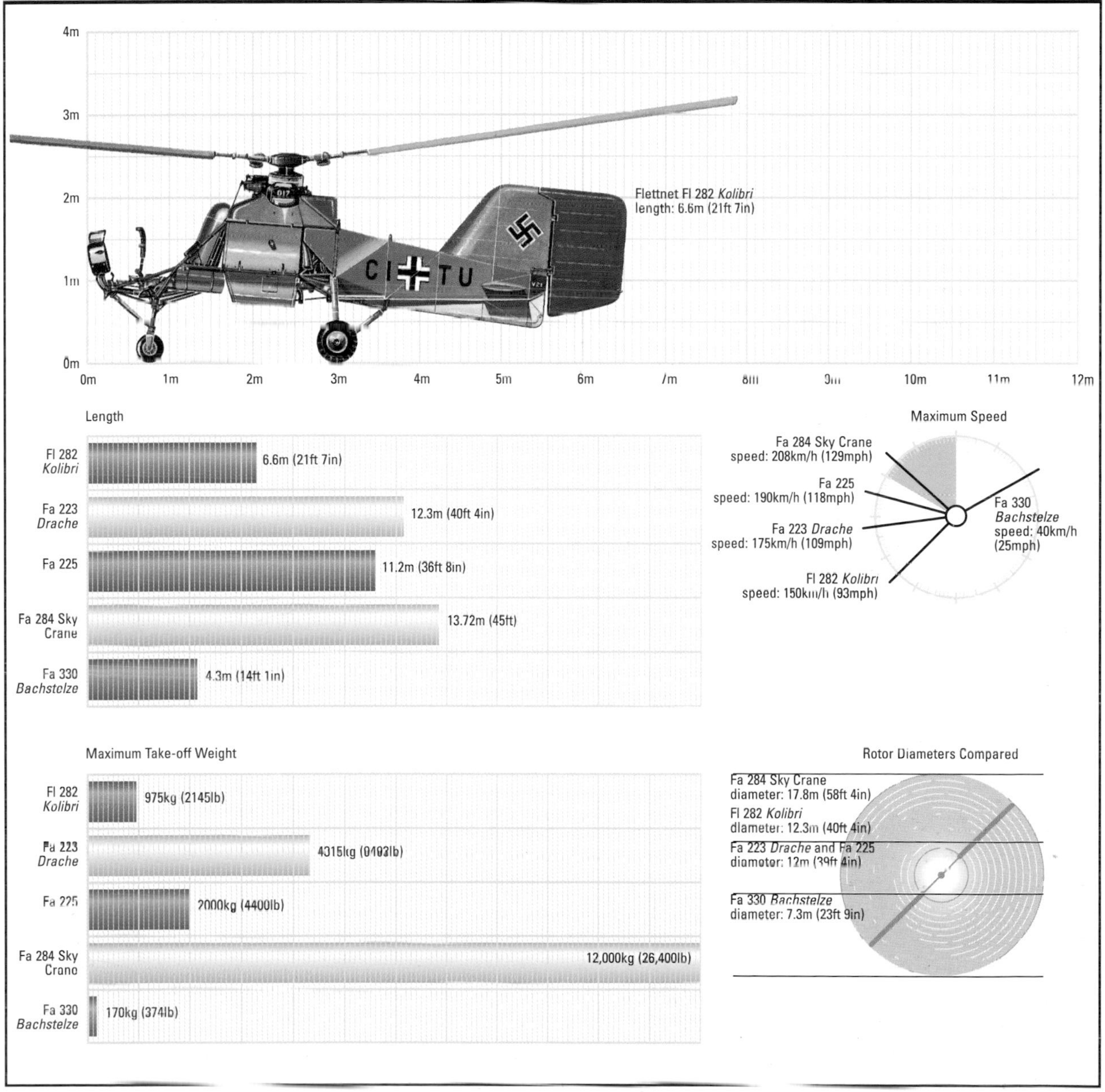
4m
3m
2m
1m
0m
Flettnet Fl 282 *Kolibri*
length: 6.6m (21ft 7in)
0m
1m
2m
3m
4m
5m
6m
10m
11m
12m
Length
Fl 282 *Kolibri*
6.6m (21ft 7in)
Fa 223 *Drache*
12.3m (40ft 4in)
Fa 225
11.2m (36ft 8in)
Fa 284 Sky Crane
13.72m (45ft)
Fa 330 *Bachstelze*
4.3m (14ft 1in)
Maximum Speed
Fa 284 Sky Crane
speed: 208km/h (129mph)
Fa 225
speed: 190km/h (118mph)
Fa 223 *Drache*
speed: 175km/h (109mph)
Fl 282 *Kolibri*
speed: 150km/h (93mph)
Fa 330 *Bachstelze*
speed: 40km/h (25mph)
Maximum Take-off Weight
Fl 282 *Kolibri*
975kg (2145lb)
Fa 223 *Drache*
4315kg
Fa 225
2000kg (4400lb)
Fa 284 Sky Crane
12,000kg (26,400lb)
Fa 330 *Bachstelze*
170kg (374lb)
Rotor Diameters Compared
Fa 284 Sky Crane
diameter: 17.8m (58ft 4in)
Fl 282 *Kolibri*
diameter: 12.3m (40ft 4in)
Fa 223 *Drache* and Fa 225
diameter: 12m (39ft 4in)
Fa 330 *Bachstelze*
diameter: 7.3m (23ft 9in)

FOCKE-WULF *TRIEBFLUGEL*

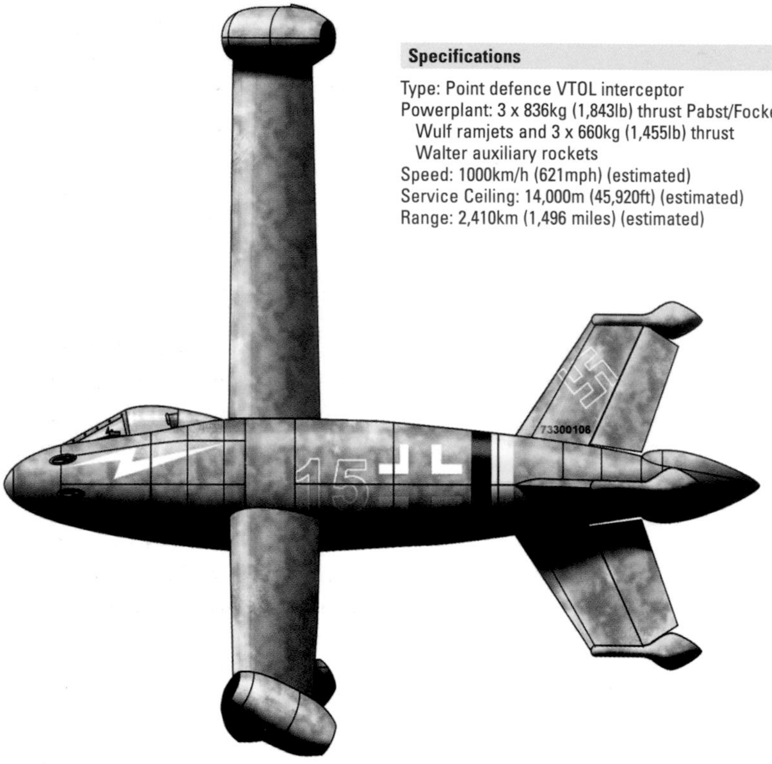

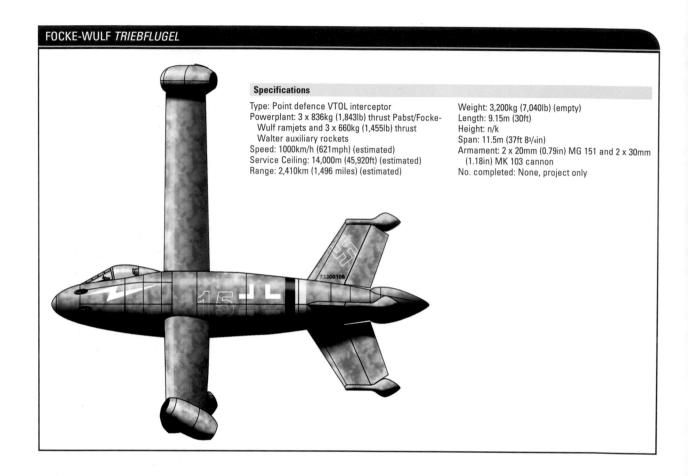

Specifications

Type: Point defence VTOL interceptor
Powerplant: 3 x 836kg (1,843lb) thrust Pabst/Focke-Wulf ramjets and 3 x 660kg (1,455lb) thrust Walter auxiliary rockets
Speed: 1000km/h (621mph) (estimated)
Service Ceiling: 14,000m (45,920ft) (estimated)
Range: 2,410km (1,496 miles) (estimated)
Weight: 3,200kg (7,040lb) (empty)
Length: 9.15m (30ft)
Height: n/k
Span: 11.5m (37ft 8¾in)
Armament: 2 x 20mm (0.79in) MG 151 and 2 x 30mm (1.18in) MK 103 cannon
No. completed: None, project only

Radar and Radio Guidance Systems

During the 1930s, German research into radar and radio guidance systems was highly advanced. The Lorenz blind-landing system provided the basis for the development of highly effective bombing guidance systems, while German radars were technically well ahead of their British and US counterparts.

Radio Guidance Systems

Knickebein (Crooked Leg)
This was the first such guidance system to be used operationally in 1940 and was a direct development of the Lorenz radio navigation system. Lorenz transmitted a signal that sent a stream of short signal 'dots' to the left of the centre line of the radio beam that was aligned with the centre of the runway, and a stream of long signal 'dashes' to the right. Aircraft to the right of the runway centre line would receive a much stronger 'dash' while those to the left would receive a stronger 'dot'.

The two signals overlapped along a relatively narrow centre line, and since the received strengths of the dashes matched those of the dots, a continuous 'equisignal' was received. Lorenz had a range of about 48km (30 miles) and allowed an aircraft to fly a straight course with sufficient accuracy to find the runway visually in all but the worst conditions.

Knickebein operated at far higher power to reach British targets. Two transmitters were set up at Stollberg in northern Germany near the Danish border and the other at Kleve (Cleves), almost the most westerly point in Germany. The aerials could be rotated to make the two beams cross over the target. The bombers would follow one beam of one until they heard the tones from the other, using a second receiver. When the steady 'on course' sound was heard from the second beam, they dropped their bombs.

Fortunately, it proved to be relatively simple to jam *Knickebein* by transmitting false signals on the same frequency and its threat had been largely negated by September 1940.

X-Gerät

Knickebein was rapidly superseded by the far more accurate *X-Gerät,* which operated at a much higher frequency using three cross-beams and incorporated an automatic bomb-release signal as the aircraft reached their target. The system's accuracy was roughly 91m (100yd) at a range of 320km (200 miles), good enough to hit a large factory. Once again, a jamming system was devised which transmitted a false bomb release signal, but before it was perfected, *X-Gerät's* potential was demonstrated by the raid on Coventry on 14–15 November 1940 that devastated five major factories and much of the city centre.

Y-Gerät

In an attempt to counter the jamming of the two existing systems, the Germans developed *Y-Gerät*, an even more accurate automatic single beam guidance system. However, it operated on a frequency of 45mHz, which had been used by the BBC's pre-war TV channel. British TV services had been suspended for the duration of the war and it proved to be relatively easy for the otherwise redundant BBC transmitters to jam the *Y-Gerät* signals.

Radars

Freya

By 1940, the Germans had eight operational *Freya* early warning radar stations. These were greatly outnumbered by the technically inferior British Chain Home radars and most importantly, were never integrated into a really effective early warning system. The system was used as the basis for the much larger and more powerful *Mammut* (Mammoth) and *Wasserman* (Waterman) early warning radars, both of which entered service in 1942. *Mammut's* range was about 320km (200 miles), whilst *Wasserman* could track Allied bomber formations at up to 240km (150 miles).

Würzburg and *Giant Würzburg*

Würzburg and its derivates were very sophisticated gun-laying radars which began to enter service in 1941, primarily with AA batteries. Almost 4000 *Würzburgs* of various models were produced between 1940 and 1945.

Jagdschloss (Hunting Lodge)

Although *Freya* and its derivatives were very good radars, they were blinded as soon as the Allies began using 'Window'. This was simply bundles of aluminium foil strips that were dropped at regular intervals by Allied bombers. The strips were cut to match the operating frequencies of known German radars and produced strong multiple returns on radar screens, obscuring the weaker returns from the aircraft. The basic system is still used by modern military aircraft, but is now known as chaff. *Jagdschloss* became operational in 1944, operating on a frequency that was immune to 'Window' jamming, and proved to be an effective early warning radar, with a range of up to 120km (75 miles).

Lichtenstein B/C

This was the first operational German AI radar that equipped night fighters (primarily the Me 110 and Ju 88) from spring 1942. It had a maximum range of 4km (2.5 miles), but was vulnerable to the Allied 'Window' jamming system.

Lichtenstein SN-2

Fortunately for the *Luftwaffe's* night fighters, the improved *Lichtenstein SN-2* was introduced just as Allied bombers began to use 'Window' in summer 1943. This operated on a different frequency to the earlier system and could cut through all jamming until the Allies countered with the introduction of 'Rope', a new version of 'Window', in mid-1944.

CHAPTER 7

Missiles and Air-Launched Weapons

German designers probably achieved more 'firsts' in these fields than in any others, including the first cruise missile, the first short-range ballistic missile, the first guided surface-to-air missiles, and the first anti-ship missiles.

The sheer number of missile projects was staggering – approximately 90 were under way by 1945. As with so many other aspects of German weapons development, there was considerable duplication of effort as the Luftwaffe*, army,* Kriegsmarine *and SS all pursued their own programmes. Many promising projects, such as the surface-to-air missiles, which had the potential to affect the course of the war by checking the Allied bombing campaign, never achieved operational status due to the diversion of resources to the V-1 and V-2 systems.*

A V-2 rocket is test-fired. Experimental missiles were painted in a distinctive black and white colour scheme to help track their flight path after launch.

Surface-to-Surface Missiles

Although they were far from being the decisive weapons that Hitler had envisaged, the V-1 and V-2 inflicted significant damage to their targets and compelled the Allies to divert considerable resources to countering the threat that they posed.

V-1

In common with many other countries, Germany had experimented with unmanned aircraft during the inter-war years, but had never seriously considered their potential as flying bombs. Tentative proposals for such weapons were rejected in 1939 and 1941, but by 1942, the erosion of German air superiority prompted the *Luftwaffe* to reconsider the matter and begin the development of a small, cheap flying bomb, with a range of about 250km (155 miles) and a 800kg (1760lb) warhead, that could hit an area target, evading interception by flying in at high speed and low altitude. The project was given the cover designation of *Flakzielgerät 76* (FZG 76) – 'AA target equipment 76'.

The FZG 76 was powered by an Argus pulse jet – a simple tube containing a fuel injection system and a spark plug, with its front covered by a screen of spring-loaded flaps. In flight, the airflow forced the flaps open, which operated a valve spraying fuel into the tube. The fuel/air mix was ignited by the spark plug and the explosion blew the flaps shut, producing a brief burst of thrust before the flaps were again forced open by the airflow to restart the operating cycle. At full speed, the engine produced these pulses at an approximate rate of 42 per second. While it was a crude engine, which could only operate effectively at low altitude, it would run well on low octane petrol and was ideally suited to power a flying bomb.

The initial test flight of an air-launched unpowered prototype was made in early December 1942, with the first powered flight following on Christmas Eve, when a missile was air-launched from a Focke-Wulf Fw 200 Condor from Peenemünde.

New launch system

Considerable development work was still required, but by mid-1943, a workable catapult launching system had been devised. A gyrocompass-based autopilot guidance system had been adopted which gave sufficient accuracy for use against area targets and selection of launch sites began. Potential launch sites were fewer than had been anticipated, as steadily increasing weight had degraded the missile's performance. It had been estimated that it would have a range of 483km (300 miles) and a speed of 720–800km/h (450–500mph) but in practice these figures were reduced to approximately 240km (150 miles) and 560–640km/h (350–400mph).

Production examples of the V-1 were fitted with an odometer driven by a vane anemometer on the nose that determined when the target area had been reached. Before launch, the counter was set to a value that would reach zero upon arrival at the target in the prevailing wind conditions. As the missile flew, the airflow turned the propeller, with every 30 rotations counting down one number on the counter. This counter triggered the arming of the warhead after about 60km (38 miles). When the counter reached zero, two explosive bolts were fired and two spoilers on the elevator were released, the linkage between the elevator and servo was jammed and a guillotine device cut off the control hoses to the rudder servo, setting the rudder in neutral. These actions put the V-1 into a steep dive.

RHEINBOTE, V-1, V-2, AND A9/A10 SIZES COMPARED

Missile	Length	Max Diameter	Span
Rheinbote	11.5m (37ft 6in)	0.535m (1ft 9in)	1.49m (4ft 10in)
V-1	8m (26ft)	0.84m (2ft 9in)	5m (17ft)
V-2	14m (46ft)	1.68m (5ft 6in)	3.5m (11ft 6in)
A-9/A-10 *Amerikarakete*	25.8m (84ft 8in)	4.3m (14ft 1in)	9m (29ft 6in)

SURFACE-TO-SURFACE MISSILES COMPARED

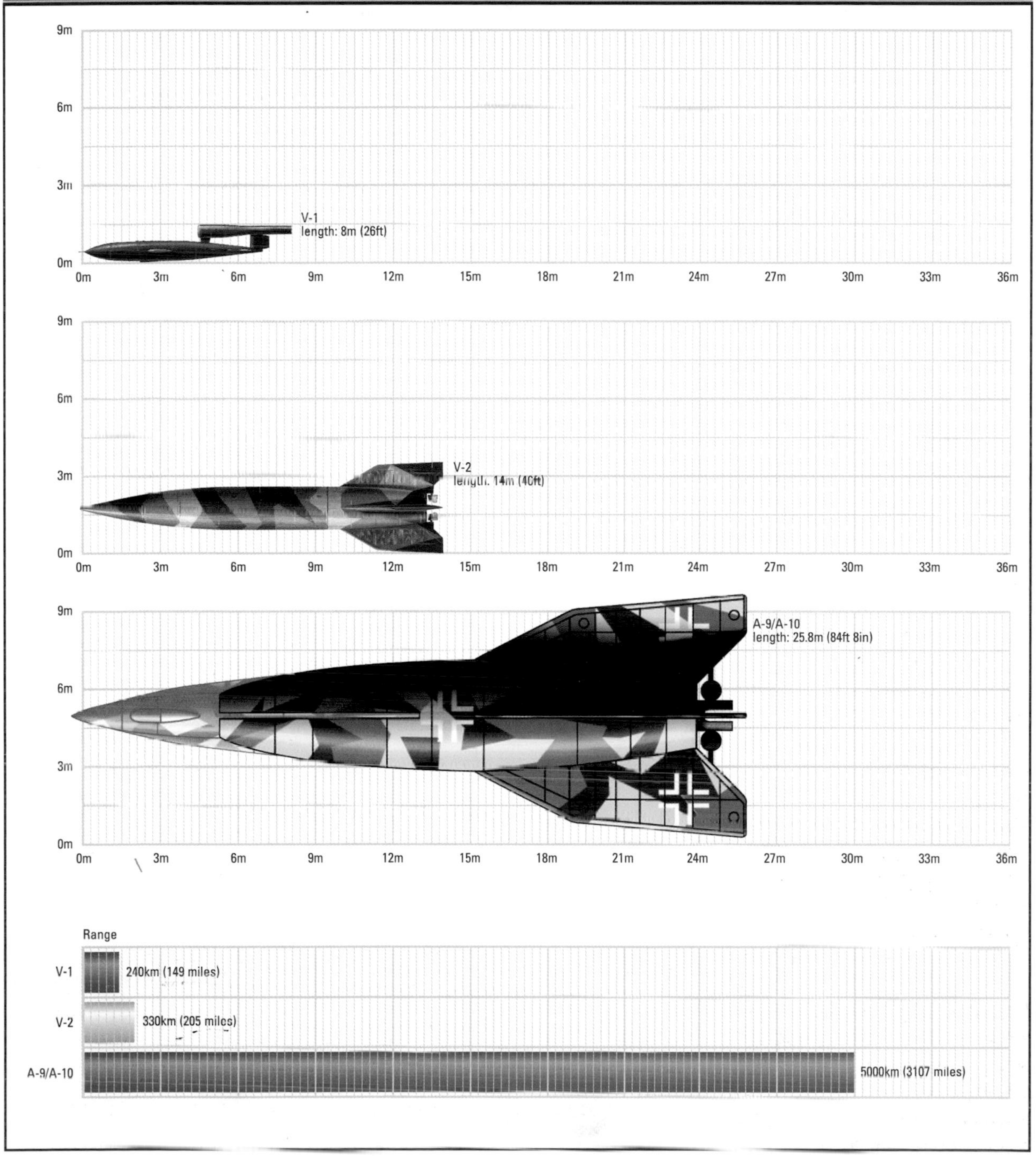
9m
6m
3m
0m
V-1
length: 8m (26ft)
0m
3m
6m
9m
12m
15m
18m
21m
24m
27m
30m
33m
36m
V-2
length: 14m (46ft)
A-9/A-10
length: 25.8m (84ft 8in)
Range
V-1
240km (149 miles)
V-2
330km (205 miles)
A-9/A-10
5000km (3107 miles)

RHEINBOTE, V-1, V-2, AND A-9/A-10 WARHEADS COMPARED

Missile	*Warhead Weight*	*Range*
Rheinbote	40kg (88lb) HE	220km (137 miles)
V-1	830kg (1826lb)	240km (149 miles)
V-2	975kg (2145lb)	330km (205 miles)
A-9/A-10 *Amerikarakete*	1000kg (2200lb)	5000km (3107 miles)

It was initially intended to build five major heavily protected bunker complexes for missile storage, servicing and launching, with approximately a further 100 smaller launch sites, in a belt just behind the Channel coast running from Le Havre to Calais. These smaller sites were dubbed 'ski sites' by Allied intelligence, since their missile storage buildings resembled giant skis laid on their sides. These prominent installations acted as magnets for Allied air attacks and they were steadily replaced by a network of far less conspicuous, well-camouflaged sites, many of which were never detected.

Fiesler Fi-103

The flying bomb was officially designated the Fiesler Fi-103 or FZG-76, but was more commonly referred to as the V-1 – *Vergeltungswaffe Einz* (Vengeance Weapon 1). It was a simple weapon, eminently suitable for assembly by a semi-skilled workforce and production was scheduled to begin in September 1943 with a target rate of 1400 V-1s per month by January 1944, increasing to 8000 per month by September 1944. It was intended to begin sustained attacks on British targets – primarily London – in mid-February 1944, by which time a stockpile of at least 1400 missiles should have been assembled. While the manufacturing process itself was relatively straightforward, Allied bombing of both the Peenemünde research establishment and the factories badly disrupted production and the first 1000 missiles were not completed until April 1944.

Centralization of production at the massive underground factory at Nordhausen dramatically improved the numbers being made and almost 12,000 V-1s were ready by the time that operational launches began in June 1944.

In August 1943, Flak Regiment 155(W) – FR 155(W) – was formed to operate the V-1. It had a total strength of 3500 personnel divided between four *Abteilung* (Battalions). Each *Abteilung* had two service and supply sections, plus four firing teams. As each firing team could man four launch sites, in theory, a total of 64 V-1s could be fired simultaneously.

Air-launched V-1s

At approximately the same time, III/KG3 began re-equipping with the first examples of the Heinkel He 111H-22, each of which could air-launch a single V-1. Although the Heinkel was very sluggish while

SURFACE-TO-SURFACE MISSILES: PAYLOADS

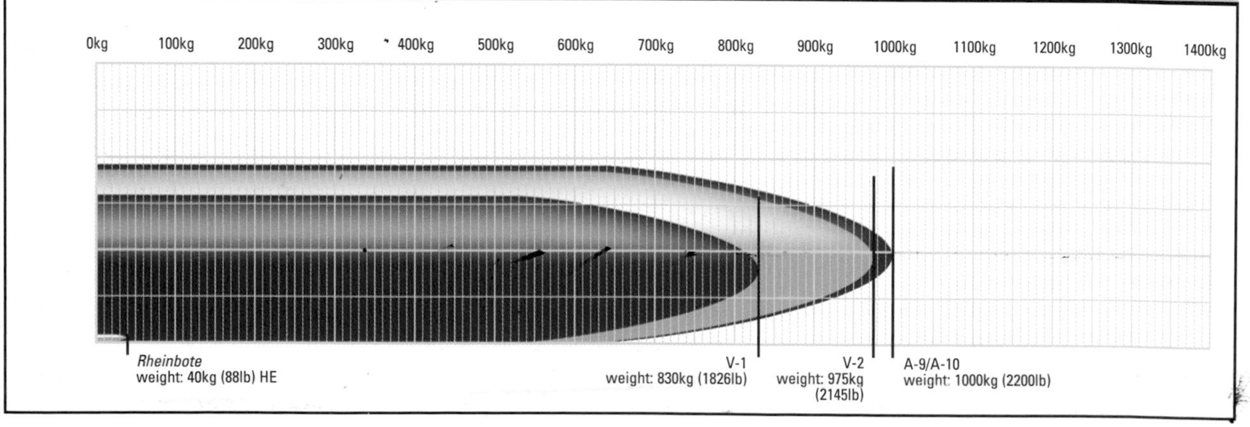
0kg
100kg
200kg
300kg
400kg
500kg
600kg
700kg
800kg
900kg
1000kg
1100kg
1200kg
1300kg
1400kg
Rheinbote
weight: 40kg (88lb) HE
V-1
weight: 830kg (1826lb)
V-2
weight: 975kg (2145lb)
A-9/A-10
weight: 1000kg (2200lb)

carrying the missile, this aspect of the development programme was largely trouble-free and the unit was able to steadily work up as aircraft and missiles became available.

The D-Day landings prompted Hitler to demand retaliation and the first V-1 attacks were made on 9 June 1944 when III/KG3 began operations from bases in the Netherlands. The Heinkels fired their V-1s over the North Sea at night, approaching the launch points at 'wave-top' height to minimise the risk of radar detection. They would then climb to an altitude of about 450m (1476ft) to release their missiles before running for home at low level. The first series of airborne launches lasted until early September when the Allied advance forced the unit to redeploy to Germany. During this time 300 V-1s were launched against London, 90 against Portsmouth and Southampton, 20 against Bristol and 23 against Paris. Despite the hazardous nature of the attacks – each firing dramatically lit up the launch aircraft for the benefit of any Allied night fighters in the vicinity – III/KG3 only lost two aircraft.

First ground launches

An initial handful of ground-launched V-1s were fired on the evening of 12 June 1944. The launching programme then escalated from the night of 15–16 June when 244 missiles were fired at London and a further 53 at Portsmouth and Southampton. At first, mechanical failures were responsible for most missile losses – 45 of the 244 V-1s aimed at London on 15–16 June crashed soon after launch, compared to 25 destroyed by AA fire and seven shot down by Allied fighters.

Despite the missiles' inaccuracy and unreliability, they had the potential to inflict serious damage – in total they destroyed or damaged over 100,000 houses. The 830kg (1826lb) warhead had a lethal blast radius of approximately 15m (49ft) and would destroy most buildings within a radius of 69m (226 feet) whilst causing structural damage at up to 183m (600ft).

AA shield

Allied bombing of the launch and storage sites was stepped up, while fighter and AA defences were strengthened. Initially, much of the effort was ill-directed, with the AA batteries frequently having to cease fire to avoid hitting Allied fighters attempting to intercept the missiles. Both discovered that the V-1s were hard targets as they flew too high for light AA weapons, but too low for heavy AA guns to track them effectively. Their speed was such that only the fastest Allied fighters such as the Tempest, Meteor and Mustang could catch them and shooting them down was a dangerous business, given the risk of cannon or machine gun fire detonating the warhead.

Eventually the AA guns were redeployed in protective belts, from which Allied fighters were banned. These belts underwent several moves to counter the changing nature of the threat: first, in mid-June 1944, from positions on the North Downs to the south coast of England, in a cordon closing the Thames Estuary to attacks from the east. In September 1944, a new defence line was formed on the coast of East Anglia, and finally in December there was a further extension along the Lincolnshire–Yorkshire coast. In the first week of their deployment on the south coast, the guns destroyed 17 per cent of all flying bombs entering their engagement zone. This figure rose to 60 per cent by 23 August and 74 per cent in the last week of the month, when 82 per cent were shot down in one day. The rate of destruction improved from an initial figure of one V-1 destroyed for every 2500 shells fired, to one for every 100.

The AA guns' effectiveness was significantly improved by the introduction of the US SCR-548 gun-laying radar, which was used in conjunction with an early analogue computer as one of the first automated fire-control systems. The ammunition itself was also dramatically improved by the issue of radio proximity fuses, which detonated shells as they came to within lethal range of targets, instead of relying on time fuses set before firing. The V-1's straight and level flight path made it a relatively easy target for the new automated AA gun system, and as gun crews became more experience with their new tools, the number of kills rose dramatically. A total of 20 SCR-584s were assigned to reinforce the AA belt, together with 80 x 90mm (3.54in) guns and supplies of proximity-fused ammunition. In a single day in August 1944 these batteries claimed a total of 97 V-1s using the new proximity-fused ammunition.

The Allied advance following the break out from the Normandy

V-2/A-4b DESIGNS

V-2

Length: 14m (46ft)
Max. Diameter: 1.68m (5ft 6in)
Span: 3.5m (11ft 6in)
Launch Weight: 12,870kg (28,314lb)
Warhead: 975kg (2145lb)
Range: 330km (205 miles)

A-4b (Unmanned)

Length: 14m (46ft)
Max. Diameter: 1.68m (5ft 6in)
Span: 3.99m (13ft 1in)
Launch Weight: 13,000kg (28,600lb)
Warhead: 975kg (2145lb)
Range: 600km (373 miles)

beachhead overran the last of the launch sites by early September 1944, forcing a hasty resumption of the German air-launched offensive as soon as the squadrons had completed their redeployment to more secure bases. III/KG3 was joined by KG 53 with a combined strength of roughly 100 bombers in this renewed offensive.

In contrast to the earlier operations, the Heinkels took heavy losses from night fighters and accidents. In order to counter the bombers' 'wave-top' approach beneath ground-based radar, a Wellington bomber was modified for use by the RAF's Fighter Interception Unit into what would now be described as an Airborne Early Warning and Control (AWACS) aircraft. By the time that a combination of crippling losses (a total of 77 bombers) and fuel shortages ended the air-launched missile campaign in mid-January 1945, a total of 1776 V-1s had been dropped, but no more than 388 landed in England, of which only 66 hit London.

New targets

As the Allied advance across Europe slowed in autumn 1944, the ground-launched V-1s were redeployed against other targets. Brussels and Liège were hit, but the greatest effort was directed against the key supply port of Antwerp. By the time that the attacks ended in March 1945, a total of 8896 V-1s had been fired at Antwerp, 3141 at Liège and 151 at Brussels.

The final V-1s to be launched were a new type, the extended-range Fi-103E-1. This had an enlarged fuel tank, but a smaller warhead to give a maximum range of 400km (250 miles) which brought London within range of Dutch launch sites. These missiles did not become available until early 1945 and a total of 275 were fired against London during March, of which only 13 hit London. These were the last of approximately 10,000 V-1s to be fired at England, of which 2419 reached London, killing 6184 people and injuring 17,981.

CAMPAIGNS COMPARED: V-1 VERSUS THE *BLITZ* (US INTELLIGENCE ASSESSMENT, DECEMBER 1944)

Cost to Germany	*Blitz*	*V1*
Sorties	90,000	8025
Weight of Bombs, Tonnes (tons)	67,631 (61,149)	14,834 (14,600)
Fuel Consumed, Tonnes (tons)	72,847 (71,700)	4756 (4681)
Aircraft Lost	3075	0
Men Lost	7690	0
Results	*Blitz*	*V1*
Houses Damaged/Destroyed	1,150,000	1,127,000
Casualties	92,566	22,892
Rate Casualties/Bombs Tonnes (tons)	1.63 (1.6)	1.63 (1.6)
Allied Air Effort	*Blitz*	*V1*
Sorties	86,800	44,770
Planes Lost	1260	351
Men Lost	2233	805

From A-1 to V-2

German rocket development began in the early 1930s with the activities of the Berlin amateur rocket society whose members included Werner von Braun. Army interest in their research led to the appointment of Captain Walter Dornberger to lead a team to investigate the military potential of rockets. In 1933, Dornberger began to gather a team of specialists including von Braun and, by the end of the year, it had completed the small 300kg (660lb) thrust lox alcohol liquid-fuel rocket, designated A-1. This was test-fired at the Kummersdorf artillery range but proved to be unstable.

Work then began on the more sophisticated gyroscopically stabilized A-2, two of which were successfully launched from Borkum Island in December 1934. Development continued and by 1936, the team had expanded to about 150 specialists who were able to stage an impressive demonstration of a new 1500kg (3300lb) thrust rocket motor for the Commader-in-Chief, General Frisch. This secured funding for a purpose-built research centre at Peenemünde, which was not completed until 1941.

In the meantime, the A-3 rocket was designed around the new motor – this was the team's largest rocket yet, with a length of 7.6m (25ft). Four were test-fired during the winter of 1937–38, all of which crashed. It was realized that more research was needed before production of the much larger A-4 could start. A heavily modified version of the A-3 was developed as the A-5, a test-bed for extensive aerodynamic and control systems trials which ran until 1941.

A-4 success

As data from the A-5 was assessed, work began on the A-4. The first airframes underwent wind-tunnel trials in 1940–41 and flight-capable prototypes were completed in 1942. After two failed launches in June and August 1942, the Peenemünde site launched its first successful A-4 on 3 October 1942. This missile reached an altitude of 96.5km (60 miles) and range of 201km (125 miles) in a 296-second flight, coming within 4km (2.5 miles) of its target and reaching a top speed of 5280km/h (3300mph).

On 22 November 1942, Hitler accepted the missile for service use and a month later, Armaments Minister Speer appointed Gerhard Degenkolb as the director of the A-4 production programme. Degenkolb was selected as a result of his achievement in dramatically increasing annual locomotive production at the Krupp and Henschel factories from 1900 in 1941 to 5500 by 1943.

Despite his abilities, it was a challenging project as the A-4 had never been designed for mass production – each of the existing examples had been hand-built by a highly skilled workforce and there was no production line equipment. However, plans were rapidly drawn up for A-4 factories to be established

V-2 PRODUCTION FIGURES

Period	*Production*
Up to 15 Sept 1944	1900
15 Sept–29 Oct 1944	900
29 Oct–24 Nov 1944	600
24 Nov 1944–15 Jan 1945	1100
15 Jan–15 Feb 1945	700
Total	5200

at Peenemünde itself, the Zeppelin GmbH works in Friedrichshafen and the Henschel-Raxwerke near Wiener Neustadt, Austria.

Production and costs

Initial monthly production targets were for 300 missiles to be completed during October 1943, rising to 900 by December. In July 1943, the December target figure was raised to 2000 – the additional rockets were to be produced by Demag at Falkensee. After destructive RAF raids on Friedrichshafen, Wiener Neustadt and Peenemünde in August 1943, A-4 production was centralized at the underground Mittelwerk factory at Nordhausen, in the Harz Mountains. However, the assembly facilities at Peenemünde were largely undamaged and were used to produce an initial batch of missiles for field training with *Lehr und Versuchs Batterie 444*, the unit formed to carry out field trials of the A-4, now increasingly referred to as the V-2 – *Vergeltungswaffe Zwei* (Vengeance Weapon 2). Peenemünde subsequently manufactured a total of roughly 250 A-4s for use in its research programme.

The initial cost of producing a V-2 rocket was 100,000 Reichsmarks (RM) (excluding the warhead) but the average cost was later reduced to 75,110RM. At Peenemünde, each V-2 took between 10,000 and 20,000 man-hours to produce, while at Mittelwerk the figure dropped to approximately 7500. The V-2 workforce at Mittelwerk totalled 2000 civilian technicians and approximately 10,000 slave labourers who lived in nearby

DR WERNER MAGNUS MAXIMILIAN FREIHERR VON BRAUN

■ Werner von Braun (with his arm in a cast) immediately after his surrender to US forces, May 1945.

Von Braun began his life-long interest in rocketry and space flight as a teenager, when he joined the German Spaceflight Society. He subsequently carried out research work on the military application of solid-fuel rockets before becoming Technical Director of the Peenemünde Rocket Research Centre, where he played a key role in the development of the V-2 ballistic missile and the *Wasserfall* anti-aircraft missile.

BIRTH:	23 March 1912
DEATH:	16 June 1977
PLACE OF BIRTH:	Wirstz, Prussia (now Wyrzysk, Poland)
FATHER:	Magnus Alexander Maximilian Freiherr von Braun
MOTHER:	Emmy von Braun (née von Quistorp)
SIBLINGS:	Sigismund von Braun (1911–98) Magnus von Braun (1919–2003)
PERSONAL RELATIONSHIPS:	Maria Louise von Quistorp, married 1 March 1947. Three children – Iris Careen (1948), Margrit Cecile (1952) and Peter Constantine (1960)
MILITARY SERVICE:	n/a
KEY PRE-WAR AND WARTIME POSITIONS:	Ordnance Department Researcher (1932–37). Technical Director Peenemünde Rocket Research Centre (1937–45).

barracks camp known as 'Dora', which became the main camp of *Konzentrationslager* Mittelbau in October 1944. The 'Dora' prisoners lived in terrible conditions, especially during the first few months before their barracks were completed and they were forced to live underground. Conditions again deteriorated sharply in the last few months of the war, when the food supply worsened and many prisoners from Auschwitz and other eastern camps were dumped into Mittelbau-Dora. About half of the 20,000 deaths in the camp can be ascribed to the V-2 programme.

Operational structure

Three missile launching battalions (*Artillerie Abteilungen 485, 836 and 191 Motorised*) had been formed to operate the V-2 alongside *Batterie 444* in late 1943 and a Waffen-SS unit, *SS-Werfer Batterie* 500 began training with the missile in spring 1944. It had been intended to launch the V-2s from a small number of heavily protected bunkers near the Channel coast, but these were destroyed by Allied bombing and all operational missiles were fired from road-mobile launchers.

As with all early liquid-fuelled missiles, the launch procedure was complex and took between four and six hours, 90 minutes of which was spent in final preparations at the launch site. Each battery deployed a total of 32 vehicles to handle, service and fuel the V-2s, which were delivered to the launch areas by rail and transferred to a *Vidalwagen* transporter for the short journey to the field storage site. The battery's technical section would then check

A-10 *AMERIKARAKETE*

Specifications

Length: 25.8m (84ft 8in)
Max. Diameter: 4.3m (14ft 1in)
Span: 9m (29ft 6in)
Launch Weight: 101,000kg (222,200lb)
Warhead: 1000kg (2200lb)
Range: 5000km (3107 miles)

each missile and fit its warhead, before loading it on to the *Meillerwagen* transporter/erector trailer for transfer to the actual launch site.

On arrival, the *Meillerwagen* lifted the V-2 onto its launch pad, where the missile was fuelled and the final pre-launch checks carried out. The battery's vehicles then pulled back to a safe distance and the missile was launched, after which the unit cleared the area to avoid the air attacks that would follow if the launch had been spotted by Allied aircraft.

The V-2 continued to suffer from serious technical problems that delayed its combat use until autumn 1944 and it was not until 8 September that the first two operational rockets were fired at Paris by *Batterie 444*, from launch sites in the Ardennes. The first apparently disintegrated in flight, but the second worked perfectly and exploded near the Porte d'Italie. Later the same day, a battery of *Abteilung 485* fired two missiles against London and during the first ten days of operations a total of 43 V-2s were fired: 26 at London and 17 at other targets, mainly in France.

Antwerp and London

The Allied airborne offensive, Operation Market Garden, disrupted the missile offensive as the V-2 batteries in the Netherlands were temporarily withdrawn, but they returned as soon as the situation had stabilized and resumed launches from sites around the Hague.

In October 1944, Hitler ordered that launches against secondary targets should cease and that the batteries should concentrate their fire on London and the vital supply port of Antwerp. Attacks against Antwerp were stepped up in December 1944 in support of the Ardennes Offensive, which had the city as its ultimate objective.

In fact, Antwerp was hit by an average of 100 missiles per week in the second half of the month. During the same period, a number of V-2s were also fired at other Belgian targets and by the end of 1944, a total of 1561 had been launched. Of these, 491 had been aimed at London, 924 at Antwerp and the remainder at various French and Belgian cities.

Missile launches from Dutch sites peaked in February 1945, before tailing off as Allied bombing disrupted V-2 production – the last rockets were fired against London and Antwerp on 27 March. Earlier in the month, the V-2 was used against a point target for the first time, when a total of 11 were launched in an attempt to destroy the Ludendorff Bridge across the Rhine at Remagen following its capture by US forces on 7 March.

Remarkably, two of the missiles fired on 17 March were near misses and the bridge collapsed on the same day. It is possible that the shock of the missiles' impact at Mach 3, coupled with the detonation of their 975kg (2145lb) warheads was enough to bring down the bridge that had

SURFACE-TO-SURFACE MISSILE RANGES

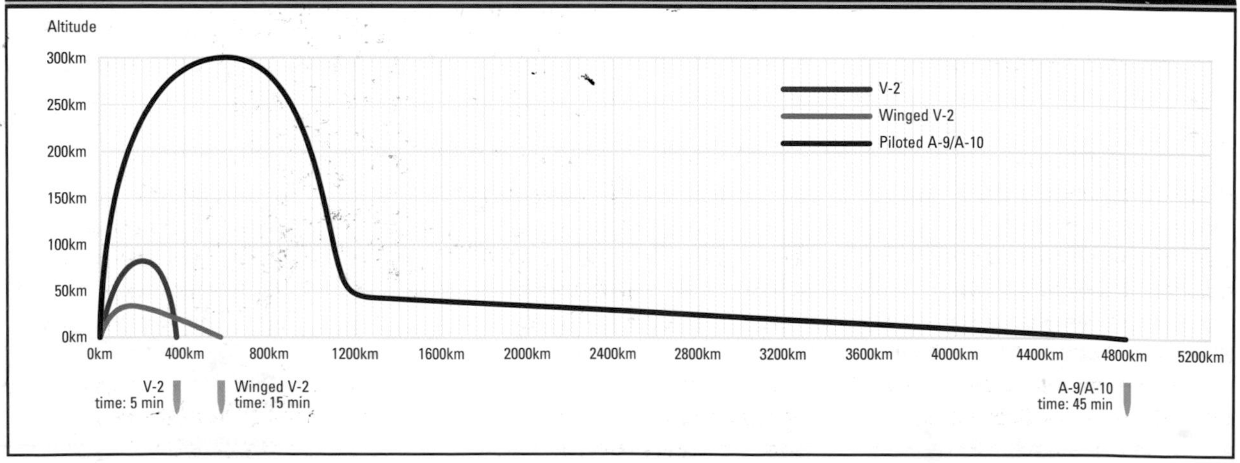
Altitude
300km
250km
200km
150km
100km
50km
0km
V-2
Winged V-2
Piloted A-9/A-10
0km
400km
800km
1200km
1600km
2000km
2400km
2800km
3200km
3600km
4000km
4400km
4800km
5200km
V-2
time: 5 min
Winged V-2
time: 15 min
A-9/A-10
time: 45 min

V-2 ROCKET – INTERNAL VIEW

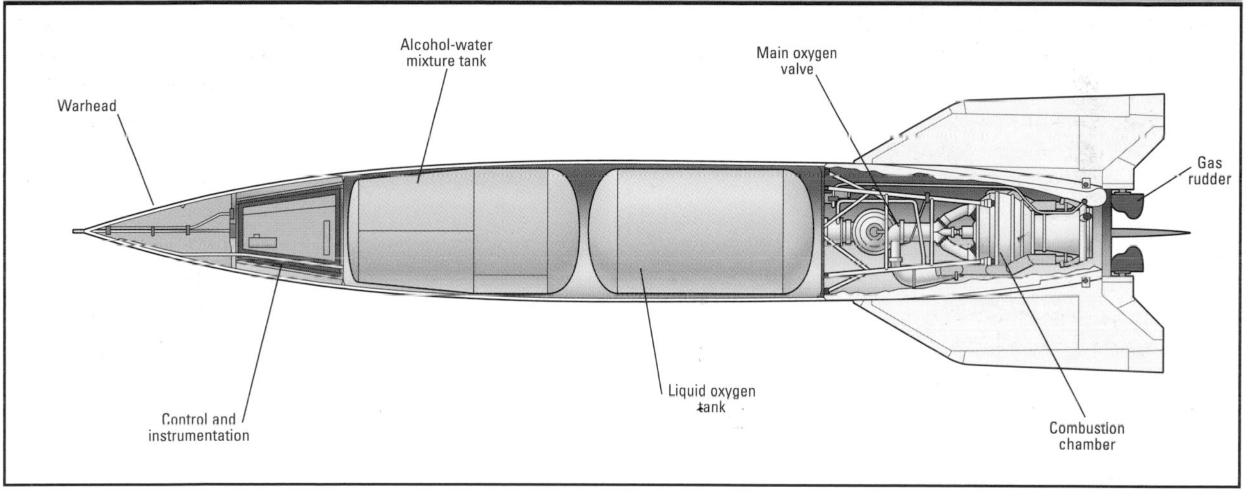
Alcohol-water mixture tank
Main oxygen valve
Warhead
Gas rudder
Control and instrumentation
Liquid oxygen tank
Combustion chamber

already been weakened by the initial botched demolition attempt.

Poor accuracy

In many respects, the operational V-2 was an ineffective weapon – the accuracy of a standard gyroscopically guided missile was insufficient for its conventional warhead of less than 1000kg (2200lb) to have much chance of inflicting significant damage on a point target and its high-speed impact meant that much of the blast effect was dissipated in gouging out a large crater.

However, up to 20 per cent of V-2s were fitted with the *Leitstrahlstellung,* a radio beam guidance system which improved their accuracy and made them more suitable for point target attacks. It seems that these were only issued to *SS-Werfer Batterie 500* operating from the Dalfsen/Hellendoorn area in the Netherlands. Significantly, it was missiles fired by this unit that almost hit and destroyed the Ludendorff Bridge.

On the drawing board – V-2 derivatives

One of the most spectacular proposed V-2 modifications was designed in 1944 as a method of bombarding 'prestige' targets in the eastern United States, such as New York and Washington. Designated Project *Prufstand XII*, the design was a 500 tonne (492 ton) watertight cylindrical container containing a slightly modified V-2. Three such containers could be towed across the Atlantic by a submerged Type XXI U-boat. On arrival at the launch area, the containers' ballast tanks were to be flooded to bring them to the vertical. The missiles would then be fuelled and have their guidance systems set before being launched, after which the containers would be sunk. Orders for three containers were placed in December 1944 and at least one is believed to have been completed by the end of the war.

While it was an ingenious idea, it seems unlikely that even a Type XXI could evade Allied anti-submarine forces while towing three unwieldy containers. It is even more unlikely that it would be able to spend 90 minutes or so surfaced just off the US coast while the missiles were prepared for launching.

A-9/A-4b/A-10

The development of these missiles started in late 1939 when research began into ways of increasing the range of the A-4. It was calculated that fitting properly designed wings could extend the A-4's range to approximately 550km (342 miles). Wind-tunnel tests were extremely promising and the new design was designated A-9. A manned version of this missile was also designed that could reach a conventional airfield 600km (373 miles) from the launch point in only 17 minutes, landing at a speed of 160km/h (100mph)

NUMBERS OF V-2s FIRED AT TARGETS IN EUROPE

Location	*Total*
Belgium	**1664**
Antwerp	1610
Liège	27
Hasselt	13
Tournai	9
Mons	3
Diest	2
UK	**1402**
London	1358
Norwich	43
Ipswich	1
France	**76**
Lille	25
Paris	22
Tourcoing	19
Arras	6
Cambrai	4
Netherlands (Maastricht)	**19**
Germany (Remagen)	**11**

Work on the A-9 was officially halted in 1943 in order to concentrate on getting the V-2 into service. However, it seems that some clandestine research continued, under the cover of a 'paper project', designated A-4b. In 1944, this project was revived to fulfil both its original role and as the second stage of a true intercontinental ballistic missile (ICBM), referred to as the A-4b/A-10 or the A-9/A-10.

Two prototype A-4bs were test-fired in December 1944 and January 1945, the first crashing soon after launch, while the second was lost when a wing broke away just after the missile began the gliding phase of its flight. Despite these failures, von Braun was confident that the design was sound, but the deteriorating military situation forced the evacuation of the Peenemünde site before any further trials could be carried out.

A final variant of the A-4b was intended to be fitted with a ring of 10 solid propellant booster rockets to achieve a speed of Mach 6 at an altitude of 20km (12 miles), extending the range of the missile to 950–1000km (590–621 miles).

First ICBM

The first stage of the proposed ICBM, the A-10, was to be powered by six modified V-2 rocket engines and was intended to carry the second stage A-4b/A-9 embedded in its nose. The problem of achieving any sort of accuracy against US targets was considerable, given the limitations of 1940s technology.

Two options were seriously considered, the first was guidance by radio beacons which were to be set up by German agents operating in the USA and the second was to utilize a manned version of the A-4b/A-9. In theory, the pilot was to eject after setting the missile on course to its target.

The A4b/A-10 combination was designed in parallel with the A-9/A-4b and its development was also officially suspended in 1943 to free resources for the V-2 programme. However, there is some surprising evidence to the contrary at two locations in Normandy, one at Haut Mesnil, near Caen and the other at La Meauffe, near St Lo. Both were quarries that had been taken over for conversion to V-2 storage areas in 1942, but little work was completed up to the end of 1943. In early 1944, urgent construction work suddenly began at both sites and after their capture, Allied intelligence teams found that they contained networks of tunnels and loading equipment for missiles almost twice the size of the V-2. Perhaps, therefore, work on A-4b/A-10 was much closer to completion than official historical research suggests.

Rheinbote (Rhine Messenger)

In the late 1930s, the armaments firm Rheinmetall-Borsig had built up considerable expertise in the development of solid fuel rockets for army use in the short-range bombardment role (the 28/32cm (11/12.6in) NbW 41 series). It appears that there were some misgivings at this time about the feasibility of the large, liquid-fuelled missiles under development at Peenemünde and that Rheinmetall-Borsig were requested to design a solid fuel missile to act as back-up in the event of the failure of the V-1 or V-2 design and construction projects.

By May 1942, plans had been drawn up for a multi-stage, solid fuel rocket carrying a 1225kg (2695lb) warhead to a maximum range of 241km (150 miles). Although a production contract was issued, it soon became apparent that development would be a lengthy business and attention turned to smaller versions of the missile that could be brought into service more quickly. The selected type, the Rh-Z-61/9, was dubbed *Rheinbote* and was a four-stage, fin-stabilized missile with no guidance or control system that had to be accurately aimed at its target before launch to have any chance of hitting it.

General Dornberger expressed deep reservations about the practicality of the design which used a 1715kg (3775lb) multi-stage missile to inaccurately deliver a 40kg (88lb) warhead containing only 20kg (44lb) of explosives. However, the SS believed that the system had real potential to damage Allied targets and used their increasing influence over missile development to issue a production order for the *Rheinbote* in November 1944.

The *Rheinbote* trials unit was accordingly mobilized as *Artillerie Abeitlung 709* and deployed to Nunspeet in the Netherlands to take part in the massive bombardment of Antwerp, which was an important supply port. The unit was supposed to be equipped with 12 launchers, but only seems to have received four.

The launcher was the *FR-Wagen*, a modification of the *Meillerwagen* transporter/erector trailer used for the V-2. The missile was fired from a launch rail mounted on the erector frame rather than from a separate launch pad, as in the case of the V-2.

Combat Effectiveness

The shortage of launchers accentuated the ineffectiveness of the *Rheinbote* bombardment which began on Christmas Eve and continued into January 1945. The average rate of fire for each launcher seems to have been roughly one missile per hour – estimates of the

V-2 LAUNCH SITES AND TARGETS

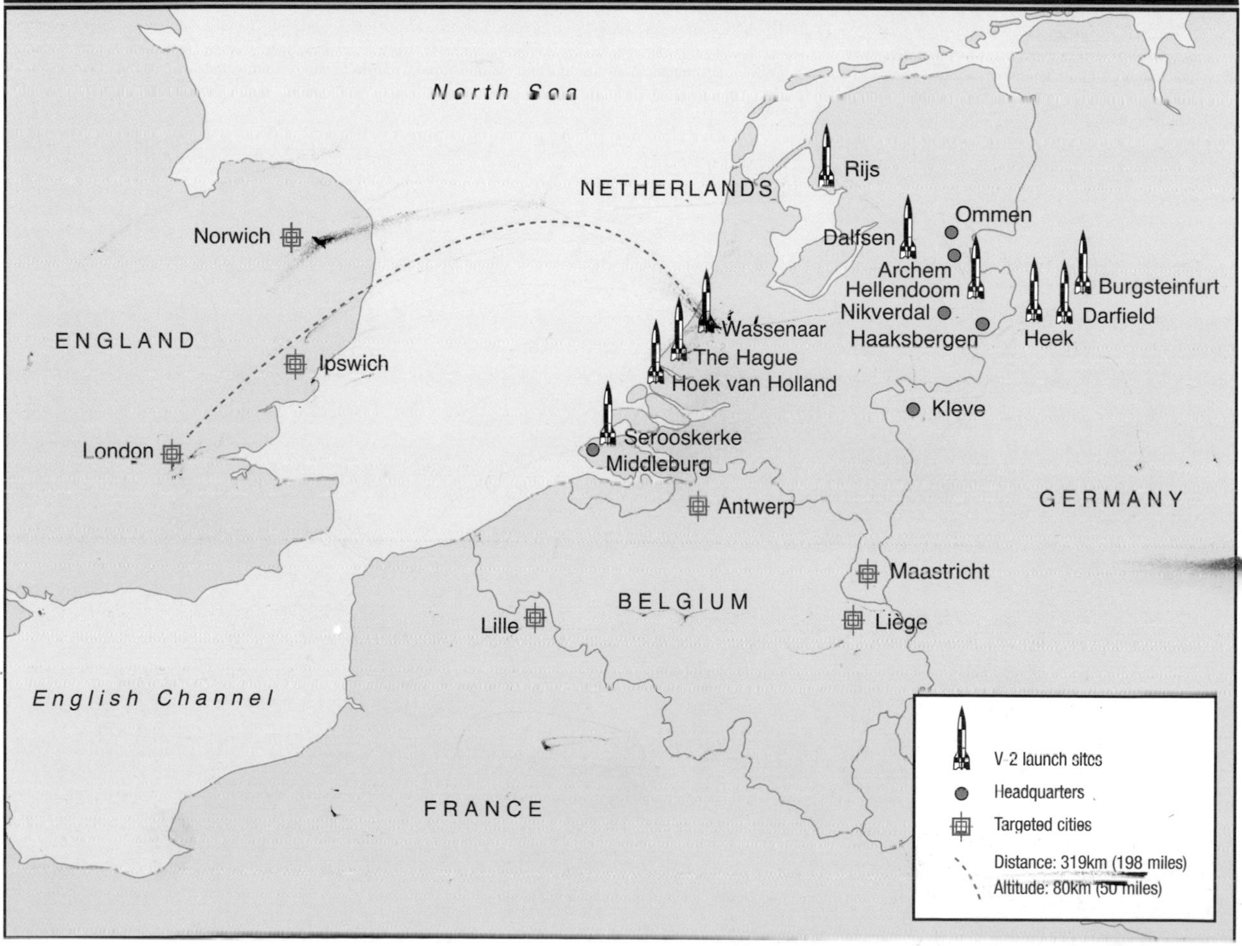
North Sea
NETHERLANDS
Rijs
Ommen
Dalfsen
Archem
Hellendoom
Nikverdal
Haaksbergen
Heek
Burgsteinfurt
Darfield
Norwich
ENGLAND
Ipswich
London
Wassenaar
The Hague
Hoek van Holland
Kleve
Serooskerke
Middleburg
Antwerp
GERMANY
Maastricht
BELGIUM
Lille
Liège
English Channel
FRANCE
V-2 launch sites
Headquarters
Targeted cities
Distance: 319km (198 miles)
Altitude: 80km (50 miles)

LAUNCH SCHEDULE: V-2 ROCKETS, BATTERY 444 (OCTOBER 1944)

Date	Time	Launch Site	Damage
1 Oct	1850 hours	Rijsterbos, Middenleane	Rocket fired, impacted farm at Bedingham, close to the Sycamore farm, wounding 4 persons. Farm had major damage, crater 9m (30ft) wide and 1.5m (5ft) deep
3 Oct	0930 hours	Rijsterbos, Middenleane	Rocket fired, impacted in a forest near the village of Beeston St Lawrence
3 Oct	1015 hours	Rijsterbos, Middenleane	Rocket fired, impacted in North Sea
3 Oct	1330 hours	Rijsterbos, Middenleane	Rocket fired, impacted a pasture near farm at Lowestoft, three persons serious injuries, and major damage to farm. Five people had minor injuries
3 Oct	1650 hours	Rijsterbos, Middenleane	Rocket fired, impacted near Great Witchingham with no damage. Crater 15m (49ft) wide and 6m (20ft) deep
3 Oct	1945 hours	Rijsterbos, Middenleane	Rocket fired, impacted in Norwich, much damage. The missile broke up over the Mile Cross housing-estate, Norwich, the warhead hit the Royal Norwich Golf Club, Hellesdon 400 houses were damaged, and one person died
3 Oct	2000 hours	Rijsterbos, Middenleane	Rocket fired, impacted in Denton, the impact was about 10 minutes later (longer than normal) creating much damage
4 Oct	1219 hours	Rijsterbos, Middenleane	Rocket fired, impacted shoreline called California, 8km (5 miles) north of Great Yarmouth
4 Oct	1336 hours	Rijsterbos, Middenleane	Rocket fired, impacted near school at Rockland St Mary, minor injuries and one serious
4 Oct	1643 hours	Rijsterbos, Middenleane	Rocket fired, impacted at Crostwick, very close to the air base at Rackheath. It landed in area known locally as Mud Corner, only about 0.4km (1/4 mile) away from the Base Bomb Dump
4 Oct	1733 hours	Rijsterbos, Middenleane	Rocket fired, impacted at Spixworth, no damage. This rocket fell apart before impact scattered over a large area. The entire engine, parts of the radio, etc., recovered and sent to research institute for Air Travel at Farnborough
5 Oct	0959 hours	Rijsterbos, Middenleane	Rocket fired, impacted at a forest near Taverham
5 Oct	1237 hours	Rijsterbos, Middenleane	Rocket fired, impacted near Great Yarmouth in the sea
5 Oct	1440 hours	Rijsterbos, Middenleane	Rocket fired, impacted at Surlingham. Ten wounded and 36 houses damaged
5 Oct	–	Rijsterbos, Middenleane	Rocket fired, impact unknown, this rocket possibly canted horizontal at lift off and crashed near Mirnser cliff at IJsselmeer (IJssel Lake) according to local newspaper accounts
6 Oct	1020 hours	Rijsterbos, Middenleane	Rocket fired, impacted at swamp near Shotesham All Saints, 43 buildings damaged
9 Oct	1040 hours	Rijsterbos, Middenleane	Rocket fired, impacted at Cantley, two cows died
9 Oct	1042 hours	Rijsterbos, Middenleane	Rocket fired, impacted at Brooke
9 Oct	1800 hours	Rijsterbos, Middenleane	Rocket fired, fell in sea south of Orfordness
10 Oct	0720 hours	Rijsterbos, Middenleane	Rocket fired, impacted North Sea near Frinton (airburst)
10 Oct	0929 hours	Rijsterbos, Middenleane	Rocket fired, impact unknown
10 Oct	1557 hours	Rijsterbos, Middenleane	A-4 rocket fired, exploded 1,200m (3936ft) high above the harbor of Harwich
10 Oct	1750 hours	Rijsterbos, Middenleane	Rocket fired, impacted at Woods End, minor injuries to two persons
11 Oct	0805 hours	Rijsterbos, Middenleane	Rocket fired, impacted at Haddiscoe. Slight damage to property
11 Oct	1049 hours	Rijsterbos, Middenleane	Rocket fired, impacted in sugar beet field near Rockland St Mary, Norfolk. Slight damage
11 Oct	1355 hours	Rijsterbos, Middenleane	Rocket fired, impact unknown
11 Oct	1419 hours	Rijsterbos, Middenleane	Rocket fired, impacted in field at Playford, Suffolk. Slight damage
11 Oct	1807 hours	Rijsterbos, Middenleane	Rocket fired, crashed near launch site between Rijs and Bakhuizen, killing two cows
*11 Oct	+1800 hours	Rijsterbos, Middenleane	Rocket fired (impact unknown)
12 Oct	+/-0735 hours	Rijsterbos, Middenleane	Rocket fired, impacted near Ingworth, Norfolk. Minor damage
13 Oct	0940 hours	Rijsterbos, Middenleane	Rocket fired, first V-2 impact in Antwerp. Impacted at the corner of the Schildersstraat and the Karel Rogierstraat; 32 people were killed, 45 were injured and 80 houses including a museum were damaged, with 43 houses totally destroyed
13 Oct	1311 hours	Rijsterbos, Middenleane	Rocket fired, impacted Borsbeek. No casualties
13 Oct	1545 hours	Rijsterbos, Middenleane	Rocket fired, impact unknown
13 Oct	1610 hours	Rijsterbos, Middenleane	Rocket fired, impacted Lange Loebroekstraat, Antwerp; 12 dead, 20 injured
13 Oct	1905 hours	Rijsterbos, Middenleane	Rocket fired, impact unknown

total number of missiles fired vary, but it was certainly no more than 200. As predicted, the effectiveness of these missiles was very limited and by the end of January 1945, even the SS appreciated that the rocket was militarily useless and the project was finally cancelled the following month.

While the service version of *Rheinbote* was a total disaster, there were designs derived from the original study that could have been at least as effective as the V-2. The most advanced of these seems to have been the *Rheinbote III,* which had a 771kg (1700lb) warhead and a range of 241km (150 miles).

LAUNCH SCHEDULE: V-2 ROCKETS, BATTERY 444 (OCTOBER 1944) (CONT.)

Date	Time	Launch Site	Damage
14 Oct	0800 hours	Rijsterbos, Middenleane	Rocket fired, impact unknown
14 Oct	1500 hours	Rijsterbos, Middenleane	Rocket fired, impact unknown
14 Oct	1600 hours	Rijsterbos, Middenleane	Rocket fired, impact unknown
14 Oct	1700 hours	Rijsterbos, Middenleane	Rocket fired, impact unknown
15 Oct	0800 hours	Rijsterbos, Middenleane	Rocket fired, impact unknown
15 Oct	0930 hours	Rijsterbos, Middenleane	Rocket fired, impact unknown
15 Oct	1130 hours	Rijsterbos, Middenleane	Rocket fired, impact unknown
15 Oct	1215 hours	Rijsterbos, Middenleane	Rocket fired, impact unknown
16 Oct	0800 hours	Rijsterbos, Middenleane	Rocket fired, impact unknown
16 Oct	1300 hours	Rijsterbos, Middenleane	Rocket fired, impact unknown
16 Oct	1530 hours	Rijsterbos, Middenleane	Rocket fired, impact unknown
16 Oct	1800 hours	Rijsterbos, Middenleane	Rocket fired, impact possibly at dock in Antwerp harbour
17 Oct	0700 hours	Rijsterbos, Middenleane	Rocket fired, impact unknown
17 Oct	0945 hours	Rijsterbos, Middenleane	Rocket fired, impact possibly in the Bouwhandelstraat in Borgerhout; 25 houses demaged and no victims
17 Oct	1200 hours	Rijsterbos, Middenleane	Rocket fired, impact unknown
19 Oct	0730 hours	Rijsterbos, Middenleane	Rocket fired, impact at the Fonteinstraat and Engelschelei at Borgerhout; two people were killed, eight were injured, two houses destroyed and 34 damaged
19 Oct	1050 hours	Rijsterbos, Middenleane	Rocket fired, impact unknown
19 Oct	1345 hours	Rijsterbos, Middenleane	Rocket fired, impact unknown
19 Oct	1625 hours	Rijsterbos, Middenleane	A-4 rocket crashed near launching site
27 Oct	0646 hours		Rocket fired, impacted Windsor Great Park, near Egham, Surrey
27 Oct	1015 hours		Rocket fired, impacted Swanley, Kent. Two persons suffered slight injuries
27 Oct	1115 hours		Rocket fired, impacted Leyton. Direct hit on house. six dead, 30 seriously injured. Six properties demolished
27 Oct	1200 hours		Rocket fired, impacted on forest land in Chingford. Hotel and historic hunting lodge damaged. Two persons suffered slight injuries. The crater from this incident still exists
27 Oct	1355 hours	Wassenaar, Beukenhorst	Rocket fired, rises about 90m (295ft), then falls back onto launch site killing 12 German soldiers, damaging launch vehicles and equipment. This was the worst firing site accident that the Germans had during the Den Haag/Wassenaar launch period. The Beukenhorst was cleared
27 Oct	1600 hours		Rocket fired (failure)
27 Oct	1855 hours		Rocket fired, impacted on open ground in Wanstead. No damage, but one person killed, another seriously injured
27 Oct	2315 hours		Site 176, rocket fired, impacted West Ham. 14 seriously injured. Six properties demolished
27 Oct	2340 hours	Site 164	Rocket fired, impacted on waste ground in Lewisham. Slight damage. One person seriously injured

*Source: courtesy http://www.v2rocket.com/start/deployment-start.html

Surface-to-Air Rockets and Missiles

German surface-to-air rockets and missiles included advanced design features such as jettisonable boosters and multiple homing systems that were widely adopted by post-war Western and Soviet missile-designers.

Despite these advances, it is arguable that the programmes suffered from excessive attention to missile design and insufficient attention to the more critical technological hurdles of their associated radars and fire control systems.

Henschel Hs 117 *Schmetterling* (Butterfly)

The Hs 117 originated with a 1941 design by Dr Wagner. It was rejected as an unnecessary weapon as it was thought at the time that the war would be over before such rockets could enter production. The deteriorating military situation led to the revival of the project in 1943, with a projected in-service date of early 1945.

The first prototype was completed in early 1944 and resembled a miniature aircraft with swept wings and cruciform tail surfaces. It was powered by a liquid-fuelled BMW 109-558 motor, but later examples switched to a Walther HWK 109-729, using *R-Stoff* hypergolic liquid and *SV*- or *S-Stoff* propellants. At take-off, the main engine was supplemented by two jettisonable Schmidding 109-553 solid-fuel booster rockets that fired for approximately five seconds.

Flight-testing began in May 1944, with the first 28 prototype missiles using the BMW engine. All test firings used the Strassburg-Kehl system of radio command guidance and the 25kg (55lb) warhead was detonated by an AEG Fuchs radio proximity fuse. A total of 59 launches were carried out, 29 of which were successful, with low-level targets being engaged at ranges of up to 32km (20 miles). In trials against high altitude targets, it was established that *Schmetterling's* operational ceiling was 10,976m (36,000ft). The type was approved for service with a target production figure of 3000 missiles per month, but it seems unlikely that manufacture actually began in the chaos of the last months of the war.

Wasserfall (Waterfall)

Design studies for *Wasserfall* began in 1941, and were completed in November 1942. It was essentially a scaled-down AA version of the V-2 missile, which retained the same general configuration, although it was fitted with additional mid-fuselage fins to improve manoeuvrability. Prototypes of the liquid-fuelled rocket motor were test-

■ **Test-firing of the *Wasserfall* missile.**

***WASSERFALL* W-10 SPECIFICATIONS**	
Specification	*Amount*
Length:	6.13m (20ft 1in)
Max Diameter:	0.72m (2ft 4in)
Span:	1.58m (5ft 2in)
Launch Weight:	3500kg (7700lb)
Warhead:	306kg (673lb)
Range:	26.4km (16.4 miles)

HENSCHEL Hs 117 *SCHMETTERLING*

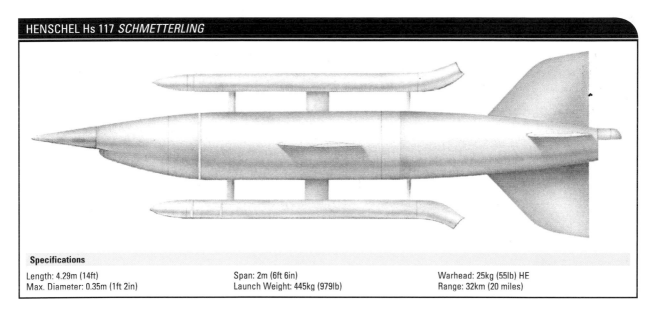

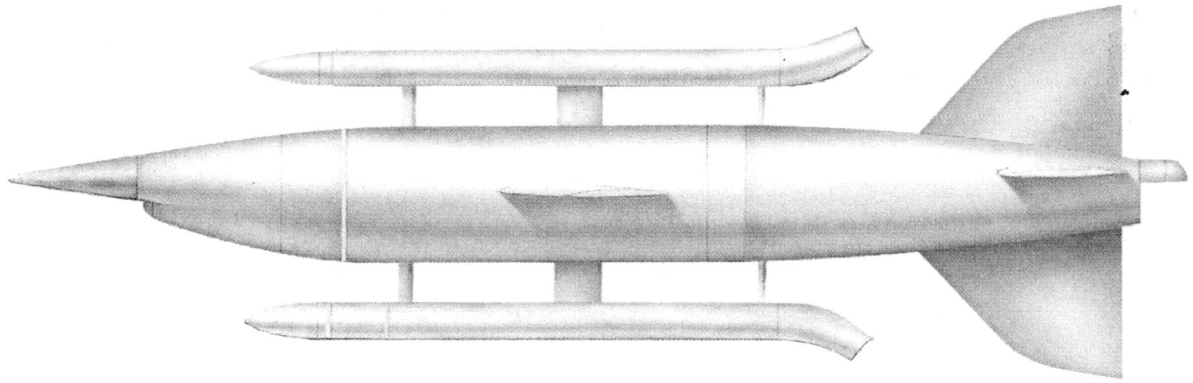

Specifications

Length: 4.29m (14ft)	Span: 2m (6ft 6in)	Warhead: 25kg (55lb) HE
Max. Diameter: 0.35m (1ft 2in)	Launch Weight: 445kg (979lb)	Range: 32km (20 miles)

run early in 1943, but the programme was badly disrupted when its designer, Dr Walter Thiel, was killed in the RAF bombing of Peenemünde in August 1943.

As an AA weapon, *Wasserfall* would have to be constantly ready for launching and remain fully fuelled for months at a time, so the liquid oxygen/alcohol fuel system of the V-2 could not be used. Instead, *Visol* (vinyl isobutyl ether) and *SV-Stoff*, or *Salbei* (90 per cent nitric acid, 10 per cent sulphuric acid) were used. This hypergolic mixture was forced into the combustion chamber by pressurized nitrogen.

Guidance was to be a simple radio control 'manual command to line of sight' (MCLOS) system for clear weather use, but effective engagement of targets at night or in bad weather was far more complex. For these circumstances, a new system known as *Rheinland* was under development that used a radar unit to track the target and a simple analogue computer to guide the missile into the tracking radar beam as soon as possible after launch. The operator could then see both 'blips' on a single display, and guide the missile onto the target.

Steering during the launch phase was carried out by four graphite rudders in the rocket exhaust after which the four fin-mounted control surfaces took over. Commands were sent to the missile using a modified version of the Strassburg-Kehl radio-command link, code named *Burgund*.

A second development was underway that used only a single cross-shaped radar beam that was rotated while pointing at the target. Like the *Rheinland* system, the missile was first directed into the beam, after which it would keep itself centered in the beam by means of a negative feedback system that listened to the radar signal; if it was off course, it would hear pulses instead of a steady signal, and automatically steer itself back into the centre of the beam. However *Wasserfall*'s speed of up to Mach 2 meant that the accuracy of the system would have to be very high in order to get the missile within lethal range of its target, and it was generally accepted that a type of infrared terminal guidance system would have to be added to achieve this.

The original design had specified a 100kg (220lb) warhead, but because of doubts about the missile's accuracy, it was replaced with a much larger one of 306kg (673lb). It was intended to fit a type of proximity fuse, together with a back-up command detonation system.

The first successful launch was made on 8 March 1944, and a total of 35 *Wasserfalls* had been test-fired by the time that Peenemünde was evacuated in February 1945. The system undoubtedly had great potential – Speer later wrote that:

To this day, I am convinced that substantial deployment of Wasserfall *from the spring of 1944 onwards, together with an uncompromising use of the jet fighters as air defence interceptors, would have essentially stalled the Allied strategic bombing offensive against our industry. We would have well been able to do that – after all, we managed to manufacture 900 V-2 rockets per month at a later time when resources were already much more limited.*

■ **A rare archive photo of the *Rheintochter* missile in flight.**

Enzian (Gentian)

This was a very powerful missile that strongly resembled a miniature Messerschmitt Me 163. It began life as the *Flak Rakete 1* (FR 1) in June 1943 and a number of FR models were designed before the project was renamed *Enzian* in early 1944.

The missile was rail-launched from a modified 88mm (3.5in) gun mounting, using four jettisonable solid-fuel Rheinmetall-Borsig RI-503 booster rockets to augment the thrust of the main liquid-fuelled Walter HWK 109-739 rocket motor. Constant delays with the Walter motor eventually led to its replacement with the cheaper and simpler VFK 613-A01 rocket motor.

It was initially proposed that the missile would be steered by a command guidance system to a point just ahead of a bomber formation where its warhead would be detonated by a radio link. It was thought that the enormous blast effect of its 500kg (1100lb) warhead would be sufficient to destroy several aircraft without the need for any elaborate terminal guidance system. Studies soon indicated that this was impractical and the prototypes flew with the Strassburg-Kehl III VHF radio command link, which was intended to be supplanted in production missiles with the L-band *Telefunken Kogge* system. At least two terminal seekers were planned: the *Kepka 'Madrid'*, a scanning infrared homing seeker; and the *Elsass* (Alsatian), an active radar-homing seeker.

Three alternative warheads were considered. The first was a thin metal casing containing a payload of 25mm (0.98in) steel pellets filled with an incendiary compound and cast into explosive. The second warhead was a container which fired 550 small rockets in a conical pattern ahead of the missile with an effective range of roughly 500m (545yd). The third was a simple HE warhead, with an estimated lethal blast radius of 45m (148ft). A number of proximity fuses were proposed, including the *Marabu* or *Fuchs* radio proximity fuses and the *Paplitz* infrared fuse.

A successful series of 38 flight tests began in May 1944, but the project was cancelled in January 1945 as part of the emergency programme to free resources for Me 262 and He 162 development.

RHEINTOCHTER SPECIFICATIONS

Specification	*Amount*
Length:	4.75m (15ft 7in)
Max. Diameter:	0.537m (1ft 9in)
Span:	2.65m (8ft 8in)
Launch Weight:	1746kg (3841lb)
Warhead:	150kg (330lb) HE
Range:	12.1km (7.5 miles)

Rheintochter (Rhine Maiden)

Rheinmetall-Borsig began development of the two stage *Rheintochter R I* in 1942 and the prototype first flew in August 1943.

Unusually for a German missile of the period, it used solid propellant rockets for both stages, which simplified construction and maintenance. Guidance was via a radio command link, with the operator optically tracking flares on the missile's tail. The 150kg (330lb) HE warhead was detonated by a *Kranich* acoustic fuse, which sensed changes in the Doppler shift of the target's propeller sound to trigger the warhead.

A total of 82 R Is were test-fired, with only four failures, but the type's ceiling was only 6098m (20,000ft), well below the minimum of 8232m (27,000ft) that was considered essential at this stage of the war. Accordingly, the R III variant was designed, which retained much of the R I's second stage but introduced a simpler cruciform wing and a pair of external strap-on boosters replacing the first stage of the R I.

No fewer than five different guidance systems were developed for different versions of *Rheintochter*:

- *Burgund*: optical tracking with radio command guidance
- *Franken*: optical tracking and radio guidance on the 10m (33ft) band
- *Alsace*: radio tracking and radio guidance on the UHF band
- *Brabant*: radio tracking and radio control on the 10m (33ft) band
- *Ganza*: panoramic observation and radio beam guidance on the 10m (33ft) band

Although initial assessments indicated that *Rheintochter III* should fully meet its specifications, it was one of the numerous projects cancelled in January 1945.

ENZIAN MISSILE

Specifications

Length: 4m (13ft 1in)
Max. Diameter: 0.88m (2ft 11in)
Span: 4m (13ft 1in)
Launch Weight: 1800kg (3960lb)
Warhead: 500kg (1100lb)
Range: 25.7km (16 miles)

Air-to-Surface Rockets and Missiles

The Henschel Hs 293/294 series and the Fritz-X *guided bomb were sophisticated weapons whose effectiveness was compromised by over-reliance on easily jammed radio-command guidance systems.*

Henschel Hs 293

Development of the Hs 293 began in July 1940, using the 1939 Gustav Schwartz Propellerwerke-designed glide bomb as a starting point. The first Hs 293V-1 prototypes were unpowered radio-controlled glide bombs based on a standard 500kg (1100lb) SC-500 (*Sprengbombe Cylindrisch*) general purpose bomb that was fitted with wings and control surfaces. These were tested successfully and were followed by a number of similar Hs 293V-2 prototypes with modified controls. The final batch of Hs 293V-3 prototypes were used to evaluate the *Strassburg-Kehl* radio control system.

The trials indicated that it was extremely difficult to guide a glide bomb as it was rapidly overtaken by the launch aircraft, causing the controller to lose sight of the target. The next version, the Hs 293A-0, was powered by a Walter 109-507B liquid-fuel rocket motor in a ventral pod to overcome this problem and to increase the range so that the launch aircraft could stay beyond AA fire. Results were very satisfactory and, with a few further changes, the weapon went into production as the Hs 293A-1.

The Hs 293A-1 used the *Strassburg-Kehl* radio control system which could be preset to one of 18 different frequencies in the 48:50 MHz band, to allow up to 18 bombers to each drop and control a glide bomb simultaneously. The operator guided the bomb with a joystick wired to the *Strassburg-Kehl* transmitter, tracking its course with the aid of a bright red flare in its tail.

The Dornier Do 217 was the first aircraft cleared for operational use of the Hs-293A, followed by the Focke-Wulf Fw 200 and the Heinkel He 177. The missile was also launched from the Heinkel He 111, but solely for trials purposes.

In theory, carrier aircraft would carry two Hs-293As, one under each wing, but in practice, Do 217s tended to carry only one, plus a drop-tank under the other wing. Engine exhaust was piped into the bombs to keep the propellants warm.

Depending on the glide angle, the bomb could reach terminal velocities of 435–900km/h (270–560mph) and had a range of roughly 5km (3 miles) after launch at an altitude of 4000m (13,123ft).

Operations

Luftwaffe aircraft armed with these missiles went into action in the summer of 1943, attacking Allied shipping in the Bay of Biscay. On 25 August 1943, they sank the sloop HMS *Egret* and badly damaged the destroyer HMCS *Athabascan,* forcing the Admiralty to order warships to stay at least 320km (200 miles) from the French coast until counter-measures could be devised.

The *Strassburg-Kehl* control system was quickly identified as the missile's weakest point – the British Type 650 transmitter jammed the intermediate frequency receiver (3MHz) quite successfully. This was primarily because it automatically defeated the receiver regardless of which radio frequency had been selected for an individual missile.

At much the same time the US Naval Research Laboratory developed the XCJ jamming

AIR-TO-SURFACE ROCKETS AND MISSILES: SPECIFICATIONS COMPARED

Specification	Fritz-X	*Hs 293*	*Hs 294*
Length:	3.32m (11ft)	3.82m (12ft 6in)	6.12m (20ft 1in)
Max Diameter:	0.853m (2ft 8in)	0.47m (1ft 6.5in)	0.62m (2ft)
Span:	1.5m (4ft 11in)	3.14m (10ft 4in)	4.025m (13ft 2in)
Launch Weight:	1362kg (3000lb)	1045kg (2304lb)	2107kg (4645lb)
Warhead:	320kg (705lb) APHE	295kg (650lb) HE	656kg (1445lb) HE
Range:	5km (3 miles)	5km (3 miles)	14km (9 miles)

AIR-TO-SURFACE ROCKETS COMPARED

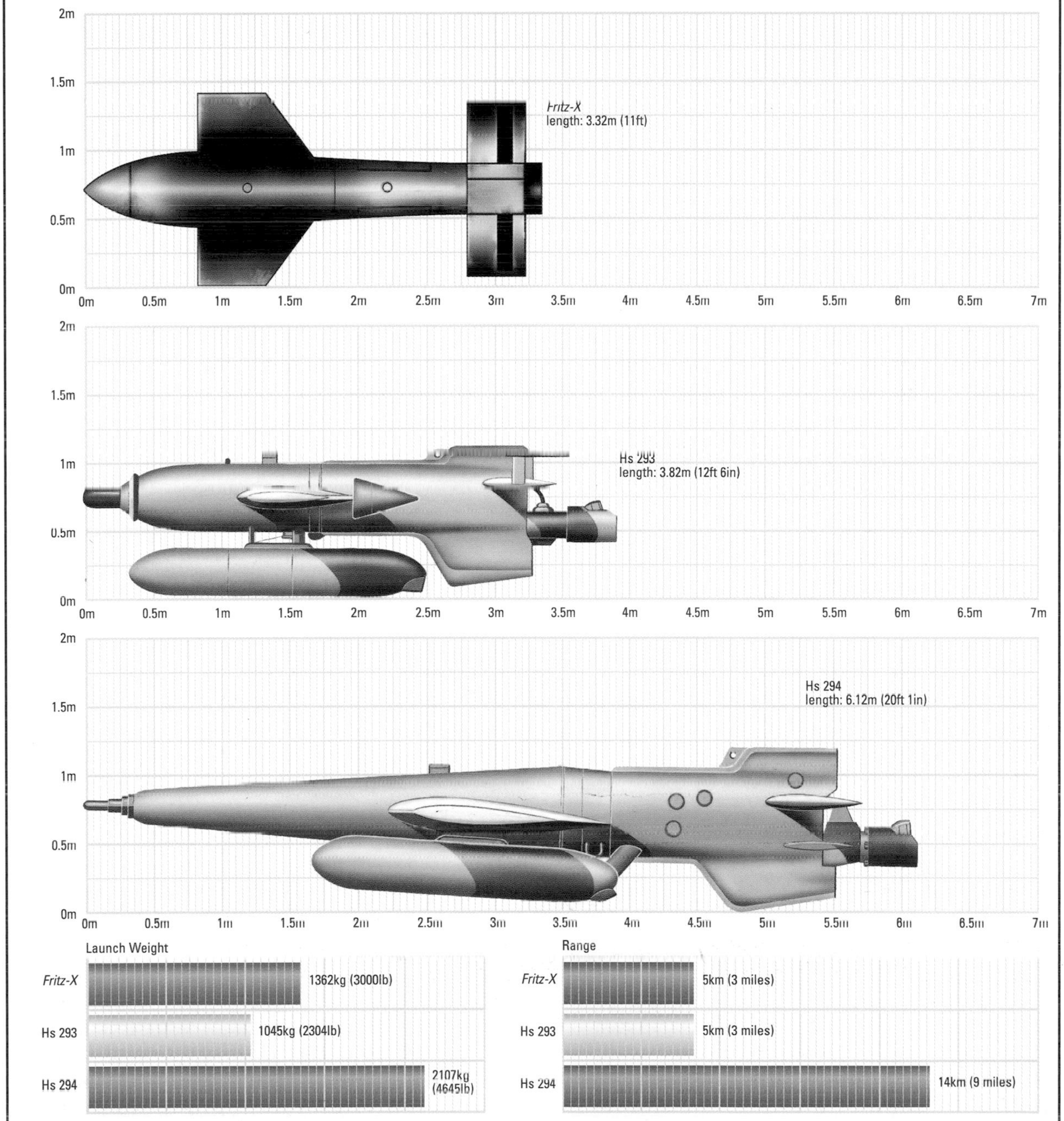

Fritz-X
length: 3.32m (11ft)
Hs 293
length: 3.82m (12ft 6in)
Hs 294
length: 6.12m (20ft 1in)
Launch Weight
Fritz-X 1362kg (3000lb)
Hs 293 1045kg (2304lb)
Hs 294 2107kg (4645lb)
Range
Fritz-X 5km (3 miles)
Hs 293 5km (3 miles)
Hs 294 14km (9 miles)

transmitter which was installed aboard the destroyer escorts USS *Herbert C. Jones* and *Frederick C. Davis* in late September 1943, but which proved to be ineffective because the frequencies selected for jamming were incorrect. This was replaced in time for the Anzio landings by the XCJ-1 system, which replaced the XCJ in *Herbert C. Jones* and *Frederick C. Davis* and also equipped the destroyers USS *Woolsey, Madison, Hilary P. Jones* and *Lansdale*. These six ships saw service at Anzio, with three deployed at any one time.

The XCJ-1 system was also fairly successful, although it could be swamped if large numbers of missiles had to be engaged as the operator had to find which of the 18 *Strassburg-Kehl* command frequencies were in use and then manually tune the jamming transmitter.

Despite these increasingly sophisticated counter-measures, the Hs 293 could still be terrifyingly effective when intelligently deployed, as was proved on 26 November 1943 when a missile launched by a Heinkel He 177 sank the 8738 tonne (8600 ton) troopship HMT *Rohna* off the Algerian coast, with the loss of 1050 of the 2000 US servicemen on board.

Variants

Henschel constantly developed new variants of the Hs-293. The Hs 293A-2 substituted a simpler spoiler control system for the conventional control surfaces of the A-1. Allied success in jamming the *Strassburg-Kehl* system led to the introduction of the Hs-293B, which had a range of 30km (19 miles), using the *Dortmund-Duisburg* wire guidance system.

Approximately 200 of these were converted from Hs 293A missiles and were used in limited numbers in the Mediterranean by bombers operating from northern Italy in the closing stages of the war.

Although the vast majority of operational Hs 293s were launched against naval targets, a number of Hs 293Bs were used in attacks on bridges over the river Oder in hope of slowing down the Soviet advance on Berlin in April 1945.

A variety of other Hs 293 derivatives were produced in small numbers, including:

- The Hs 293C, which was intended to dive into the sea just short of its target, continuing to 'fly' underwater and operate as a 'rocket torpedo'. Only a few were completed late in the war and the type was never used operationally
- The Hs 293D was a television-guided version that was tested in 1942, but the TV system was not

FOCKE-WULF FW 200C-6: HS-293 LAUNCH AIRCRAFT

Specifications

Type: Long-range maritime reconnaissance-bomber
Powerplant: 4 x 895kW (1200hp) Bramo 323R 9-cylinder radial piston engines
Speed: 360km/h (224mph)
Service Ceiling: 6000m (19,684ft)
Range: 3560km (2212 miles)
Weight: 17,005kg (37,490lb) (empty) 24,520kg (50,057lb) (maximum take-off)
Length: 23.45m (76ft 11¹/₄in)
Height: 6.3m (20ft 8in)
Span: 32.85m (107ft 9¹/₄in)
Armament: 1 x 20mm (0.79in) MG 151/20 cannon, 1 x 15mm (0.59in) MG 151 cannon, 3 x 13mm (0.51in) MG 131 and 1 x 7.92mm (0.31in) MG 15 plus 2 x Henschel Hs 293 anti-shipping missiles
No. completed: 280 of all versions, including prototypes

sufficiently developed for effective combat use.

Henschel Hs 294

The Hs 294 was a derivative of the Hs 293C that was optimized for underwater performance. It had a more streamlined 650kg (1430lb) warhead and twin Walter 109-507B liquid-fuel rocket motors in ventral pods. The first prototypes used the standard *Strassburg-Kehl* guidance system and, on hitting the water about 40m (131ft) short of the target vessel, explosive bolts were intended to blow off the wings, tail and propulsion unit. The warhead would then continue on a steady underwater course to hit the target like a torpedo.

Initial trials were promising, but the detonations of the explosive bolts were liable to throw the warhead off course and on later prototypes they were replaced by 'frangible joints', which broke up as soon as the missile hit the water. This worked well, but concerns about the *Strassburg-Kehl's* vulnerability to jamming led to a re-design to incorporate wire guidance. In 1944, just as it seemed that production could finally begin, it was suddenly decided to switch to TV guidance, using a small camera built into the front of one of the motor pods. As with the Hs 293D, the limitations of 1940s TV technology were simply too great to produce a viable system and the entire Hs 294 project was cancelled in early 1945 before any missiles entered service.

Fritz-X

In 1938, Dr Max Kramer of the *Deutsche Versuchsansalt fuer Luftfahrt* (DVL) (German Aviation Research Institute) began a series of trials to test the feasibility of adding a guidance system to conventional free-fall bombs. Development of the *Fritz-X* (also known as the *Ruhrstahl SD 1400 X*, *Kramer X-1*, PC 1400X or FX 1400) began in 1939 and the following year, the Ruhrstahl company was brought into the programme to share their expertise in bomb production.

The *Fritz-X* was based on the 1400kg (3080lb) PC-1400 armour-piercing bomb with a new nose cone and four stubby fixed wings arranged in a cruciform pattern around the bomb's centre of gravity. The box-shaped 12-sided tail-framed vertical and horizontal fins were fitted with spoilers to provide aerodynamic control. The bomb was guided by a *Strassburg-Kehl* system as used by the Hs 293A and also had an internal gyro system to prevent rolling. No boost motor was fitted, but a tracking flare was mounted in the tail.

Unlike the Hs 293, which was deployed against merchant ships and light warships, the *Fritz-X* was intended to be used against armoured vessels, such as heavy

DORNIER DO 217E-5: HS-293 LAUNCH AIRCRAFT

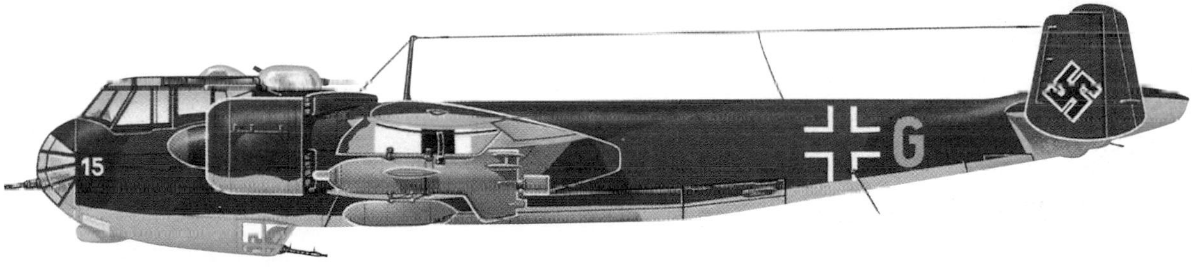
15
G

Specifications

Type: Four-seat anti-shipping bomber
Powerplant: 2 x 1147kW (1539hp) BMW 801C 14-cylinder radial piston engines
Speed: 515km/h (320mph)
Service Ceiling: 9500m (31,170ft)
Range: 2300km (1429 miles)
Weight: 8840kg (19,489lb) (empty) 16,465kg (36,299lb) (maximum take-off)
Length: 18.2m (60ft)
Height: 5m (16ft 4¾in)
Armament: 1 x 20mm (0.79in) MG 151/20 cannon, 1 x 15mm (0.59in) MG 151 cannon, 2 x 13mm (0.51in) MG 131 and 3 x 7.92mm (0.31in) MG 15 plus 2 x Henschel Hs 293 anti-shipping missiles
No. completed: 1730 of all versions, including prototypes

AIR-TO-SURFACE ROCKET AND MISSILE WARHEADS: WEIGHT COMPARED

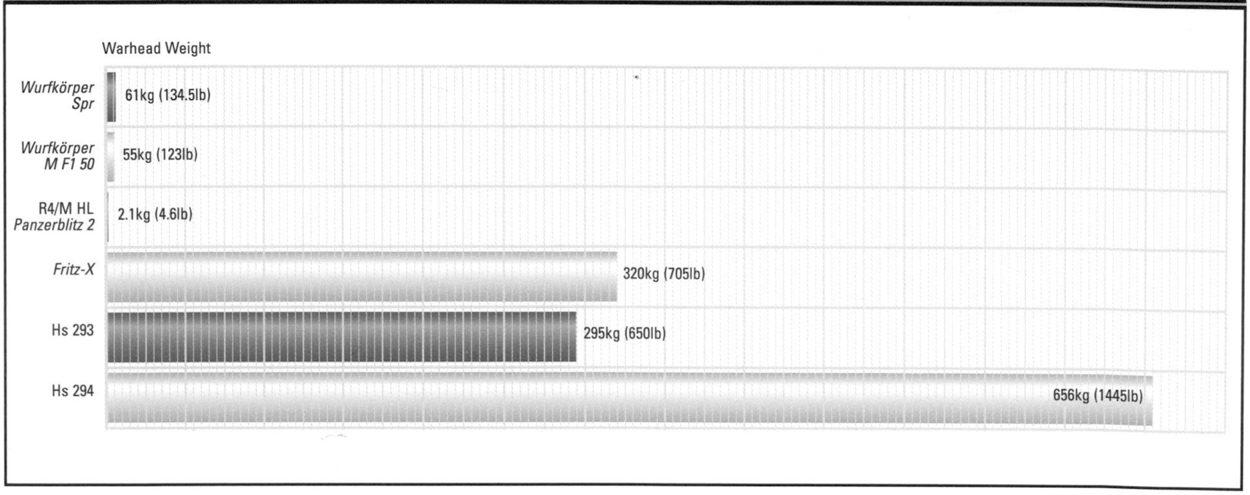
Warhead Weight
Wurfkörper Spr
61kg (134.5lb)
Wurfkörper M F1 50
55kg (123lb)
R4/M HL *Panzerblitz 2*
2.1kg (4.6lb)
Fritz-X
320kg (705lb)
Hs 293
295kg (650lb)
Hs 294
656kg (1445lb)

cruisers and battleships. The minimum release height was 4000m (13,120ft) and a release height of 6100m (20,008ft) was preferred to give the bomb sufficient terminal velocity to pierce armoured decks with a total thickness of up to 130mm (5.1in). The bomb was aimed by means of a standard *Lotfe 7* bomb sight. After release, the pilot throttled back and climbed to rapidly reduce speed and hold the aircraft over the bomb's trajectory so that the bomb aimer could maintain visual contact and steer the *Fritz-X* to its target. The control system could make a maximum correction of 500m (1640ft) in range and 350m (1148ft) in bearing.

The only *Luftwaffe* unit to use the *Fritz-X* was III/KG 100, which flew the Dornier Do 217 K-2 bomber on the vast majority of its operational sorties, although these were later supplemented by small numbers of Do 217 K-3 and Do 217 M-11 variants. Heinkel He 111s had been used for trials with the *Fritz-X* and a few

AIR-TO-SURFACE ROCKET AND MISSILE WARHEADS: RANGE COMPARED

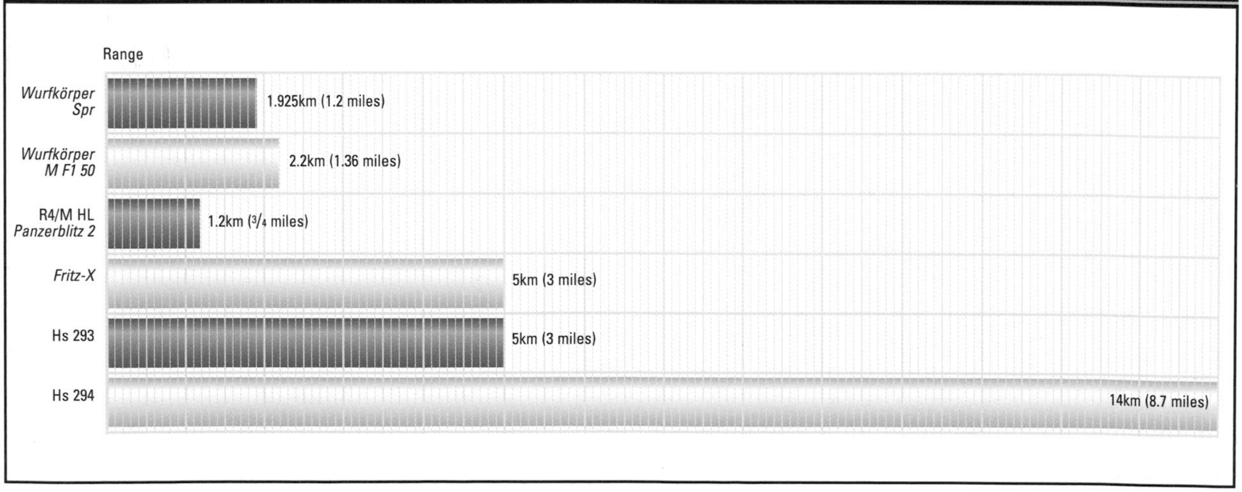
Range
Wurfkörper Spr
1.925km (1.2 miles)
Wurfkörper M F1 50
2.2km (1.36 miles)
R4/M HL *Panzerblitz 2*
1.2km (3/4 miles)
Fritz-X
5km (3 miles)
Hs 293
5km (3 miles)
Hs 294
14km (8.7 miles)

variants of the Heinkel He 177 were also equipped to carry the weapon, but neither of these combinations saw combat action.

Fritz-X was first deployed on 21 July 1943 in a raid on Augusta harbour in Sicily. A number of further attacks were made on Allied shipping off Sicily, but no hits were scored and it seems that the Allies were unaware that radio-guided bombs were being used.

Successful strike

On 9 September 1943, the *Luftwaffe* achieved their deadliest success with the weapon against the Italian fleet, which was on its way to Malta to surrender to the Allies. Six Dornier Do 217 K-2s of III/KG100 took off from Marseilles, each carrying a single *Fritz-X* and found the fleet off Sardinia. The flagship, the battleship *Roma*, took two hits and one near miss, and sank after her magazines exploded, killing 1352 men, including Admiral Carlo Bergamini. Her sister-ship, *Italia*, was also damaged but reached Malta.

III/KG 100 scored another success with *Fritz-X* against HMS *Warspite*, which was providing gunfire support off Salerno during the Allied invasion of southern Italy on 16 September. One bomb penetrated six decks before exploding in Number 4 boiler room, putting out all her boilers and blowing out the double bottom. She took on a total of 5080 tonnes (5000 tons) of water and lost steam and power, but suffered only a few casualties. HMS *Warspite* was towed to Malta before returning to Britain and was out of action for nearly nine months.

Hs-293 ATTACK PROFILE

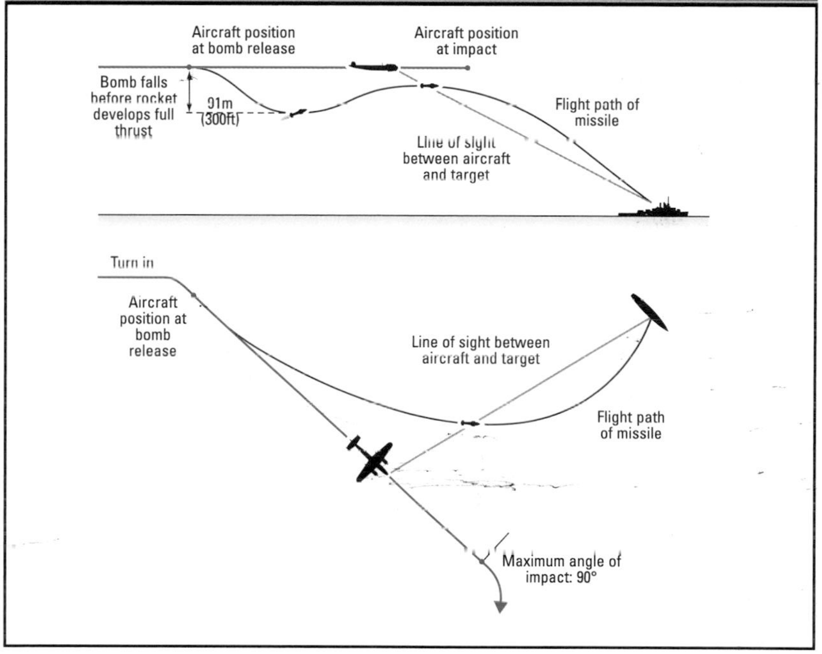
Aircraft position
at bomb release
Aircraft position
at impact
Bomb falls
before rocket
develops full
thrust
91m
(300ft)
Flight path of
missile
Line of sight
between aircraft
and target
Turn in
Aircraft
position at
bomb
release
Line of sight between
aircraft and target
Flight path
of missile
Maximum angle of
impact: 90°

FRITZ-X ATTACK PROFILE

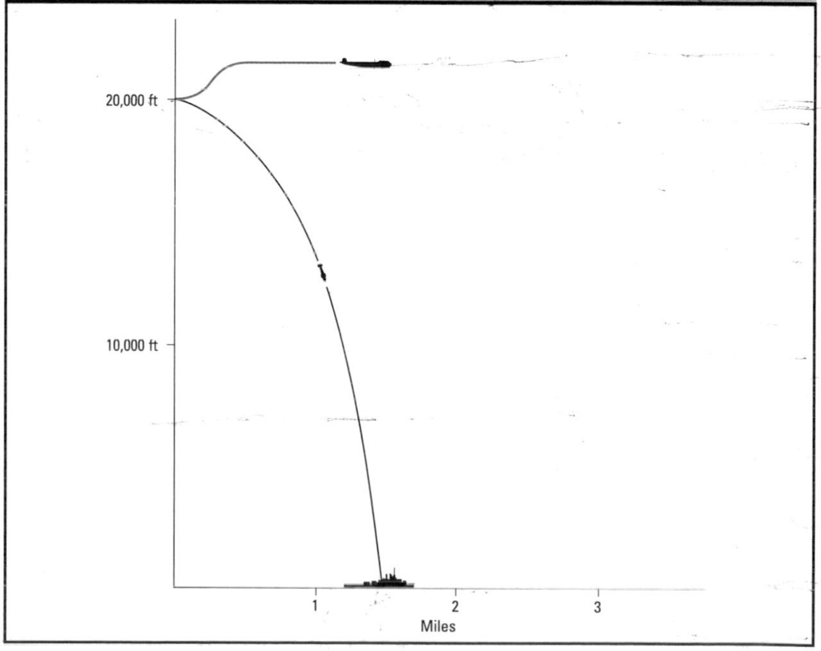
20,000 ft
10,000 ft
1
2
3
Miles

ANTI-SHIPPING STRIKES: ALLIED COMBAT LOSSES, 1943

Ship/Vessel	*Type*	*Campaign/Operation*	*Cause*	*Damage*	*No. Killed*
HMS *Bideford*	Sloop	ASW Patrol – Biscay	Hs-293 rocket-propelled glide bomb	Damaged	–
HMS *Landguard*	Sloop	ASW Patrol – Biscay	Hs-293 rocket-propelled glide bomb	Damaged	–
HMS *Egret*	Corvette	ASW Patrol – Biscay	Hs-293 rocket-propelled glide bomb	Sunk	194
HMCS *Athabaskan*	Destroyer	ASW Patrol – Biscay	Hs-293 rocket-propelled glide bomb	Damaged	–
HMS *Intrepid*	Destroyer	Aegean	Hs-293 rocket-propelled glide bomb	Sunk	–
RHS *Vasillisa Olga*	Destroyer	Aegean	Hs-293 rocket-propelled glide bomb	Sunk	–
HMS *Dulverton*	Destroyer	Aegean	Hs-293 rocket-propelled glide bomb	Sunk	–
HMS *Rockwood*	Destroyer	Aegean	Hs-293 rocket-propelled glide bomb	Damaged	–
SS *Delius*	Transport	Atlantic	Hs-293 rocket-propelled glide bomb	Damaged	–
HMT *Rohna*	Troopship	KMF-26 Mediterranean	Hs-293 rocket-propelled glide bomb	Sunk	1152
RN *Roma*	Battleship	Cape Testa – Sardinia	SD-1400X *Fritz-X* glide bomb	Sunk	1352
RN *Littorio*	Battleship	Cape Testa – Sardinia	SD-1400X *Fritz-X* glide bomb	Damaged	–
USS *Philadelphia*	Cruiser	Salerno	SD-1400X *Fritz-X* glide bomb	Damaged	–
HMS *Warspite*	Battleship	Salerno	SD-1400X *Fritz-X* glide bomb	Damaged	9
USS *Savannah*	Cruiser	Salerno	SD-1400X *Fritz-X* glide bomb	Damaged	200
HMHS *Newfoundland*	Hospital Ship	Salerno	Hs-293 rocket-propelled glide bomb	Sunk	–
SS *Bushrod Washington*	Transport	Salerno	Hs-293 rocket-propelled glide bomb	Sunk	–
HMS *Uganda*	Cruiser	Salerno	SD-1400X *Fritz-X* glide bomb	Damaged	16

ANTI-SHIPPING STRIKE COMBAT LOSSES, 1944

Ship/Vessel	*Type*	*Campaign/Operation*	*Cause*	*Damage*	*No. Killed*
HMS *Spartan*	Destroyer	Anzio	Hs 293 rocket-propelled glide bomb	Sunk	35
SS *Elihu Yale*	Transport	Anzio	Hs 293 rocket-propelled glide bomb	Sunk	12
SS *Samuel Huntingdon*	Transport	Anzio	Hs 293 rocket-propelled glide bomb	Sunk	–
LCT-35	Landing Craft	Anzio	Hs 293 rocket-propelled glide bomb	Sunk	–
USS *Herbert C. Jones*	Destroyer	Anzio	Hs 293 rocket-propelled glide bomb	Damaged	–
HMS *Jervis*	Destroyer	Anzio	Hs 293 rocket-propelled glide bomb	Damaged	–
HMHS *St David*	Hospital Ship	Anzio	Hs 293 rocket-propelled glide bomb	Sunk	–
HMHS *St Andrew*	Hospital Ship	Anzio	Hs 293 rocket-propelled glide bomb	Sunk	–
USS *Prevail*	Minesweeper	Anzio	Hs 293 rocket-propelled glide bomb	Damaged	–
HMS *Boadicea*	Destroyer	Normandy	Hs 293 rocket-propelled glide bomb	Sunk	175
USS *Meredith*	Destroyer	Normandy	Hs 293 rocket-propelled glide bomb	Sunk	–
LST-282	Landing Ship	St Raphael, France	Hs 293 rocket-propelled glide bomb	Sunk	–
LST-312	Landing Ship	Salerno	Hs 293 rocket-propelled glide bomb	Damaged	–
HMS *Spartan*	Cruiser	Anzio	SD-1400 *Fritz-X* glide bomb	Sunk	46

Air-to-Air Missiles and Guns

The increasingly urgent need to counter Allied heavy bombers led the Luftwaffe *to adopt a wide range of heavy cannon and rockets. By the end of the war, the first air-to-air guided missiles were on the point of entering service.*

***Werfer-Granate 21* (Wfr. Gr. 21)**
This was the first air-to-air rocket to be taken into service by the *Luftwaffe* in 1943. It was based on the rocket fired by the army's 21cm (8.3in) *Nebelwerfer 42*, which was modified by fitting a larger time-fused 40.8kg (90lb) HE warhead. The idea was to use the rockets to break up US bomber formations so that isolated aircraft could be easily dealt with by conventionally armed fighters.

A number of Bf 109s and Fw 190s were fitted with a single launch tube under each wing, while some Bf 110s and Me 410s carried two under each wing. Their earliest known use was by JG 1 and JG 11 on 29 July 1943 against American bombers attacking Kiel and Warnemünde. When the rockets hit, the results could be spectacular – in one incident, it was claimed that a rocket exploded just beneath a B-17, which was blown into the next bomber in the formation. Debris from both aircraft then brought down a third B-17.

However, such successes were rare – the high drag caused by the launchers reduced the speed and manoeuvrability of the launching aircraft, which could be lethal if Allied fighters were encountered. The worst aspect of the system was its inaccuracy – it was very difficult to assess the correct range at which to

AIR-TO-AIR MISSILES: SPECIFICATIONS COMPARED

Specification	Wurfgranate 21 *Rocket*	*R4M Rocket*	*X-4 Missile*
Length:	1.177m (3ft 10in)	0.812m (2ft 8in)	2.01m (6ft 7in)
Max Diameter:	21.4cm (8.4in)	5.5cm (2.17in)	22cm (8.7in)
Span:	n/a (spin-stabilized)	n/k (folding fin stabilization)	0.726m (2.38in)
Launch Weight:	112.5kg (248lb)	3.85kg (8.49lb)	60kg (132lb)
Warhead:	40.8kg (90lb) HE	0.815kg (1.8lb)	20kg (44lb) HE
Range:	1.2km (3/4 mile)	1.1km (7/10 mile)	3.5km (2 1/5 miles)

AIR-TO-AIR AIRCRAFT GUNS COMPARED

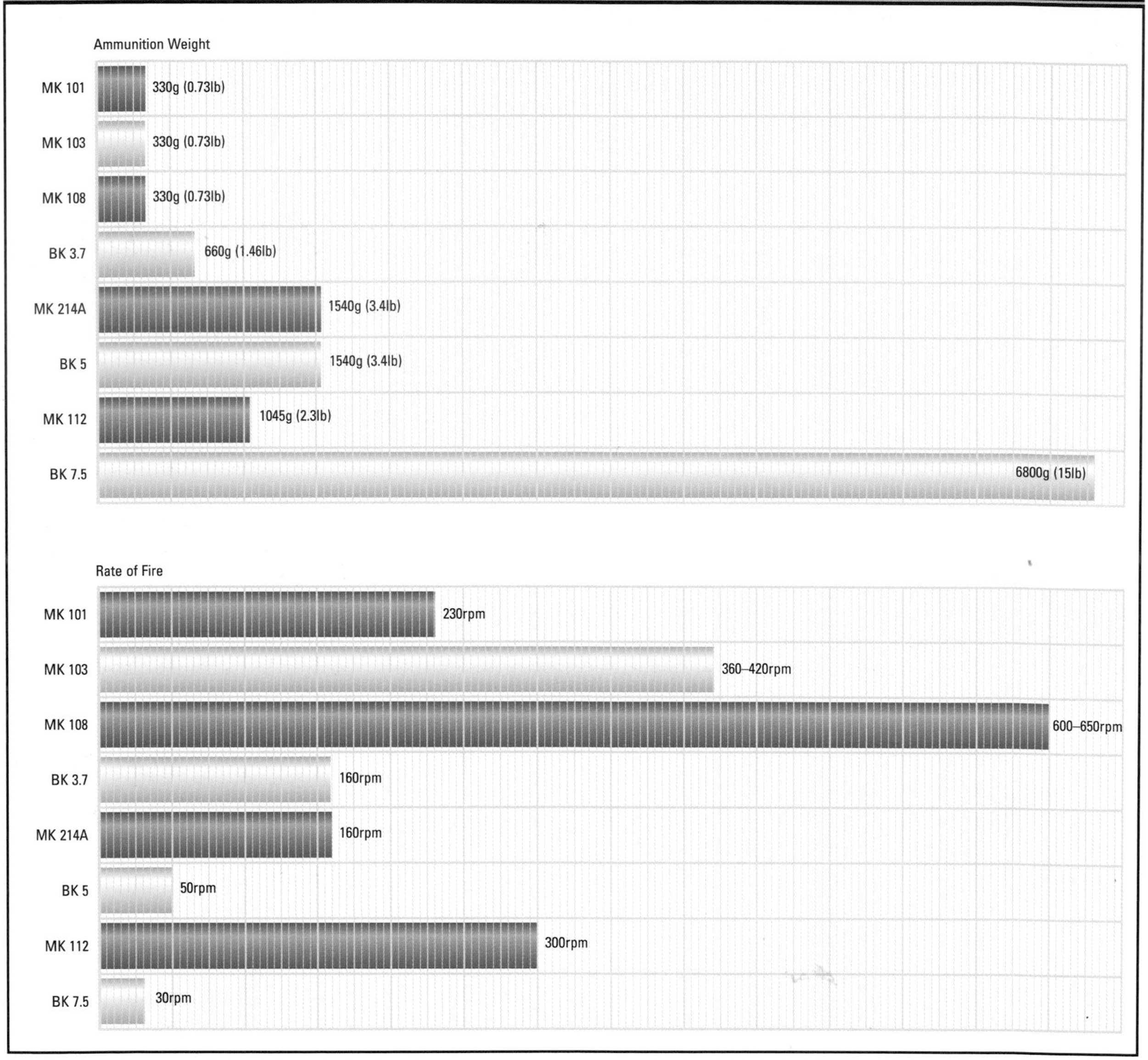
Ammunition Weight
MK 101
330g (0.73lb)
MK 103
330g (0.73lb)
MK 108
330g (0.73lb)
BK 3.7
660g (1.46lb)
MK 214A
1540g (3.4lb)
BK 5
1540g (3.4lb)
MK 112
1045g (2.3lb)
BK 7.5
6800g (15lb)
Rate of Fire
MK 101
230rpm
MK 103
360–420rpm
MK 108
600–650rpm
BK 3.7
160rpm
MK 214A
160rpm
BK 5
50rpm
MK 112
300rpm
BK 7.5
30rpm

■ **The increasing threat posed by the Allied bombing campaign from 1942–43 onwards led to the development of heavy cannon that were more effective against four-engined bombers than the machine guns and 20mm (0.8in) cannon of the early war years. Some of these, such as the MK 101, BK 3.7 and BK 5, proved to be too heavy and slow-firing to be effective as air-to-air weapons. The enormous BK 7.5 was briefly considered for use in the anti-bomber role, but the problems experienced with the BK 3.7 and BK 5 led to all three types being reserved for use by the *Luftwaffe*'s anti-tank squadrons. Recoilless large calibre guns seemed to have potential as anti-shipping weapons, but their development was abandoned after the Junkers Ju 88 used for trials suffered extensive damage from the *Duka 88*'s enormous back-blast.**

AIRCRAFT GUNS COMPARED

Specification	*MK 101*	*MK 103*	*MK 108*	*BK 3.7*	*MK 214A*	*BK 5*	*MK 112*	*BK 7.5*
Ammunition	30 x 184B	30 x 184B	30 x 90RB	37 x 263B	50 x 419R	50 x 419R	55 x 175RB	75 X714R
Ammunition weight, grams (lb)	330 (0.73)	330 (0.73)	330 (0.73)	660 (1.46)	1540 (3.4lb)	1540 (3.4)	1045 (2.3)	6800 (15)
Rate of fire (rpm)	230	360–420	600–650	160	160	50	300	30
Muzzle velocity, m/s (ft/s)	920 (3018)	860 (2821)	505 (1656)	810 (2657)	920 (3018)	920 (3018)	595m/s (1952f/s)	790 (2591)
Gun weight, kg (lb)	180 (396)	141 (310)	60 (132)	295 (649)	490 (1078)	540 (1188)	274 (603)	705 (1551)

fire the rockets, and the vast majority exploded well short of their targets.

RECOILLESS AIRCRAFT GUNS COMPARED

Specification	*Gerat 104*	*Dusenkanone Duka 88*
Weight:	4837kg (10,630lb)	1000kg (2200lb)
Length:	10m (32ft 9½in)	4.7m (15ft 5in)
Barrel Length:	10m (32ft 9½in)	–
Calibre:	356mm (14in)	88mm (3.46in)
Shell Weight:	700kg (1543lb)	9.2kg (20lb)
Range:	3.54km (2.2 miles)	1.5km (0.93 miles)

R4M *Orkan* (Hurricane)

The problems of the Wfr. Gr. 21 were solved with the introduction of the R4M rocket in 1945. It was an unguided solid-fuelled rocket that was light enough to be carried by all *Luftwaffe* fighters, although it seems that it only saw action with the Me 262.

The standard R4M was a folding fin rocket fitted with a warhead containing a 520g (17.6oz) explosive charge, virtually guaranteeing a kill with each hit. The Me 262 carried 12 under each wing on light wooden racks which barely affected the aircraft's flying performance. Although the rocket's maximum range was over 1000m (3280ft), they were generally fired from no more than 600m (1968ft) since within that range their ballistics matched those of the Me 262's 30mm (1.18in) MK 108 cannon, which greatly simplified aiming using the standard gun sights.

Only small numbers of rockets reached combat units but they were highly effective – in March 1945, a flight of six R4M-armed Me 262s from the Oberammergau flight test centre and led by General Gordon Golloband claimed to have shot down 14 B-17s in a single mission.

Ruhrstahl X-4

The X-4 was the most sophisticated air-to-air weapon to come close to service status during the war. It originated with a series of design studies by Dr Max Kramer in 1943, and prototypes were completed the following year.

The missile was liquid fuelled, although it was intended to fit a solid fuel motor in later production examples. Two wing-mounted flares were fitted to help the operator track the missile, which was controlled by a small cockpit-mounted joystick. Guidance commands were transmitted through two wires that unwound from spools in the missile and corrected its course by operating tail-mounted control surfaces.

The 20kg (44.1lb) HE warhead had a lethal radius of about 8 metres (25 feet) and was triggered by a Kranich acoustic proximity fuse. This operated within 40 metres (131 feet) of the target and had a delayed-action mechanism to allow the range to close to within five metres (16 feet) before detonating the warhead.

The first flight test took place on 11 August 1944 when a prototype was launched by a Fw 190. Later tests involved the Ju 88 and Me 262 and showed that the X-4 was not really practical as a weapon for single-seat fighters due to the difficulty experienced by a lone pilot in controlling both his aircraft and the missile in combat. Production missiles were accordingly earmarked for multi-seat types, such as the Ju 88.

By early 1945, Ruhrstahl's Brackwede factory had completed over 1000 airframes, but was awaiting their rocket motors, which were delayed by bomb damage to BMW's Stargard factory. It is possible that a handful of X-4s were used in the closing weeks of the war, although the type never formally entered service with the *Luftwaffe*.

FES

CHAPTER 8

Chemical and Nuclear Weapons

The highly advanced German chemical industry had given the Imperial German Army a head start in the gas warfare of 1914–18. The lurid portrayal of the subject in the mass media during the inter-war years (and the Italian use of mustard gas in their conquest of Abyssinia) led to a popular belief that the next war would begin with massed bombers making large scale gas attacks on civilian targets. The absence of any such attacks in 1939 caused considerable speculation, but public awareness of the subject gradually faded as the war progressed and the realities of conventional warfare proved equally destructive. However, the Germans were steadily accumulating stockpiles of nerve agents, far more deadly than anything deployed during World War I.

The potential use of nuclear fission to produce a bomb of unprecedented power was investigated by German scientists from 1939 onwards, but they were crucially just behind the US and UK in developing an operational weapon.

A US ammunition technician examines some of the 500,000 *Tabun*-filled nerve gas artillery shells found at the end of the war.

Nerve Agents

During the 1930s, German researchers investigated the potential use of organophosphate compounds as commercial insecticides. While many were highly effective in agriculture, a few were found to be deadly nerve agents.

All nerve agents function by interrupting the neurotransmitters that signal muscles to contract, preventing them from relaxing. Initial symptoms following exposure are a runny nose, tightness in the chest and constriction of the pupils. Shortly afterwards, the victim has difficulty in breathing, together with nausea. The symptoms progress to include involuntarily salivation, urination and defecation, often coupled with gastrointestinal pain and vomiting. Blistering and burning of the eyes and/or lungs may also occur. This phase is followed by twitching and jerking and ultimately the victim will become comatose and suffocate as a consequence of convulsive spasms. In high doses, death occurs before many of these symptoms have time to develop.

Tabun

In December 1936, Dr Gerhard Schrader of the I.G. Farbenindustrie laboratory in Leverkusen first developed *Tabun* (ethyl dimethyl-phosphoramidocyanidate) as an insecticide, only discovering its effects on humans the following month when a drop of *Tabun* was spilled on a laboratory bench. Within minutes he and his assistant began to experience constriction of the pupils, dizziness and severe shortness of breath. It took them three weeks to fully recover – given its lethality, they were extremely lucky to survive.

A sample of *Tabun* was sent to the chemical warfare (CW) section of the Army Weapons Office at Berlin-Spandau in May 1937 and Schrader was summoned to Berlin to give a demonstration, after which his patent application was classified as secret. Colonel Rüdiger, the head of the CW section, ordered the construction of new facilities for the development of *Tabun* and other organophosphate compounds and Schrader soon moved to a new research establishment at Wuppertal-Elberfeld in the Ruhr.

In 1939, trials to confirm the practicality of large scale *Tabun* manufacture were successfully carried out at an experimental plant at Munsterlager on Luneberg Heath. In January 1940, work began on the full-scale production facility, code named *Hochwerk*, at Dyernfurth-am-Oder (now Brzeg Dolny in Poland). The factory complex was run by an I.G. Farbenindustrie subsidiary, Anorgana GmbH, and was completely self-contained, synthesizing all intermediates as well as *Tabun* itself. The facility had an underground plant for filling munitions, which were then stored at Krappitz (now Krapowice) in Upper Silesia.

Although construction work began in January 1940, the factory only began production in June 1942. Its total output was between 10,160–30,480 tonnes (10,000–30,000 tons) of *Tabun*. This delay was primarily due to the extremely dangerous and highly corrosive chemicals involved in the manufacturing process.

Tabun's extreme toxicity forced the adoption of elaborate safety precautions – the final production areas of the factory were enclosed in double glass-lined walls, with a stream of pressurized air circulating between them. All units were regularly decontaminated with steam and ammonia.

The Dyernfurth-am-Oder workforce totalled 3000, all of whom were German nationals. They were equipped with respirators and protective suits made from a composite rubber-cloth-rubber material that were incinerated after the tenth wearing. Despite these safety measures, over 300 accidents occurred before production began, and a number of workers were killed. *Tabun*'s lethality was dramatically illustrated by the following incidents:

- Liquid *Tabun* drained onto four pipe-fitters who all died before their rubber suits could be removed
- Two litres (3.5 pints) of *Tabun* poured down the neck of a worker's rubber suit – he died within two minutes

TOXICITY OF WARTIME NERVE AGENTS

The values are estimates of the lethal doses (LD) for humans. LD50 is the lethal dose at which 50 per cent of those exposed to the nerve agent will die as a result of their injuries. A different measure is used for inhalation, which is a sum of concentration (C) and length of exposure (t). As before, L stands for lethal and 50 for a 50 per cent effect. The toxicity sequence is the same for the two types of exposure but the differences are much greater in skin exposure. This is mainly due to the more volatile nerve agents evaporating from naked skin.

Agent	LD50 Skin mg/individual	LCt50 Inhalation mg min/m^3
Tabun	4000	200
Sarin	1700	100
Soman	300	100

- Seven workers were hit in the face by a high-pressure stream of *Tabun* that penetrated their respirators; only two survived despite desperate resuscitation measures.

Sarin

In 1938, a second potent organophosphate nerve agent was discovered. This agent, *Sarin* (methylethyl methylphosphonofluoridate), was named after its four discoverers: Schrader, Ambros, Rüdiger and van der Linde. In June 1939, *Sarin's* formula and a sample of the compound were passed to the CW section of the Army Weapons Office. A number of potential manufacturing processes were investigated, but all involved the use of hydrogen fluoride, which caused severe corrosion problems.

As with *Tabun*, the only practical solution was the use of quartz- or silver-lined containers. Experimental production was undertaken at Spandau, Munsterlager, and Building 144 in Dyernfurth-am-Oder. A factory capable of producing 508 tonnes (500 tons) per month was under construction at Falkenhagen near Berlin at the end of the war, but it seems unlikely that total German *Sarin* production exceeded 10 tonnes (10 tons).

Soman

Richard Kuhn discovered *Soman* (Pinacolyl methylphosphonofluoridate) in spring 1944 while working for the German Army on the pharmacology of *Tabun* and *Sarin*. The Russians produced *Soman* post-war after discovering research papers on the nerve agent which had been buried in a mineshaft near Berlin.

No 'first use'

Although 500,000 artillery shells and 100,000 bombs filled with *Tabun* had been stockpiled by the end of the war, none were ever used, most likely because the Germans thought the Allies were well ahead in the production of nerve agents and believed that any 'first use' would provoke overwhelming retaliation.

Nuclear Weapons

After the reality of nuclear atomic fission had been demonstrated in 1938, several German nuclear physicists saw the possibility of creating a 'super-explosive' on the basis of the concentrated energy in the heart of an atom's nucleus.

The physicists included Paul Harteck, director of the physical chemistry department at the University of Hamburg, who was also an advisor to the *Heereswaffenamt* (HWA), the Army Ordnance Office. In April 1939, he contacted officials of the *Reichskriegsministerium* (RKM), the Reich War Ministry, to alert them to

NUCLEAR WEAPONS COMPARED

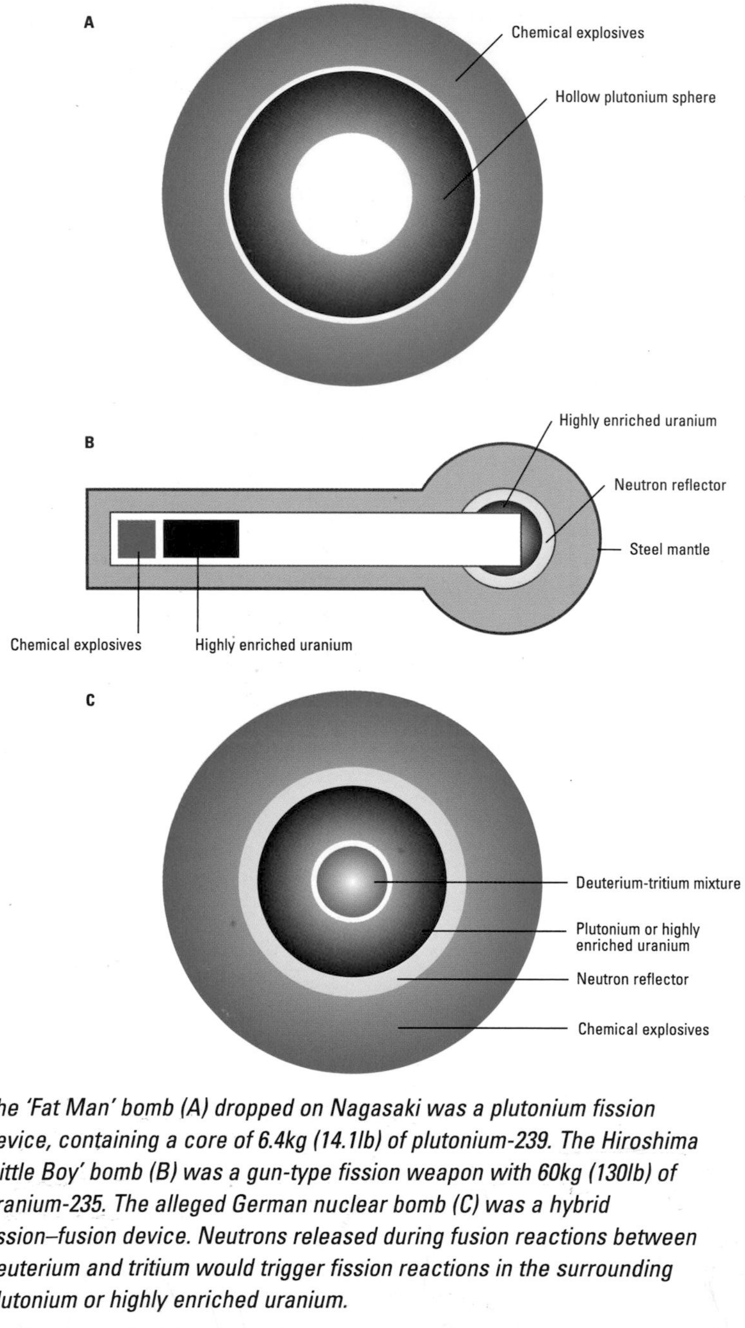
A
Chemical explosives
Hollow plutonium sphere
B
Highly enriched uranium
Neutron reflector
Steel mantle
Chemical explosives
Highly enriched uranium
C
Deuterium-tritium mixture
Plutonium or highly enriched uranium
Neutron reflector
Chemical explosives

The 'Fat Man' bomb (A) dropped on Nagasaki was a plutonium fission device, containing a core of 6.4kg (14.1lb) of plutonium-239. The Hiroshima 'Little Boy' bomb (B) was a gun-type fission weapon with 60kg (130lb) of uranium-235. The alleged German nuclear bomb (C) was a hybrid fission–fusion device. Neutrons released during fusion reactions between deuterium and tritium would trigger fission reactions in the surrounding plutonium or highly enriched uranium.

the potential military applications of nuclear chain reactions. Several other physicists also passed on similar advice to official bodies at about the same time and in April 1939, a small group of scientists known as the first *Uranverein* (Uranium Club) began informal studies of potential nuclear weapons at the Georg-August University of Göttingen. This first study group only existed for a few months and was broken up when its members were conscripted as Germany mobilized for the invasion of Poland.

Uranium stockpile

By mid-1939, the Berlin electrical engineering group Auergesellschaft had accumulated a substantial amount of uranium which was then regarded as little more than a waste product from radium manufacture. The group's scientific director, Nikolaus Riehl, recognized a potential market for this stockpile after reading a paper on the potential use of uranium as a source of nuclear energy. Accordingly, he contacted the HWA and secured its backing for setting up uranium production facilities at the Auergesellschaft factory in Oranienburg. This supplied the uranium cubes for the experimental *Uranmaschine* (Uranium machine), an early nuclear reactor at the *Kaiser-Wilhelm Institut für Physik* (KWIP – Kaiser-Wilhelm Institute for Physics) and the *Versuchsstelle* (testing station) of the HWA in Gottow.

The second *Uranverein* began after the HWA took control of the German nuclear energy project. It was formed on 1 September 1939 and its first meeting was held on 16 September 1939. This was organised by Kurt Diebner, advisor to the HWA, and held in Berlin. The invitees included Walther Bothe, Siegfried Flügge, Hans Geiger, Otto Hahn, Paul Harteck, Gerhard Hoffmann, Josef Mattauch, and Georg Stetter. A second meeting was held shortly afterwards which included Klaus Clusius, Robert Döpel, Werner Heisenberg and Carl Friedrich von Weizsäcker. At the same time, the HWA tightened its grip on the nuclear research programme by effectively taking control of the KWIP and appointing Diebner as its director.

When it was apparent that the nuclear research programme would not make a decisive contribution to winning the war quickly, control of the KWIP was returned in January 1942 to its umbrella organization, the *Kaiser-Wilhelm Gesellschaft* (KWG – Kaiser Wilhelm Society). In July 1942, the HWA's control of the programme was relinquished to the *Reichsforschungsrat* (RFR – Reich Research Council).

The nuclear energy project thereafter maintained its *kriegswichtig* (important for the war) designation and funding continued from the military. However, the administration of the research programme was then fragmented into several areas, principally uranium and heavy water production, uranium isotope separation, and the nuclear reactor.

The 'official' story

The generally accepted history of German nuclear research indicates that from 1942 onwards, little

GERMAN NUCLEAR DEVICE

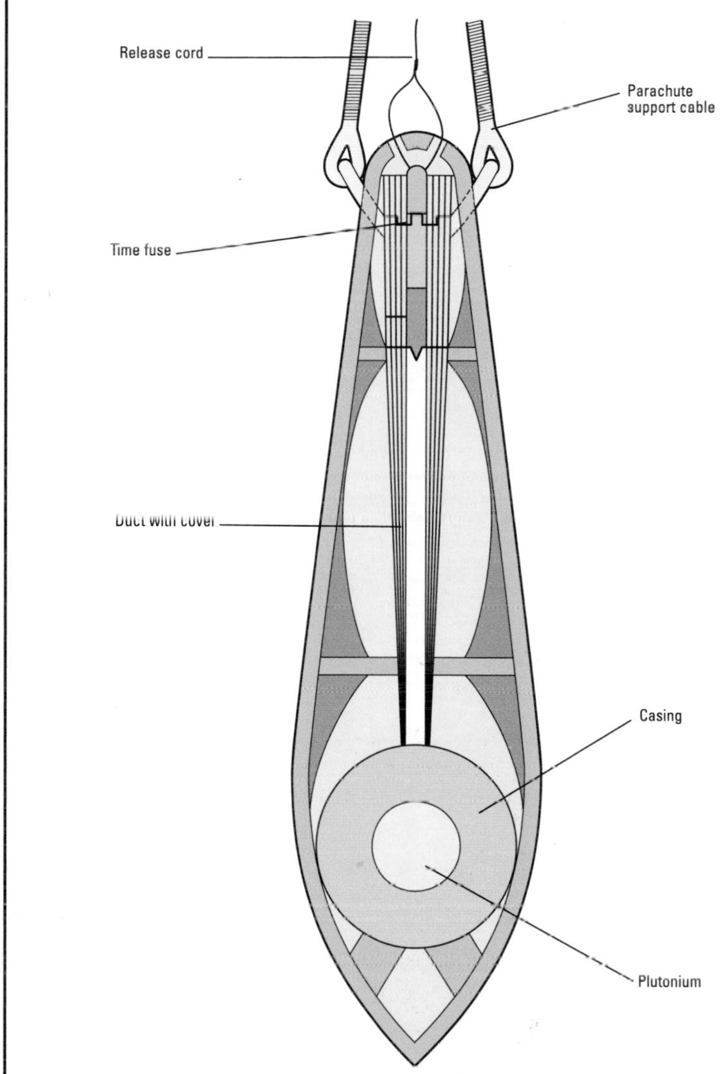
Release cord
Parachute support cable
Time fuse
Duct with cover
Casing
Plutonium

This is the only known German diagram of a nuclear weapon, which was discovered in an incomplete report compiled shortly after the war. Although the diagram is very basic and is far from being a detailed design for a nuclear bomb, the report contains an accurate assessment of the critical mass required for a plutonium bomb, which was almost certainly derived from German wartime research. The report also indicates that German scientists had carried out extensive theoretical work on hydrogen bombs.

practical progress was made towards a viable weapon – Speer attempted to get Professor Werner Heisenberg, one of the principal experts in the field, to give him some straight answers about the feasibility of producing an atomic weapon in a reasonable time-scale. Heisenberg supposedly told him that even with generous funding, it would take at least three or four years, at which point Speer recalled that, 'we scuttled the project to develop an atomic bomb'.

Thereafter, research efforts were largely concentrated on building practical nuclear reactors. The programme was hampered by shortages of essential materials (principally uranium and heavy water) and only two small unsuccessful experimental reactors were found by Allied technical investigation teams at the end of the war.

A campaign of 'disinformation'

The accepted history paints a picture of sustained German incompetence in the field of nuclear research that is in marked contrast to their achievements in other areas of military technology. This account begins to look increasingly improbable as closer examination of the period throws up a number of inconsistencies.

In 1941–42, the German chemical consortium I.G. Farben invested heavily in the construction of what was officially a huge *'Buna'* – synthetic rubber – factory at Monowitz, only 6km (4km) from the main Auschwitz concentration camp. Sensing the large profits to be made, the Farben directors decided to finance the enormous factory complex from company funds, rather than waiting for official grants or loans and earmarked 900,000,000 Reichsmarks – nearly 250 million dollars in 1945 prices or over 2 billion dollars today – to the project.

Yet despite massive funding and almost unlimited slave labour from the concentration camp complex, the factory apparently never produced any *Buna* at all. It is true that it was bombed several times during 1944, but even so, some output should have been apparent, especially as it used enormous amounts of electricity, '...more than the entire city of Berlin'.

Whilst this seems incompatible with a *Buna* factory, it is consistent with the characteristics of a uranium enrichment plant. (Speculation is fuelled by anecdotal evidence that the numerous tours of Auschwitz do not include the sealed-off factory complex. Allegedly, even private tour guides refuse to take visitors there, which inevitably leads to spectulation as to what took place there.

At much the same time as I.G. Farben were planning their Monowitz factory in 1941, Carl Friedrich von Weizsäcker, one of the members of the second *Uranverein*, filed a draft patent application indicating that the production of plutonium and its military potential were well understood. The application includes the following summary:

The production of element 94 [plutonium] in practically useful amounts is best done with the 'uranium machine' [nuclear reactor]. It is especially advantageous – and this is the main benefit of the invention – that the element 94 thereby produced can easily be separated from uranium chemically.

The document also specifically goes on to note the use of plutonium to produce an exceptionally powerful bomb:

With regard to energy per unit weight, this explosive would be around 10 million times greater than any other [existing explosive] and comparable only to pure uranium 235.

A later section of the patent application describes:

... a process for the explosive production of energy from the fission of element 94, whereby element 94 ... is brought together in such amounts in one place, for example a bomb, so that the overwhelming majority of neutrons produced by fission excite new fissions and do not leave the substance.

Possible security measures

The patent was resubmitted in November 1941, in the name of the KWIP, with all references to nuclear weapons removed – it seems as though someone had belatedly appreciated that it need to be treated as highly classified material.

It is certainly possible that the fragmentation of the German nuclear research programme in 1942 was a security measure. The most promising lines of development were shrouded in the tightest security measures and 'buried' beneath a layer of relatively easily accessible

NUCLEAR EXPLOSIONS AND THE FISSION BOMB

SEQUENCE

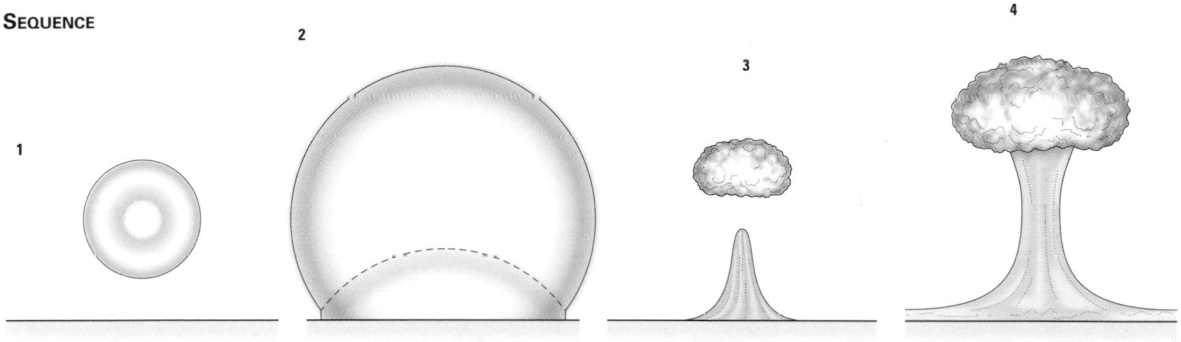
1
2
3
4

1. A blinding flash of bluish-white and ultraviolet light; air is heated to 10 million degrees centigrade (50 million degrees fahrenheit) a fireball. This generates heat, which travels at the speed of light.

2. A blast wave develops, moving at 350m/s (1148ft/s), part of which is reflected upwards from the ground.

3. The overpressure of the blast is followed by negative pressure, drawing in winds of up to 1,078km/h (674mph).

4. If the fireball touches the ground, debris is sucked into the rising column of smoke and hot gases, forming a mushroom cloud.

FISSION BOMBS

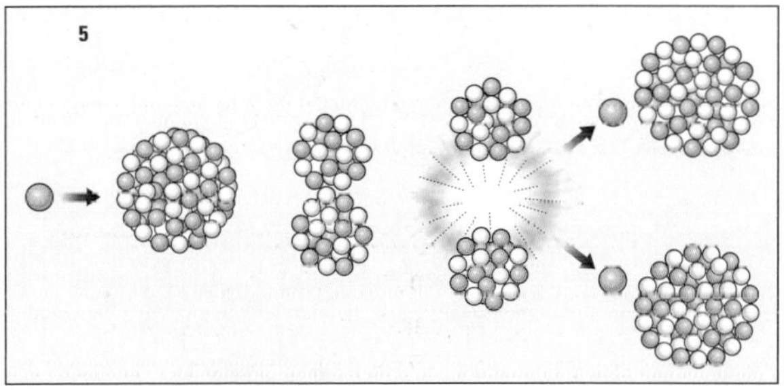
5

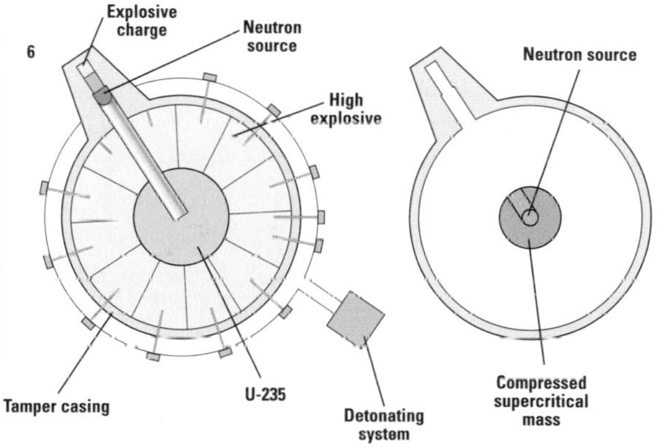
6
Explosive charge
Neutron source
High explosive
Neutron source
Tamper casing
U-235
Detonating system
Compressed supercritical mass

5. A fission bomb operates on the basis of the collision of a free neutron from one atom with another uranium atom. This causes the uranium atom to split in two; the fission releases two spare neutrons and 32 million millionths of a watt of energy. The two freed neutrons then collide with two more atoms which undergo the same reaction. As a result, 0.45kg (1lb) of U-235 can release over 36 million watts of energy.

6. A fission bomb comprises a subcritical mass of U-235 or plutonium encased in high explosive in a tamper casing. On detonation, the neutron source is fired into the U-235 or plutonium to begin fission and the high explosive detonates. This compresses the U-235 or plutonium into a supercritical mass and initiates rapid explosive fission.

■ **A map based on a 1943 original, prepared by a *Luftwaffe* study team identifying potential targets in the eastern United States, including New York City. The blast pattern is remarkably similar to that of a 15–17 kiloton nuclear bomb.**

low-priority research into atomic energy. The better-known scientists, such as Heisenberg, were deliberately assigned to the more 'open' projects as 'front men' and kept in ignorance of the most highly classified projects.

By 1943, sufficient radioactive material was available to make it worthwhile to design delivery systems. In March 1943, drawings were prepared of a new version of the V-2 with a central payload compartment, positioned as far aft as possible to ensure that the contents would be dispersed as far as possible

MAP OF PROPOSED TARGET – NEW YORK CITY

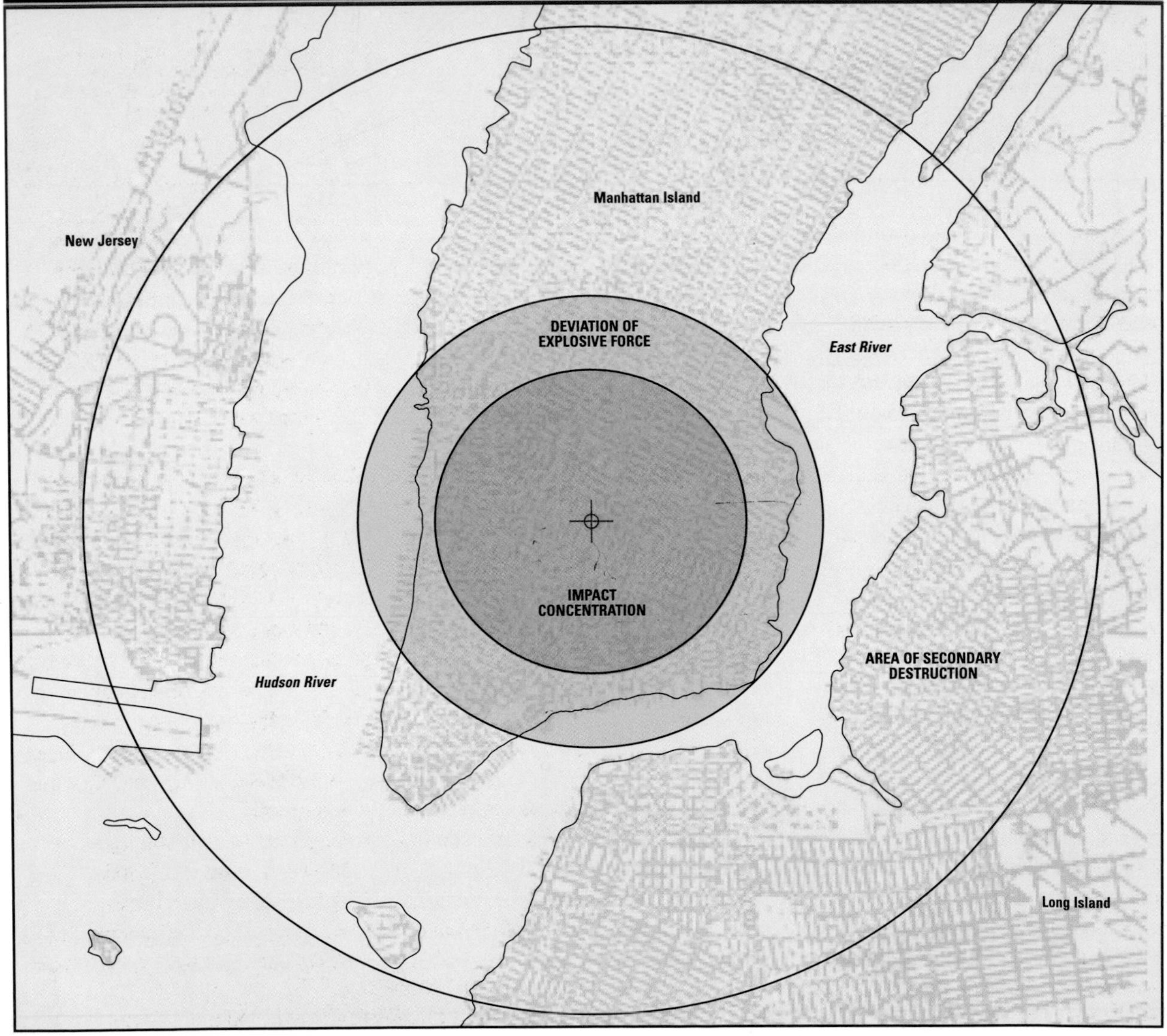
Manhattan Island
New Jersey
DEVIATION OF EXPLOSIVE FORCE
East River
IMPACT CONCENTRATION
AREA OF SECONDARY DESTRUCTION
Hudson River
Long Island

HEINKEL HE 177 A-5

V4
KN

Specifications

Type: Six-seat heavy bomber
Powerplant: 2 x 2170kW (2950hp) Daimler-Benz DB 610 (twin DB 605) 24-cylinder liquid-cooled inline engines
Speed: 488km/h (303mph) at 6098m (20,000ft)
Service Ceiling: 9390m (30800ft)
Combat radius: 1540km (960 miles)
Weight: 16,800kg (37,000lb) (empty) 31,000 kg (68,340lb) (maximum take-off)
Length: 22m (72ft 2in)
Height: 6.7m (21ft)
Armament: 2 x 20mm (0.79in) MG 151 cannon, 3 x 13mm (0.51in) MG 131 machine guns, 3 x 7.92mm (0.31in) MG 81 machine guns, plus up to 7200kg (15,873lb) of bombs

on striking the target. This could potentially point to the missile carrying either a nerve agent or radioactive waste – a 'dirty bomb'.

The next design is even clearer in its intent. In September 1944, similar plans were completed for a modified V-1, designated D-1. The most important feature of the D-1 was an entirely new warhead labelled *Schuttenbehalter fur K-stoff buschen* (Container for canned nuclear waste). The new warhead was fitted with an externally-mounted detonator in order to blow it open on impact and scatter the contents as widely as possible around the target area.

Long-range strike

A dirty bomb is the simplest military use of radioactive material, but there is a possibility that development of a much more sophisticated atomic bomb was well under way in late 1943. At that time, a *Luftwaffe* study team produced a map of lower Manhattan showing the projected blast damage from a single weapon, which was consistent with the explosion of an atomic bomb in the 15–17 kiloton range, a yield close to that of the US 'Little Boy' bomb dropped on Hiroshima.

This implies planning for a strike by a very long-range aircraft such as the Messerschmitt Me 264 or Junkers Ju 390 (both of which were under development as part of the *Amerika Bomber* project which had been authorized by *Reichsmarschall* Hermann Göring in May 1942). The Me 264 had first flown in December 1942 and the prototype Ju 390V1 flew in October 1943. It may be significant that, according to former Junkers' test pilot Hans-Joachim Pancherz' logbook, the Ju 390V1 was flown to Prague in November 1943 for a series of trials including tests of in-flight refuelling equipment and procedures.

There is a further piece of disputed evidence – it has been claimed that a single Ju 390 was attached to FAGr 5 (*Fernaufklärungsgruppe 5*), based at

■ **The He 177 was one of the few *Luftwaffe* bomber types with the potential to be a viable nuclear bomber. Some sources indicate that a prototype designated He 177V38 was being converted to this role at the end of the war.**

Mont-de-Marsan near Bordeaux in early 1944. This aircraft supposedly made a 32-hour reconnaissance flight to within 19km (12 miles) of the US coast, north of New York City. While the evidence for this flight is questionable, the *Amerika Bomber* project did specify the following priority industrial targets:

- Aluminum Corp. of America, Alcoa, Tennessee (making aluminium and light alloys)
- Aluminum Corp. of America, Massena, New York (making aluminium and light alloys)
- Aluminum Corp. of America, Badin, North Carolina (making aluminium and light alloys)
- Wright Aeronautical Corp.,

Paterson, New Jersey (making aircraft engines)

- Pratt & Whitney Aircraft, East Hartford, Connecticut (making aircraft engines)
- Allison Div. of G.M., Indianapolis, Indiana (making aircraft engines)
- Wright Aeronautical Corp., Cincinnati, Ohio (making aircraft engines)
- Hamilton Standard Corp., E. Hartford, Connecticut (making aircraft propellors)
- Hamilton Standard Corp., Pawcatuck, Connecticut (making aircraft propellors)
- Curtiss Wright Corp., Beaver, Pennsylvania (making aircraft)
- Curtiss Wright Corp., Caldwell, New Jersey (making aircraft)
- Sperry Gyroscope, Brooklyn, New York (making sighting and optical equipment
- Cryolite Refinery, Pittsburgh, Pennsylvania (smelting aluminium and alloys)
- American Car & Foundry, Berwick, Pennsylvania (making AFVs)
- Colt Manufacturing, Hartford, Connecticut (making small arms)
- Chrysler Corp., Detroit, Michigan (making AFVs)
- Allis Chalmers, La Porte, Indiana (making artillery tractors)
- Corning Glass Works, Corning, New York (making sighting and optical equipment)
- Bausch & Lomb, Rochester, New York (making sighting and optical equipment)

Since even the most optimistic production plans only envisaged the manufacture of a relatively small number of *Amerika* bombers, the bombing of such industrial targets would cause little lasting damage and would only be useful as a propaganda exercise, unless nuclear weapons were involved.

German nuclear tests

The most startling aspect of the 'revisionist theory' of German nuclear research is the possibility that it produced nuclear weapons that were actually tested. The first such test allegedly took place on the Baltic island of Rugen in October 1944, with two apparent eye-witness accounts.

The first was from Luigi Romersa, an Italian war correspondent who was sent by Mussolini to see the secret weapons that Hitler claimed would bring him victory. Romersa wrote of the devastation which resulted from this test. He recalled waiting in a bunker for several hours after the explosion to give time for the 'deathly rays, of utmost toxicity' to disperse before being allowed to leave in protective clothing.

■ **This derivative of the V-1 was designated D-1 and had the original heavy mild-steel nose cone and wings replaced with lighter wooden versions to maximize its range. Although primarily designed to carry a warhead filled with radioactive waste, it could easily have substituted a substantial payload of nerve agent.**

V-1 WITH ATOMIC OR CHEMICAL WARHEADS

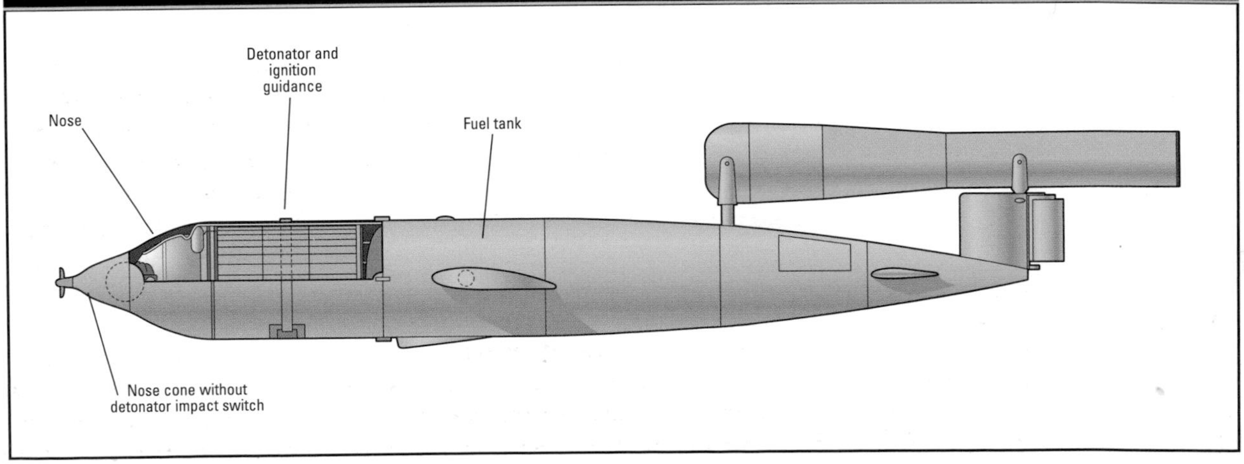
Detonator and ignition guidance
Nose
Fuel tank
Nose cone without detonator impact switch

V-2 WITH RADIOACTIVE OR CHEMICAL PAYLOAD

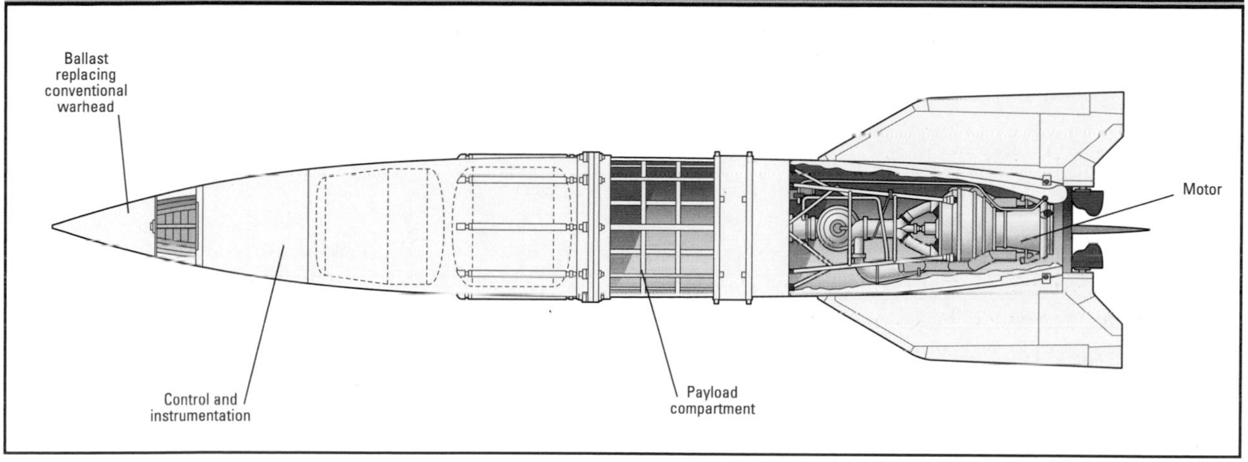
Ballast replacing conventional warhead
Motor
Control and instrumentation
Payload compartment

■ **This version of the V-2 was heavily modified with a central payload compartment for radioactive waste or nerve agent replacing the original nose-mounted HE warhead. (It is possible that some of the sabotaged V-2s found at an underground plant near Leese were of this type.)**

The other account was given by a *Luftwaffe* officer, Hans Zinsser, who was flying a Heinkel He 111 in the area. He reported that:

A cloud shaped like a mushroom with turbulent, billowing sections (at about 7000m [22,960ft] altitude) stood, without any seeming connections, over the spot where the explosion took place. Strong electrical disturbances and the impossibility to continue radio communication as by lightning, turned up.

Allowing for poor translation, there are features in the account consistent with a nuclear explosion. As well as the mushroom cloud, the reference to interference with radio communications is highly relevant – this arises from the electro-magnetic pulse (EMP) produced by a nuclear explosion. In fact, the magnitude of EMP and the extent of its effects were only gradually understood. The British nuclear tests of 1952–53 were plagued by instrumentation failures attributed to 'radioflash', the 1950s British term for EMP.

In October 1944, curious reports began circulating of a prolonged failure in the Berlin telephone system, then one of the most sophisticated in the world. The official German explanation was that the disruption was due to bomb damage, but the communications black-out lasted for at least 60 hours, far longer than the time normally taken for repairing such damage. During this October black-out, even the Swedish Foreign Office was unable to call its Berlin legation. This was in marked contrast to the situation during the bitter fighting in Berlin in April 1945, when the Berlin telephones were working almost until the end. It has been suggested that EMP may have been responsible.

The necessity of implementing improvised shielding to protect essential electronic equipment from the damaging effects of EMP may explain why the second alleged test did not take place until March 1945 at Ohrdruf in Thuringia. This seems to have involved a very small 'boosted fission' weapon, whose effects were similar to those of post-war tactical nuclear weapons.

Speculation

The true history of German nuclear research may never be known – it is a vast and highly complex subject that quickly becomes clouded by eccentric conspiracy theories. While the more extreme revisionist views seem improbable, there are inconsistencies in the mainstream historical account. Perhaps the essential requirement in studying the subject are a healthy scepticism and an open mind.

The Secrets Live On

In the closing stages of the war, each of the Allies rushed to track down 'high-tech' German weapons and their design teams. The weapons were relatively easy to find, scattered throughout the factories and bases of the ruined Reich, but finding the scientists and engineers who created them was the main prize.

Operation Paperclip

On 20 July 1945, the US Joint Chiefs of Staff merged a host of independent American intelligence-gathering projects under the code name of Operation Overcast. However, the code name was soon compromised and replaced by Operation Paperclip, which concentrated on recruiting top German scientists to aid post-war US weapons research and development.

President Harry Truman authorized Operation Paperclip in August 1945 with the proviso that anyone found...

...to have been a member of the Nazi party and more than a nominal participant in its activities, or an active supporter of Nazi militarism...

...would be excluded. This would have applied to many of the more important scientists recruited, such as Wernher von Braun, Arthur Rudolph and Hubertus Strughold, who had all been Nazi Party members and were listed as a 'menace to the security of the Allied Forces'. All were eventually cleared to work in the US after their backgrounds were 'sanitized' by the military – CVs were rewritten and links with the Nazi Party were expunged from the records. One story asserts that the operation's name was a whimsical reference to the paperclips that secured the newly-written background details to their personnel files.

Wind tunnels and missiles

As the war ended, US technical intelligence teams began frantic efforts to remove key personnel and equipment from areas which were assigned to the British, French and Soviet occupation zones. A case in point was the Hermann Göring Aeronautical Research Centre at Völkenrode. Previously undetected by Allied intelligence, it was a well-camouflaged facility of vast proportions on the outskirts of Braunschweig.

Almost 80 underground buildings, including seven wind tunnels, were expertly camouflaged with trees planted over them to blend them into the surrounding forest. Völkenrode was in the British occupation zone and US teams hastily stripped the centre of key documents and equipment before the first British troops arrived. Some of the captured wind tunnel components were still in use in US test centres 50 years later.

The greatest prizes were the German nuclear scientists (many of whom were detained as part of the joint US–UK Operation Alsos) and missile experts. Many of the latter, including Wernher von Braun, were only too happy to co-operate with Operation Overcast (Paperclip) and helped secure 100 complete V-2 missiles, plus 14.2 tonnes (14 tons) of papers relating to the project. By the late 1940s, almost 150 German experts were working in US military establishments under the auspices of Operation Paperclip.

The first of at least 63 'US' V-2s was test-fired in April 1946 and the data gathered was a vital element in the development of the US Army's Redstone surface-to-surface missile. This was designed by Wernher von Braun's team at the Redstone Arsenal, Alabama in 1950-52 and led directly to the Jupiter Intermediate Range Ballistic Missile (IRBM).

Operation Lusty and the F-86 Sabre

Although Operation Paperclip was the most famous of the operations which exploited the Reich's technology, Operation Lusty (*LUftwaffe* Secret TechnologY) was almost as important. Its validation of swept-wing aircraft designs led to dramatic revisions of several key aircraft that were still at the design stage in 1945, especially the B-47 Stratojet and the F-86 Sabre. Initial proposals for the P-86 Sabre were drawn up in late 1944 to meet a USAAF requirement for a single-seat jet fighter and were originally based on the straight wing FJ-1 Fury being developed for the US Navy. The Fury's wings, tail unit and cockpit canopy were all near-copies of those on the P-51 Mustang. Reports from Operation Lusty led to a six-month delay while the P-86 was redesigned with wings and tail surfaces incorporating a 35-degree sweep-back. The P-86, which was soon redesignated F-86, was the first American aircraft to include the results of flight research data seized from German aerodynamicists at the end of the war. The type entered service with the USAF in 1949 and a total of over 9800 were completed before production ended in 1956. It equipped over 30 air forces across the world and the last aircraft remained in service with the Bolivian Air Force until 1994.

Ta 183 PLAN VIEW

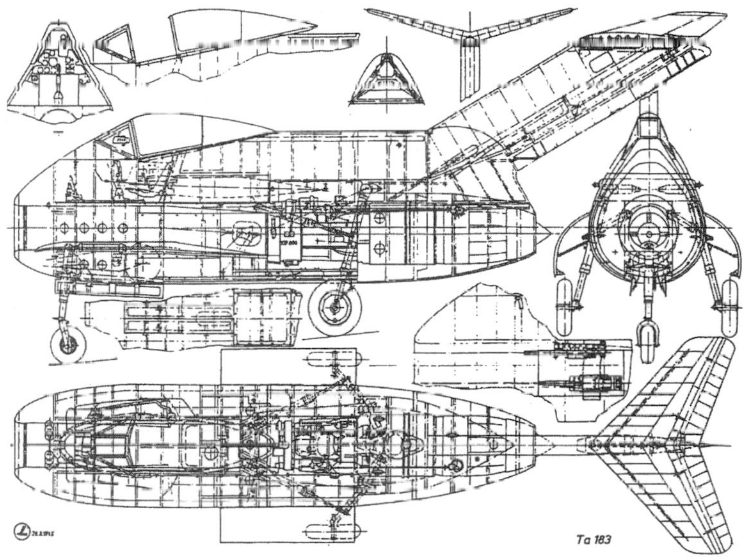
Ta 183

The Ta 183 design was remarkably similar to that of many post-war jet fighters, notably the MiG-15. Its potential was officially recognized in February 1945, when it was one of the types selected for production as a result of the Emergency Fighter Competition. The prototype's first flight was scheduled for May/June 1945, with series production to begin in October of that year, but development ended abruptly when British forces overran the Focke-Wulf factory near Bremen.

Junkers EF 132, B-47 Stratojet and the Vickers Valiant

The Junkers EF 132 was one of the German company's last aircraft projects and represented the culmination of a series of designs which included the Ju 287. The shoulder-mounted wings were swept back at 35 degrees and featured a small amount of anhedral. The six Jumo 012 jet engines were buried in the wing roots as wind tunnel tests had shown the advantages of this layout in comparison to drag-inducing under-wing nacelles. The shoulder mounted wings allowed the inclusion of a 12m (39ft) bomb bay in the centre fuselage capable of housing a bomb load of at least 5000kg (11,023lb).

The undercarriage comprised a nose wheel, two tandem main wheels beneath the centre rear fuselage and outrigger wheels under each outer wing. A fully glazed, pressurized cockpit located in the extreme fuselage nose held a crew of five. Defensive armament totalled three (dorsal, ventral and tail) remote-control turrets, each with twin 20mm (0.79in) cannon.

A wind tunnel model was tested in early 1945, and a full-scale wooden mock-up had been completed at Junkers' Dessau factory when Soviet troops overran the complex and seized all EF 132 designs and components. In the immediate post-war period, the bomb-damaged factory was partially rebuilt, the wind tunnels were repaired and the jet engine test and manufacturing facilities resumed operation.

The impressive EF 132 mock-up was inspected frequently by Soviet officials before the entire complex and its staff were moved to Russia in October 1946.

Work on the project continued at GOZ No.1 (*Gosoodarstvenny Opytnyy Zavod* – State Experimental Plant), at Dobna, near Moscow. The team, under Dr Brunholff Baade at OKB-1 (the design bureau attached to GOZ No.1), had built a glider to test the type's flight handling (which was reported to be exceptionally good) and work was well underway on the first prototype when the project was suddenly cancelled in June 1948.

B-47 Stratojet

The B-47 originated with a 1943 US Army Air Force requirement for a jet bomber and reconnaissance aircraft that could reach Germany from bases in the USA. The following year, the requirement evolved into a formal request for a bomber with a specified speed of at least 800km/h (500mph), a range of 5600km (3500 miles) and a service ceiling of 12,200m (40,000ft). The aircraft was to be powered by the General Electric TG-180 turbojet engine that was then under development. The first Boeing proposal, the Model 424, was little more than a modification of a conventional propeller-driven bomber design, essentially a scaled-down version of the Boeing B-29 Superfortress, but powered by four jet engines.

Wind tunnel tests showed that the Model 424 model suffered from excessive drag. This prompted a revised design, the Model 432, with the four engines buried in the forward fuselage, but although it had some structural advantages, there was little effect on drag. In desperation, Boeing engineers turned to the German swept-wing data provided by the firm's chief aerodynamicist, George Schairer, in May 1945. Based on this data, the Model 432 was redesigned as the Model 448, incorporating wings and tail surfaces swept back at 35 degrees. Interestingly, this angle was identical to that of the Junkers EF 132's wings and the two aircraft also featured remarkably similar undercarriage designs.

Boeing completed their redesign work in September 1946. Some further refinements were included and two prototypes based on the resulting Model 450 were ordered in April 1947 as the XB-47. Over 2000 B-47s were built and the type remained in USAF service until 1969.

Vickers Valiant

In Britain in the late 1940s, many of RAF Bomber Command's aircraft were little more than slightly improved variants of wartime aircraft, such as the Avro Lincoln, which was a development of the Lancaster. It was clear that these were rapidly becoming obsolete and a specification was issued in 1947 for a jet bomber to at least equal anything in the US and Soviet inventories.

Many British aircraft manufacturers responded – Handley-Page and Avro proposed very advanced designs that ultimately saw service as the Victor and the Vulcan, but the simpler Vickers-Armstrong Valiant was initially rejected. However, Vickers' chief designer, George Edwards, managed to sell the Vickers design on the basis that it would be available much sooner than the Victor or the Vulcan, promising delivery of a prototype in 1951 and production aircraft in 1953.

The Vickers design team kept their promises – the first prototype flew on 18 May 1951 and the first production aircraft were delivered in December 1953. While there is no evidence that they were directly copying any of the Junkers EF 132's design features, the types share a similar general configuration, with their shoulder-mounted wings and engines buried in the wing roots.

The Valiant's wing was in many respects more advanced than those of the EF 132 or the B-47 as it had a 'compound sweep' configuration (a 45-degree sweep-back at the inner third of the wing, reducing to an angle of about 24 degrees at the tips). This design allowed it to cruise at Mach 0.76 at an altitude of 15,240m (50,000ft), well above the B-47's service ceiling.

Valiants began entering squadron service in 1955 and took part in Operation Musketeer, the Suez operation the following year, dropping a total of 856 tonnes (842 tons) of bombs on Egyptian airfields. Together with the Victors and Vulcans they formed the UK's nuclear deterrent from 1954 until metal fatigue forced their withdrawal from service in 1965.

The Soviet connection

Although the US and UK secured the lion's share of German military technology, the Red Army was able to capture much useful data and equipment. Many of the early Soviet

OPERATION LUSTY: JETS COMPARED

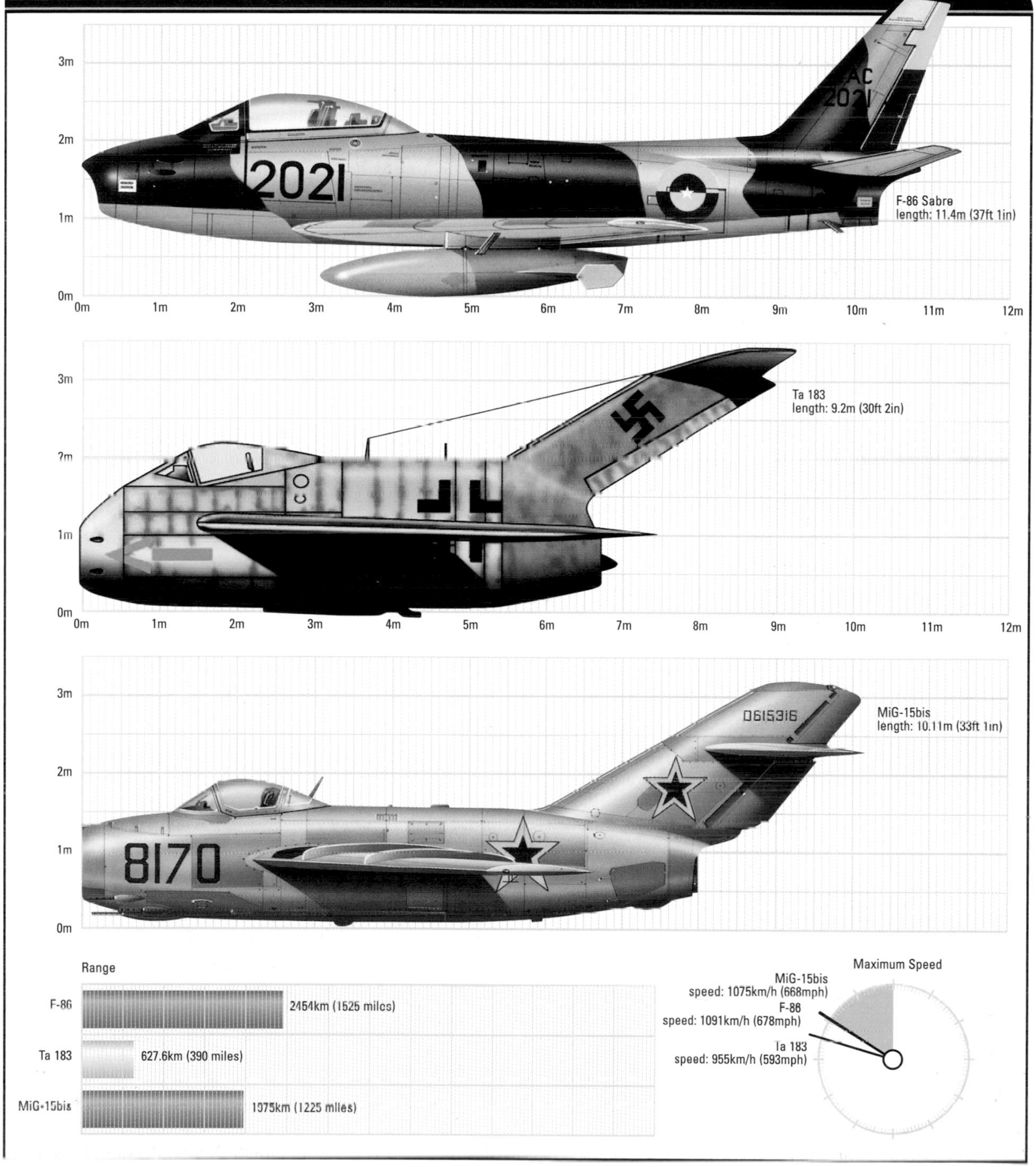
2021
F-86 Sabre
length: 11.4m (37ft 1in)
Ta 183
length: 9.2m (30ft 2in)
MiG-15bis
length: 10.11m (33ft 1in)
8170
Range
F-86
2454km (1525 miles)
Ta 183
627.6km (390 miles)
MiG-15bis
1975km (1225 miles)
Maximum Speed
MiG-15bis
speed: 1075km/h (668mph)
F-86
speed: 1091km/h (678mph)
Ta 183
speed: 955km/h (593mph)

BOMBERS COMPARED

9m
6m
3m
0m
0m
3m
6m
9m
12m
15m
18m
21m
24m
27m
30m
33m
36m
U.S. AIR FORCE
20160
B-47E
length: 32.6m (107ft 1in)
Ju-EF 132
length: 30.8m (101ft 1in)
Valiant
length: 32.99m
(108ft 3in)
XD816

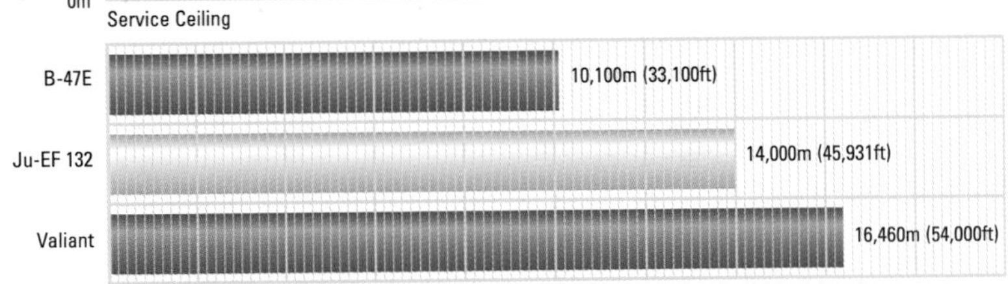
Service Ceiling
B-47E
10,100m (33,100ft)
Ju-EF 132
14,000m (45,931ft)
Valiant
16,460m (54,000ft)

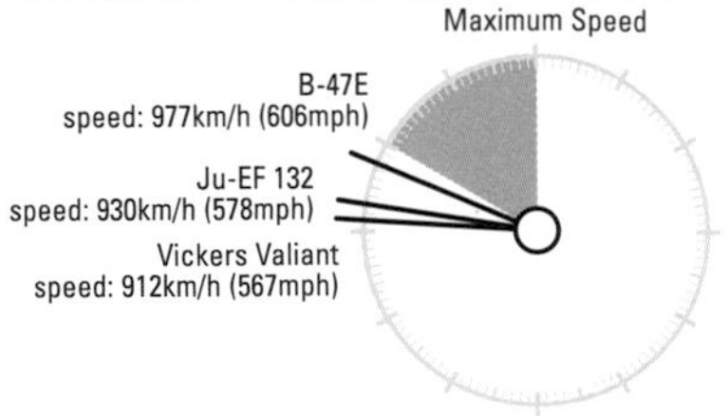
Maximum Speed
B-47E
speed: 977km/h (606mph)
Ju-EF 132
speed: 930km/h (578mph)
Vickers Valiant
speed: 912km/h (567mph)

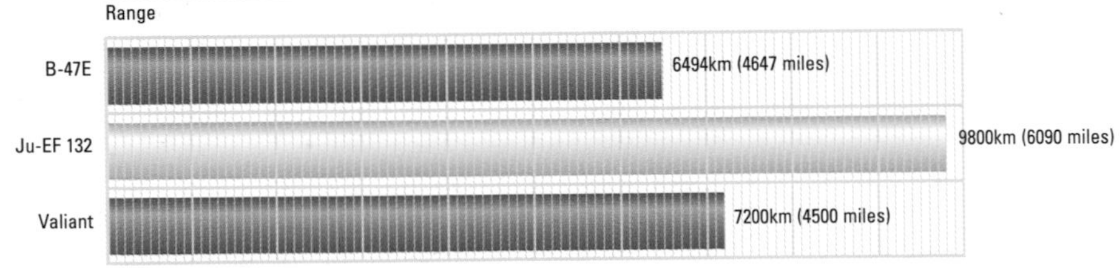
Range
B-47E
6494km (4647 miles)
Ju-EF 132
9800km (6090 miles)
Valiant
7200km (4500 miles)

jet aircraft were powered by German engines – the Yak-57 and Yak-17 were fitted with the Junkers Jumo 004B (or Soviet-built copies designated RD-10), while the MiG-9 employed the BMW 003, which was also copied as the RD-20.

Focke-Wulf Ta 183 and MiG-15

Development of the Ta 183 began in 1942 and, by 1945, the design had developed into a highly advanced jet fighter with very thin wings swept back at 40 degrees and a large fin swept back at 60 degrees.

While Soviet military sources emphatically denied any connection between the German Ta 183 and the new MiG-15, the two aircraft show a remarkable similarity in configuration. Given Stalin's personal interest in the Soviet jet fighter programme and his drastic punitive methods for dealing with perceived delays in production, it would be entirely understandable if the harassed MiG technicians chose to produce a near copy of a promising German design. The prototype MiG-15 first flew on 30 December 1947 and total production of all versions may well have exceeded 18,000 aircraft.

Developments in Missile Technology

In July 1944, US scientists and engineers at Wright Field, Ohio, test-fired a copy of the German V-1's Argus As 014 pulse jet engine that had been 'reverse-engineered' from components flown in from Britain.

Cruise missiles: V-1 to Tomahawk

The reverse engineering provided the basis for the design of America's first mass-produced cruise missile, the JB-2 'Loon', which was a 'near-copy' of the V-1. The first launch of a JB-2 took place in October 1944 and orders were placed for 2000 missiles for use in the planned Allied invasion of Japan (Operation Downfall). Production began in January 1945 and an initial batch of missiles was on its way to the Pacific for operational trials at the end of the war.

A total of 1385 JB-2s had been completed when production was cancelled in September 1945. Although the missile was never used in combat, it played a significant role in the development of more advanced surface to surface missile systems and extensive trials were carried out until the early 1950s, including numerous ground, air and submarine launches.

Matador and Regulus

The JB-2 had convinced the US military that the cruise missile was a viable weapons system and development of larger versions, capable of delivering a nuclear warhead, began in the late 1940s. In January 1949, the USAF test-fired the prototype Matador, followed by the USN's prototype, Regulus, in 1953. Both were very similar cruise missiles and formed an essential part of the US nuclear deterrent during the 1950s, pending the introduction of true intercontinental ballistic missiles (ICBMs), such as the Atlas and Polaris, in the early 1960s.

A second-generation supersonic Regulus II cruise missile, with a range of 2200km (1200 nautical miles) and a speed of Mach 2 was successfully tested but in 1958, the programme was cancelled in favour of the Polaris system.

ALCM, Tomahawk and GLCM

By the 1970s, technological advances and changing operational priorities made the cruise missile concept much more attractive and in 1974, development began of the USAF's air-launched cruise missile (ALCM), followed by the USN's Tomahawk and its derivative, the ground-launched cruise missile (GLCM). The three types became operational in 1982–83 and all, except the GLCM, remain in service. Their success was largely due to the fact that they were 'modern V-1s', whose small size, low level flight and high-subsonic speed made them very hard targets for even the most sophisticated air defence systems.

The technological advances that made them so deadly were most apparent in their guidance systems and warheads. All were fitted with terrain contour-matching guidance (TERCOM) – a pre-recorded contour map of the terrain on the flight path to the target. Computers were able to compare in-flight readings from a radar altimeter to the pre-recorded map and adjust the missile's flight accordingly. TERCOM dramatically improved the weapons' accuracy in comparison to earlier inertially guided missiles, even at their maximum range of approximately 2414km (1500 miles).

Such accuracy meant that far smaller warheads could be used – their miniaturized W80 and W84 nuclear warheads could be adjusted to produce yields between 5 and 150 kilotons.

V-1 AND TOMAHAWK COMPARED

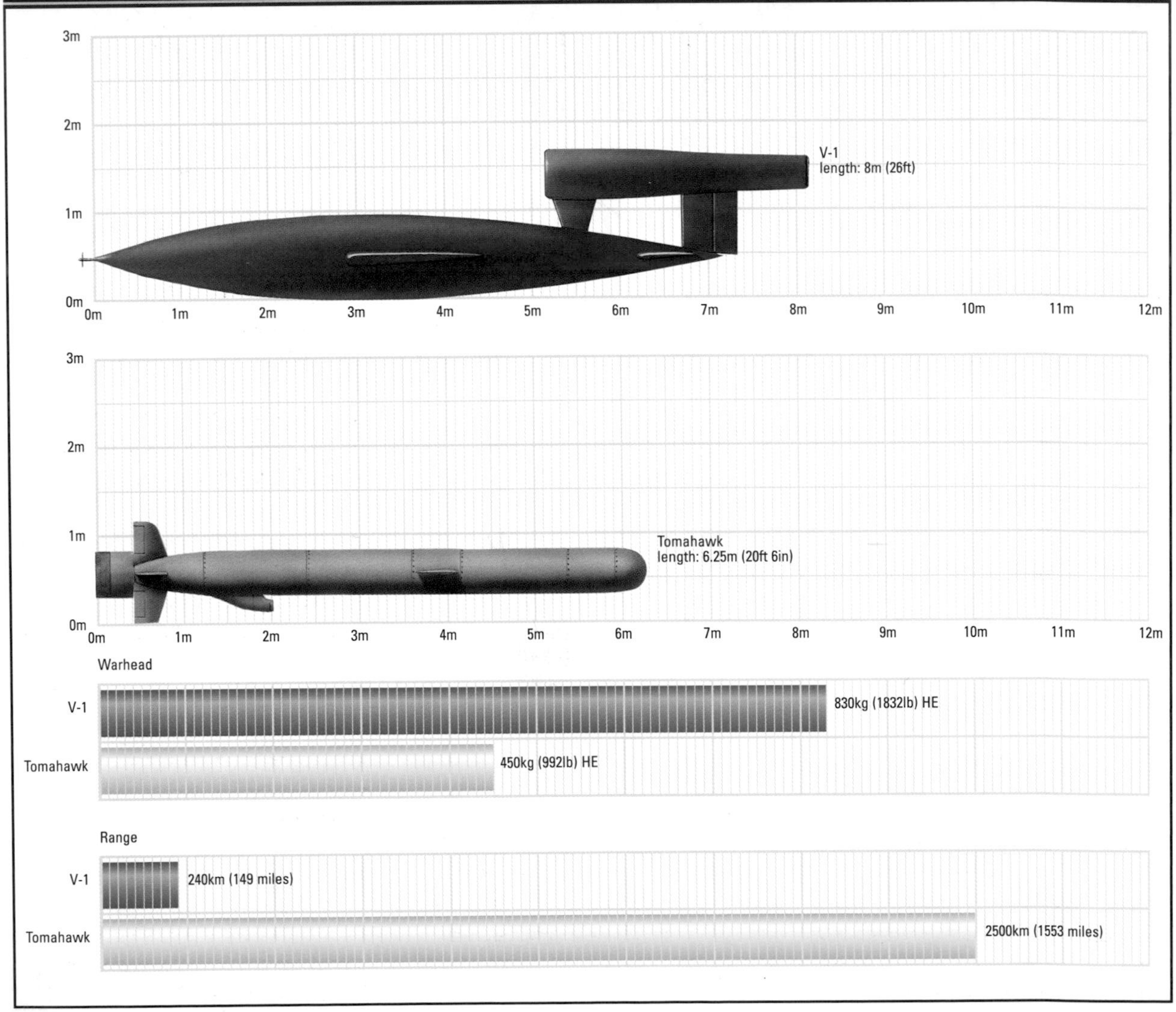

3m
2m
1m
0m
0m
1m
2m
3m
4m
5m
6m
7m
8m
9m
10m
11m
12m
V-1
length: 8m (26ft)
Tomahawk
length: 6.25m (20ft 6in)
Warhead
V-1
830kg (1832lb) HE
Tomahawk
450kg (992lb) HE
Range
V-1
240km (149 miles)
Tomahawk
2500km (1553 miles)

Glossary

Adlergerät – 'Eagle device', an infrared (IR) viewer intended to detect night bombers by the heat of their exhausts and to direct searchlights. The equipment was used in the early stages of the war until radar became widely available.

Anhedral – On an aircraft, the sloping downwards of a wing or tailplane from root to tip.

A-Stoff – Liquid oxygen. One of the fuels used in the V-2 missile.

Alberich skin – A rubberized, sonar-absorbent coating applied to some German U-Boats towards the end of the war.

Bergepanther – An armoured recovery vehicle based on the hull of the Panther medium tank.

B-Stoff – The second fuel used in the V-2 missile, comprised of a mixture of 75 per cent ethyl alcohol and 25 per cent water.

Butterblume – 'Buttercup', a type of IR system, initially intended as an airborne interception device, but which evolved into a targeting system using the heat emitted by factories, vehicle engines etc. In many respects, it was an early version of modern thermal imaging.

Claudia – A sophisticated sound locating system under development at the end of the war for use by AA batteries whose radars were jammed by Allied electronic counter-measures (ECM).

C-Stoff – A mixture of 57 per cent methanol, 30 per cent hydrazine and 13 per cent water. One of the highly toxic and volatile fuels for the Me 163's Walter rocket engine.

Eidechse – A 'frequency-hopping' device for air-defence radars that allowed rapid alteration of their operating frequencies to defeat Allied electronic counter-measures (ECM). Almost complete by the end of the war.

Erprobungskommando – 'Flight evaluation unit', a term generally applied to an operational trials unit formed to 'combat test' a new type of aircraft.

Experten – Veteran *Luftwaffe* ace pilots, many of whom flew in the Spanish Civil War.

Fallschirmjägergewehr 42 (FG 42) – 'Paratroop Assault Rifle Model 1942', an attempt to produce a selective-fire rifle/light machine gun for the *Luftwaffe's* paratroops.

Feldwebel – *Luftwaffe* rank equivalent to RAF Sergeant or USAAF Technical Sergeant.

Flak – *Flugabwehrkanone* (anti-aircraft gun). The term was widely adopted by the RAF and USAAF.

Flugdeckkreuzer – Aircraft carrier designs mounting the guns of a pocket battleship or heavy cruiser. The main drawback of the type was that its air wing was roughly half that of a conventional carrier.

Flugdeckträger – Aircraft carrier.

Hauptmann – *Luftwaffe* rank equivalent to RAF Flight Lieutenant or USAAF Captain.

Heer – 'Army', the official title of the German army from 1935–45.

Jagdgeschwader – A *Luftwaffe* fighter formation, roughly equivalent to an RAF Group or USAAF Wing, with 100–120 aircraft.

Kakadu – 'Cockatoo', a radio proximity fuse intended for the Hs 293 air-to-surface missile.

Karussell – 'Carousel', an IR homing device for the Wasserfall AA missile that was under development at the end of the war.

Kampfgeschwader – A *Luftwaffe* bomber formation, roughly equivalent to an RAF Group or USAAF Wing, with 100–120 aircraft.

Kampfgruppe – 'Battle group', an *ad hoc* force, usually including AFVs, infantry and artillery, generally formed for a particular task or operation.

Kapitänleutnant – *Kriegsmarine* rank equivalent to RN or USN Lieutenant.

Kriegsmarine – 'War Navy', the official title of the German navy from 1935–45.

Krummlauf – A curved barrel attachment for the *Sturmgewehr 44* assault rifle, primarily intended for firing from the 'pistol ports' of AFVs to shoot at Russian anti-tank teams climbing onto vehicles to set demolition charges.

Kurmark – A transmitter broadcasting imitation radar signals to mislead Allied electronic counter-measures (ECM).

K-Wagen – *GrossKampfwagen* (large battle tank). A super-heavy 'break through tank' ordered in 1917. Two prototypes were nearing completion at the end of World War I.

KwK – *Kampfwagenkanone* (tank gun). The designation applied to all guns designed for use in tanks and armoured cars.

Luftflotte Reich – 'Air Fleet Reich', one of the primary formations of the *Luftwaffe*. It was formed on 5 February 1944 in Berlin-Wannsee with the primary role of defending German air space.

Luftwaffe – The German air force, secretly formed in defiance of the terms of the Treaty of Versailles on 15 May 1933, but not officially 'unveiled' until 1935.

Major – *Luftwaffe* rank equivalent to RAF Squadron Leader or USAAF Major.

Nachtjagdgeschwader – A *Luftwaffe* night fighter formation, roughly equivalent to an RAF Group or USAAF Wing, with about 100–120 aircraft.

Naxos – An airborne receiver that allowed night fighters to home in on transmissions from RAF bombers' H2S radar.

Neubaufahrzeug – 'New construction vehicle', the cover designation applied to the 1930s heavy tank project.

Oberstleutnant – *Luftwaffe* rank equivalent to RAF Wing Commander or USAAF Lieutenant Colonel.

PaK – *Panzerabwehrkanone* (anti-tank gun), the designation applied to all guns primarily intended as anti-tank weapons.

Panzerfaust – 'Panzer fist', a single-shot, disposable infantry anti-tank weapon.

Panzerjäger – 'Tank-hunter', the German term generally applied to lighter self-propelled anti-tank guns, but occasionally used for heavier vehicles such as the *Elefant*.

Panzerschiff – 'Armoured ship', the official designation of the *Deutschland* class 'pocket battleships'. In 1940, they were reclassified by the *Kriegsmarine* as heavy cruisers.

Panzerschreck – 'Tank terror', an anti-tank rocket launcher inspired by the US Bazooka, but with better armour-piercing performance.

Paplitz – An IR proximity fuse intended for use with Wasserfall and Hs 117 AA missiles. Flight tests were carried out in March 1945 that proved that it worked well at night but was impractical for day use because of interference from sunlight.

Reichsheer – 'National Army', the official title of the German army from 1921–35.

Reichsmarine – 'National Navy', the official title of the German navy from 1921–35.

Reichswehr – 'National Defence', the official title of the German armed forces from 1921–35.

R-Stoff – Also known as Tonka and TONKA-250, this was a liquid rocket fuel, later used by North Korea and, under the name TG-02, by the Soviet Union. Its composition is approximately 50 per cent triethylamine and 50 per cent xylidine, with nitric acid as a hypergolic oxidizer.

Schornsteinfeger – 'Chimney sweep', a radar-absorbent bituminous paint.

Spähkreuzer 38 – 'Reconnaissance cruiser', a class of large destroyers capable of operating in the North Atlantic. They were intended as reconnaissance vessels for the 'Plan Z' battle fleet.

S-Stoff – A liquid rocket fuel comprised of 96 per cent nitric acid with 4 per cent ferric chloride.

SV-Stoff – A similar liquid rocket fuel comprised of 94 per cent nitric acid with 6 per cent dinitrogen tetroxide

Sturmgewehr 44 – 'Assault Rifle Model 1944', the first true assault rifle to enter service.

Trichter – A radio proximity fuse intended to convert bombs into air-to-air weapons that could be dropped onto the tight USAAF bomber formations.

T-Stoff – The second fuel used by the Me 163 comprised of 80 per cent concentrated hydrogen peroxide and 20 per cent oxyquinoline, used as hypergolic oxidizer with C-Stoff.

Unterscharführer – *Waffen-SS* rank equivalent to that of sergeant.

Waffen-SS – 'Armed SS'. By 1945, the *Waffen-SS* was effectively the fourth arm of the *Wehrmacht*, having expanded from three regiments to over 38 divisions.

Wassermaus – 'Water mouse', a photo-electric proximity fuse designed for the Wasserfall AA missile.

Wehrmacht – 'Defence Force', the title of the German armed forces from 1935–45.

Wilde Sau – 'Wild Boar', the term applied to fighter tactics for intercepting night bombers without the use of airborne radar.

Zunder-19 – A proximity fuse for 250kg (551lb) bombs, intended to detonate at 25–30m (82–98ft) above the ground. Development began in 1937, but progress was slow and the project was cancelled in 1943.

Bibliography

Books

Henshall, Philip. **Hitler's V-Weapons Sites**. *Sutton Publishing Ltd., 2002.*

Hogg, Ian V. **German Secret Weapons of the Second World War**. *Greenhill Books, 1999.*

Hogg, Ian V. **German Artillery of World War Two**. *Arms and Armour Press, 1975.*

Hyland, Gary and Gill, Anton. **Last Talons of the Eagle**. *Headline Book Publishing, 1998.*

Johnson, Brian. **The Secret War**. *Pen & Sword Military Classics, 2004.*

Zaloga, Steven J. **German V-Weapons Sites 1943–45**. *Osprey Publishing, 2007.*

Websites

http://www.luft46.com/
– A superb website detailing a host of German aircraft projects which were under development at the end of World War II.

http://www.achtungpanzer.com/achtung-panzer-home
– A great place to begin research on any aspect of wartime panzers and their associated equipment.

http://fingolfen.tripod.com/index.html
– Another excellent site on Panzer development.

http://www.navweaps.com/Weapons/index_weapons.htm
– A site with highly detailed coverage of all aspects of naval weapons.

http://uboat.net/index.html
– A site giving lots of detail on all types of U-boats and their weapons.

http://www.bibliotecapleyades.net/sociopolitica/reichblacksun/contents.htm#Contents
– A site offering an alternative view of the German nuclear weapons programme.

Index

Page numbers in *italics* refer to illustrations and tables.